VOL. 1

written by **DAVID LAPHAM**

art by **GABRIEL ANDRADE**

color by **DIGIKORE STUDIOS**

WILLIAM CHRISTENSEN editor-in-chief

MARK SEIFERT creative director

JIM KUHORIC managing editor

RICK VERBANAS director of marketing

DAVID MARKS director of events

ARIANA OSBORNE production assistant

FERALS Volume 1. Nov. 2012. Published by Avatar Press, Inc., 515 N. Century Blvd. Rantoul, IL 61866. ©2012 Avatar Press, Inc. Ferals and all related properties TM & ©2012 Avatar Press, Inc. All characters as depicted in this story are over the age of 18. The stories, characters, and institutions mentioned in this magazine are entirely fictional. Printed in Canada.

AVATAR™

www.avatarpress.com
www.twitter.com/Avatarpress
www.facebook.com/avatarpresscomics

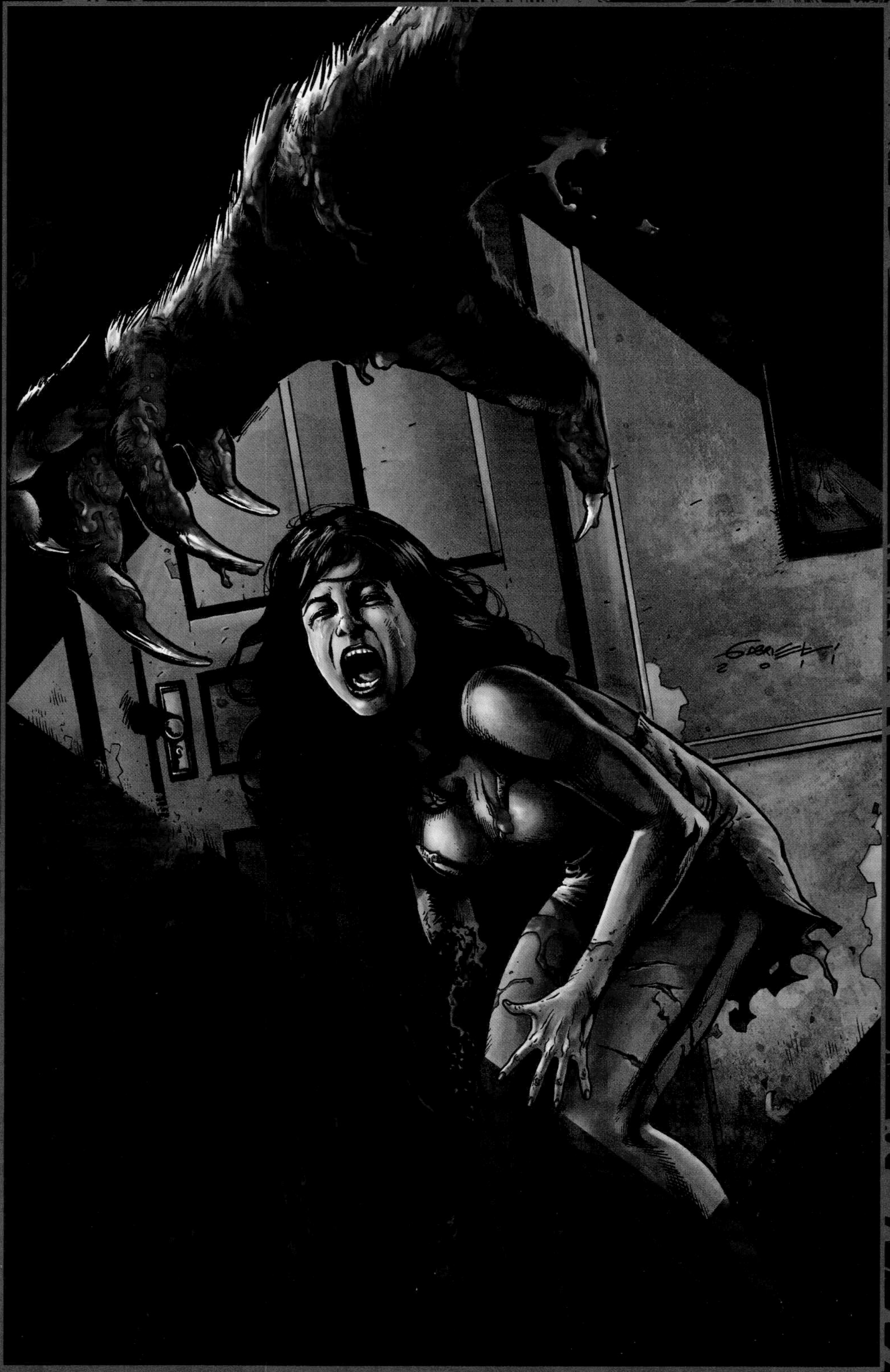

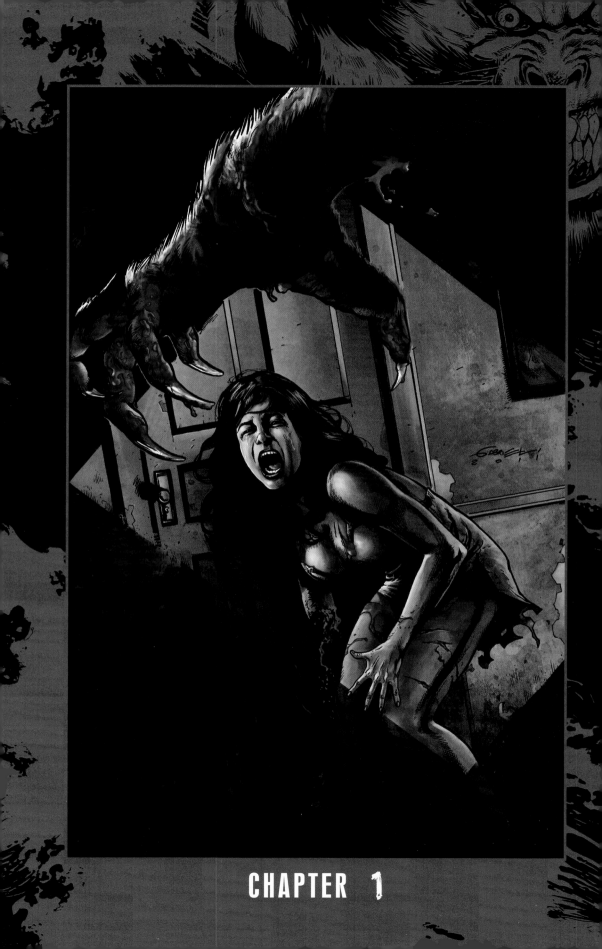

CHAPTER 1

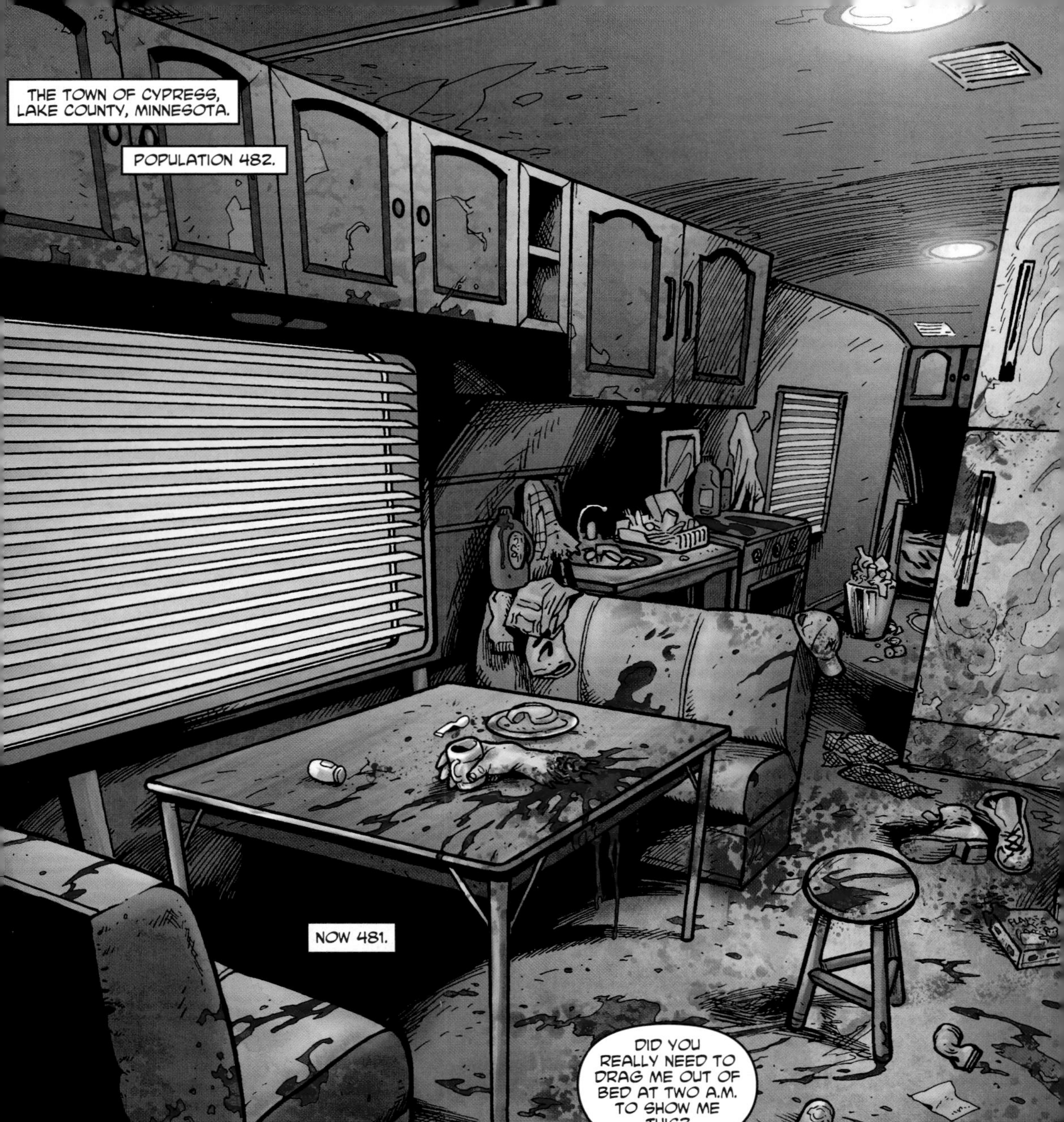
THE TOWN OF CYPRESS, LAKE COUNTY, MINNESOTA.
POPULATION 482.
NOW 481.
DID YOU REALLY NEED TO DRAG ME OUT OF BED AT TWO A.M. TO SHOW ME THIS?

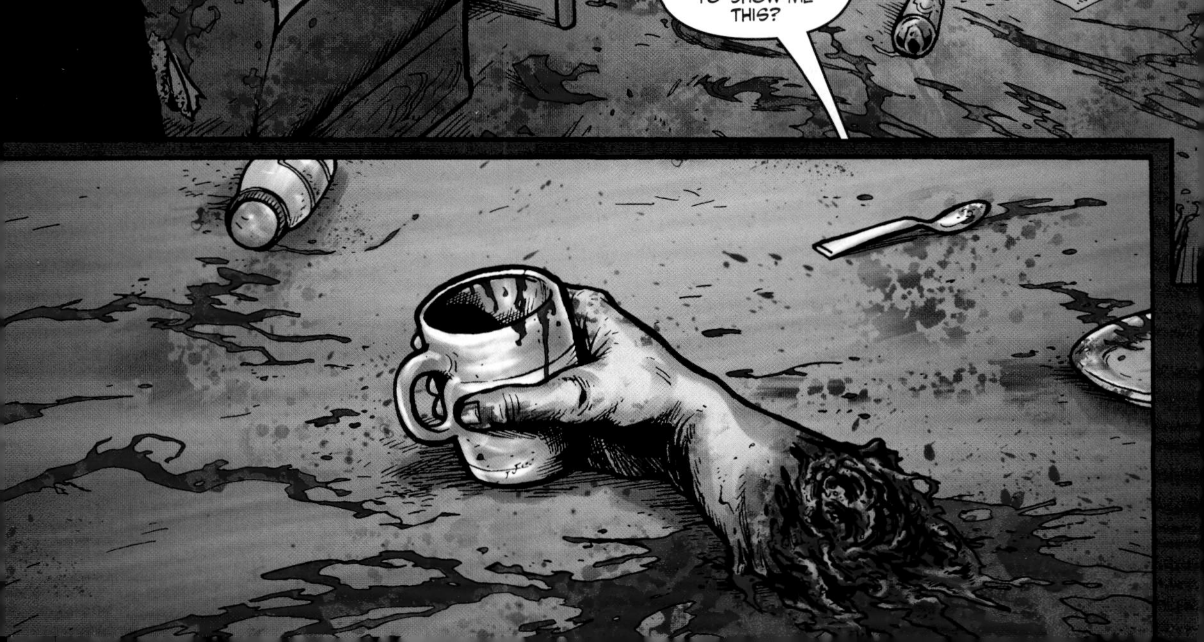

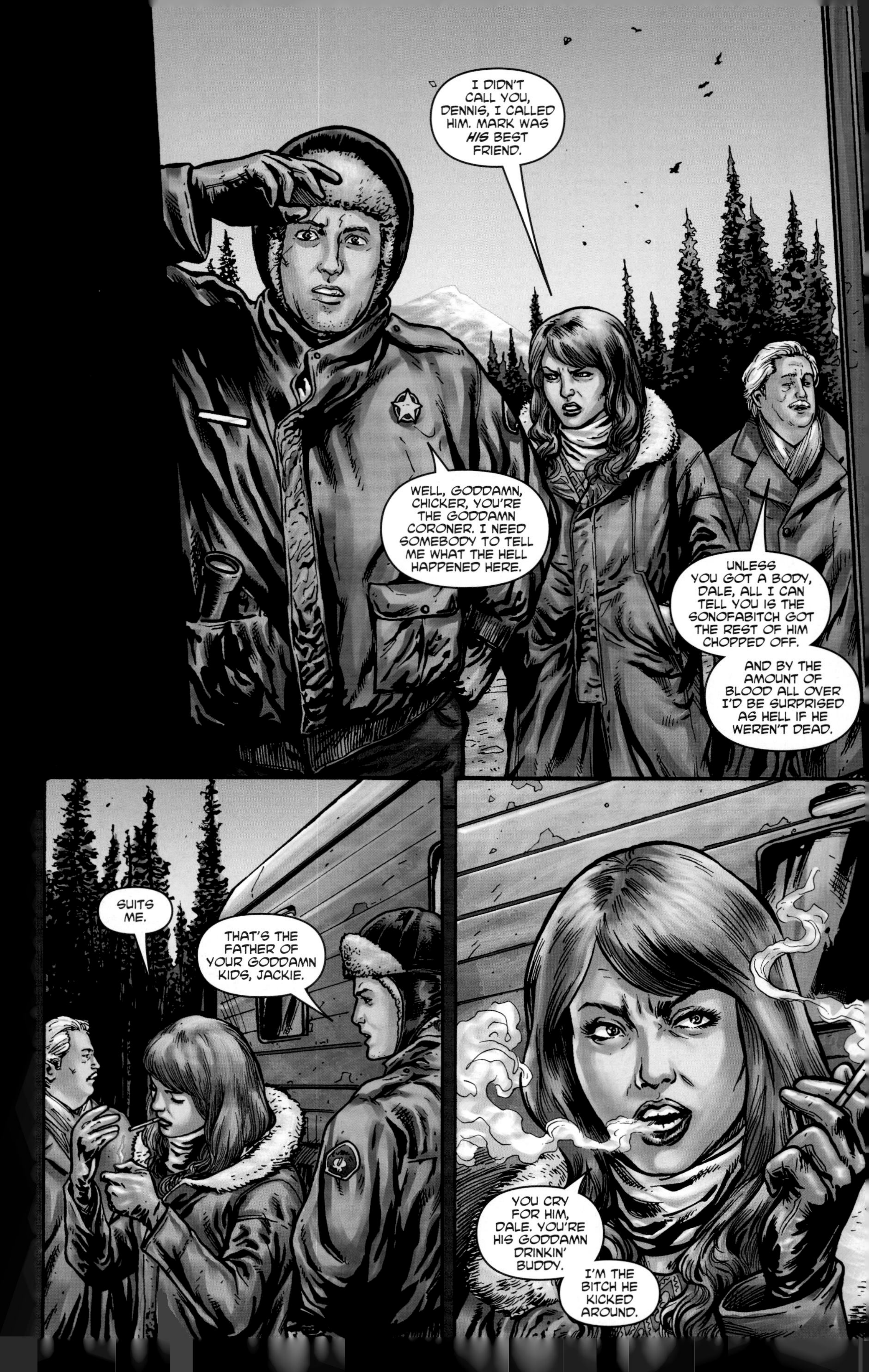

I DIDN'T CALL YOU, DENNIS, I CALLED HIM. MARK WAS *HIS* BEST FRIEND.
WELL, GODDAMN, CHICKER, YOU'RE THE GODDAMN CORONER. I NEED SOMEBODY TO TELL ME WHAT THE HELL HAPPENED HERE.
UNLESS YOU GOT A BODY, DALE, ALL I CAN TELL YOU IS THE SONOFABITCH GOT THE REST OF HIM CHOPPED OFF.
AND BY THE AMOUNT OF BLOOD ALL OVER I'D BE SURPRISED AS HELL IF HE WEREN'T DEAD.
THAT'S THE FATHER OF YOUR GODDAMN KIDS, JACKIE.
SUITS ME.
YOU CRY FOR HIM, DALE. YOU'RE HIS GODDAMN DRINKIN' BUDDY.
I'M THE BITCH HE KICKED AROUND.

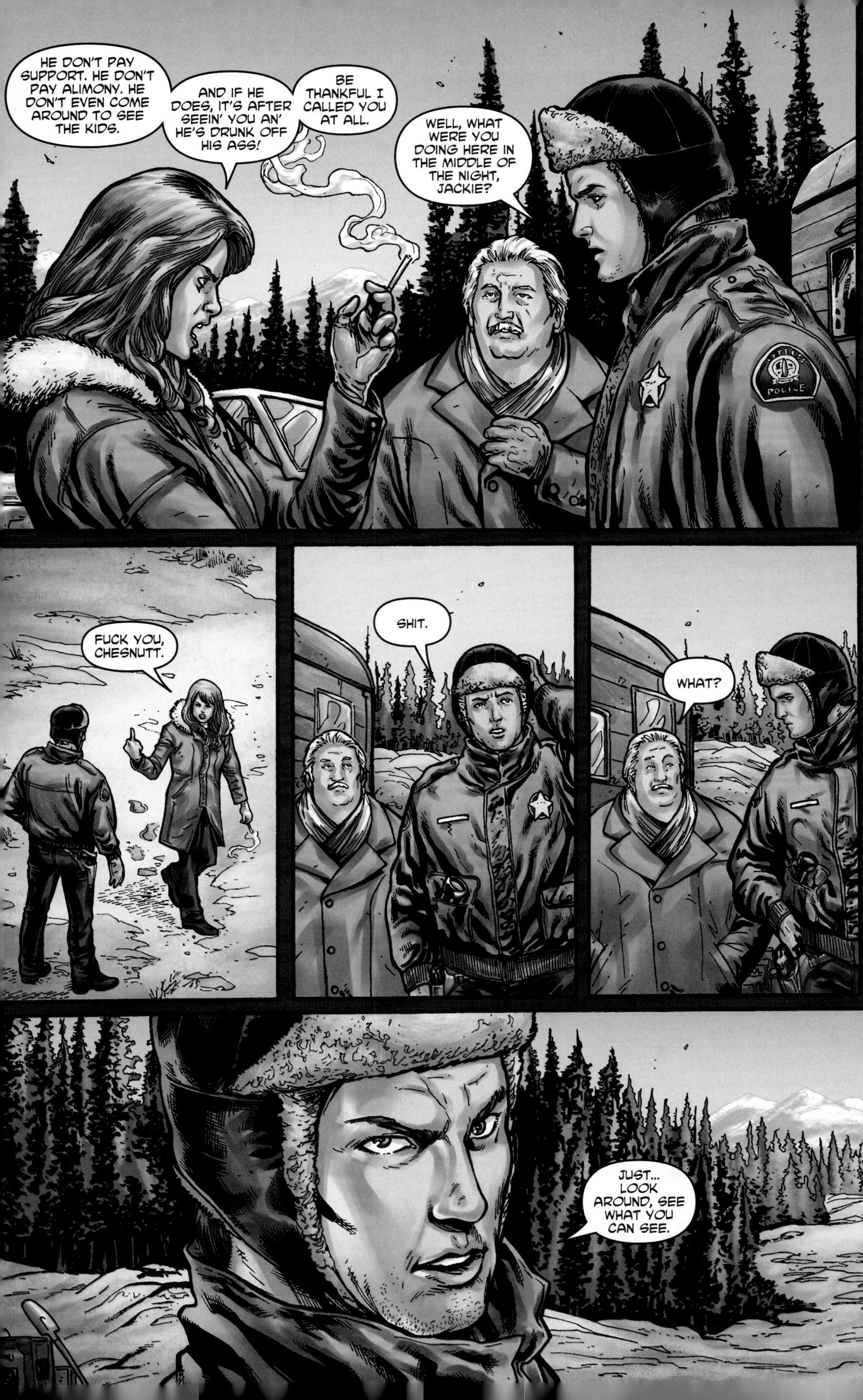
HE DON'T PAY SUPPORT. HE DON'T PAY ALIMONY. HE DON'T EVEN COME AROUND TO SEE THE KIDS.
AND IF HE DOES, IT'S AFTER SEEIN' YOU AN' HE'S DRUNK OFF HIS ASS!
BE THANKFUL I CALLED YOU AT ALL.
WELL, WHAT WERE YOU DOING HERE IN THE MIDDLE OF THE NIGHT, JACKIE?
POLICE
FUCK YOU, CHESNUTT.
SHIT.
WHAT?
JUST... LOOK AROUND, SEE WHAT YOU CAN SEE.

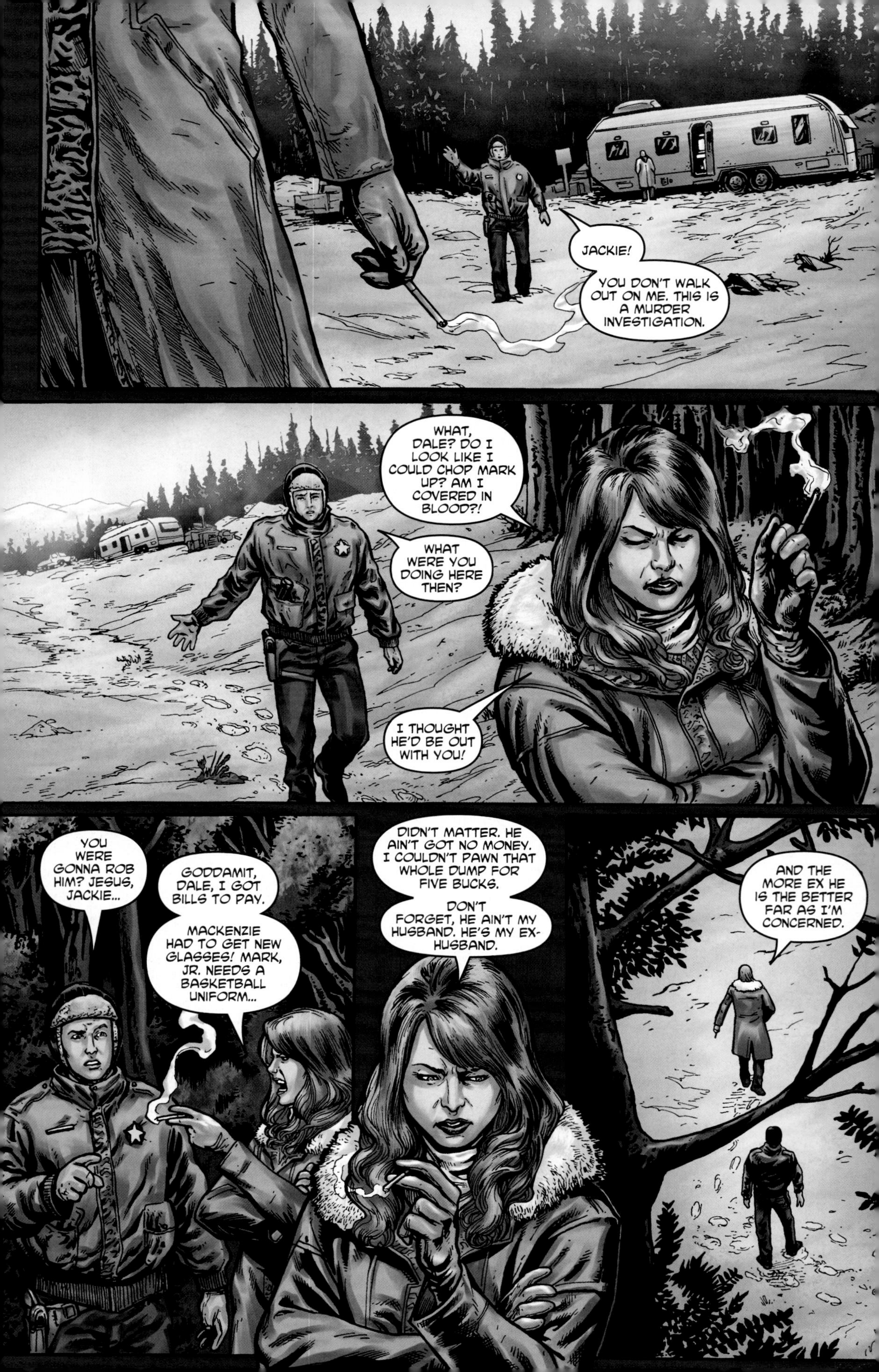

JACKIE!
YOU DON'T WALK OUT ON ME. THIS IS A MURDER INVESTIGATION.
WHAT, DALE? DO I LOOK LIKE I COULD CHOP MARK UP? AM I COVERED IN BLOOD?!
WHAT WERE YOU DOING HERE THEN?
I THOUGHT HE'D BE OUT WITH YOU!
YOU WERE GONNA ROB HIM? JESUS, JACKIE...
GODDAMIT, DALE, I GOT BILLS TO PAY.
MACKENZIE HAD TO GET NEW GLASSES! MARK, JR. NEEDS A BASKETBALL UNIFORM...
DIDN'T MATTER. HE AIN'T GOT NO MONEY. I COULDN'T PAWN THAT WHOLE DUMP FOR FIVE BUCKS.
DON'T FORGET, HE AIN'T MY HUSBAND. HE'S MY EX-HUSBAND.
AND THE MORE EX HE IS THE BETTER FAR AS I'M CONCERNED.

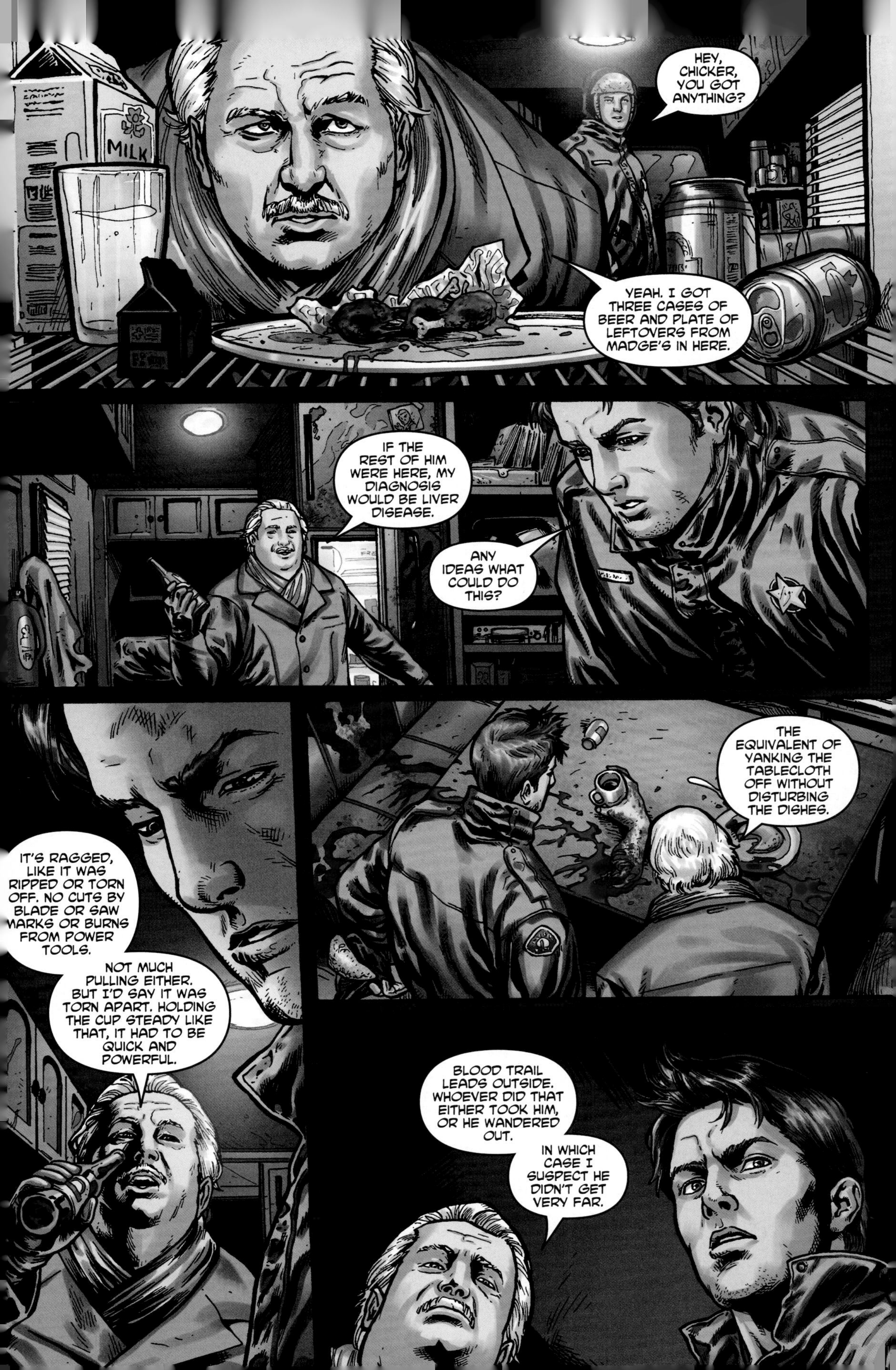
HEY, CHICKER, YOU GOT ANYTHING?
YEAH. I GOT THREE CASES OF BEER AND PLATE OF LEFTOVERS FROM MADGE'S IN HERE.
IF THE REST OF HIM WERE HERE, MY DIAGNOSIS WOULD BE LIVER DISEASE.
ANY IDEAS WHAT COULD DO THIS?
IT'S RAGGED, LIKE IT WAS RIPPED OR TORN OFF. NO CUTS BY BLADE OR SAW MARKS OR BURNS FROM POWER TOOLS.
NOT MUCH PULLING EITHER. BUT I'D SAY IT WAS TORN APART. HOLDING THE CUP STEADY LIKE THAT, IT HAD TO BE QUICK AND POWERFUL.
THE EQUIVALENT OF YANKING THE TABLECLOTH OFF WITHOUT DISTURBING THE DISHES.
BLOOD TRAIL LEADS OUTSIDE. WHOEVER DID THAT EITHER TOOK HIM, OR HE WANDERED OUT.
IN WHICH CASE I SUSPECT HE DIDN'T GET VERY FAR.

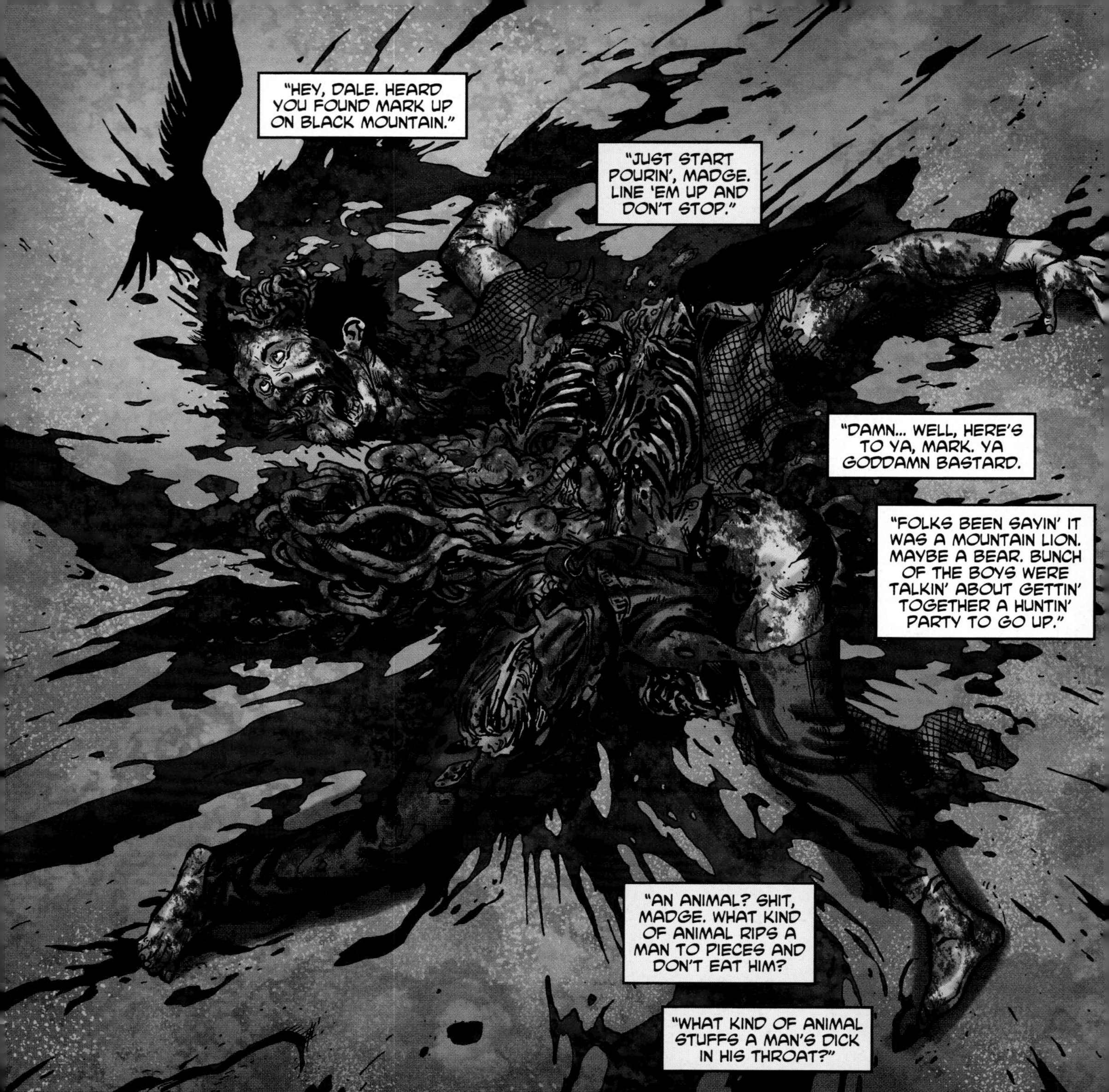
"HEY, DALE. HEARD YOU FOUND MARK UP ON BLACK MOUNTAIN."
"JUST START POURIN', MADGE. LINE 'EM UP AND DON'T STOP."
"DAMN... WELL, HERE'S TO YA, MARK. YA GODDAMN BASTARD.
"FOLKS BEEN SAYIN' IT WAS A MOUNTAIN LION. MAYBE A BEAR. BUNCH OF THE BOYS WERE TALKIN' ABOUT GETTIN' TOGETHER A HUNTIN' PARTY TO GO UP."
"AN ANIMAL? SHIT, MADGE. WHAT KIND OF ANIMAL RIPS A MAN TO PIECES AND DON'T EAT HIM?
"WHAT KIND OF ANIMAL STUFFS A MAN'S DICK IN HIS THROAT?"

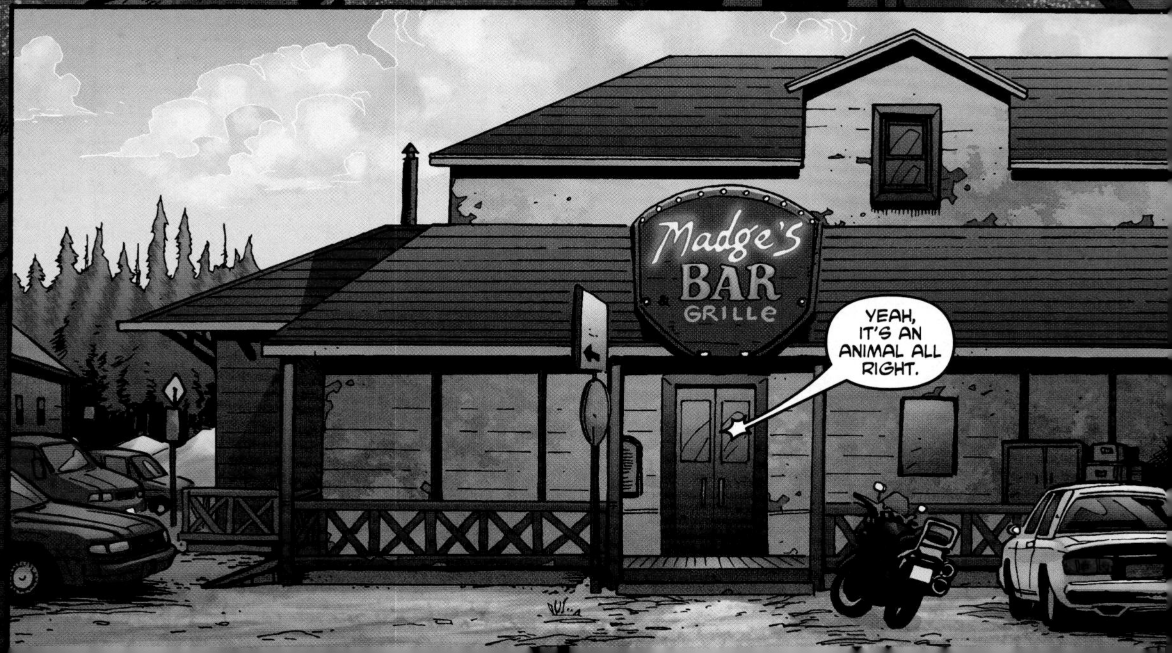
Madge's BAR GRILLE
YEAH, IT'S AN ANIMAL ALL RIGHT.

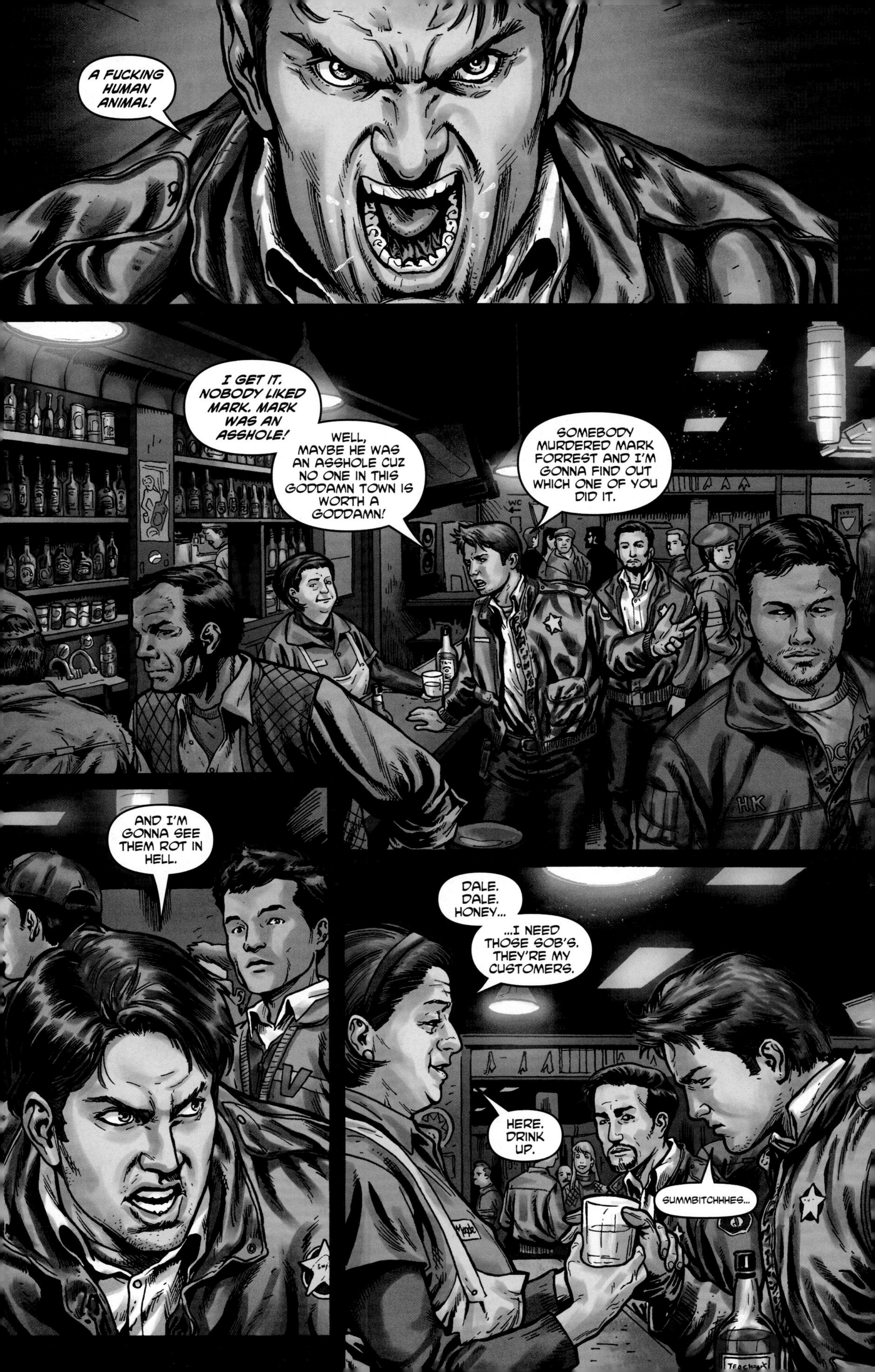
A FUCKING HUMAN ANIMAL!
I GET IT. NOBODY LIKED MARK. MARK WAS AN ASSHOLE!
WELL, MAYBE HE WAS AN ASSHOLE CUZ NO ONE IN THIS GODDAMN TOWN IS WORTH A GODDAMN!
SOMEBODY MURDERED MARK FORREST AND I'M GONNA FIND OUT WHICH ONE OF YOU DID IT.
AND I'M GONNA SEE THEM ROT IN HELL.
DALE. DALE. HONEY...
...I NEED THOSE SOB'S. THEY'RE MY CUSTOMERS.
HERE. DRINK UP.
SUMMBITCHHHES...

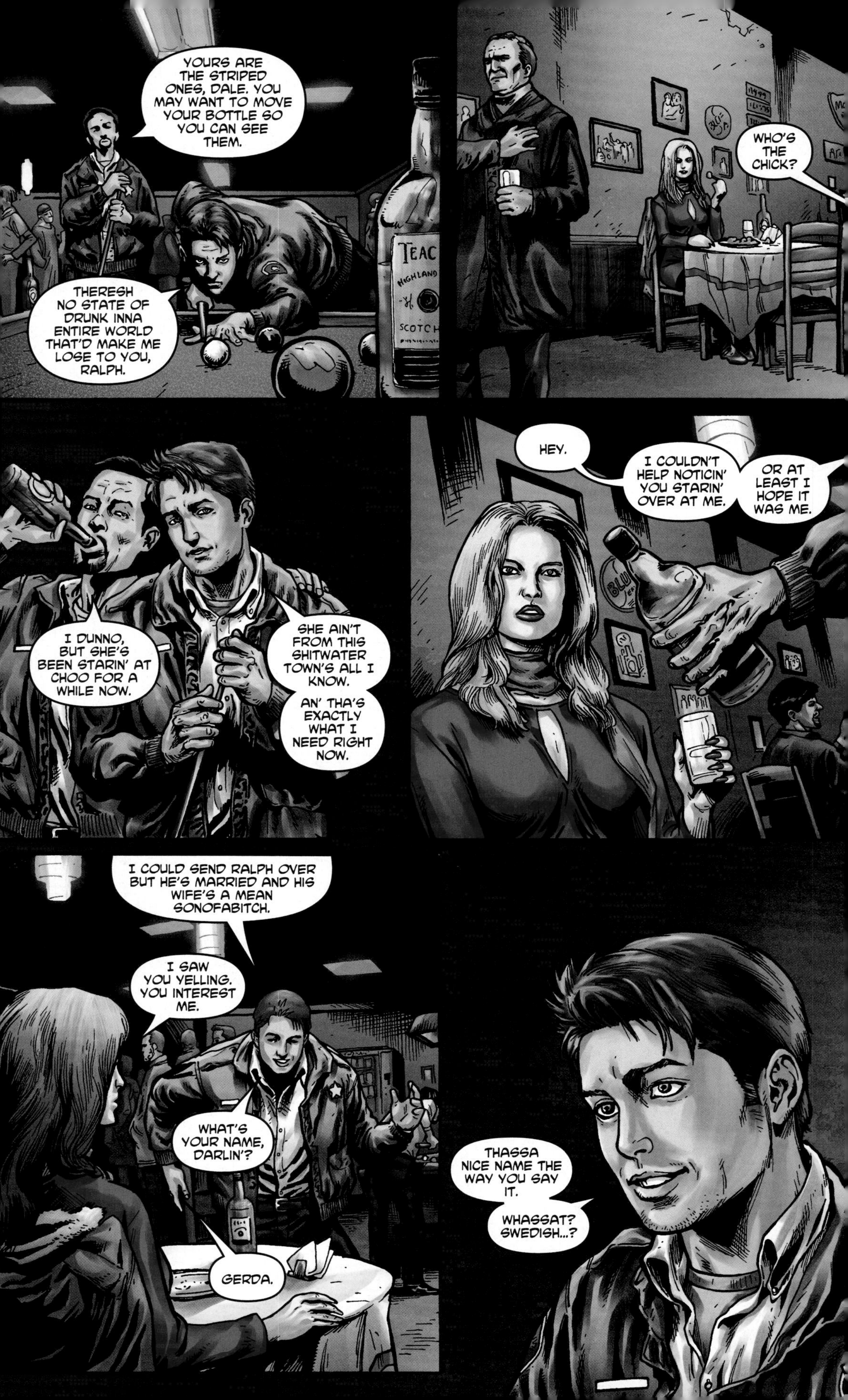
YOURS ARE THE STRIPED ONES, DALE. YOU MAY WANT TO MOVE YOUR BOTTLE SO YOU CAN SEE THEM.
THERESH NO STATE OF DRUNK INNA ENTIRE WORLD THAT'D MAKE ME LOSE TO YOU, RALPH.
TEAC
HIGHLAND
SCOTCH
WHO'S THE CHICK?
I DUNNO, BUT SHE'S BEEN STARIN' AT CHOO FOR A WHILE NOW.
SHE AIN'T FROM THIS SHITWATER TOWN'S ALL I KNOW.
AN' THA'S EXACTLY WHAT I NEED RIGHT NOW.
HEY.
I COULDN'T HELP NOTICIN' YOU STARIN' OVER AT ME.
OR AT LEAST I HOPE IT WAS ME.
I COULD SEND RALPH OVER BUT HE'S MARRIED AND HIS WIFE'S A MEAN SONOFABITCH.
I SAW YOU YELLING. YOU INTEREST ME.
WHAT'S YOUR NAME, DARLIN'?
GERDA.
THASSA NICE NAME THE WAY YOU SAY IT.
WHASSAT? SWEDISH...?

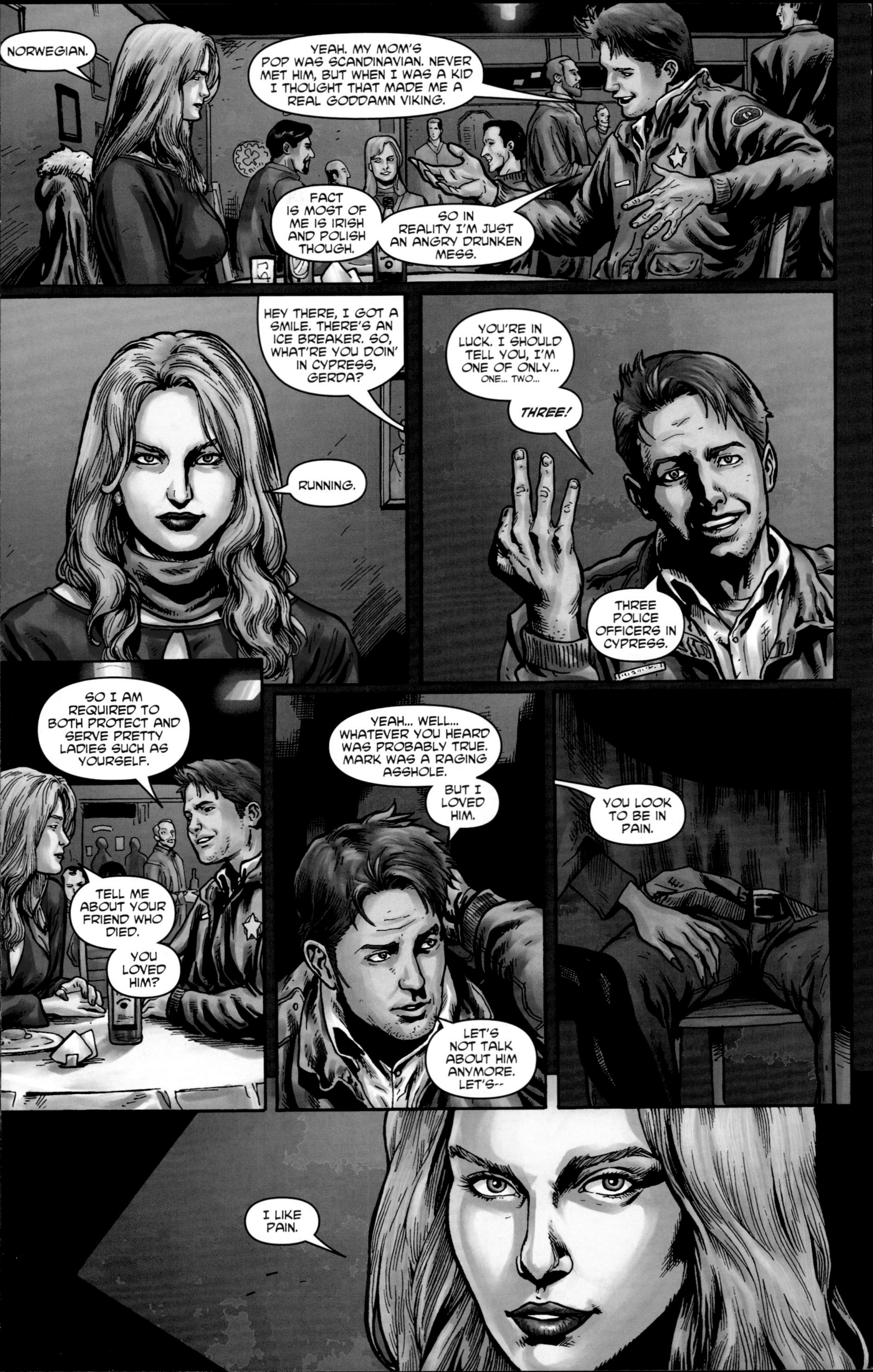
NORWEGIAN.
YEAH. MY MOM'S POP WAS SCANDINAVIAN. NEVER MET HIM, BUT WHEN I WAS A KID I THOUGHT THAT MADE ME A REAL GODDAMN VIKING.
FACT IS MOST OF ME IS IRISH AND POLISH THOUGH.
SO IN REALITY I'M JUST AN ANGRY DRUNKEN MESS.
HEY THERE, I GOT A SMILE. THERE'S AN ICE BREAKER. SO, WHAT'RE YOU DOIN' IN CYPRESS, GERDA?
RUNNING.
YOU'RE IN LUCK. I SHOULD TELL YOU, I'M ONE OF ONLY... ONE... TWO...
THREE!
THREE POLICE OFFICERS IN CYPRESS.
SO I AM REQUIRED TO BOTH PROTECT AND SERVE PRETTY LADIES SUCH AS YOURSELF.
TELL ME ABOUT YOUR FRIEND WHO DIED.
YOU LOVED HIM?
YEAH... WELL... WHATEVER YOU HEARD WAS PROBABLY TRUE. MARK WAS A RAGING ASSHOLE.
BUT I LOVED HIM.
LET'S NOT TALK ABOUT HIM ANYMORE. LET'S--
YOU LOOK TO BE IN PAIN.
I LIKE PAIN.

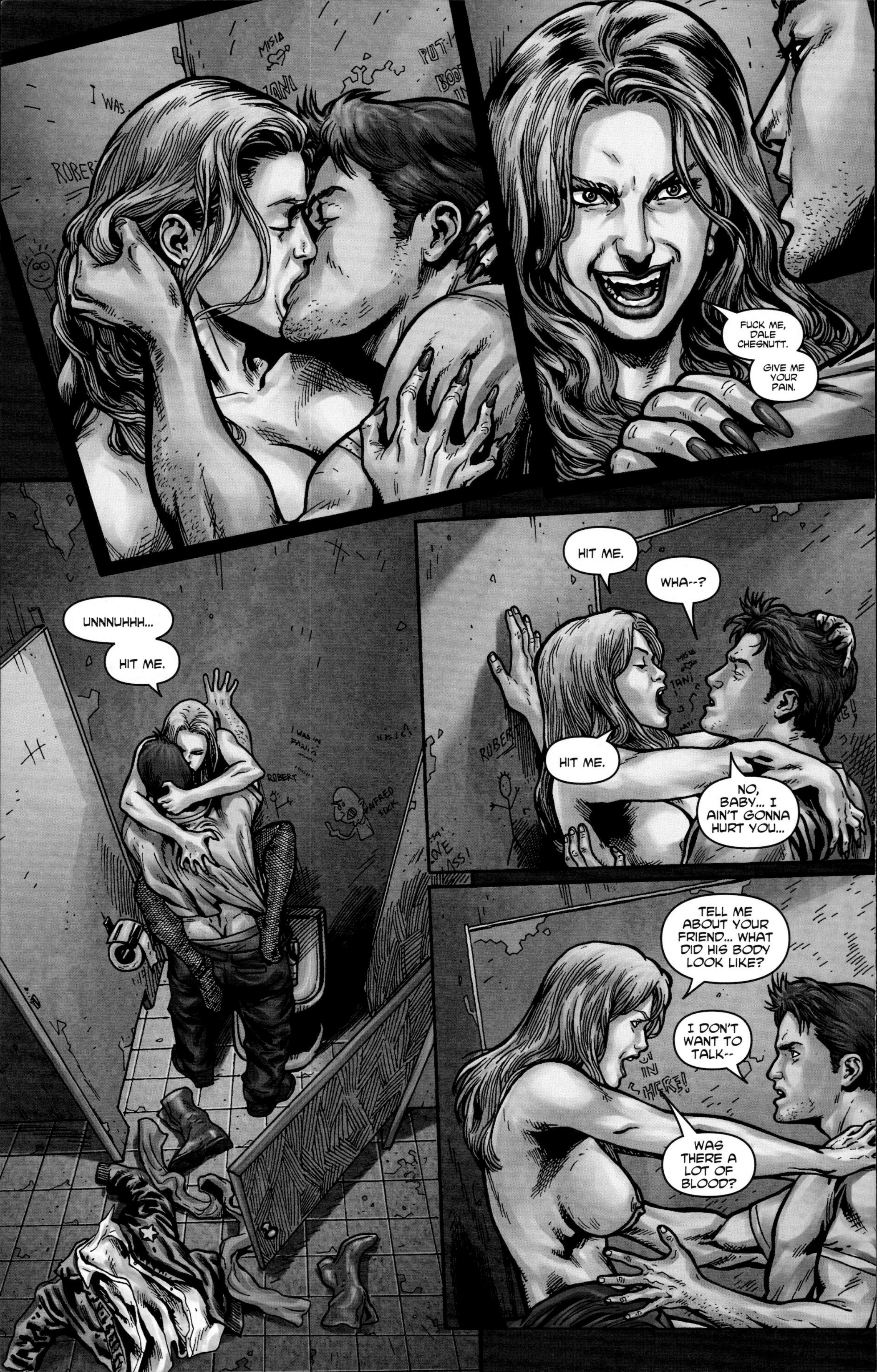
FUCK ME, DALE CHESNUTT.
GIVE ME YOUR PAIN.
UNNNUHHH...
HIT ME.
HIT ME.
WHA--?
HIT ME.
NO, BABY... I AIN'T GONNA HURT YOU...
TELL ME ABOUT YOUR FRIEND... WHAT DID HIS BODY LOOK LIKE?
I DON'T WANT TO TALK--
WAS THERE A LOT OF BLOOD?

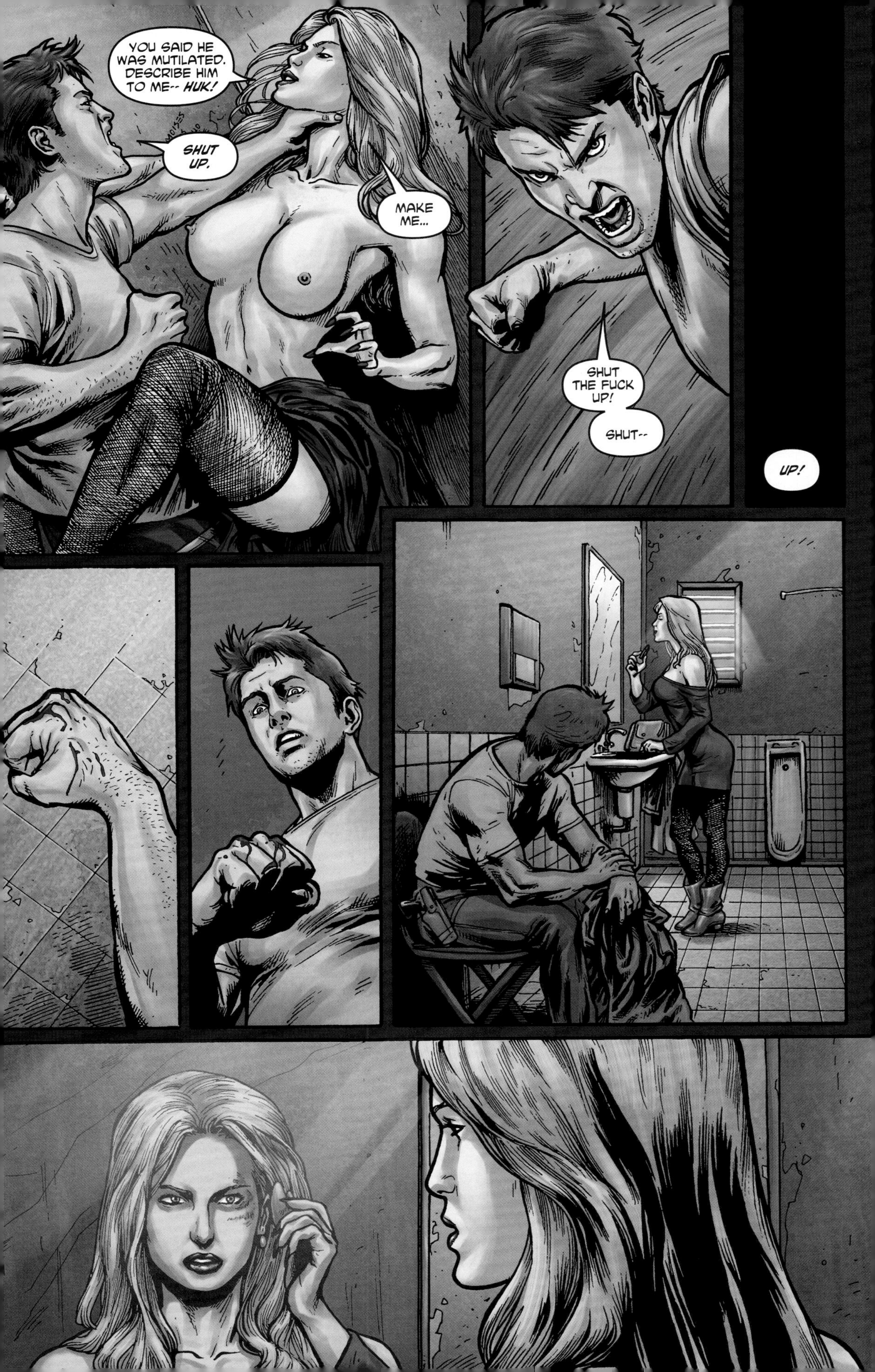

YOU SAID HE WAS MUTILATED. DESCRIBE HIM TO ME-- HUK!
SHUT UP.
MAKE ME...
SHUT THE FUCK UP!
SHUT--
UP!

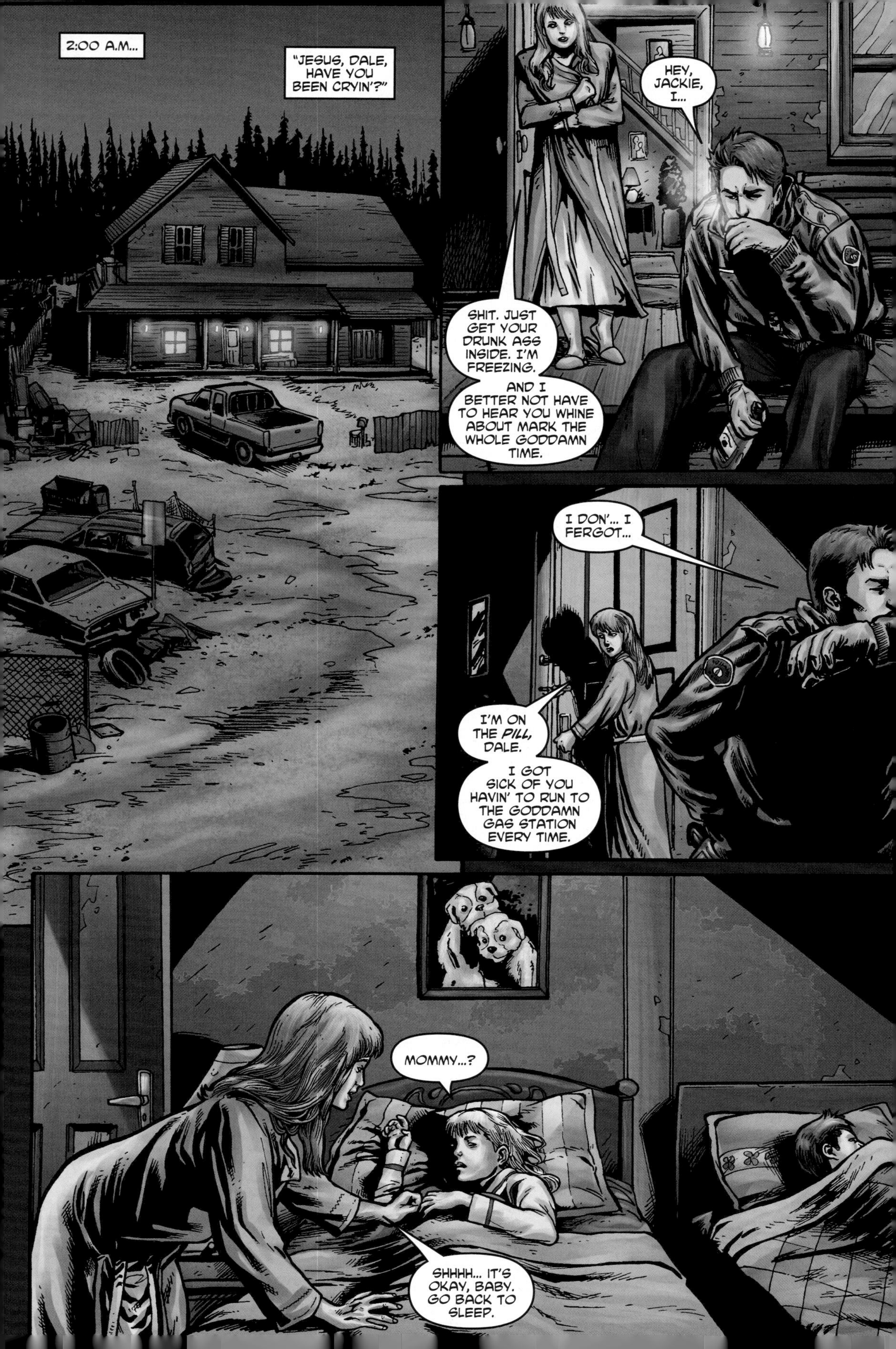
2:00 A.M...
"JESUS, DALE, HAVE YOU BEEN CRYIN'?"
HEY, JACKIE, I...
SHIT. JUST GET YOUR DRUNK ASS INSIDE. I'M FREEZING.
AND I BETTER NOT HAVE TO HEAR YOU WHINE ABOUT MARK THE WHOLE GODDAMN TIME.
I DON'... I FERGOT...
I'M ON THE *PILL,* DALE.
I GOT SICK OF YOU HAVIN' TO RUN TO THE GODDAMN GAS STATION EVERY TIME.
MOMMY...?
SHHHH... IT'S OKAY, BABY. GO BACK TO SLEEP.

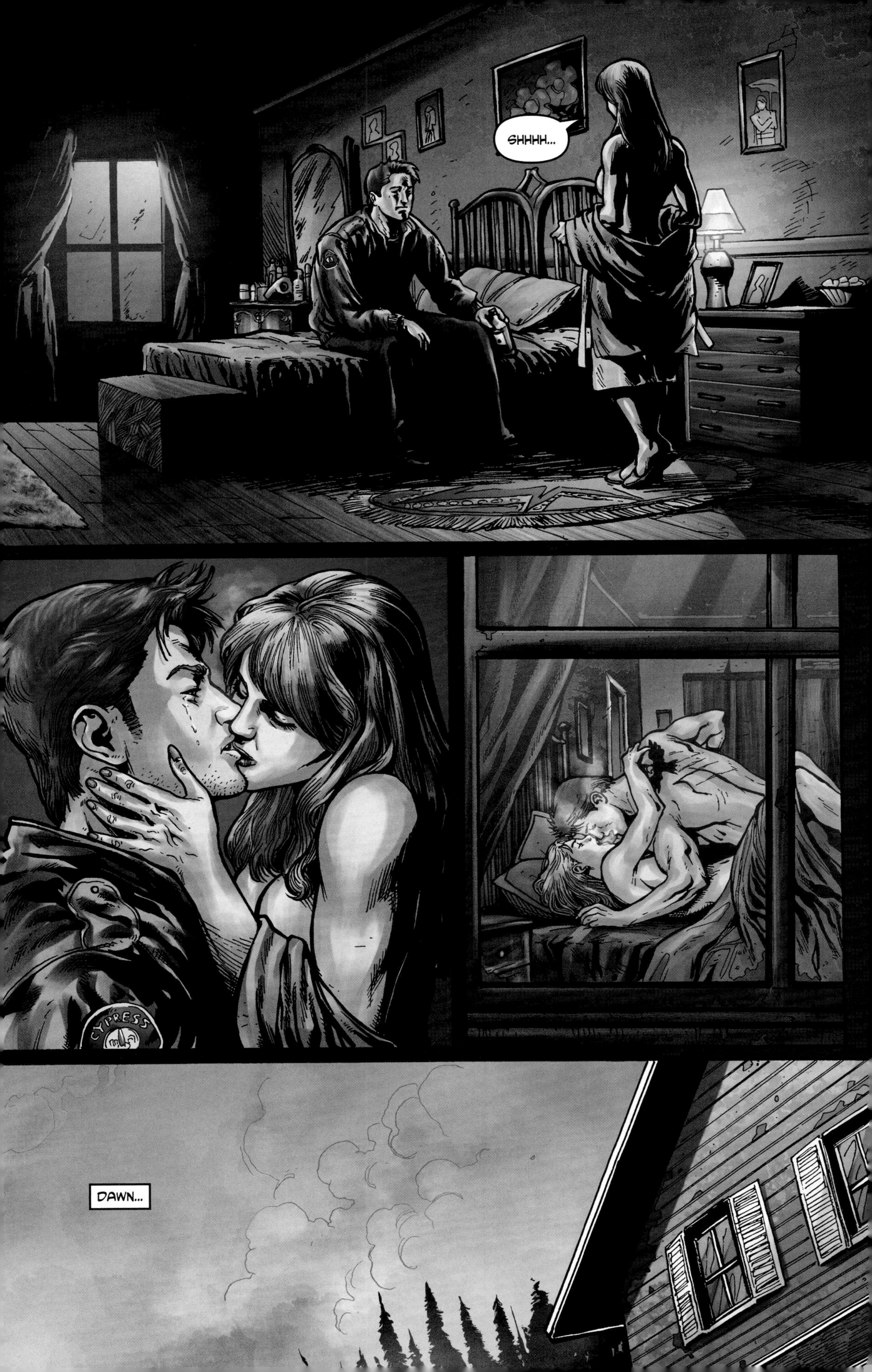
SHHHH...
CYPRESS
DAWN...

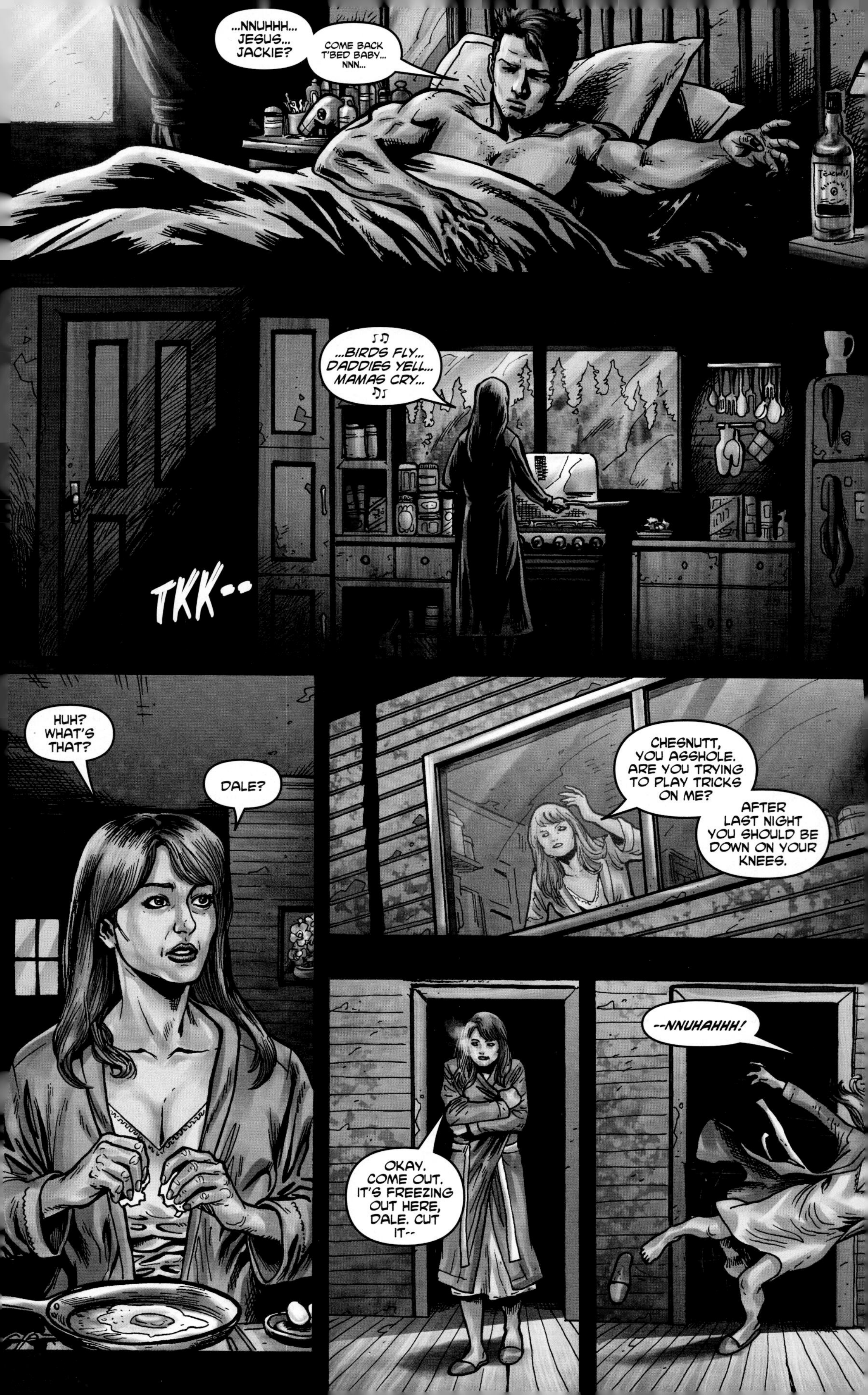
...NNUHHH... JESUS... JACKIE?
COME BACK T'BED BABY... NNN...
...BIRDS FLY... DADDIES YELL... MAMAS CRY...
TKK--
HUH? WHAT'S THAT?
DALE?
CHESNUTT, YOU ASSHOLE. ARE YOU TRYING TO PLAY TRICKS ON ME?
AFTER LAST NIGHT YOU SHOULD BE DOWN ON YOUR KNEES.
OKAY. COME OUT. IT'S FREEZING OUT HERE, DALE. CUT IT--
--NNUHAHHH!

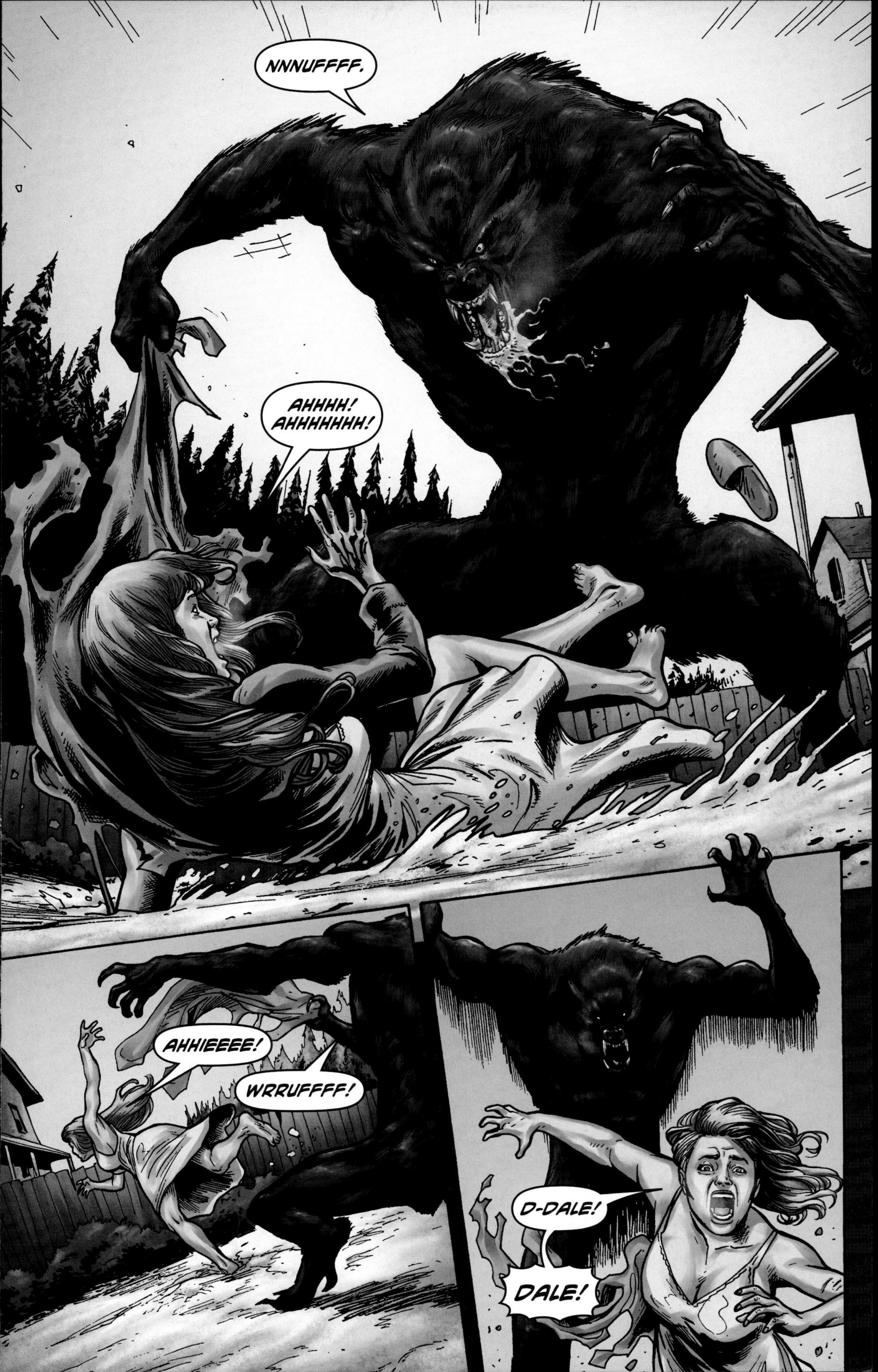
NNNUFFFF.
AHHHH! AHHHHHHH!
AHHIEEEE!
WRRUFFFF!
D-DALE!
DALE!

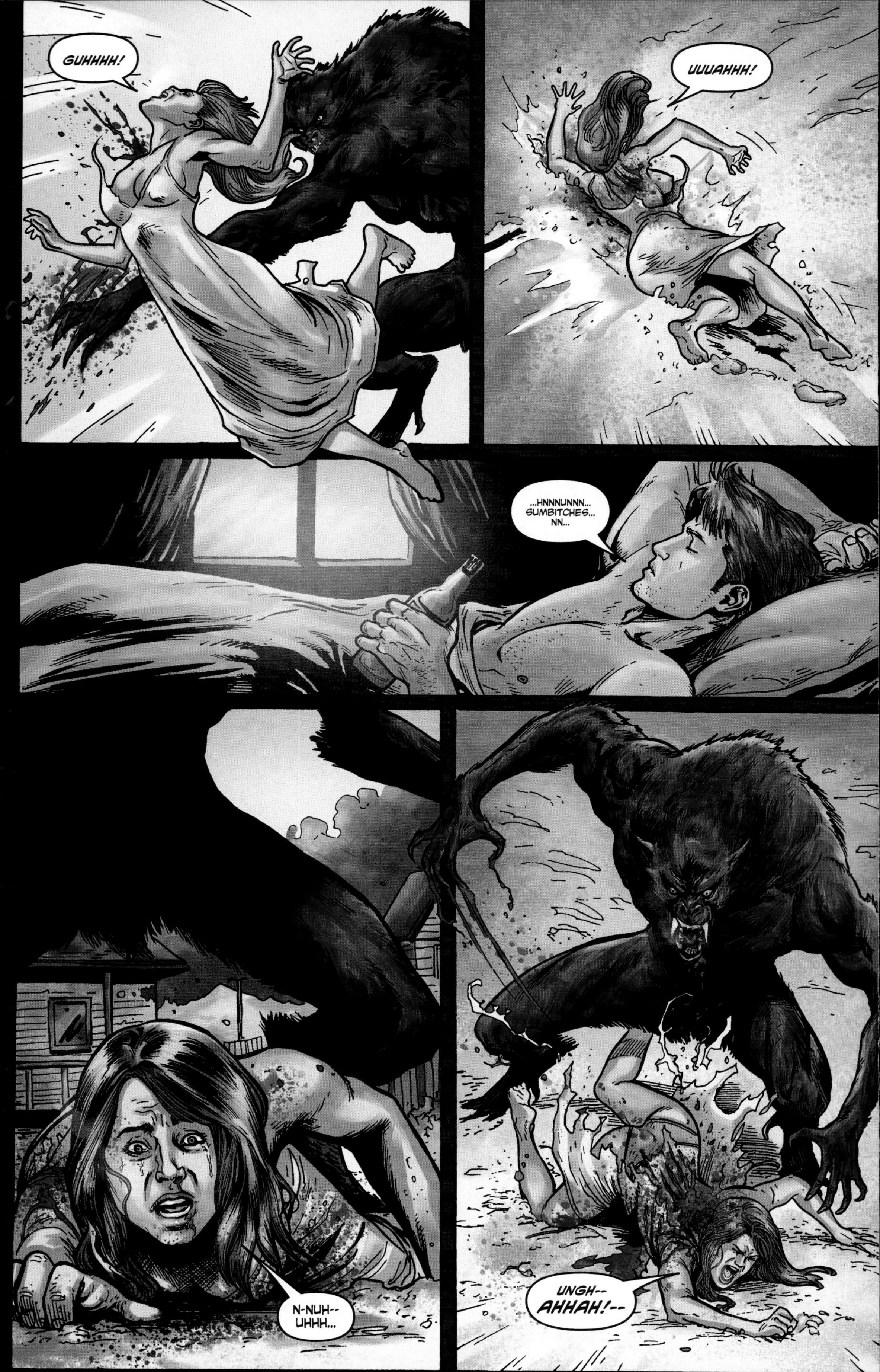
GUHHHH!
UUUAHHH!
...HNNNUNNN... SUMBITCHES... NN...
N-NUH-- UHHH...
UNGH-- AHHAH!--

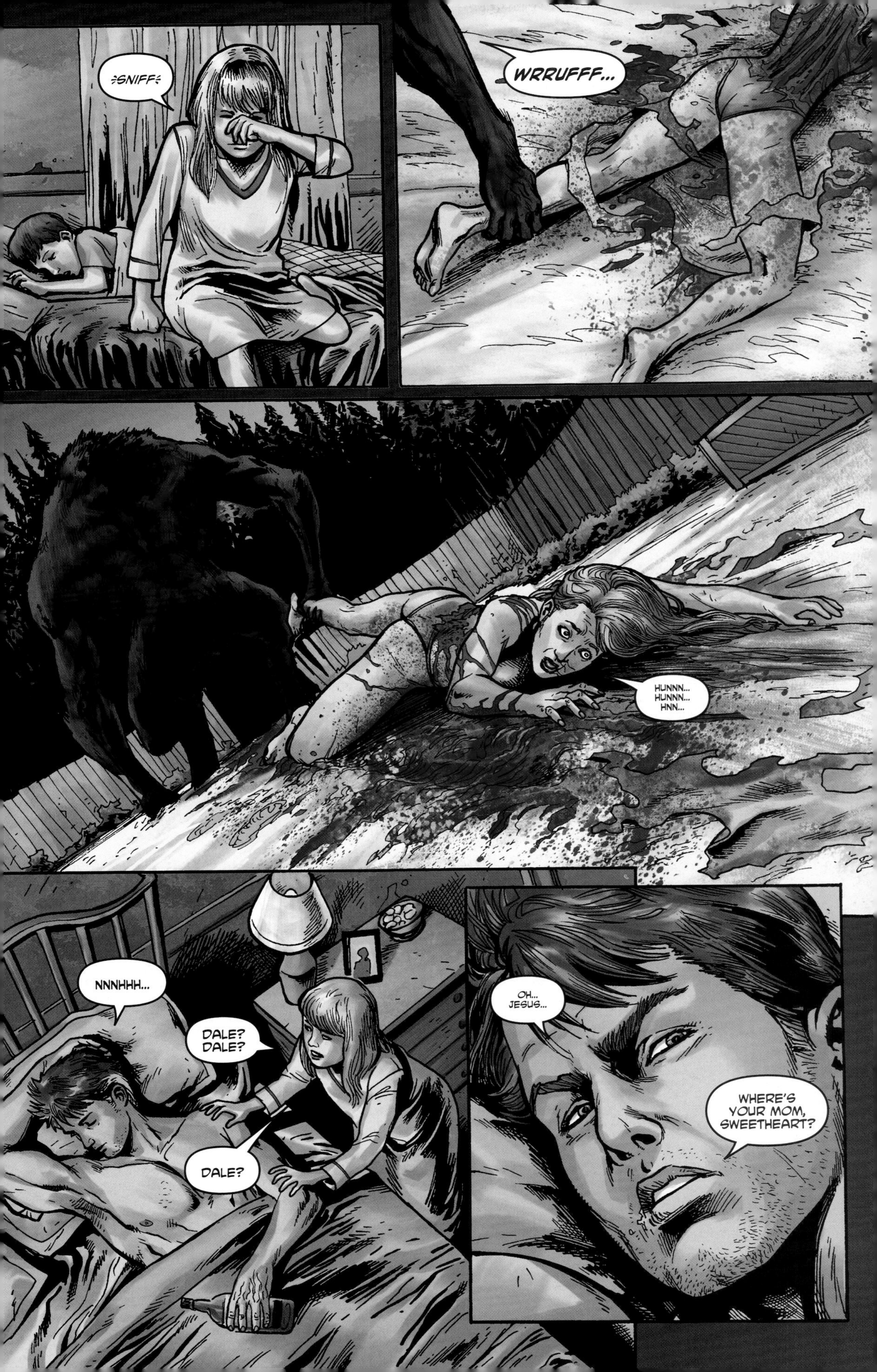

SNIFF
WRRUFFF...
HUNNN... HUNNN... HNN...
NNNHHH...
DALE? DALE?
DALE?
OH... JESUS...
WHERE'S YOUR MOM, SWEETHEART?

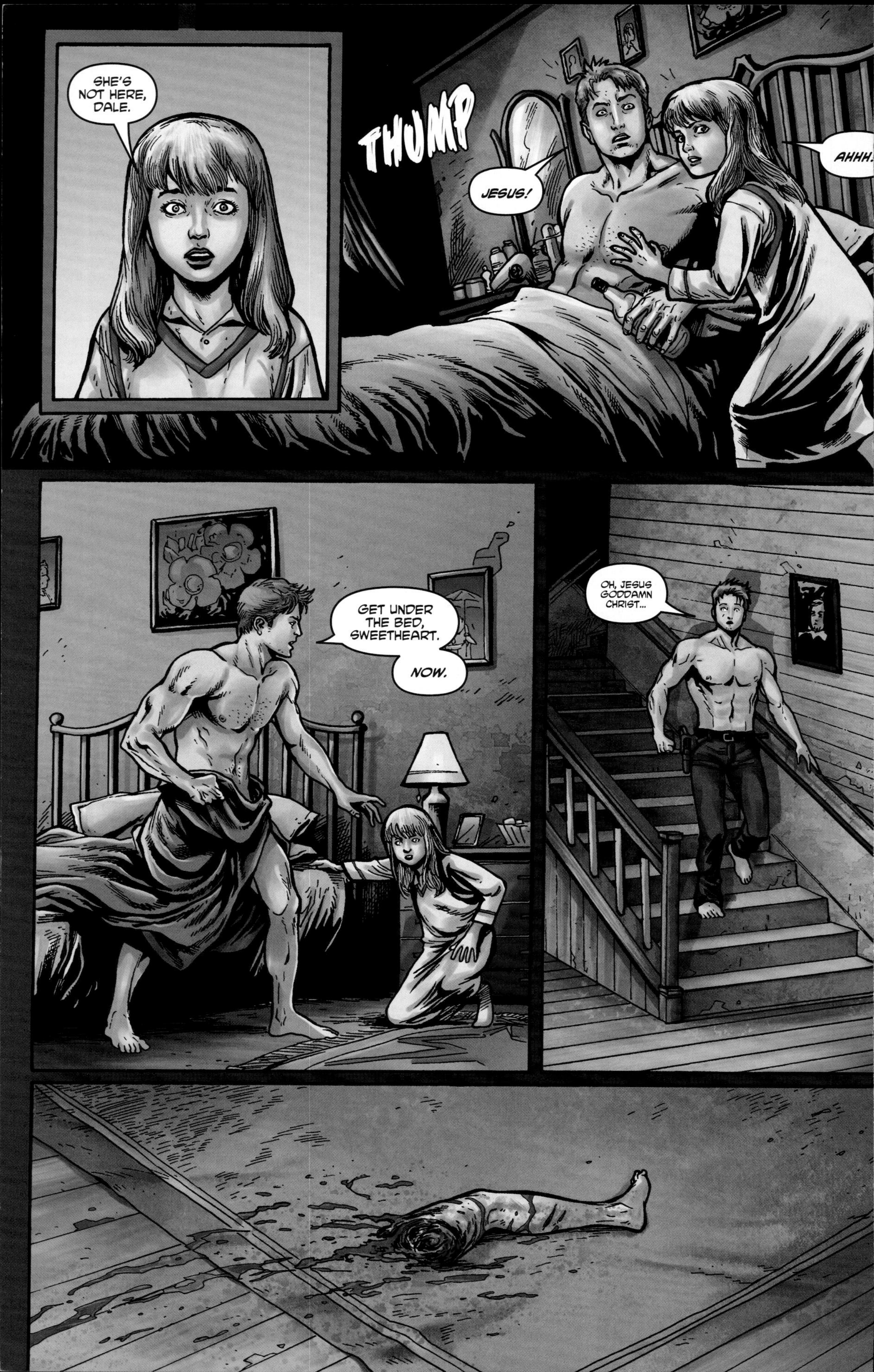
SHE'S NOT HERE, DALE.
THUMP
JESUS!
AHHH!
GET UNDER THE BED, SWEETHEART.
NOW.
OH, JESUS GODDAMN CHRIST...

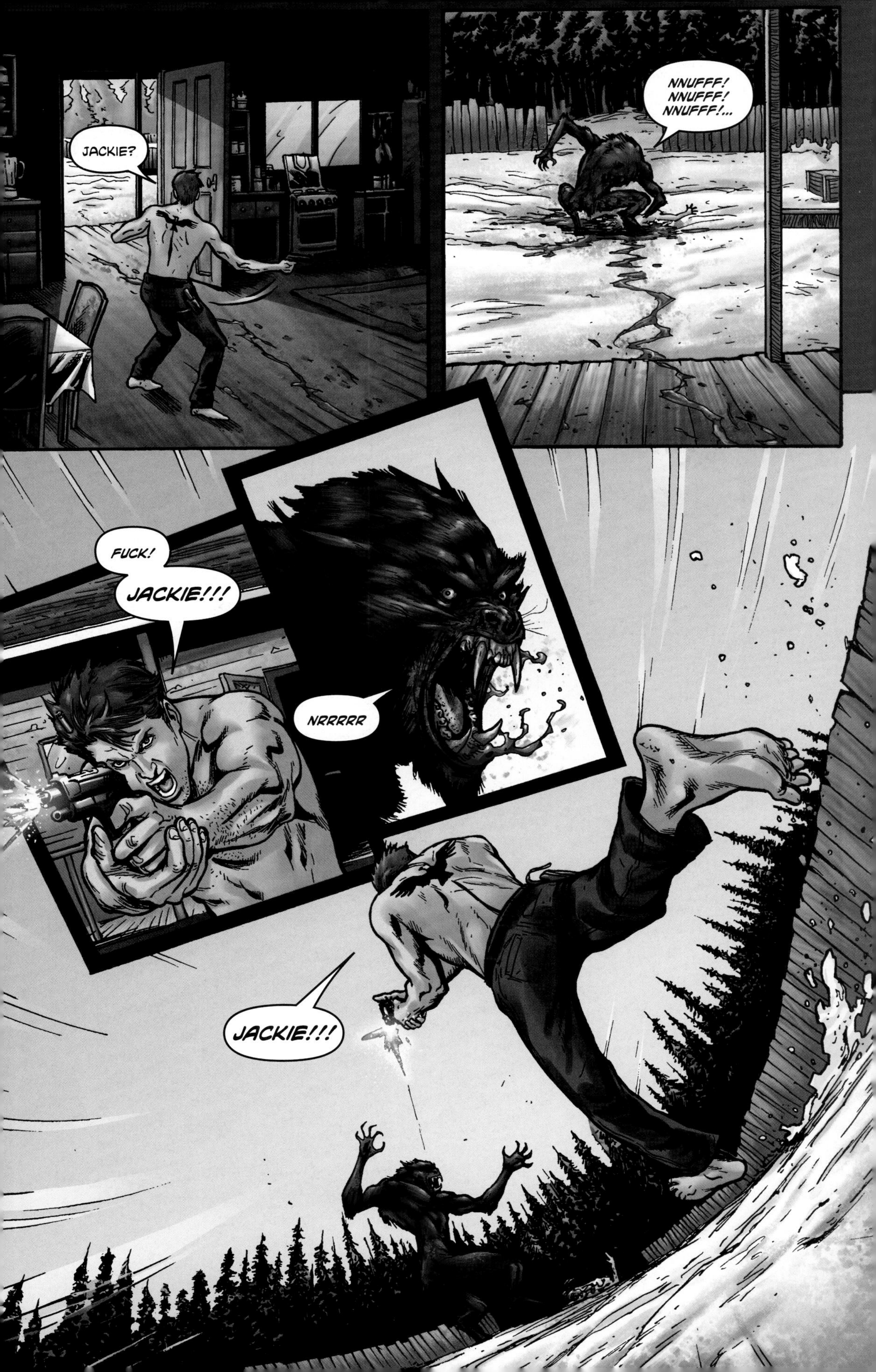
JACKIE?
NNUFFF! NNUFFF! NNUFFF!...
FUCK!
JACKIE!!!
NRRRRR
JACKIE!!!

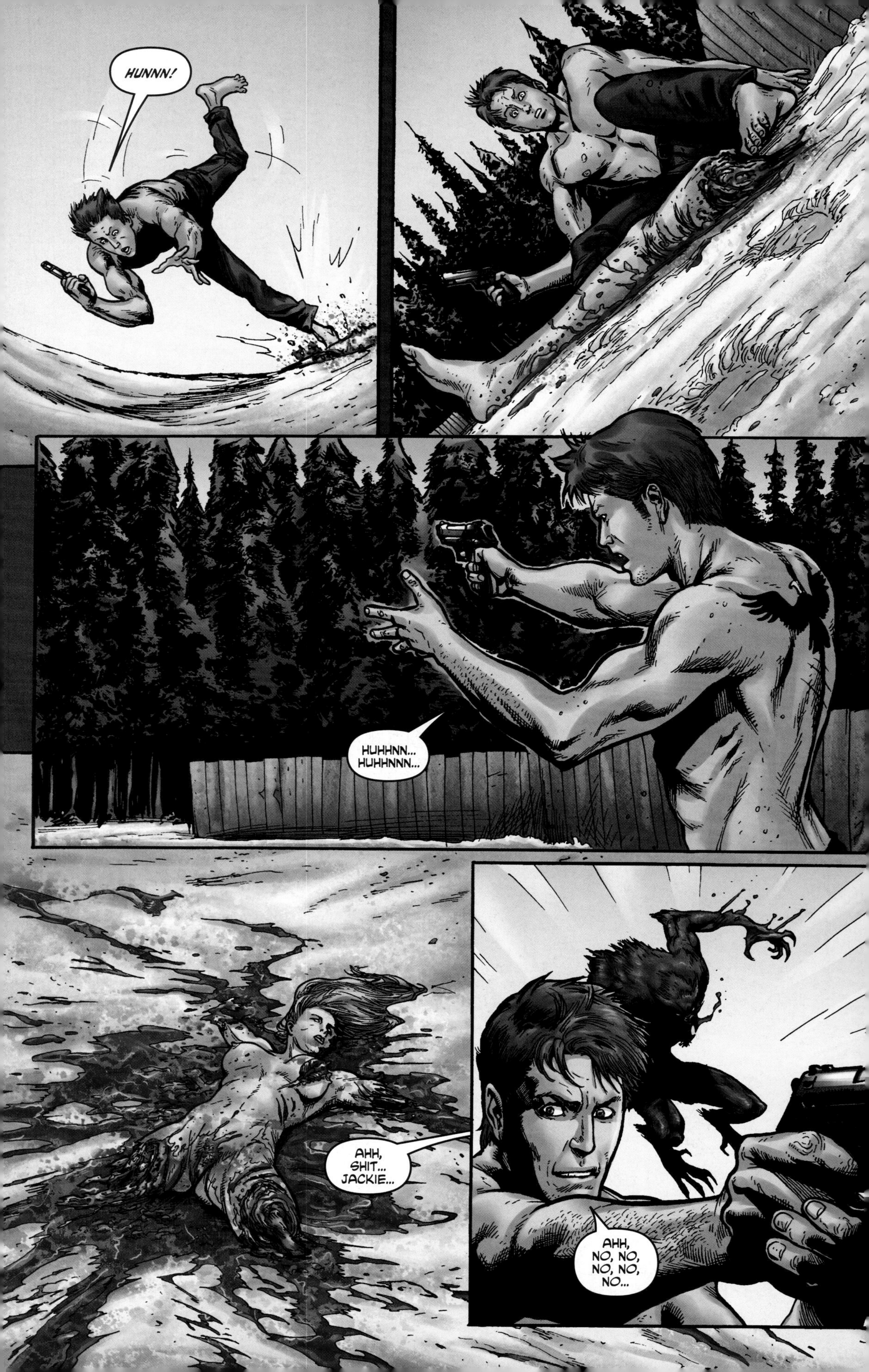
HUNNN!
HUHHNN... HUHHNNN...
AHH, SHIT... JACKIE...
AHH, NO, NO, NO, NO, NO...

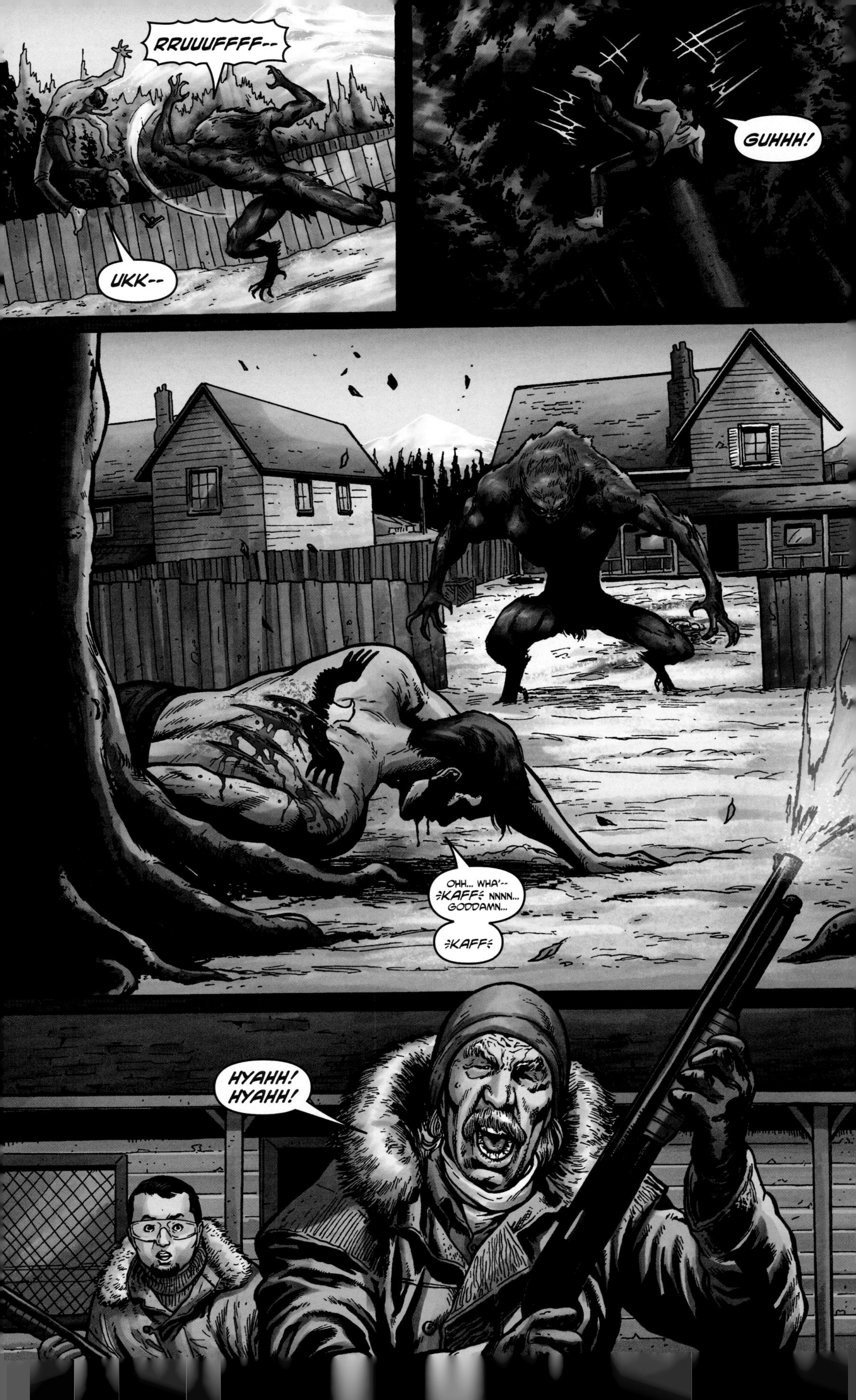
RRUUUFFFF--
UKK--
GUHHH!
OHH... WHA'-- ‹KAFF› NNNN... GODDAMN...
‹KAFF›
HYAHH! HYAHH!

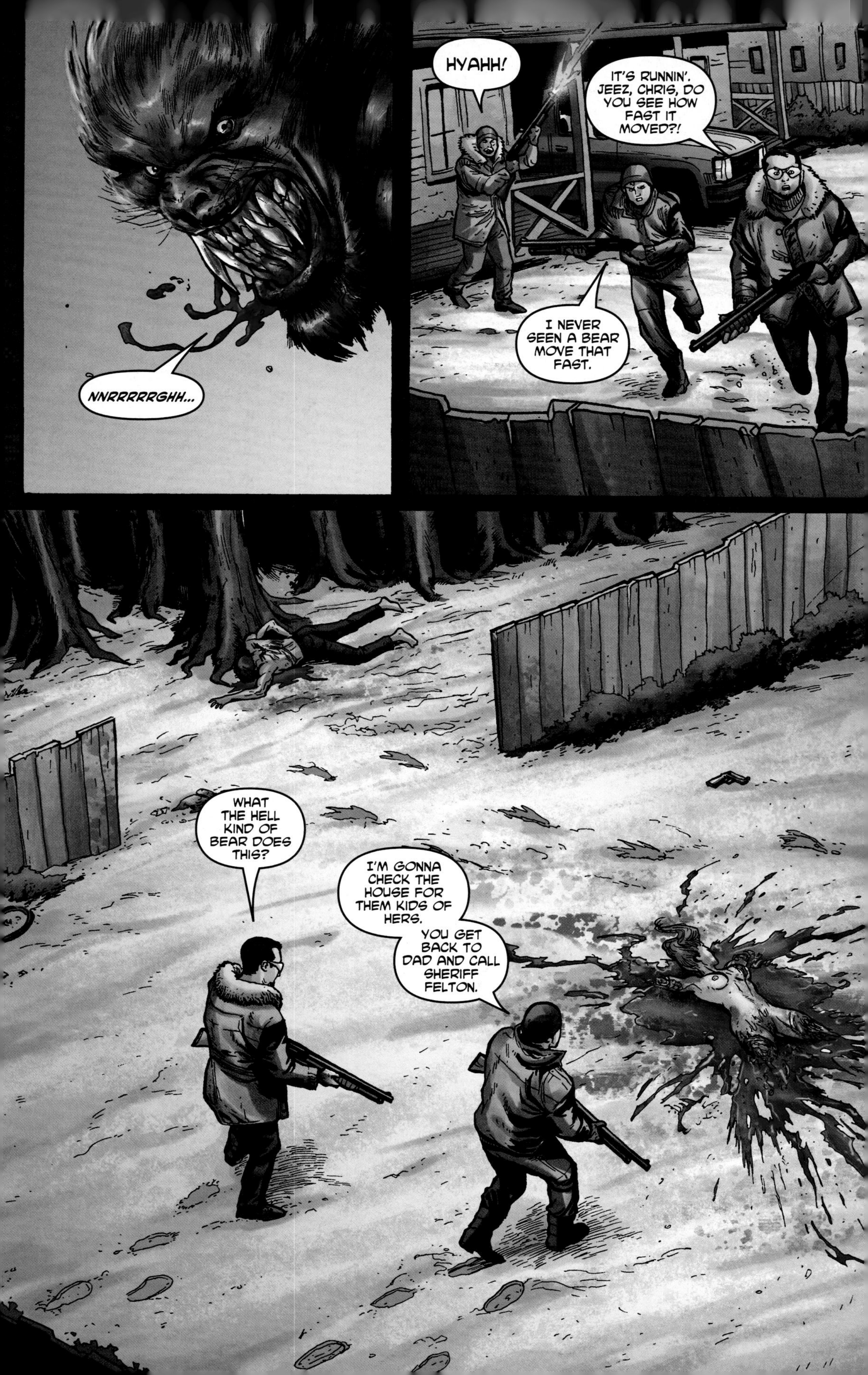
NNRRRRRRGHH...
HYAHH!
IT'S RUNNIN'. JEEZ, CHRIS, DO YOU SEE HOW FAST IT MOVED?!
I NEVER SEEN A BEAR MOVE THAT FAST.
WHAT THE HELL KIND OF BEAR DOES THIS?
I'M GONNA CHECK THE HOUSE FOR THEM KIDS OF HERS.
YOU GET BACK TO DAD AND CALL SHERIFF FELTON.

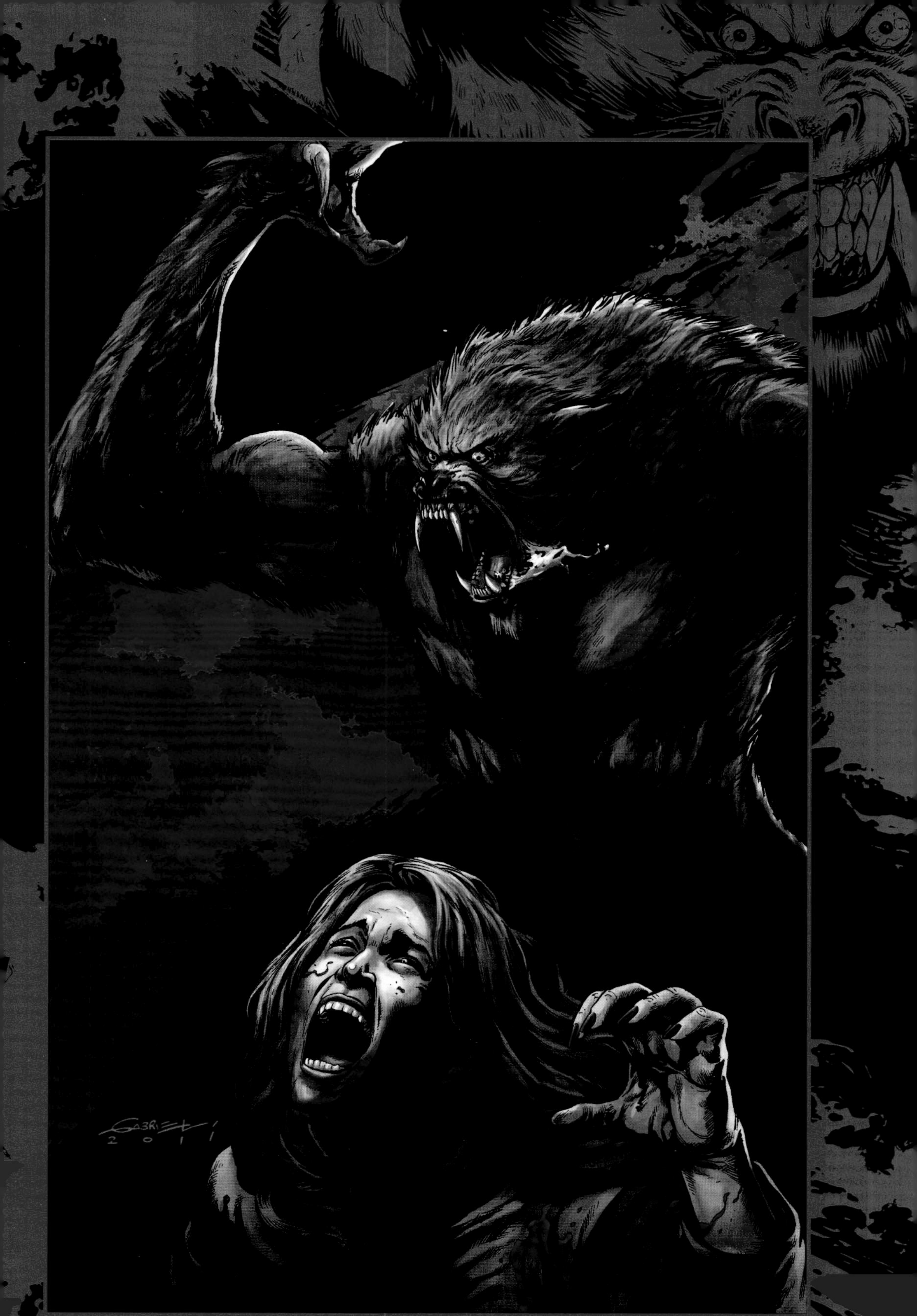

CHAPTER 2

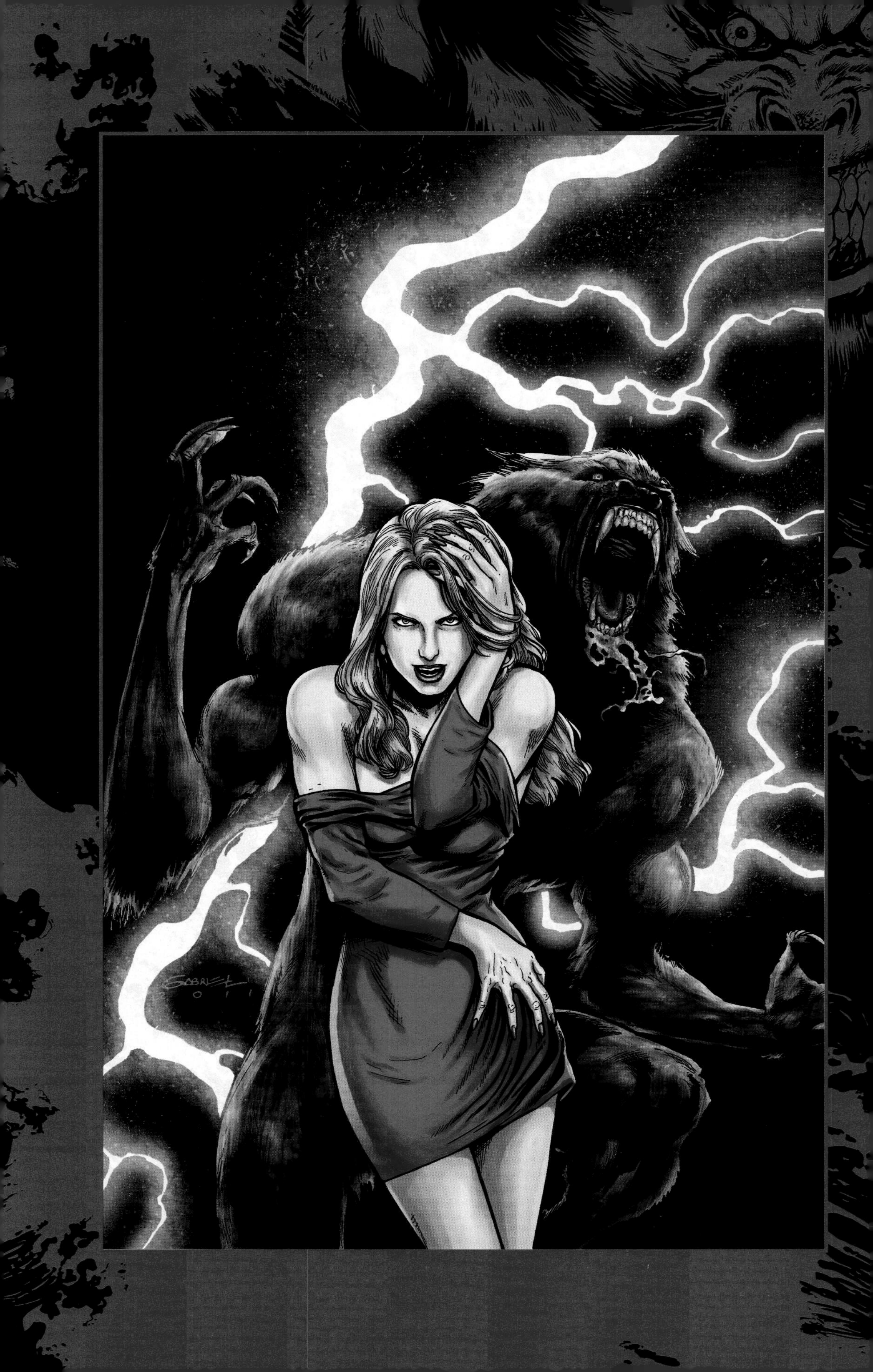

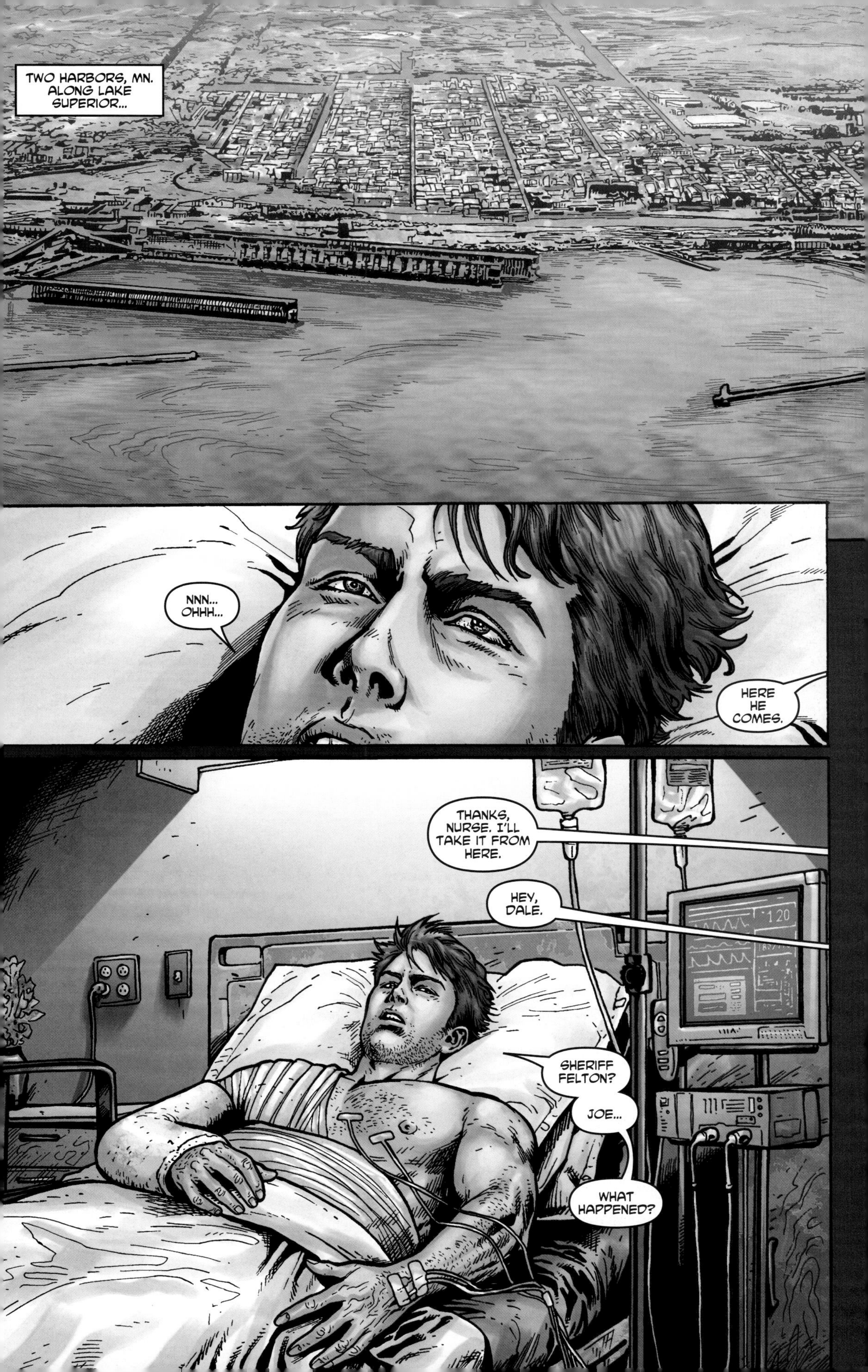
TWO HARBORS, MN. ALONG LAKE SUPERIOR...
NNN... OHHH...
HERE HE COMES.
THANKS, NURSE. I'LL TAKE IT FROM HERE.
HEY, DALE.
SHERIFF FELTON?
JOE...
WHAT HAPPENED?

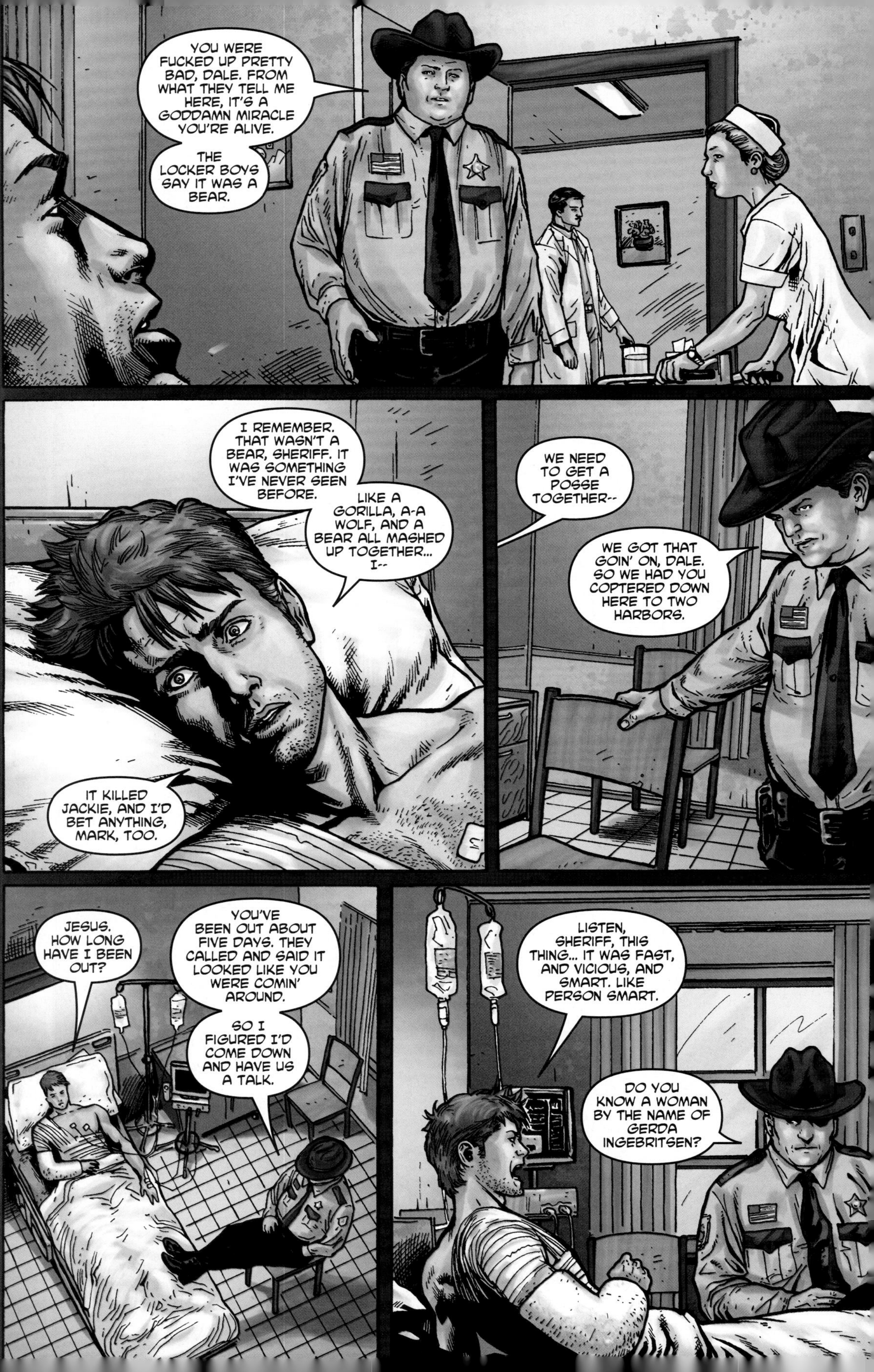
YOU WERE FUCKED UP PRETTY BAD, DALE. FROM WHAT THEY TELL ME HERE, IT'S A GODDAMN MIRACLE YOU'RE ALIVE.
THE LOCKER BOYS SAY IT WAS A BEAR.
I REMEMBER. THAT WASN'T A BEAR, SHERIFF. IT WAS SOMETHING I'VE NEVER SEEN BEFORE.
LIKE A GORILLA, A-A WOLF, AND A BEAR ALL MASHED UP TOGETHER... I--
IT KILLED JACKIE, AND I'D BET ANYTHING, MARK, TOO.
WE NEED TO GET A POSSE TOGETHER--
WE GOT THAT GOIN' ON, DALE. SO WE HAD YOU COPTERED DOWN HERE TO TWO HARBORS.
JESUS. HOW LONG HAVE I BEEN OUT?
YOU'VE BEEN OUT ABOUT FIVE DAYS. THEY CALLED AND SAID IT LOOKED LIKE YOU WERE COMIN' AROUND.
SO I FIGURED I'D COME DOWN AND HAVE US A TALK.
LISTEN, SHERIFF, THIS THING... IT WAS FAST, AND VICIOUS, AND SMART. LIKE PERSON SMART.
DO YOU KNOW A WOMAN BY THE NAME OF GERDA INGEBRITSEN?

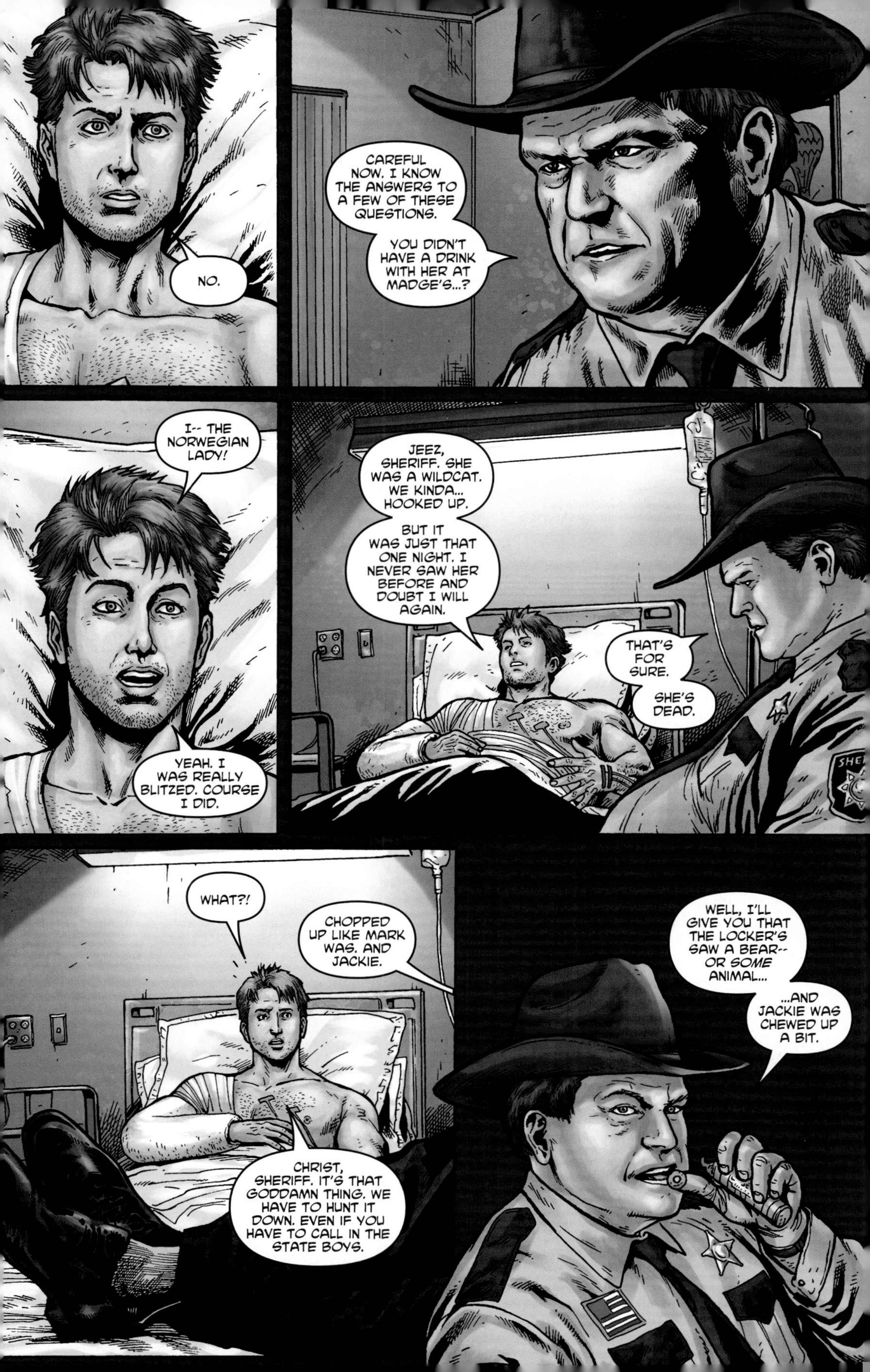
NO.
CAREFUL NOW. I KNOW THE ANSWERS TO A FEW OF THESE QUESTIONS.
YOU DIDN'T HAVE A DRINK WITH HER AT MADGE'S...?
I-- THE NORWEGIAN LADY!
YEAH. I WAS REALLY BLITZED. COURSE I DID.
JEEZ, SHERIFF. SHE WAS A WILDCAT. WE KINDA... HOOKED UP.
BUT IT WAS JUST THAT ONE NIGHT. I NEVER SAW HER BEFORE AND DOUBT I WILL AGAIN.
THAT'S FOR SURE.
SHE'S DEAD.
WHAT?!
CHOPPED UP LIKE MARK WAS. AND JACKIE.
CHRIST, SHERIFF. IT'S THAT GODDAMN THING. WE HAVE TO HUNT IT DOWN. EVEN IF YOU HAVE TO CALL IN THE STATE BOYS.
WELL, I'LL GIVE YOU THAT THE LOCKER'S SAW A BEAR-- OR *SOME* ANIMAL...
...AND JACKIE WAS CHEWED UP A BIT.

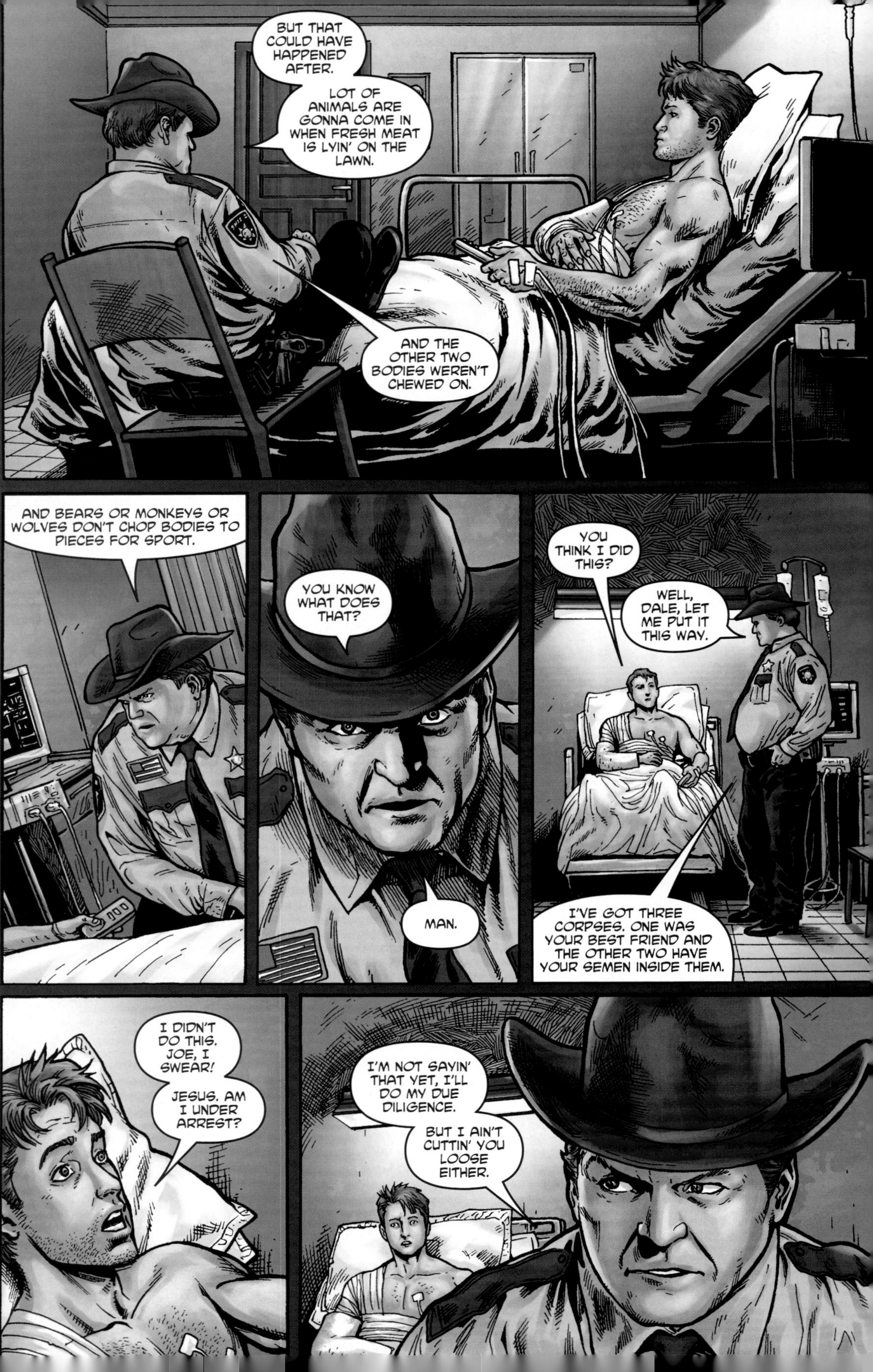
BUT THAT COULD HAVE HAPPENED AFTER.
LOT OF ANIMALS ARE GONNA COME IN WHEN FRESH MEAT IS LYIN' ON THE LAWN.
AND THE OTHER TWO BODIES WEREN'T CHEWED ON.
AND BEARS OR MONKEYS OR WOLVES DON'T CHOP BODIES TO PIECES FOR SPORT.
YOU KNOW WHAT DOES THAT?
MAN.
YOU THINK I DID THIS?
WELL, DALE, LET ME PUT IT THIS WAY.
I'VE GOT THREE CORPSES. ONE WAS YOUR BEST FRIEND AND THE OTHER TWO HAVE YOUR SEMEN INSIDE THEM.
I DIDN'T DO THIS. JOE, I SWEAR!
JESUS. AM I UNDER ARREST?
I'M NOT SAYIN' THAT YET, I'LL DO MY DUE DILIGENCE.
BUT I AIN'T CUTTIN' YOU LOOSE EITHER.

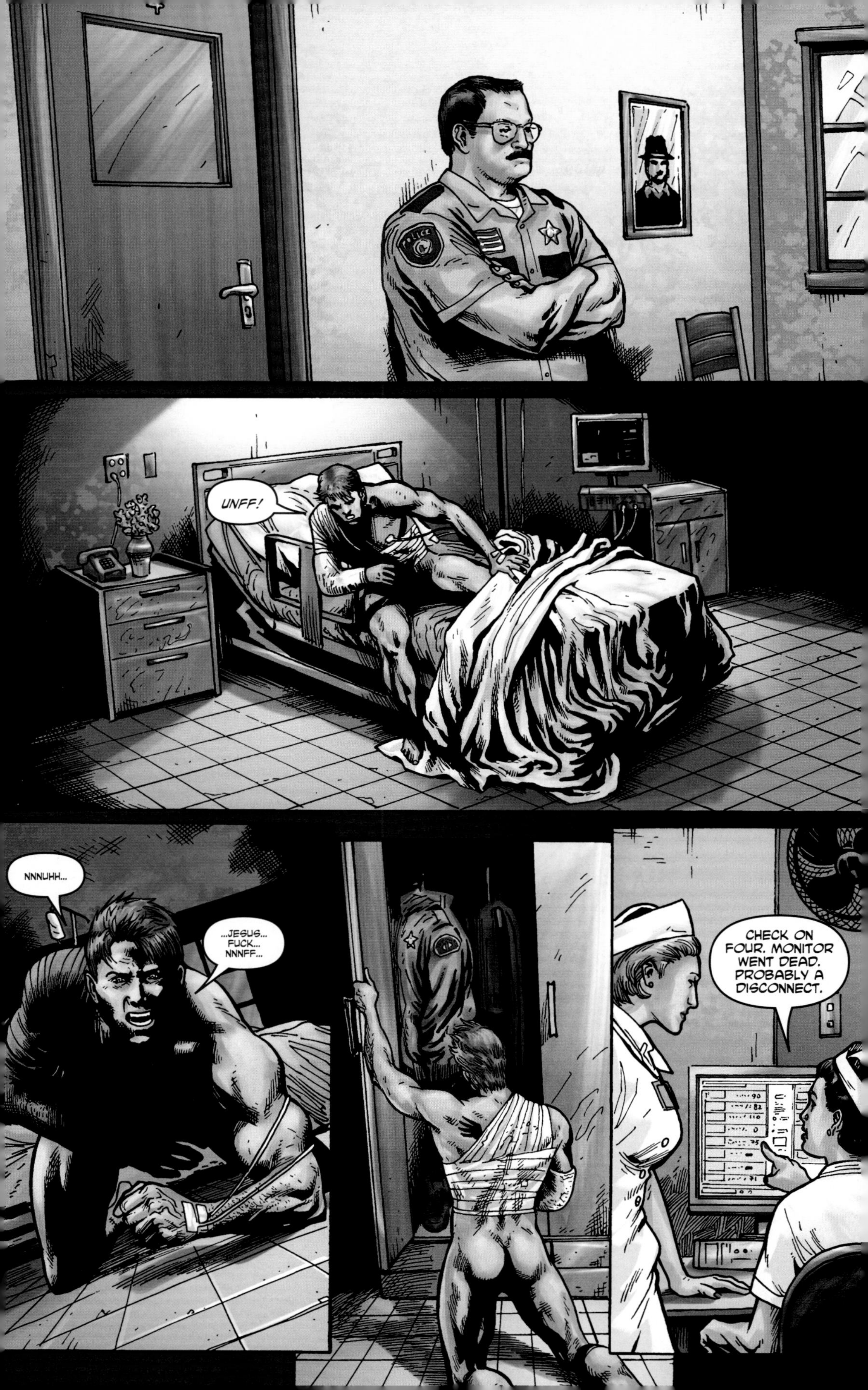
UNFF!
NNNUHH...
...JESUS... FUCK... NNNFF...
CHECK ON FOUR. MONITOR WENT DEAD. PROBABLY A DISCONNECT.

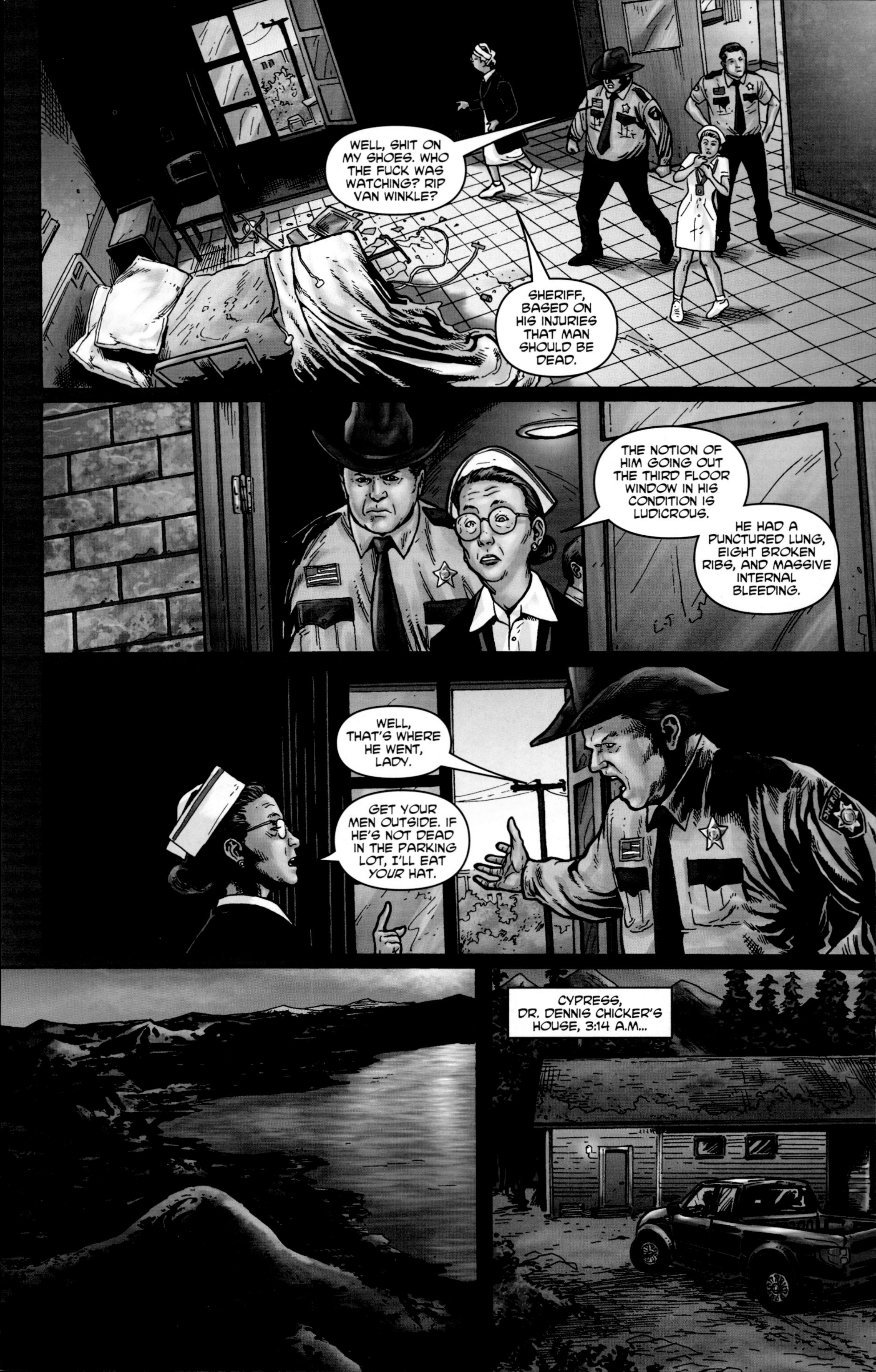
WELL, SHIT ON MY SHOES. WHO THE FUCK WAS WATCHING? RIP VAN WINKLE?
SHERIFF, BASED ON HIS INJURIES THAT MAN SHOULD BE DEAD.
THE NOTION OF HIM GOING OUT THE THIRD FLOOR WINDOW IN HIS CONDITION IS LUDICROUS.
HE HAD A PUNCTURED LUNG, EIGHT BROKEN RIBS, AND MASSIVE INTERNAL BLEEDING.
WELL, THAT'S WHERE HE WENT, LADY.
GET YOUR MEN OUTSIDE. IF HE'S NOT DEAD IN THE PARKING LOT, I'LL EAT *YOUR* HAT.
CYPRESS, DR. DENNIS CHICKER'S HOUSE, 3:14 A.M...

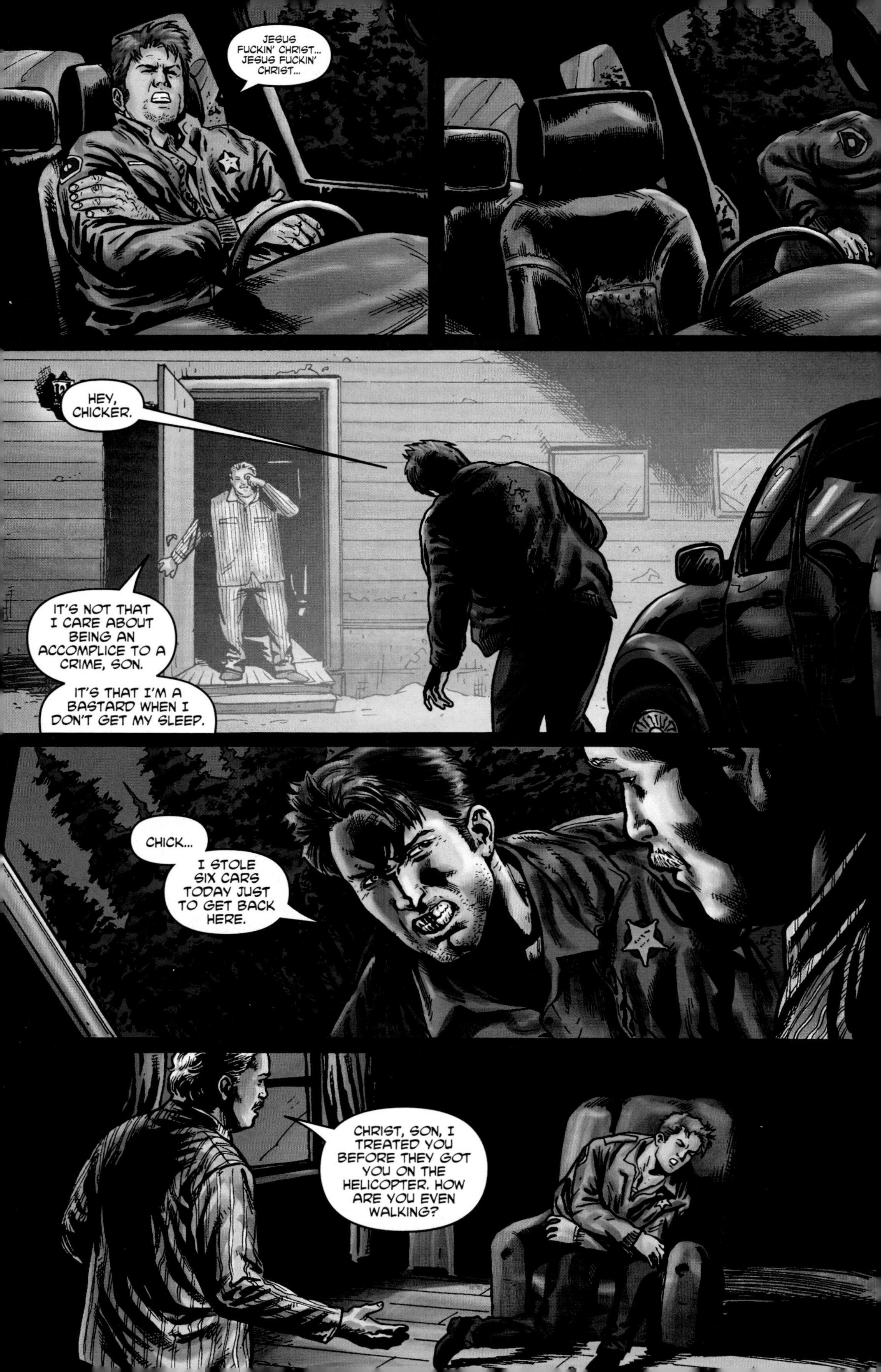
JESUS FUCKIN' CHRIST... JESUS FUCKIN' CHRIST...
HEY, CHICKER.
IT'S NOT THAT I CARE ABOUT BEING AN ACCOMPLICE TO A CRIME, SON.
IT'S THAT I'M A BASTARD WHEN I DON'T GET MY SLEEP.
CHICK...
I STOLE SIX CARS TODAY JUST TO GET BACK HERE.
CHRIST, SON, I TREATED YOU BEFORE THEY GOT YOU ON THE HELICOPTER. HOW ARE YOU EVEN WALKING?

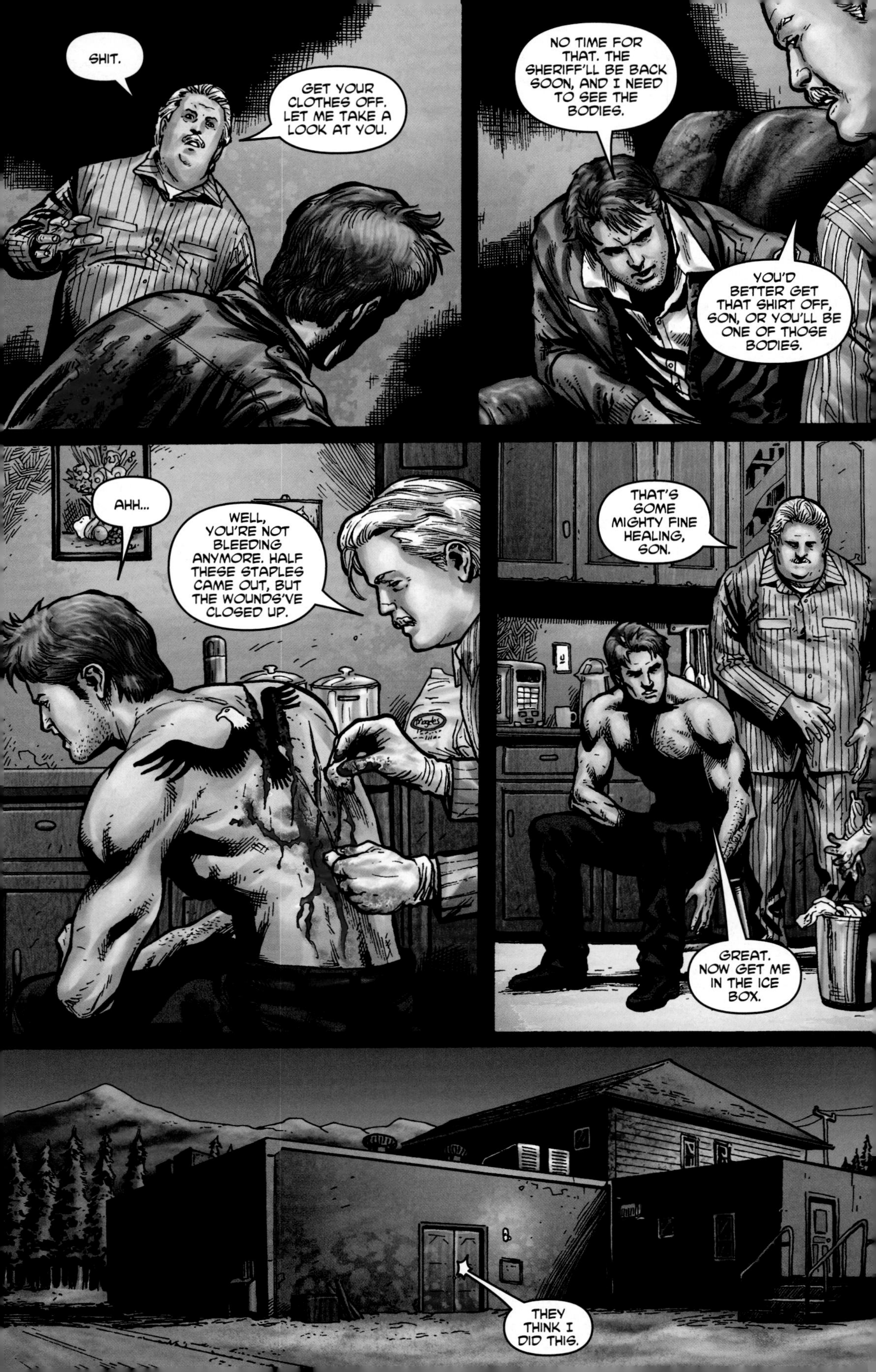
SHIT.
GET YOUR CLOTHES OFF. LET ME TAKE A LOOK AT YOU.
NO TIME FOR THAT. THE SHERIFF'LL BE BACK SOON, AND I NEED TO SEE THE BODIES.
YOU'D BETTER GET THAT SHIRT OFF, SON, OR YOU'LL BE ONE OF THOSE BODIES.
AHH...
WELL, YOU'RE NOT BLEEDING ANYMORE. HALF THESE STAPLES CAME OUT, BUT THE WOUNDS'VE CLOSED UP.
THAT'S SOME MIGHTY FINE HEALING, SON.
GREAT. NOW GET ME IN THE ICE BOX.
THEY THINK I DID THIS.

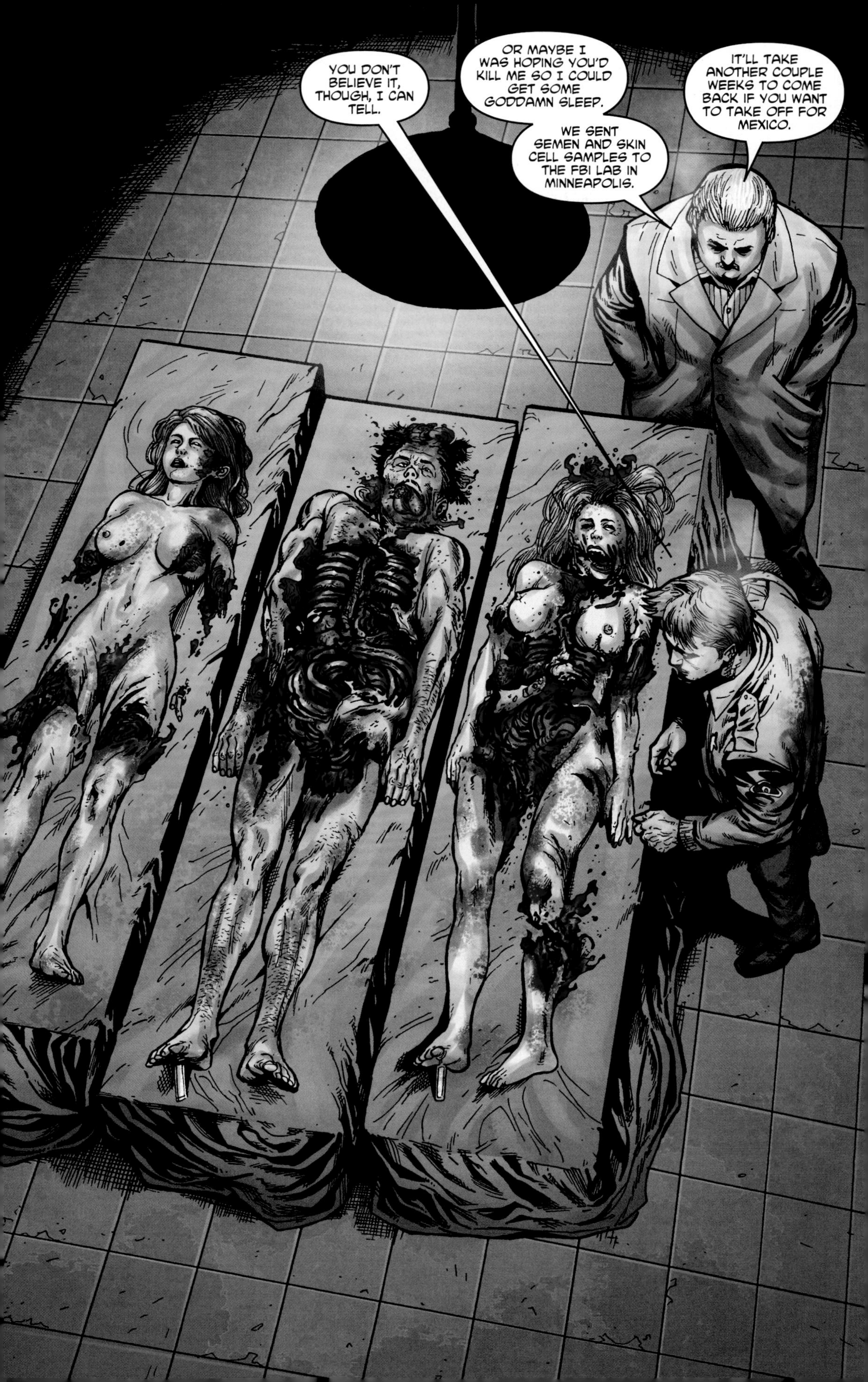
YOU DON'T BELIEVE IT, THOUGH, I CAN TELL.
OR MAYBE I WAS HOPING YOU'D KILL ME SO I COULD GET SOME GODDAMN SLEEP.
WE SENT SEMEN AND SKIN CELL SAMPLES TO THE FBI LAB IN MINNEAPOLIS.
IT'LL TAKE ANOTHER COUPLE WEEKS TO COME BACK IF YOU WANT TO TAKE OFF FOR MEXICO.

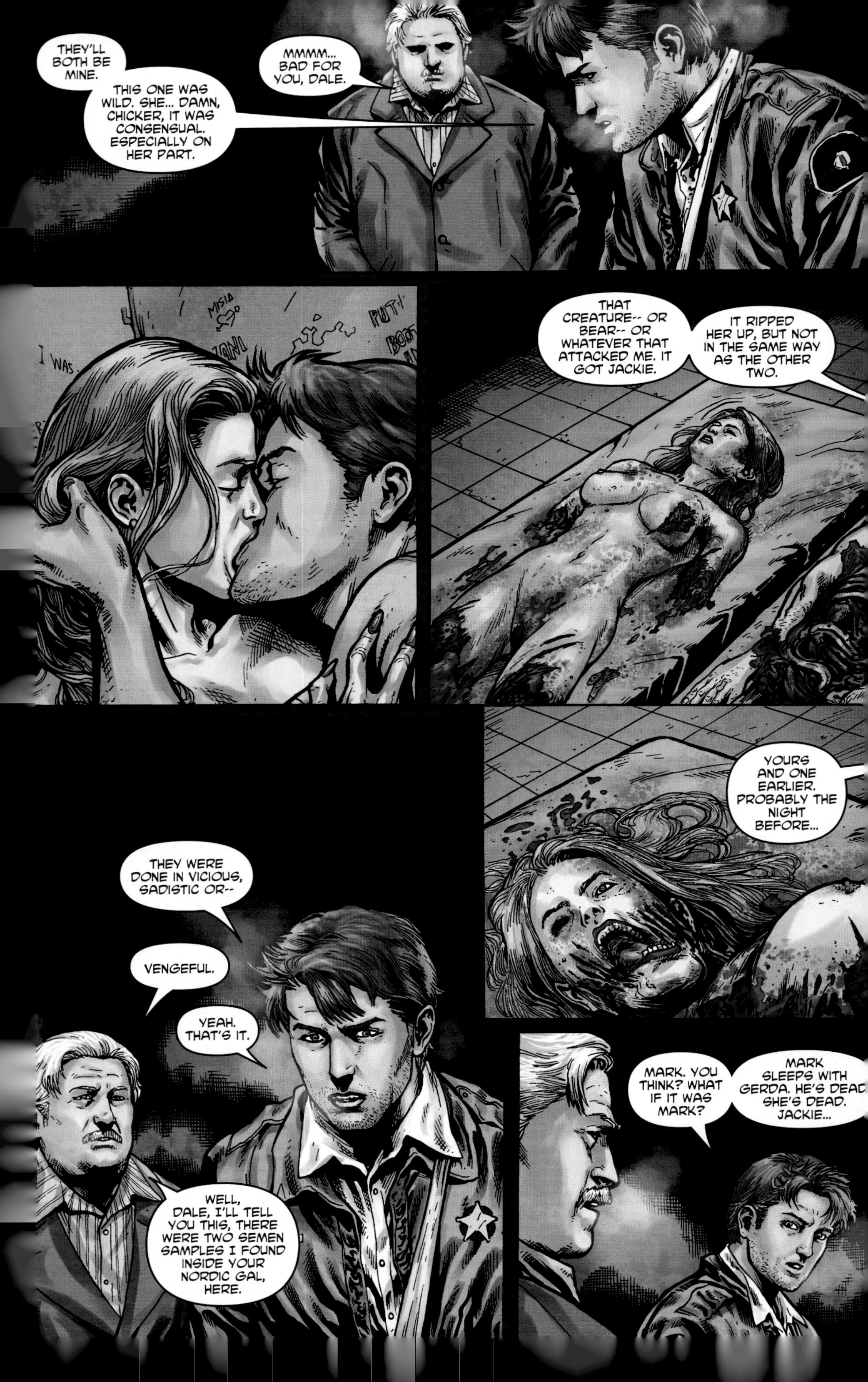
THEY'LL BOTH BE MINE.
MMMM... BAD FOR YOU, DALE.
THIS ONE WAS WILD. SHE... DAMN, CHICKER, IT WAS CONSENSUAL. ESPECIALLY ON HER PART.
THAT CREATURE-- OR BEAR-- OR WHATEVER THAT ATTACKED ME. IT GOT JACKIE.
IT RIPPED HER UP, BUT NOT IN THE SAME WAY AS THE OTHER TWO.
YOURS AND ONE EARLIER. PROBABLY THE NIGHT BEFORE...
THEY WERE DONE IN VICIOUS, SADISTIC OR--
VENGEFUL.
YEAH. THAT'S IT.
WELL, DALE, I'LL TELL YOU THIS, THERE WERE TWO SEMEN SAMPLES I FOUND INSIDE YOUR NORDIC GAL, HERE.
MARK. YOU THINK? WHAT IF IT WAS MARK?
MARK SLEEPS WITH GERDA. HE'S DEAD SHE'S DEAD. JACKIE...

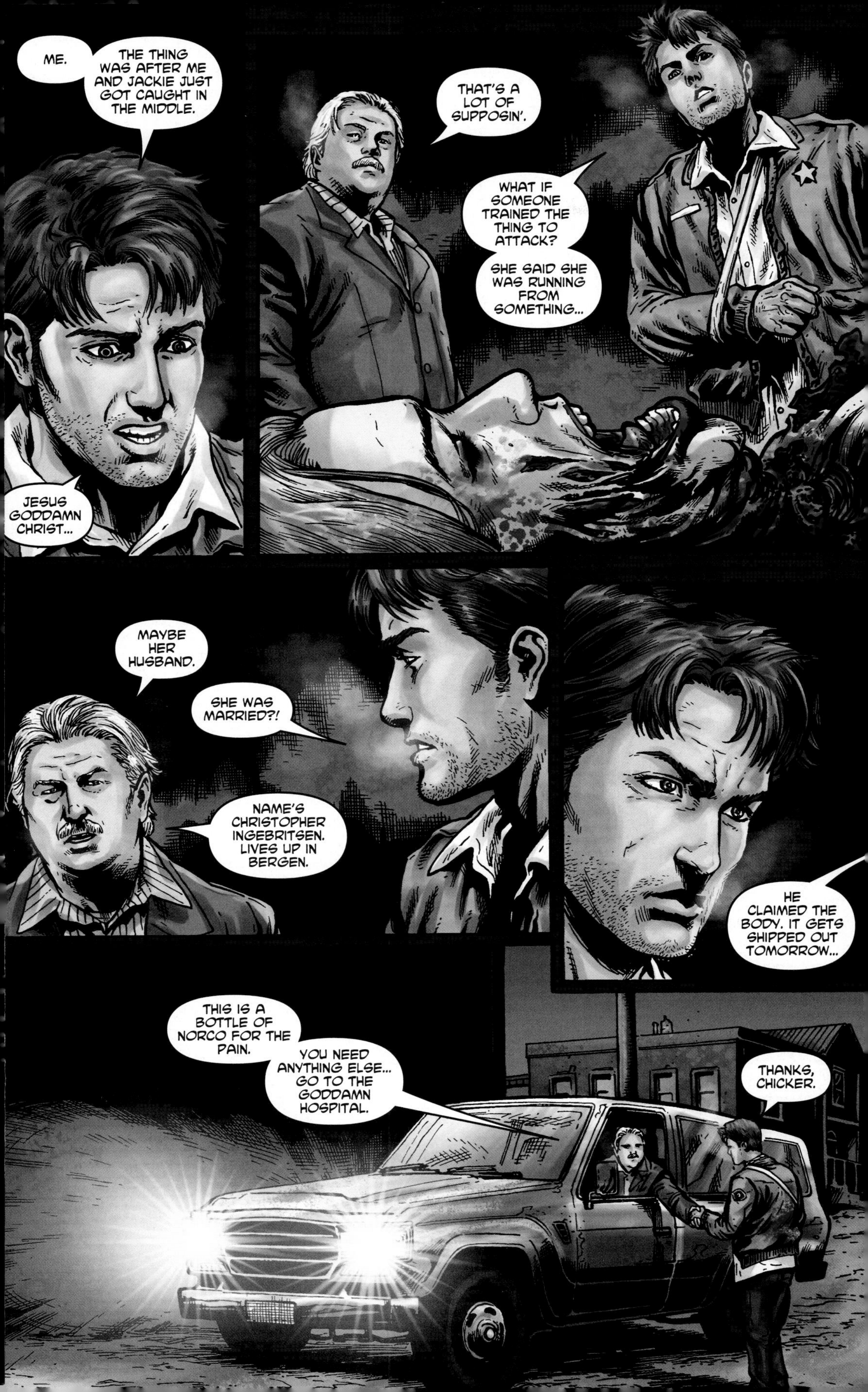
ME.
THE THING WAS AFTER ME AND JACKIE JUST GOT CAUGHT IN THE MIDDLE.
JESUS GODDAMN CHRIST...
THAT'S A LOT OF SUPPOSIN'.
WHAT IF SOMEONE TRAINED THE THING TO ATTACK?
SHE SAID SHE WAS RUNNING FROM SOMETHING...
MAYBE HER HUSBAND.
SHE WAS MARRIED?!
NAME'S CHRISTOPHER INGEBRITSEN. LIVES UP IN BERGEN.
HE CLAIMED THE BODY. IT GETS SHIPPED OUT TOMORROW...
THIS IS A BOTTLE OF NORCO FOR THE PAIN.
YOU NEED ANYTHING ELSE... GO TO THE GODDAMN HOSPITAL.
THANKS, CHICKER.

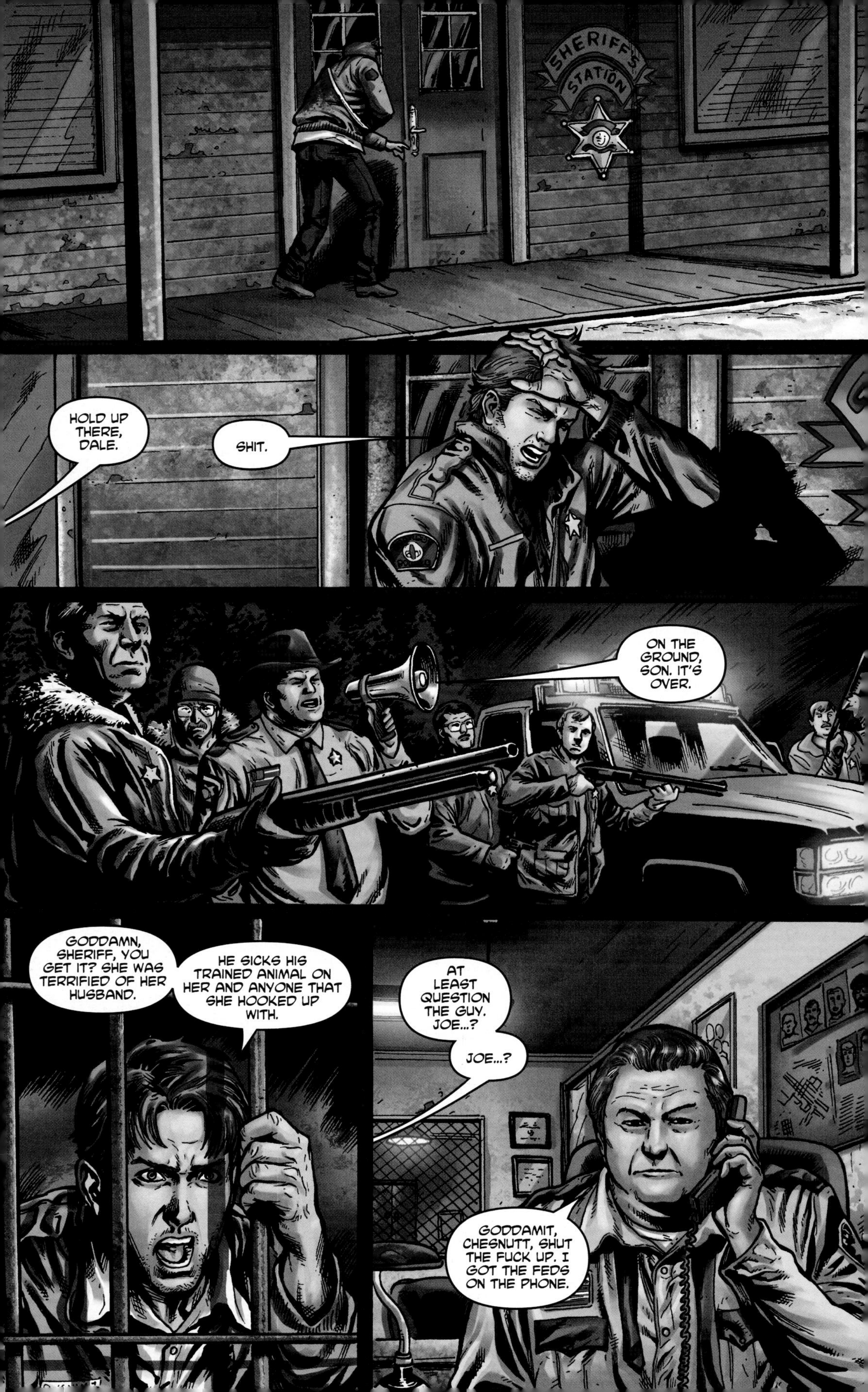
SHERIFF'S STATION
HOLD UP THERE, DALE.
SHIT.
ON THE GROUND, SON. IT'S OVER.
GODDAMN, SHERIFF, YOU GET IT? SHE WAS TERRIFIED OF HER HUSBAND.
HE SICKS HIS TRAINED ANIMAL ON HER AND ANYONE THAT SHE HOOKED UP WITH.
AT LEAST QUESTION THE GUY. JOE...?
JOE...?
GODDAMIT, CHESNUTT, SHUT THE FUCK UP. I GOT THE FEDS ON THE PHONE.

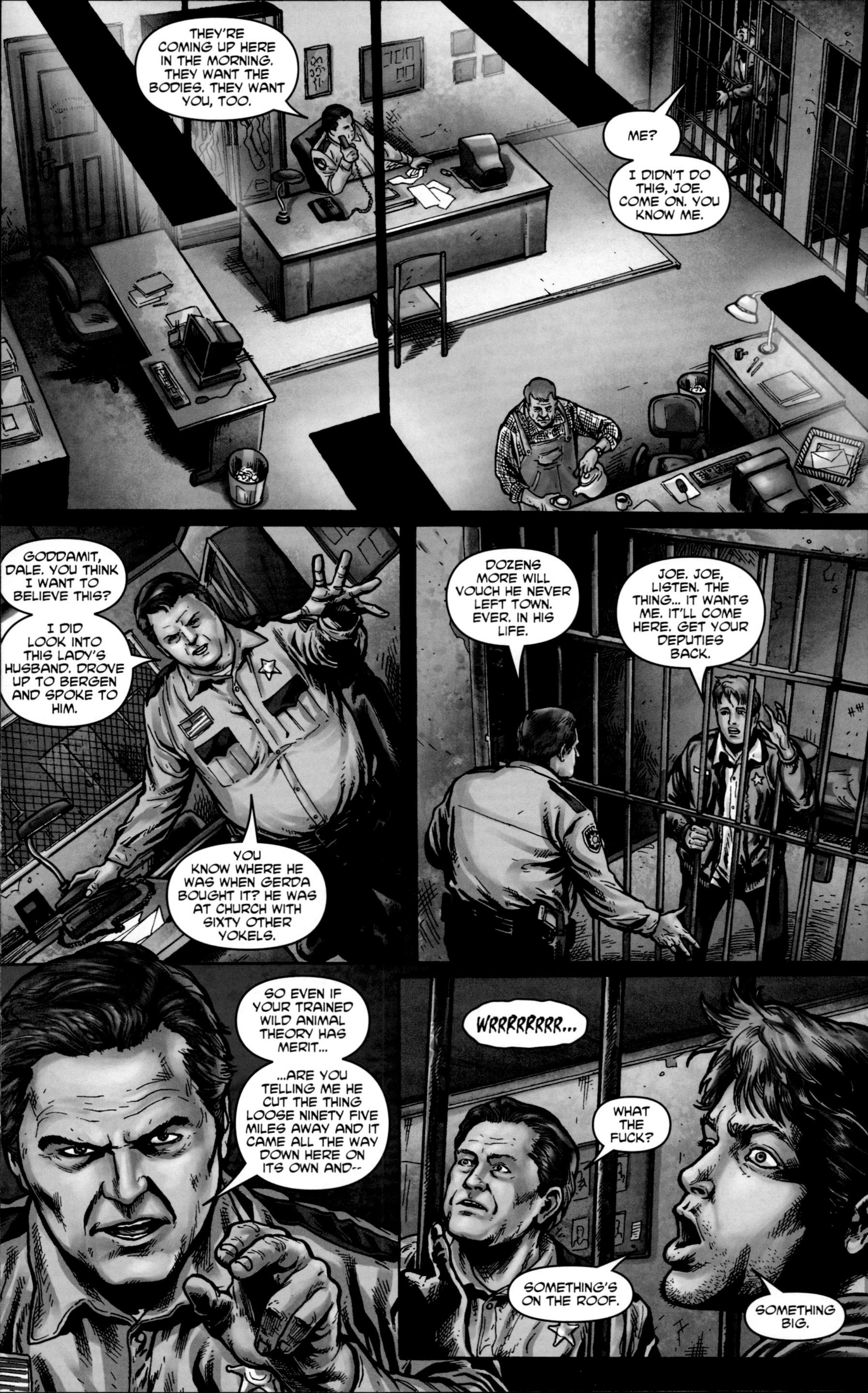
THEY'RE COMING UP HERE IN THE MORNING. THEY WANT THE BODIES. THEY WANT YOU, TOO.
ME?
I DIDN'T DO THIS, JOE. COME ON. YOU KNOW ME.
GODDAMIT, DALE. YOU THINK I WANT TO BELIEVE THIS?
I DID LOOK INTO THIS LADY'S HUSBAND. DROVE UP TO BERGEN AND SPOKE TO HIM.
YOU KNOW WHERE HE WAS WHEN GERDA BOUGHT IT? HE WAS AT CHURCH WITH SIXTY OTHER YOKELS.
DOZENS MORE WILL VOUCH HE NEVER LEFT TOWN. EVER. IN HIS LIFE.
JOE. JOE, LISTEN. THE THING... IT WANTS ME. IT'LL COME HERE. GET YOUR DEPUTIES BACK.
SO EVEN IF YOUR TRAINED WILD ANIMAL THEORY HAS MERIT...
...ARE YOU TELLING ME HE CUT THE THING LOOSE NINETY FIVE MILES AWAY AND IT CAME ALL THE WAY DOWN HERE ON ITS OWN AND--
WRRRRRRR...
WHAT THE FUCK?
SOMETHING'S ON THE ROOF.
SOMETHING BIG.

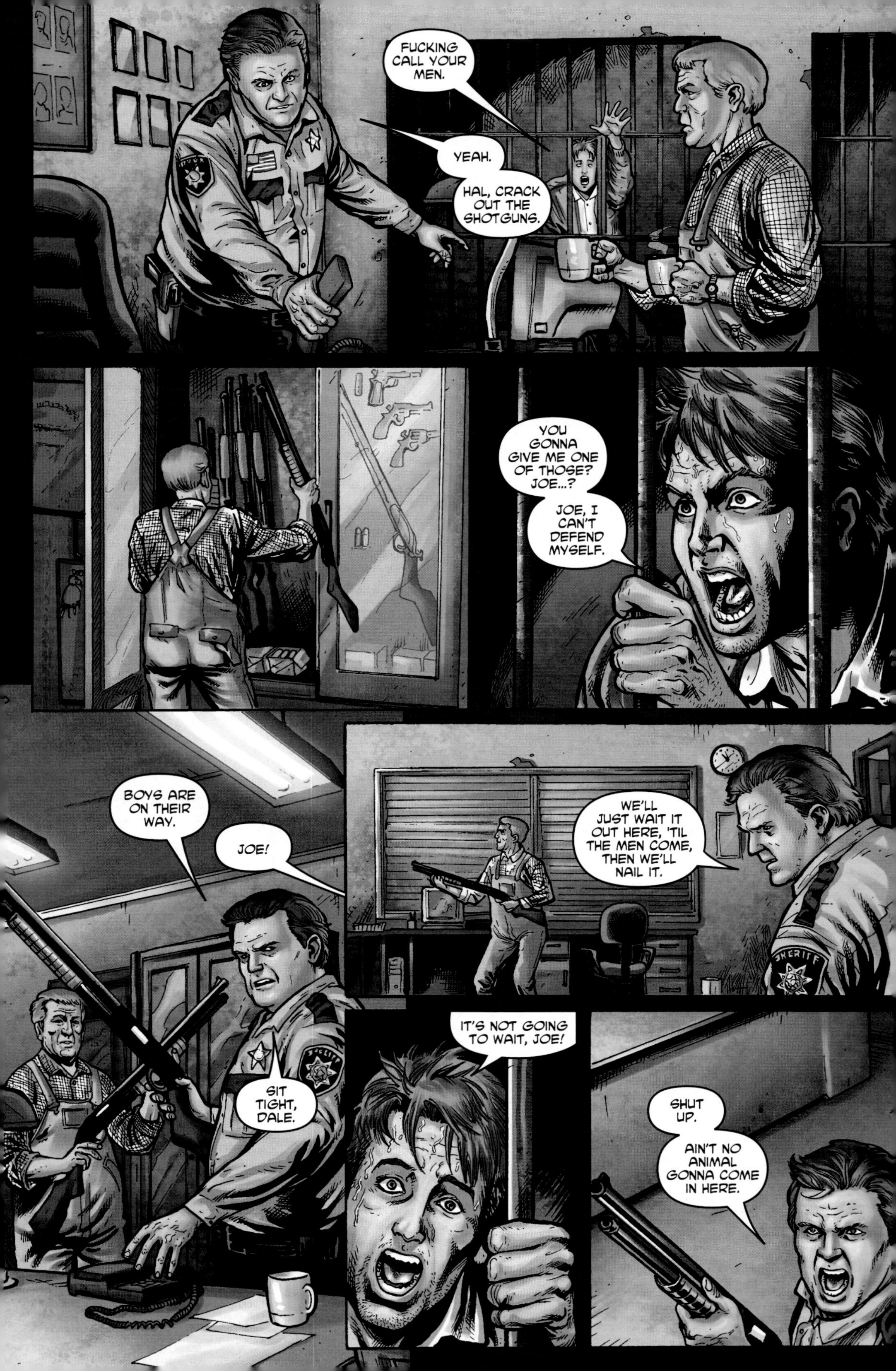
FUCKING CALL YOUR MEN.
YEAH.
HAL, CRACK OUT THE SHOTGUNS.
YOU GONNA GIVE ME ONE OF THOSE? JOE...?
JOE, I CAN'T DEFEND MYSELF.
BOYS ARE ON THEIR WAY.
JOE!
SIT TIGHT, DALE.
WE'LL JUST WAIT IT OUT HERE, 'TIL THE MEN COME, THEN WE'LL NAIL IT.
IT'S NOT GOING TO WAIT, JOE!
SHUT UP.
AIN'T NO ANIMAL GONNA COME IN HERE.

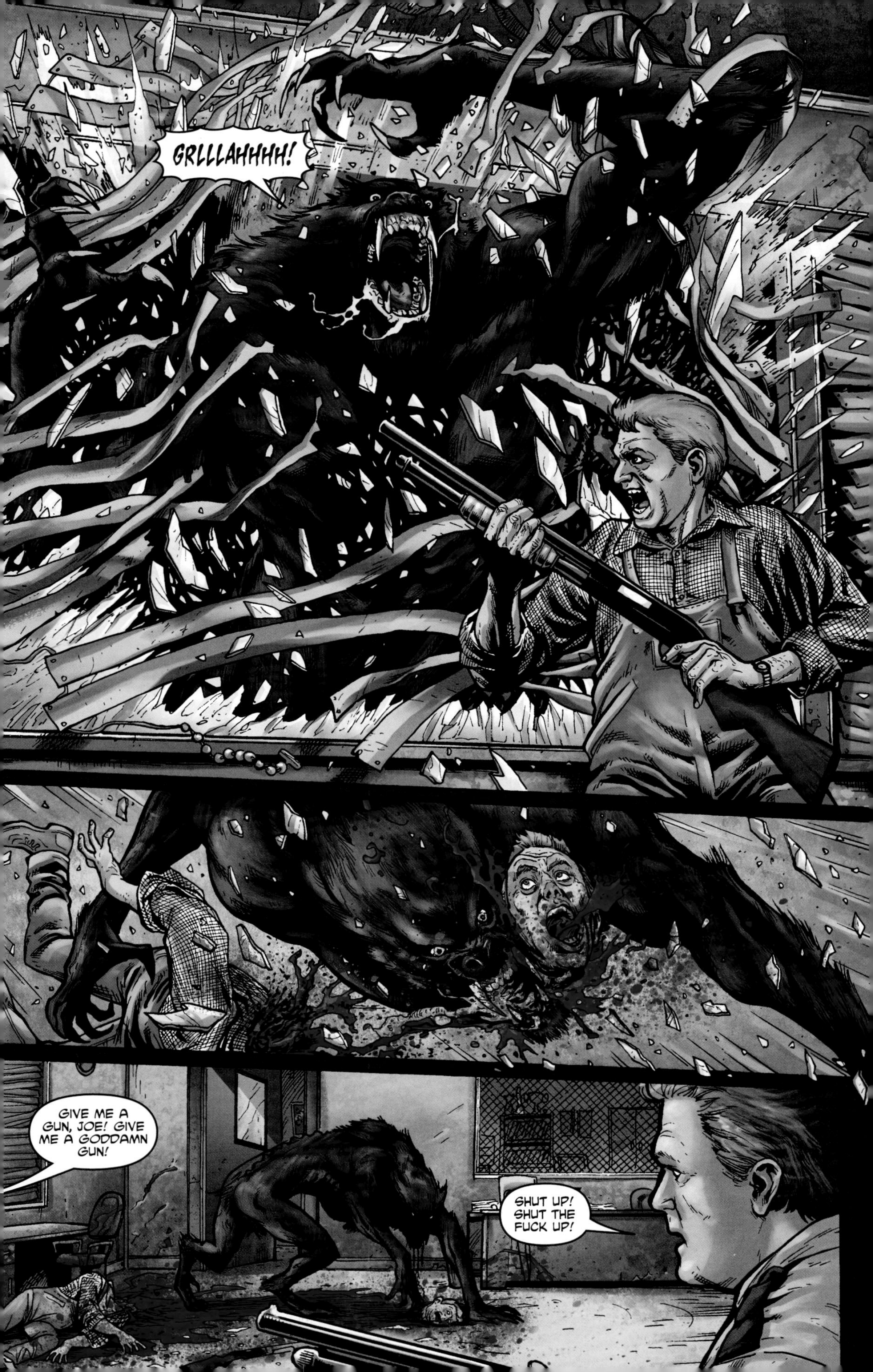
GRLLLAHHHH!
GIVE ME A GUN, JOE! GIVE ME A GODDAMN GUN!
SHUT UP! SHUT THE FUCK UP!

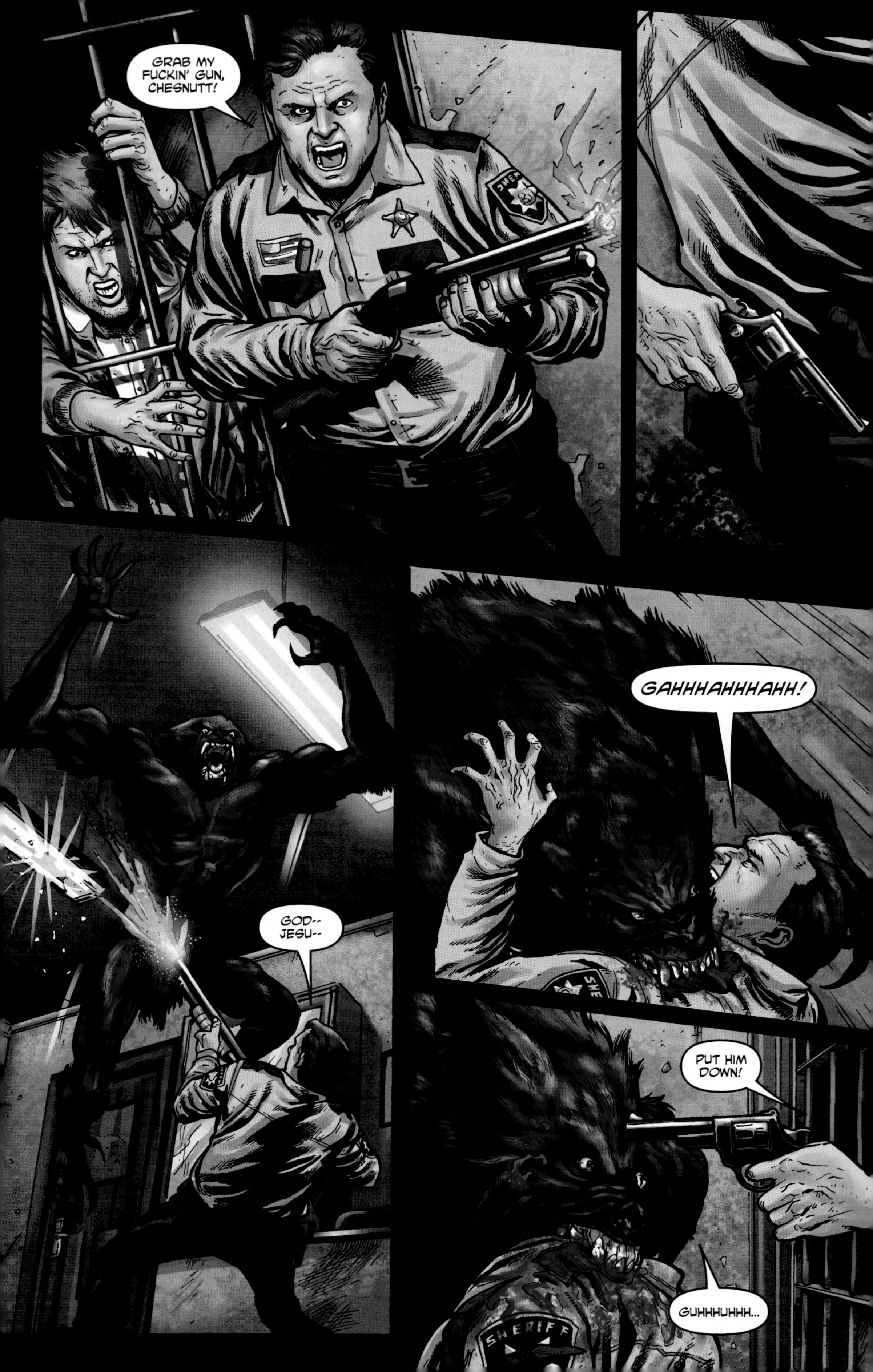
GRAB MY FUCKIN' GUN, CHESNUTT!
GOD-- JESU--
GAHHHAHHHAHH!
PUT HIM DOWN!
GUHHHUHHH...

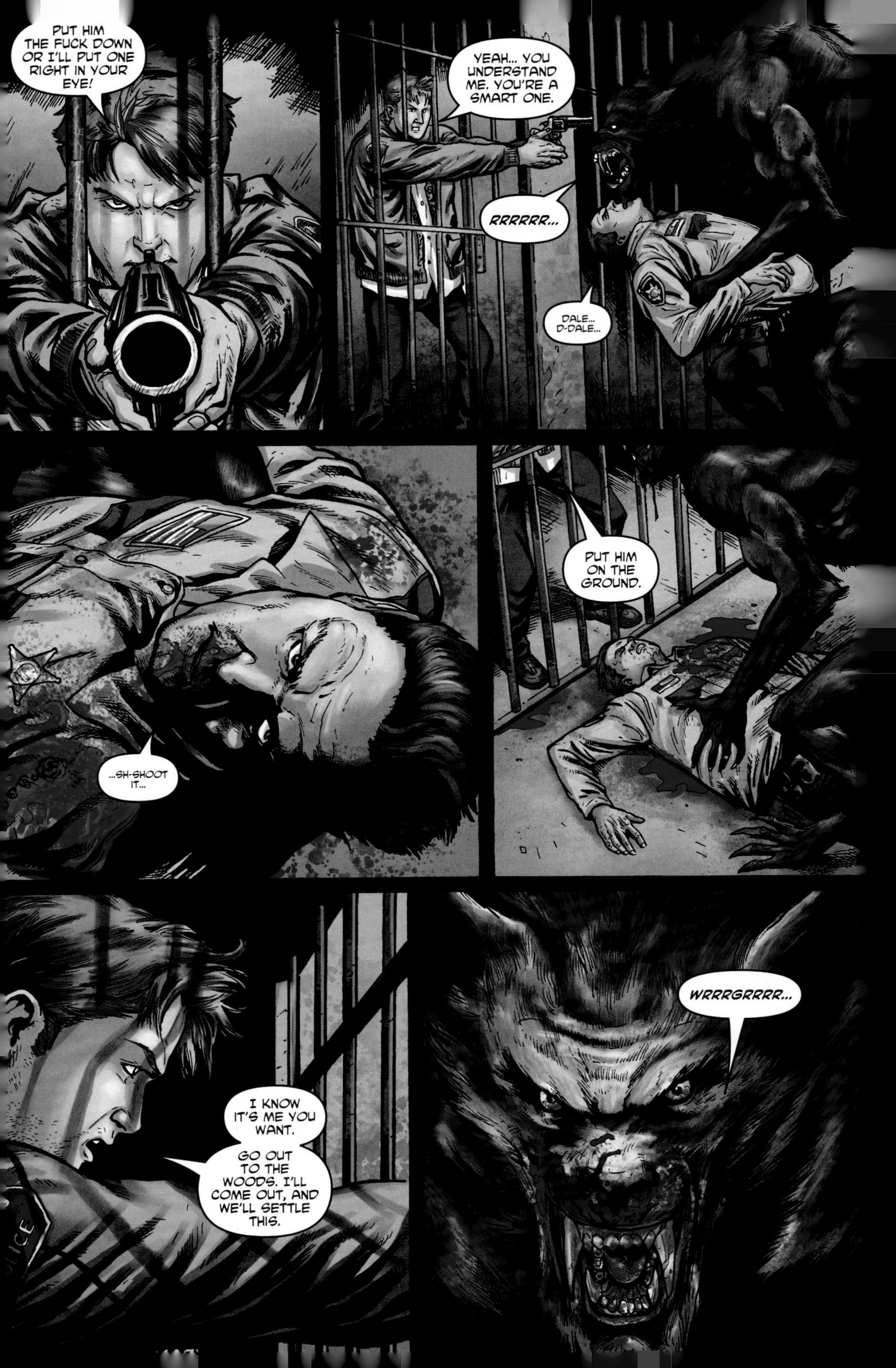
PUT HIM THE FUCK DOWN OR I'LL PUT ONE RIGHT IN YOUR EYE!
YEAH... YOU UNDERSTAND ME. YOU'RE A SMART ONE.
RRRRRR...
DALE... D-DALE...
...SH-SHOOT IT...
PUT HIM ON THE GROUND.
I KNOW IT'S ME YOU WANT.
GO OUT TO THE WOODS. I'LL COME OUT, AND WE'LL SETTLE THIS.
WRRRGRRRR...

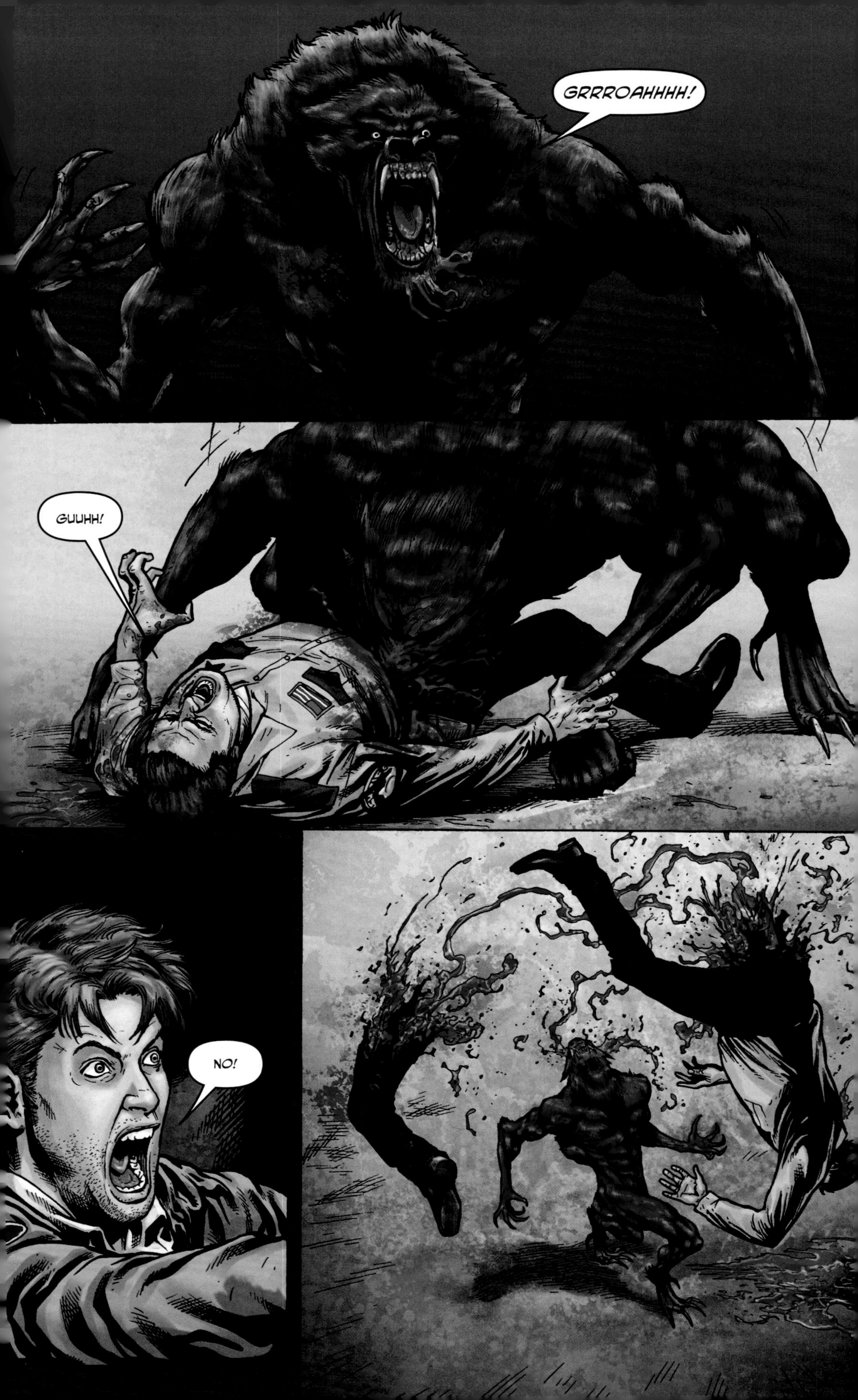
GRRROAHHHH!
GUUHH!
NO!

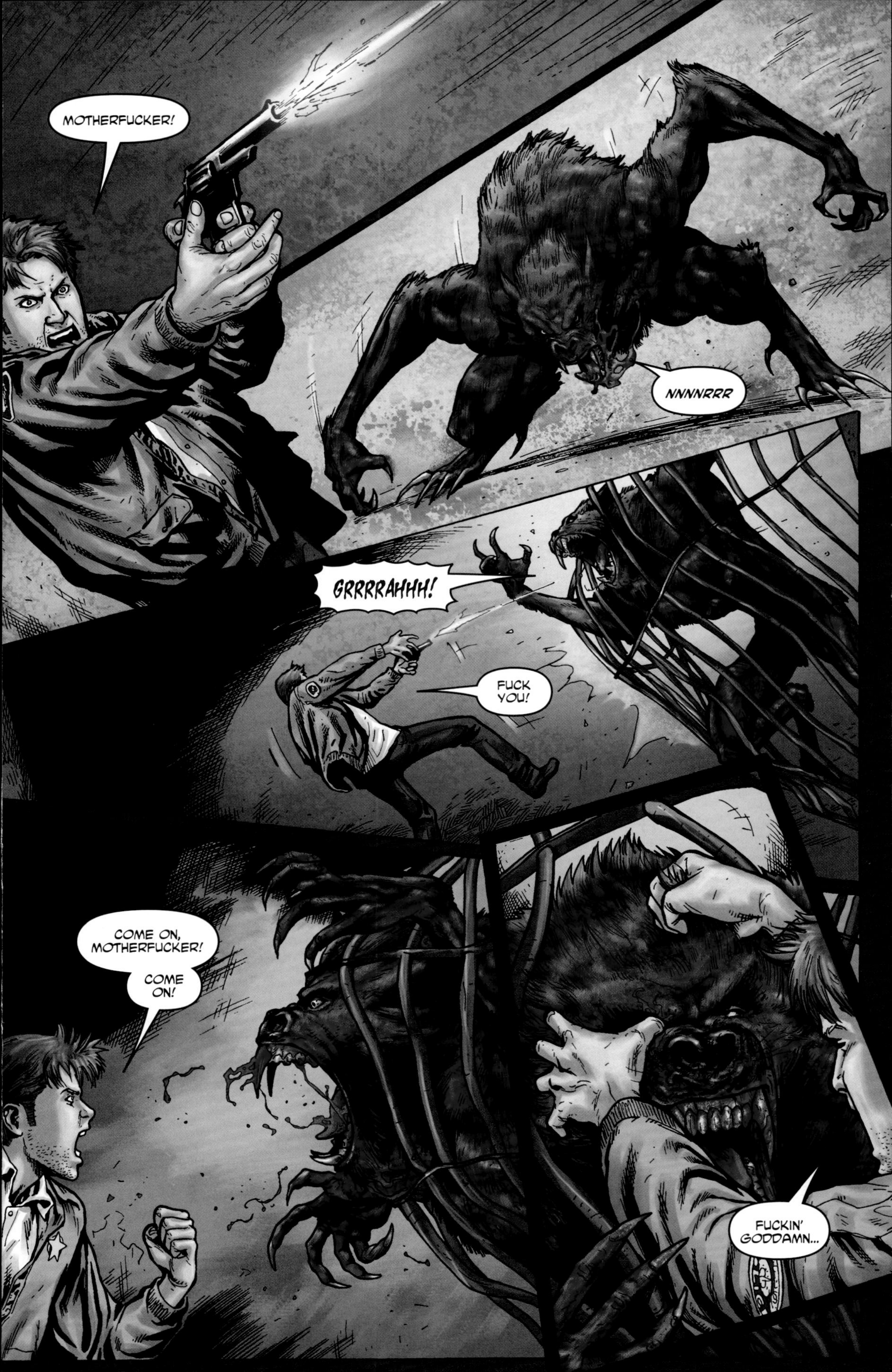
MOTHERFUCKER!
NNNNRRR
GRRRRAHHH!
FUCK YOU!
COME ON, MOTHERFUCKER!
COME ON!
FUCKIN' GODDAMN...

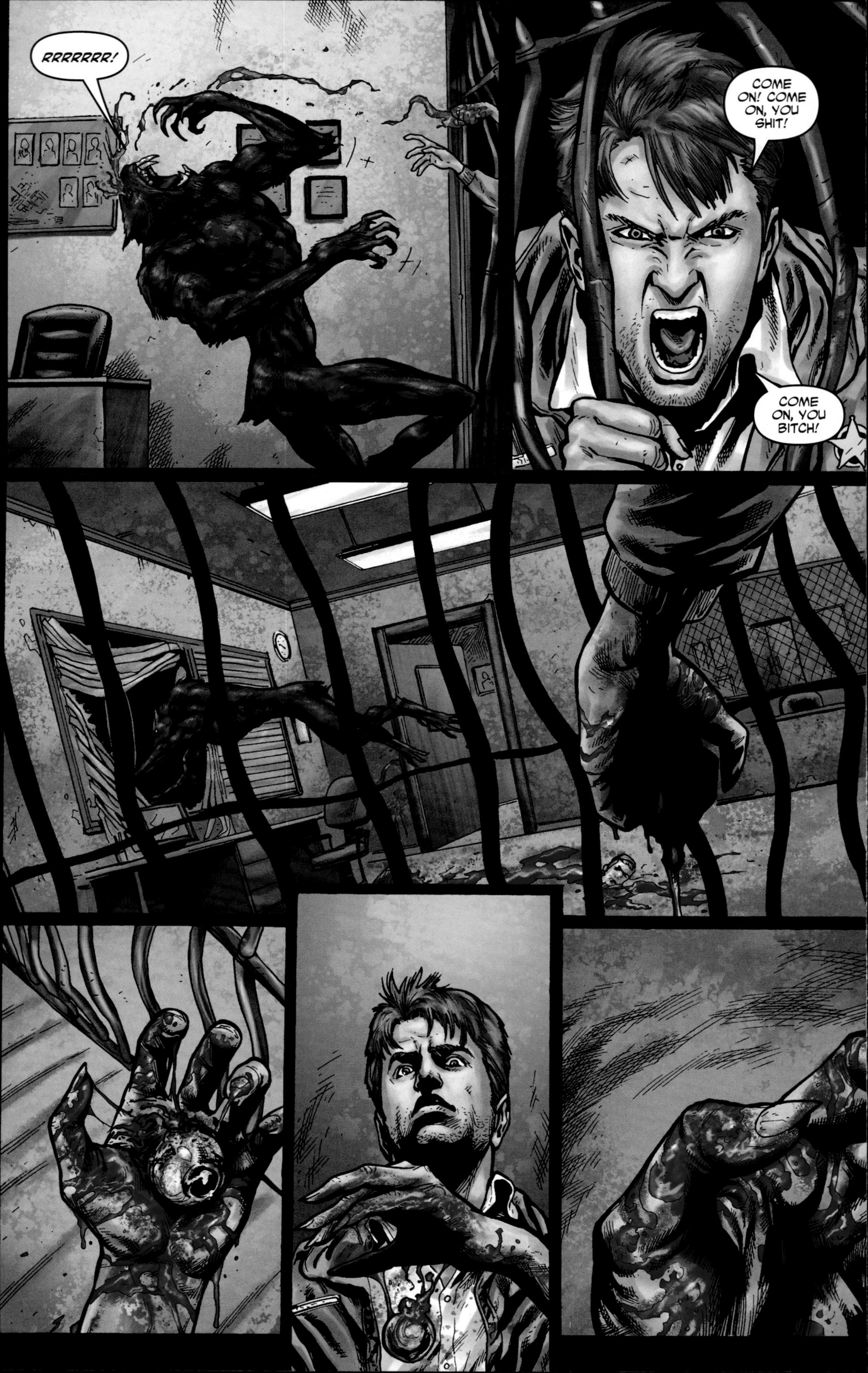
RRRRRRR!
COME ON! COME ON, YOU SHIT!
COME ON, YOU BITCH!

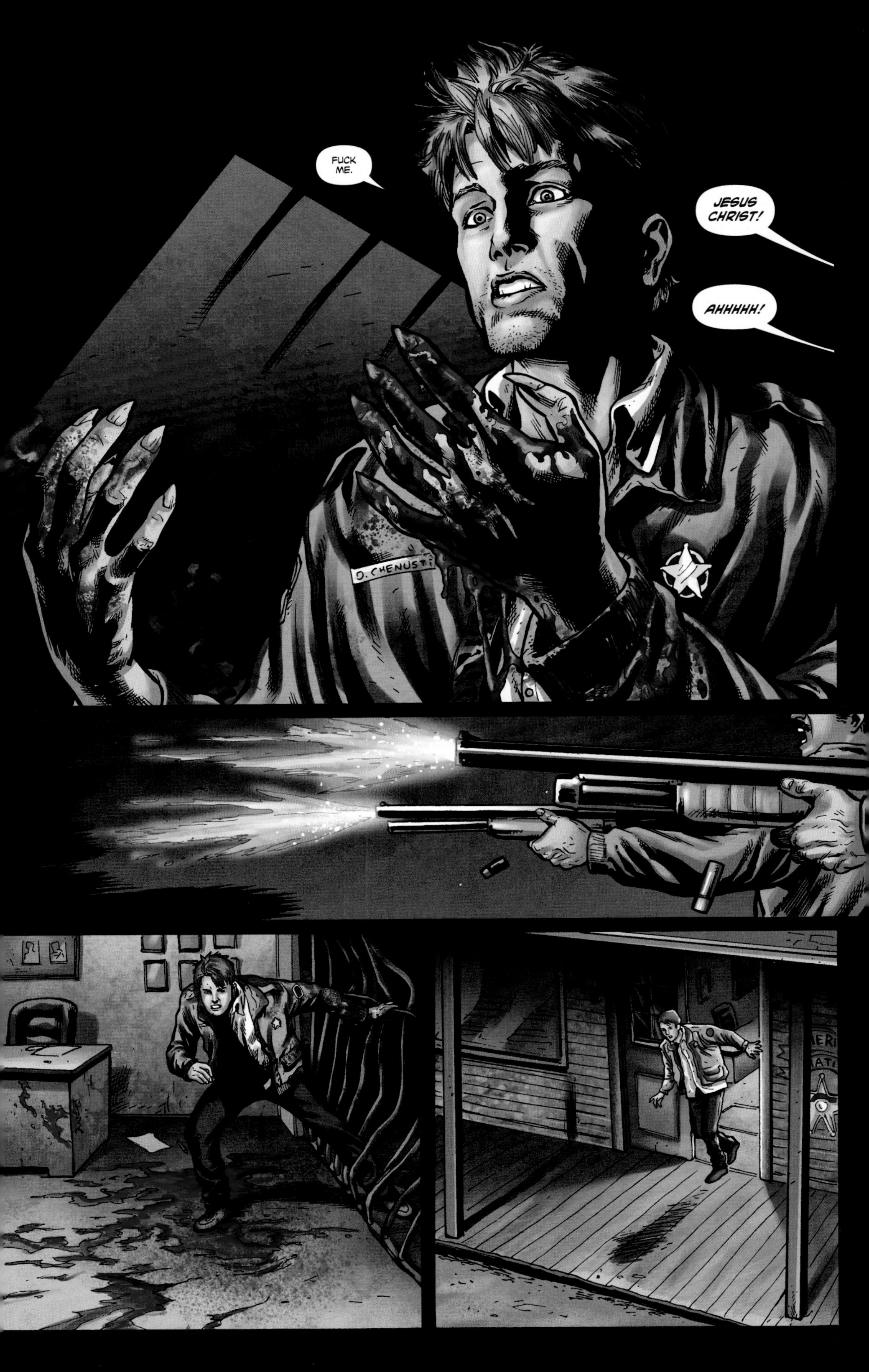
FUCK ME.
JESUS CHRIST!
AHHHHH!
D. CHENUSTI

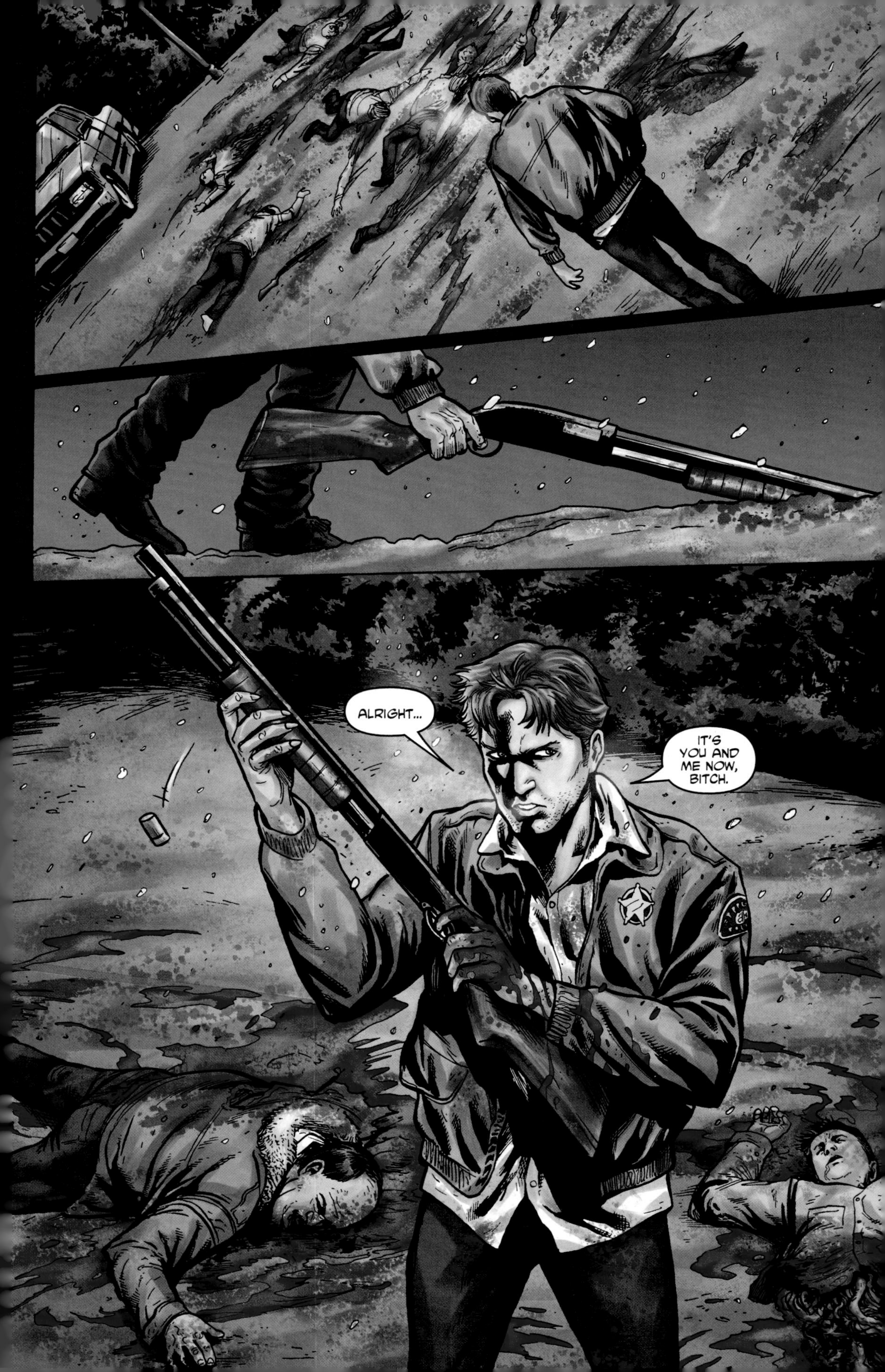
ALRIGHT...
IT'S YOU AND ME NOW, BITCH.

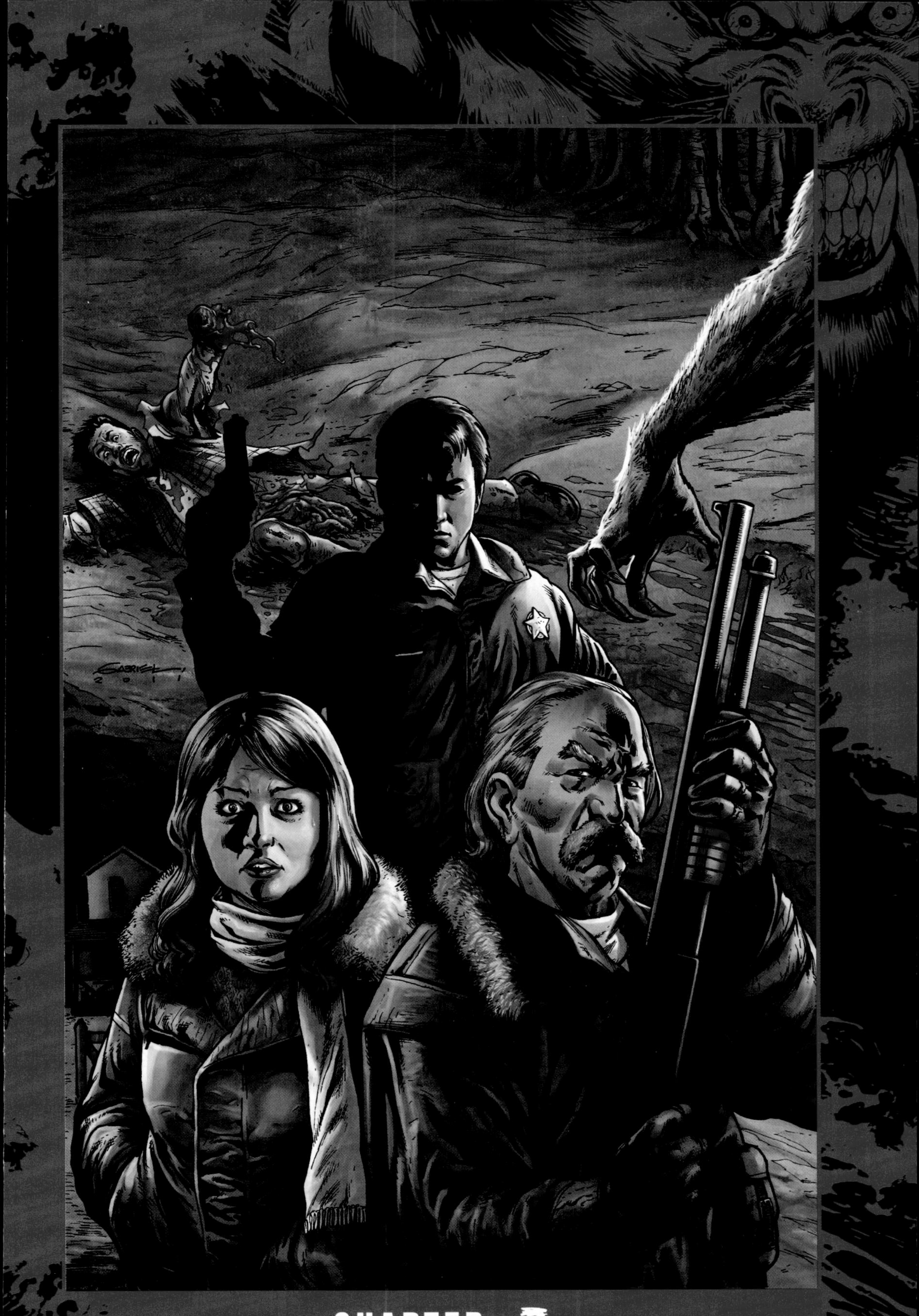
GABRIEL
2011

CHAPTER 3

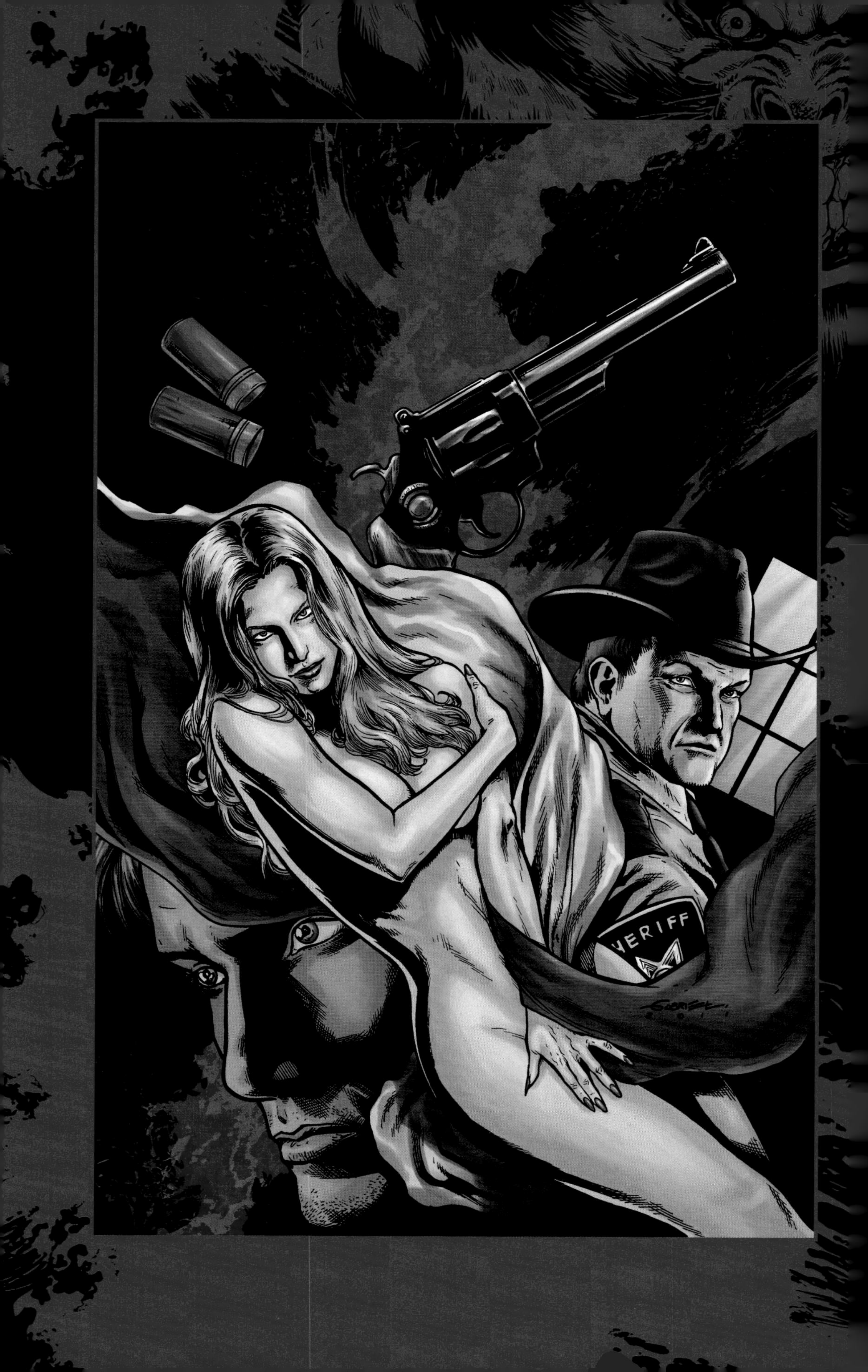
HERIFF

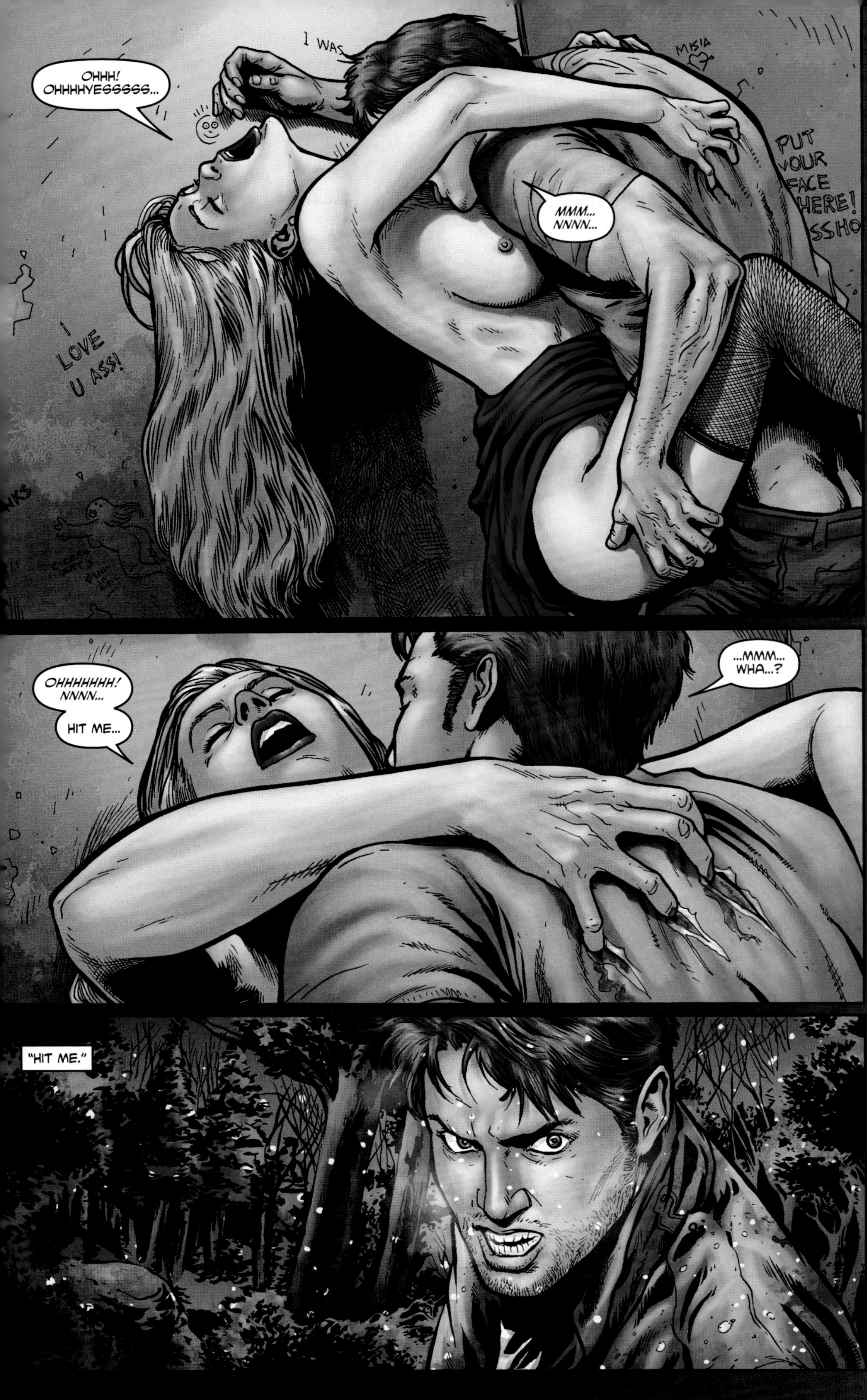
OHHH! OHHHHYESSSSS...
MMM... NNNN...
I WAS
PUT YOUR FACE HERE!
I LOVE U ASS!
OHHHHHHH! NNNN...
HIT ME...
...MMM... WHA...?
"HIT ME."

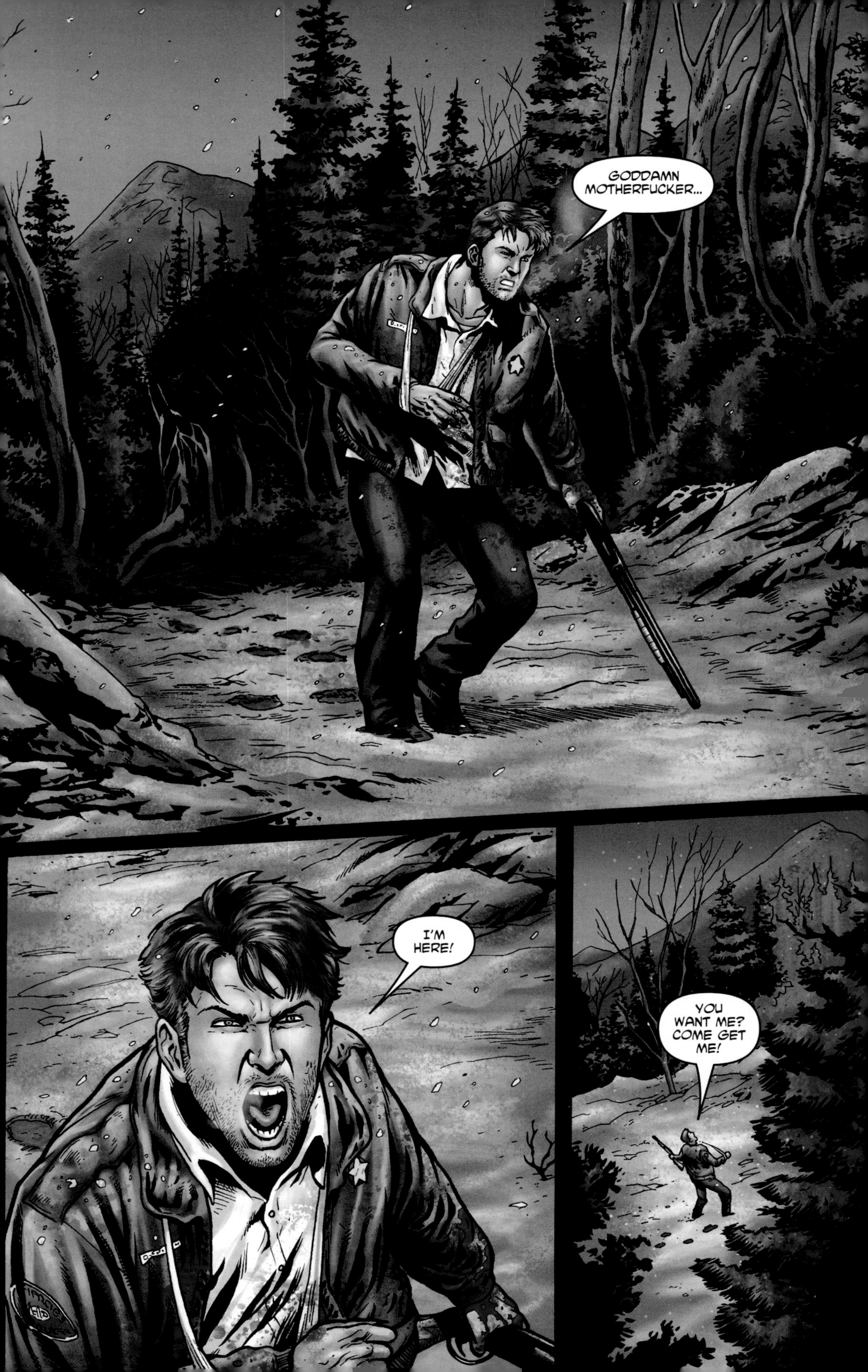
GODDAMN MOTHERFUCKER...
I'M HERE!
YOU WANT ME? COME GET ME!

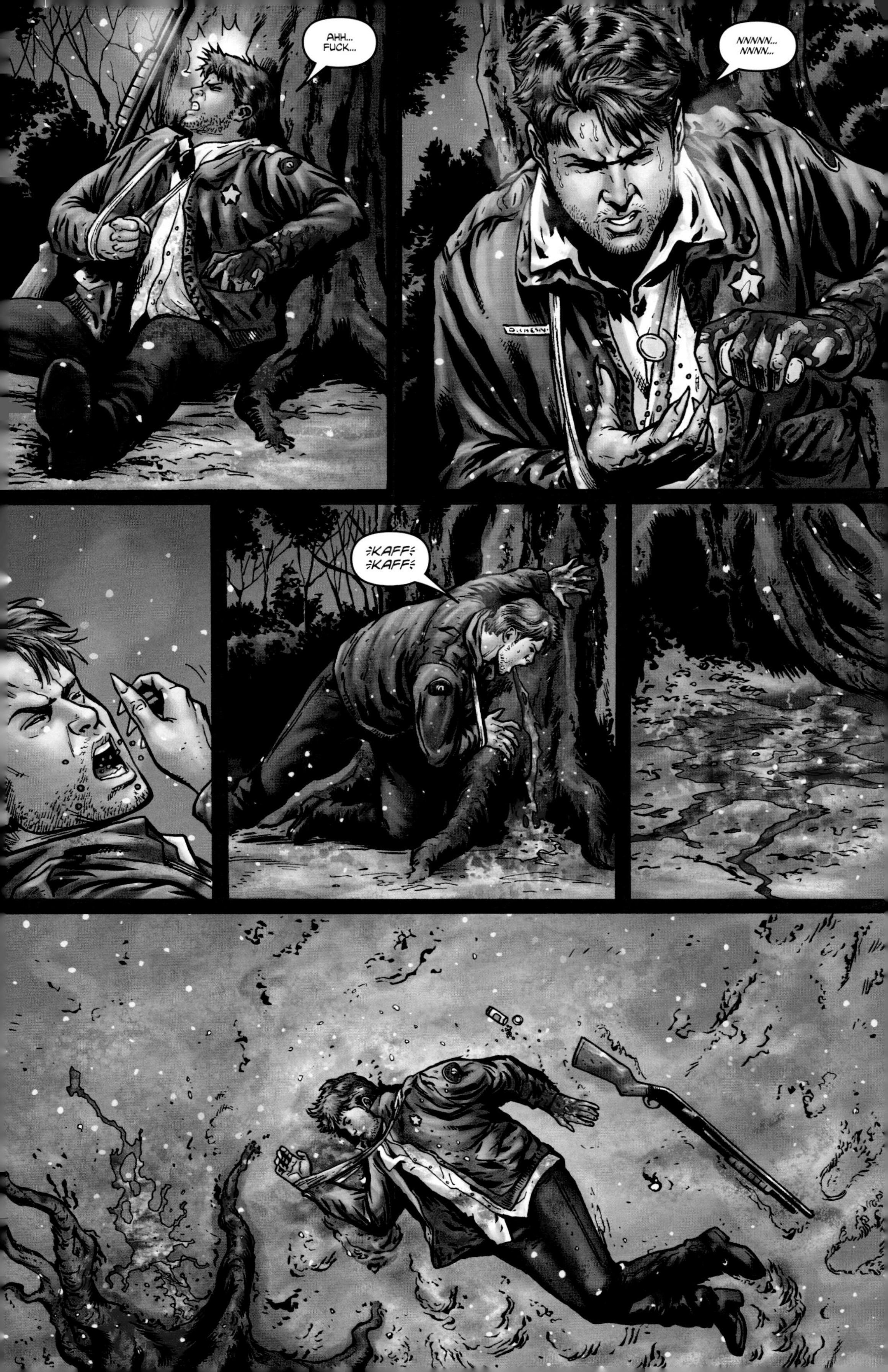
AHH... FUCK...
NNNNN... NNNN...
KAFF KAFF

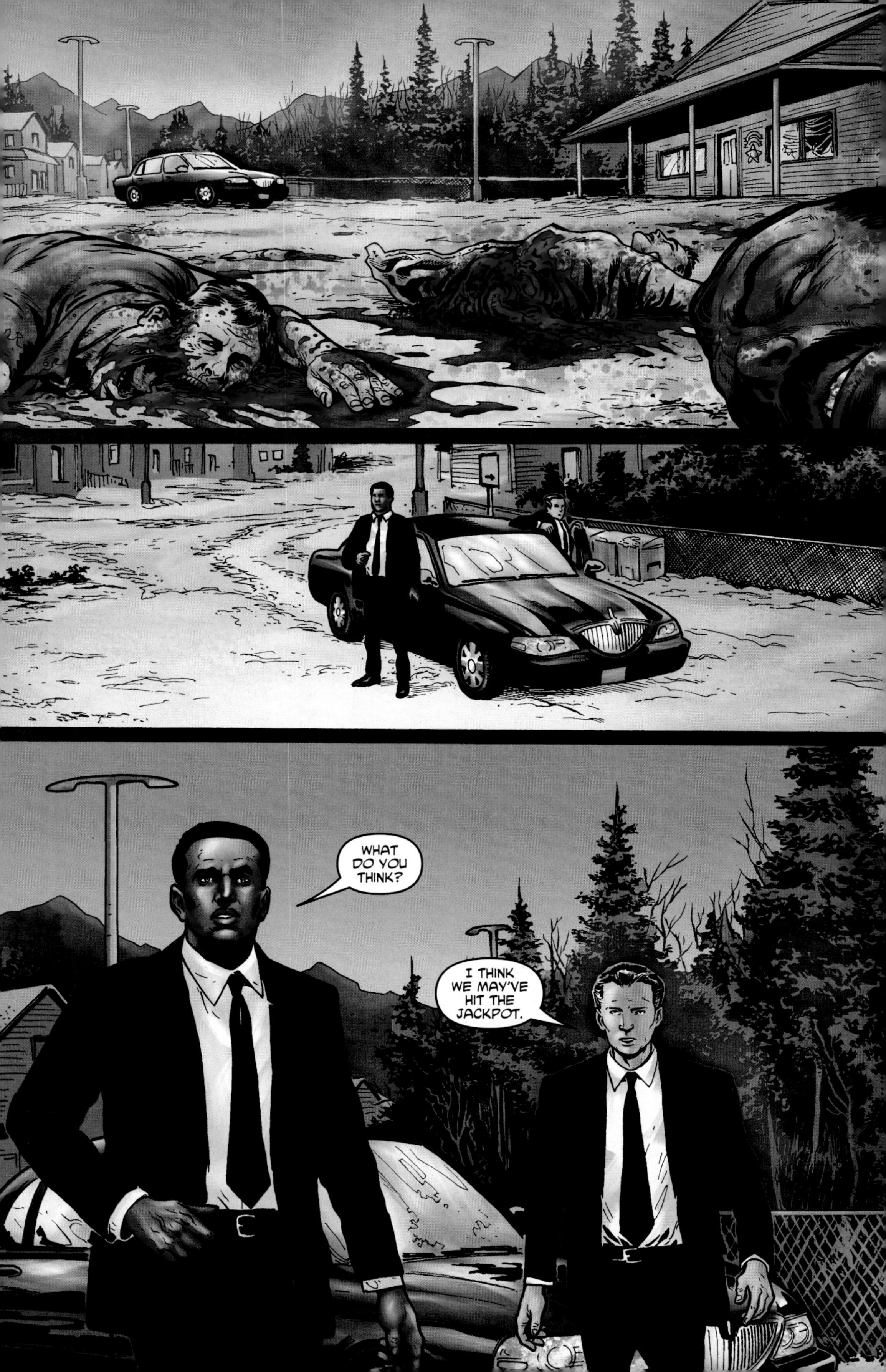
WHAT DO YOU THINK?
I THINK WE MAY'VE HIT THE JACKPOT.

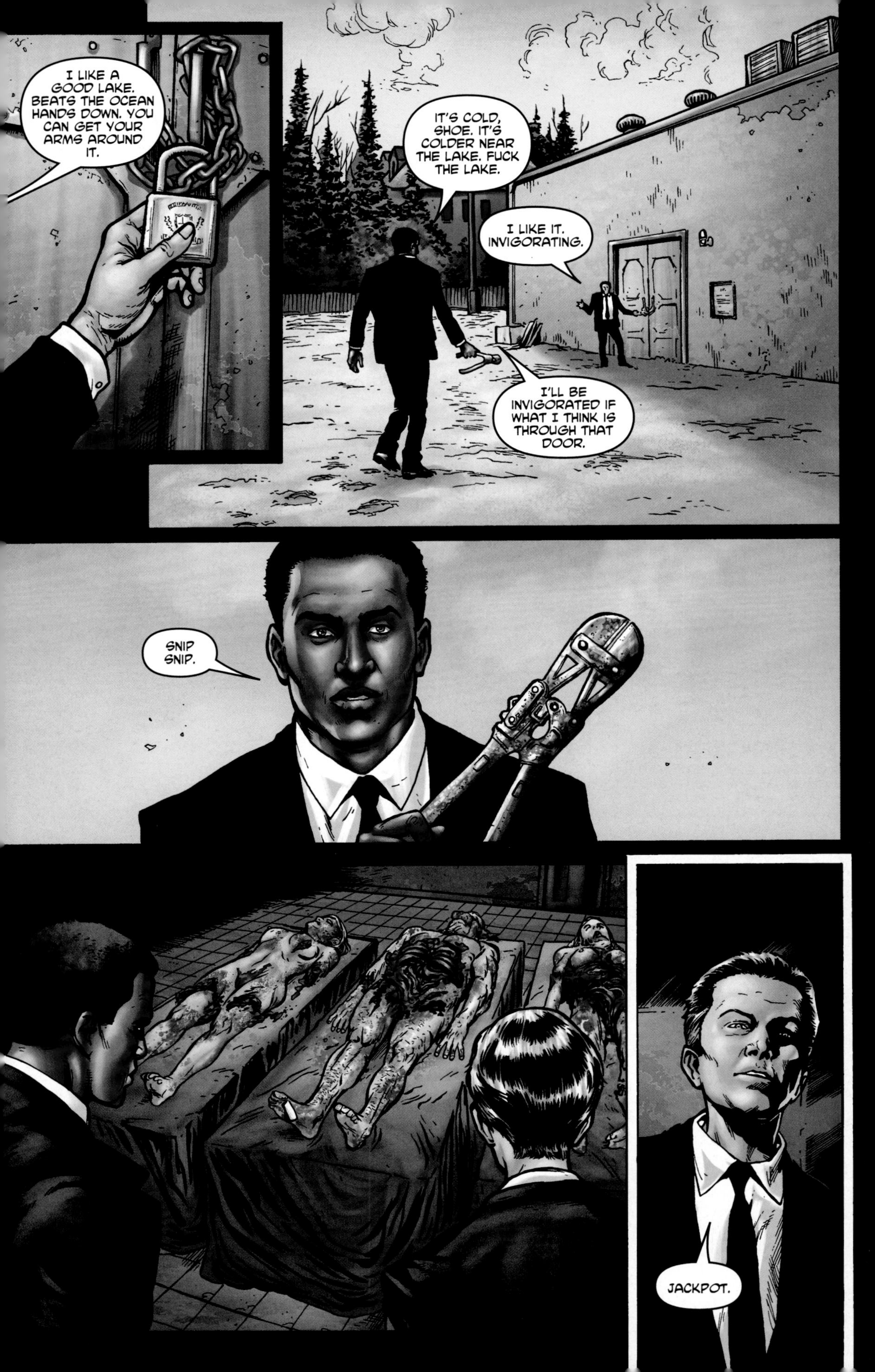
I LIKE A GOOD LAKE. BEATS THE OCEAN HANDS DOWN. YOU CAN GET YOUR ARMS AROUND IT.
IT'S COLD, SHOE. IT'S COLDER NEAR THE LAKE. FUCK THE LAKE.
I LIKE IT. INVIGORATING.
I'LL BE INVIGORATED IF WHAT I THINK IS THROUGH THAT DOOR.
SNIP SNIP.
JACKPOT.

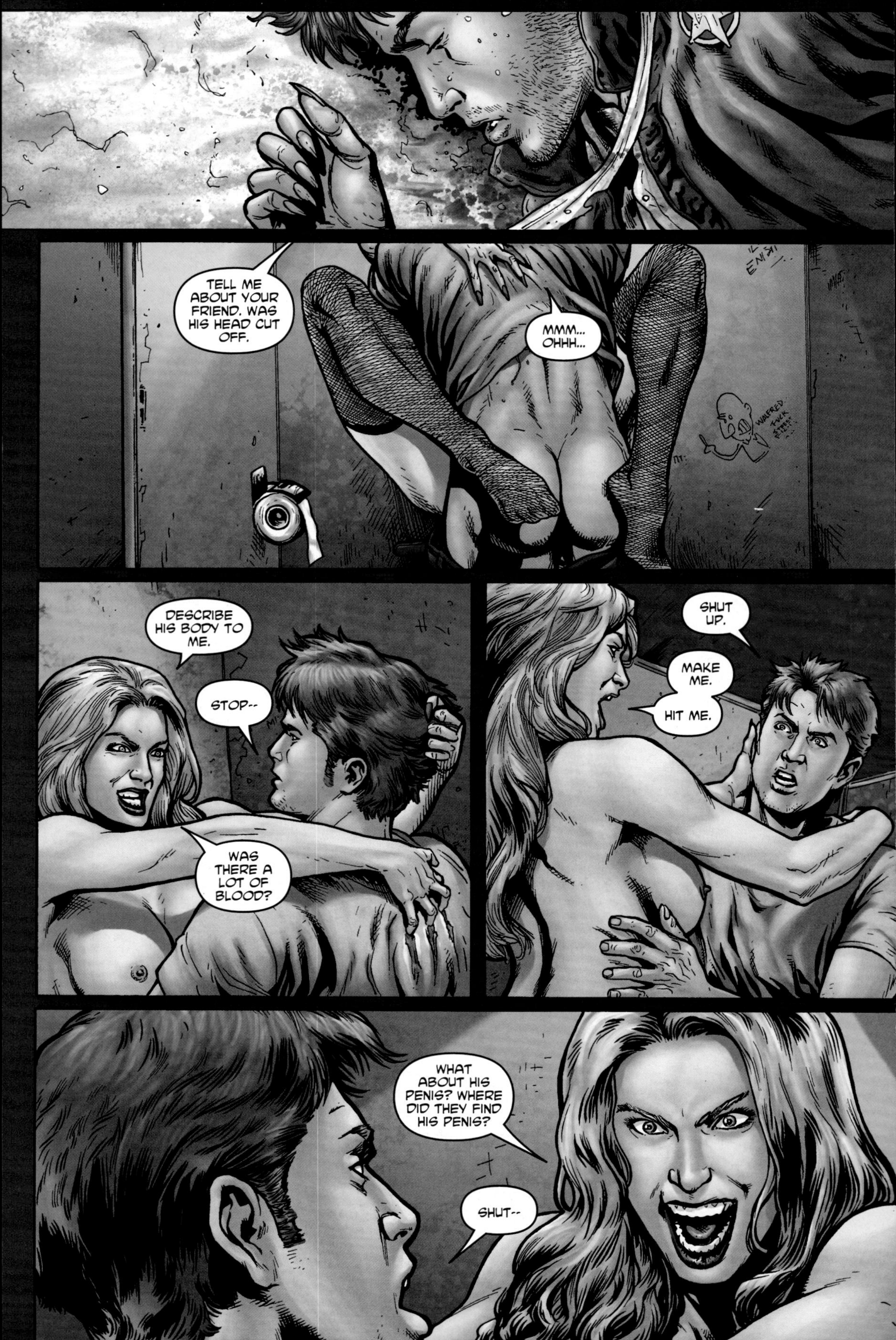
TELL ME ABOUT YOUR FRIEND. WAS HIS HEAD CUT OFF.
MMM... OHHH...
DESCRIBE HIS BODY TO ME.
STOP--
WAS THERE A LOT OF BLOOD?
SHUT UP.
MAKE ME.
HIT ME.
WHAT ABOUT HIS PENIS? WHERE DID THEY FIND HIS PENIS?
SHUT--

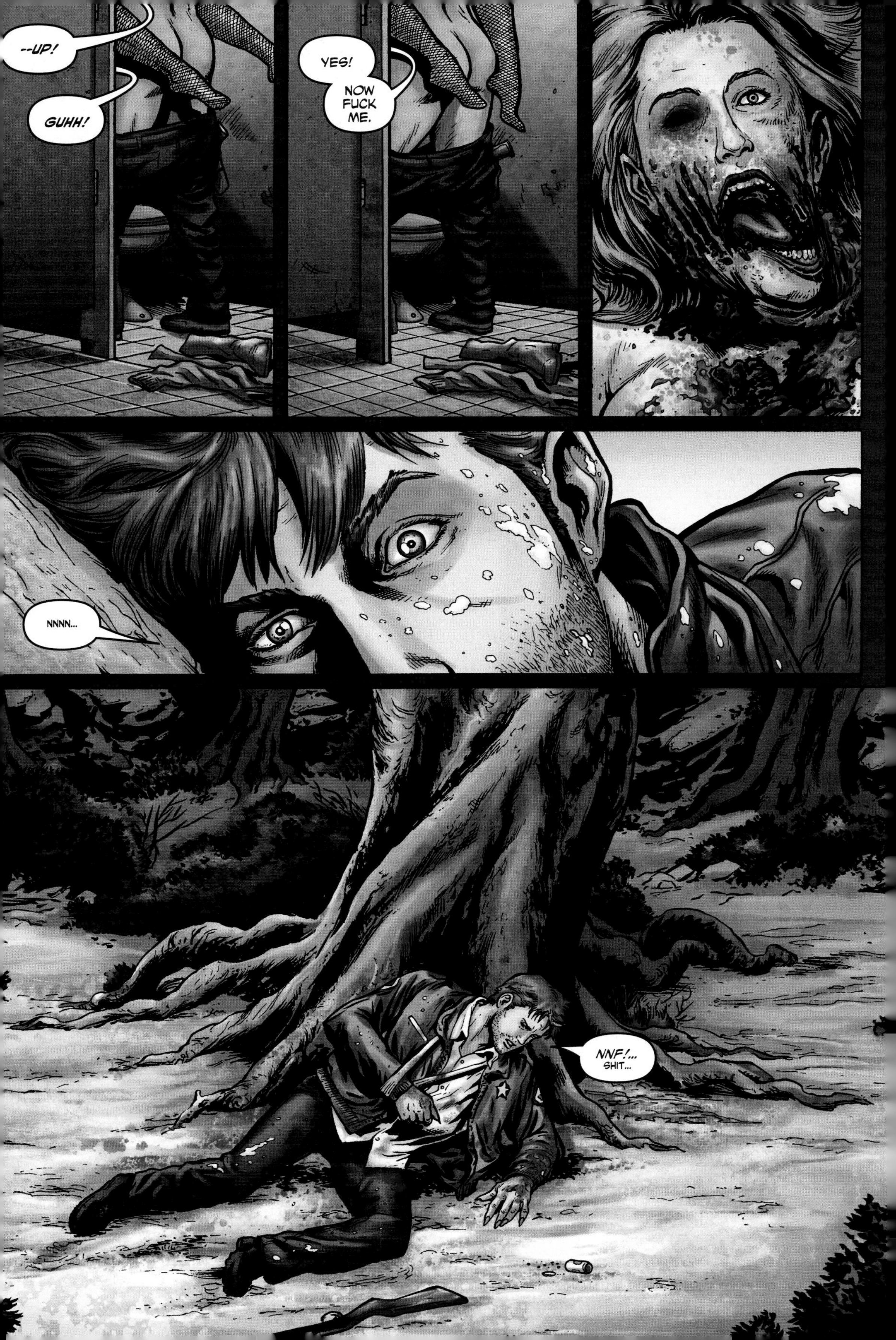
--UP!
GUHH!
YES!
NOW FUCK ME.
NNNN...
NNF!... SHIT...

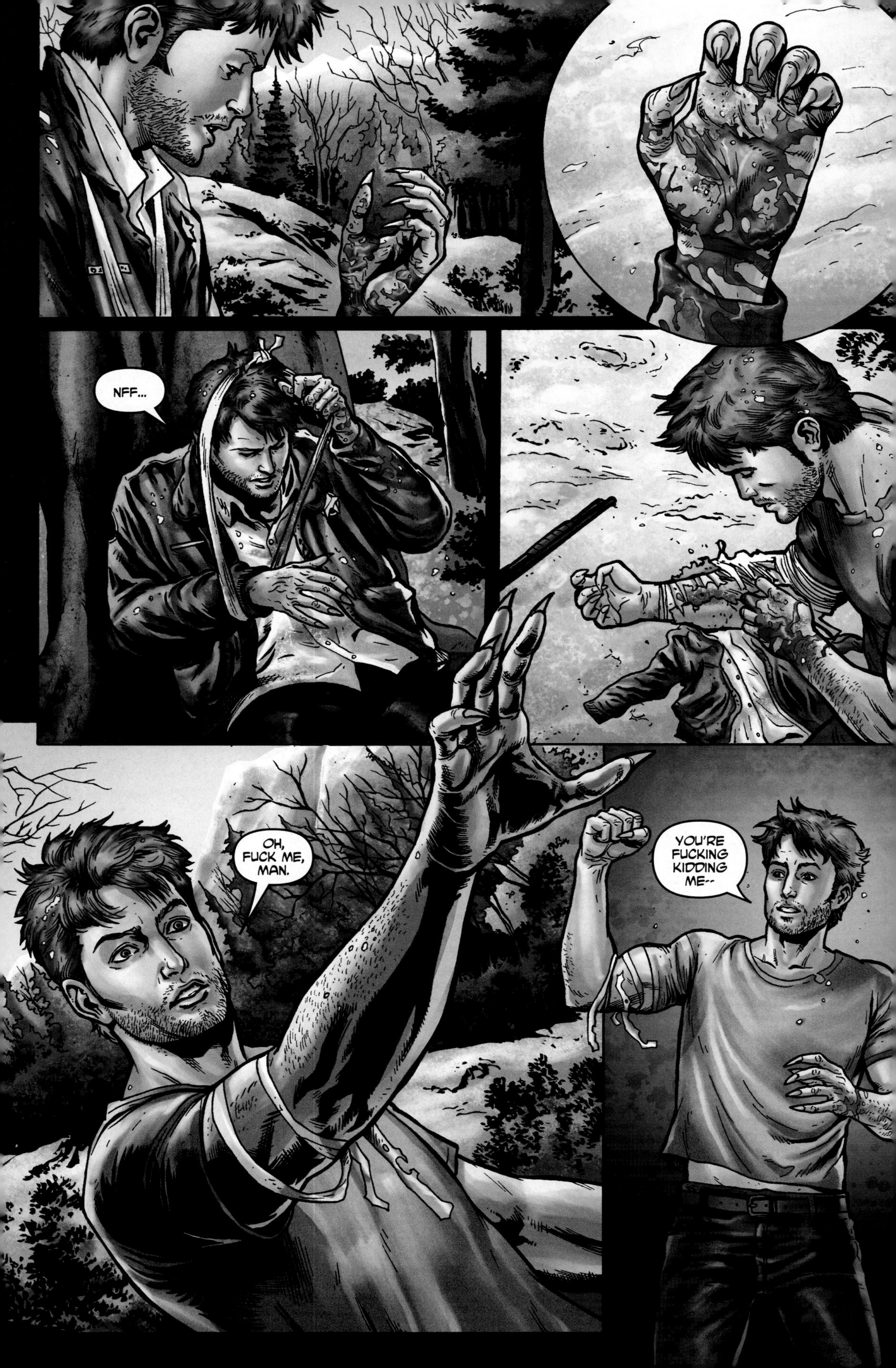
NFF...
OH, FUCK ME, MAN.
YOU'RE FUCKING KIDDING ME--

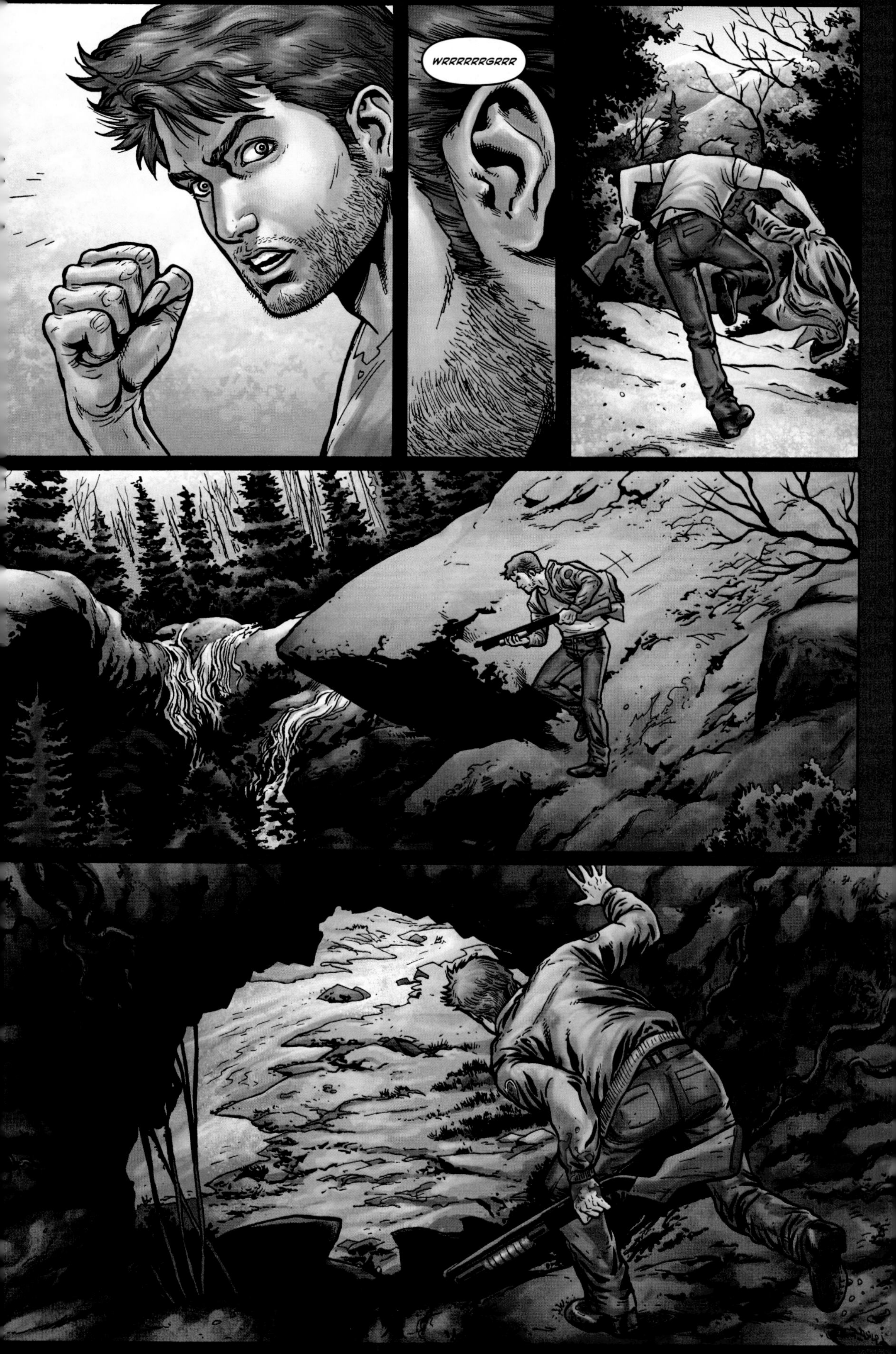
WRRRRRRGRRR

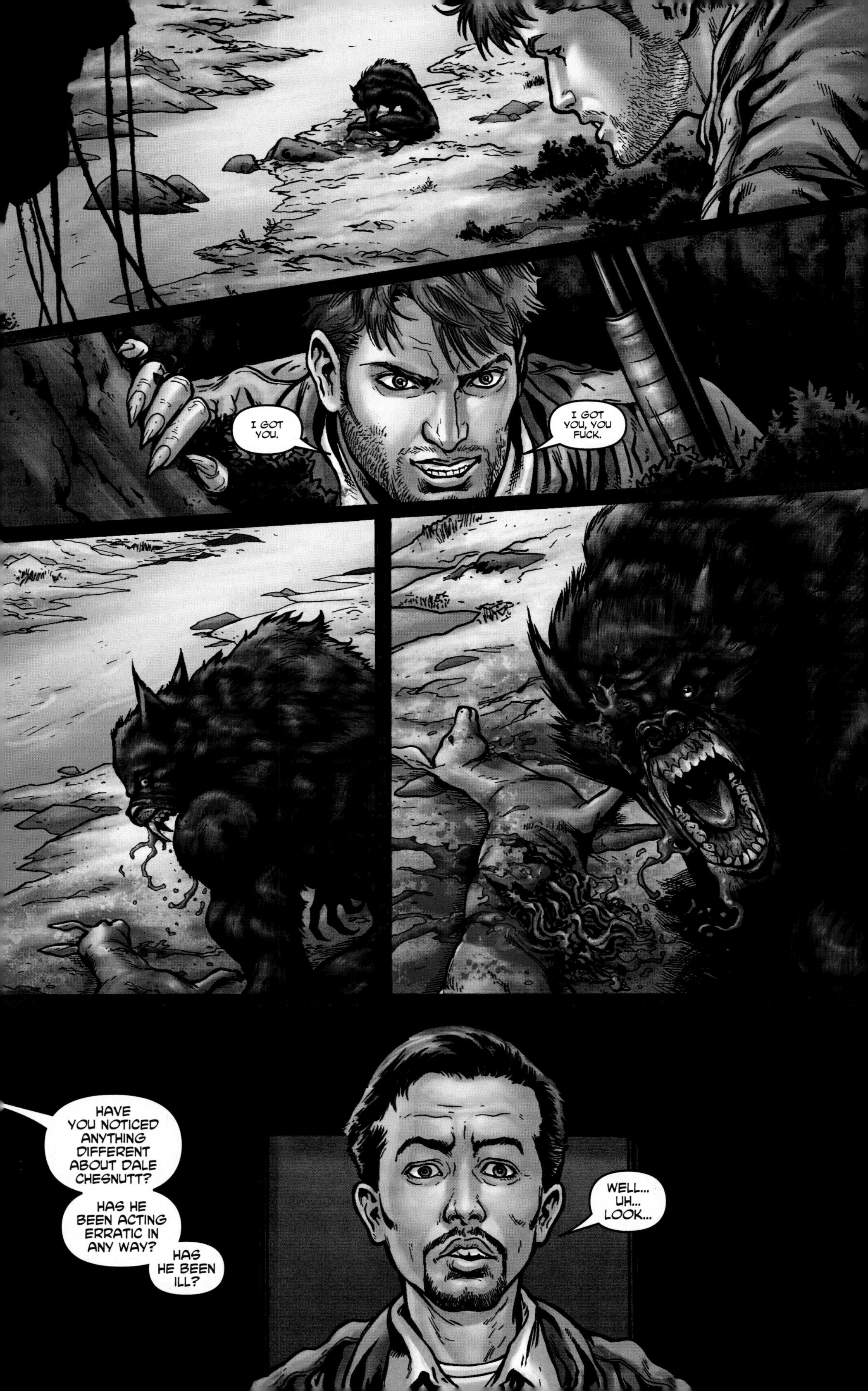
I GOT YOU.
I GOT YOU, YOU FUCK.
HAVE YOU NOTICED ANYTHING DIFFERENT ABOUT DALE CHESNUTT?
HAS HE BEEN ACTING ERRATIC IN ANY WAY?
HAS HE BEEN ILL?
WELL... UH... LOOK...

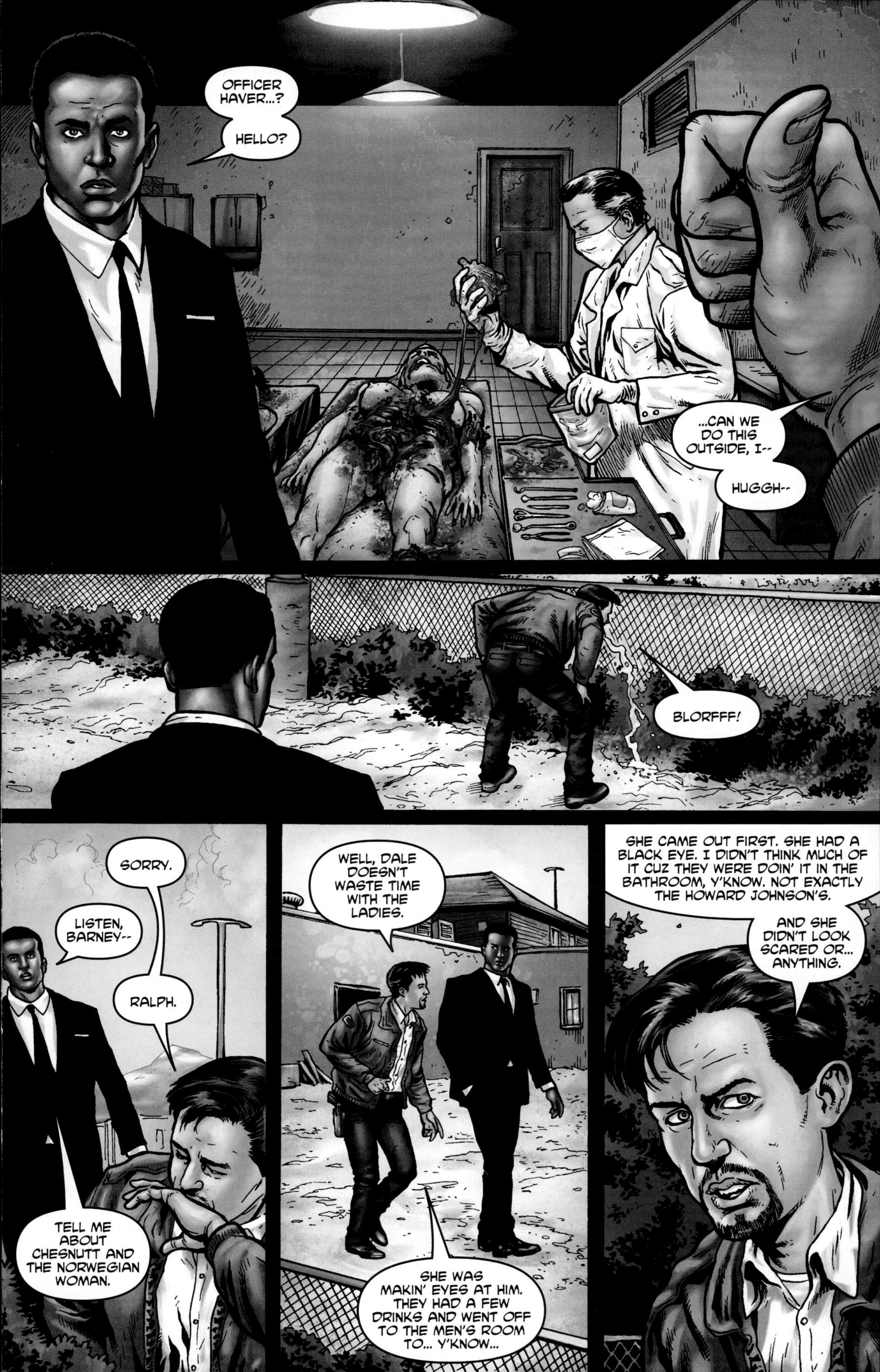
OFFICER HAVER...?
HELLO?
...CAN WE DO THIS OUTSIDE, I--
HUGGH--
BLORFFF!
SORRY.
LISTEN, BARNEY--
RALPH.
TELL ME ABOUT CHESNUTT AND THE NORWEGIAN WOMAN.
WELL, DALE DOESN'T WASTE TIME WITH THE LADIES.
SHE WAS MAKIN' EYES AT HIM. THEY HAD A FEW DRINKS AND WENT OFF TO THE MEN'S ROOM TO... Y'KNOW...
SHE CAME OUT FIRST. SHE HAD A BLACK EYE. I DIDN'T THINK MUCH OF IT CUZ THEY WERE DOIN' IT IN THE BATHROOM, Y'KNOW. NOT EXACTLY THE HOWARD JOHNSON'S.
AND SHE DIDN'T LOOK SCARED OR... ANYTHING.

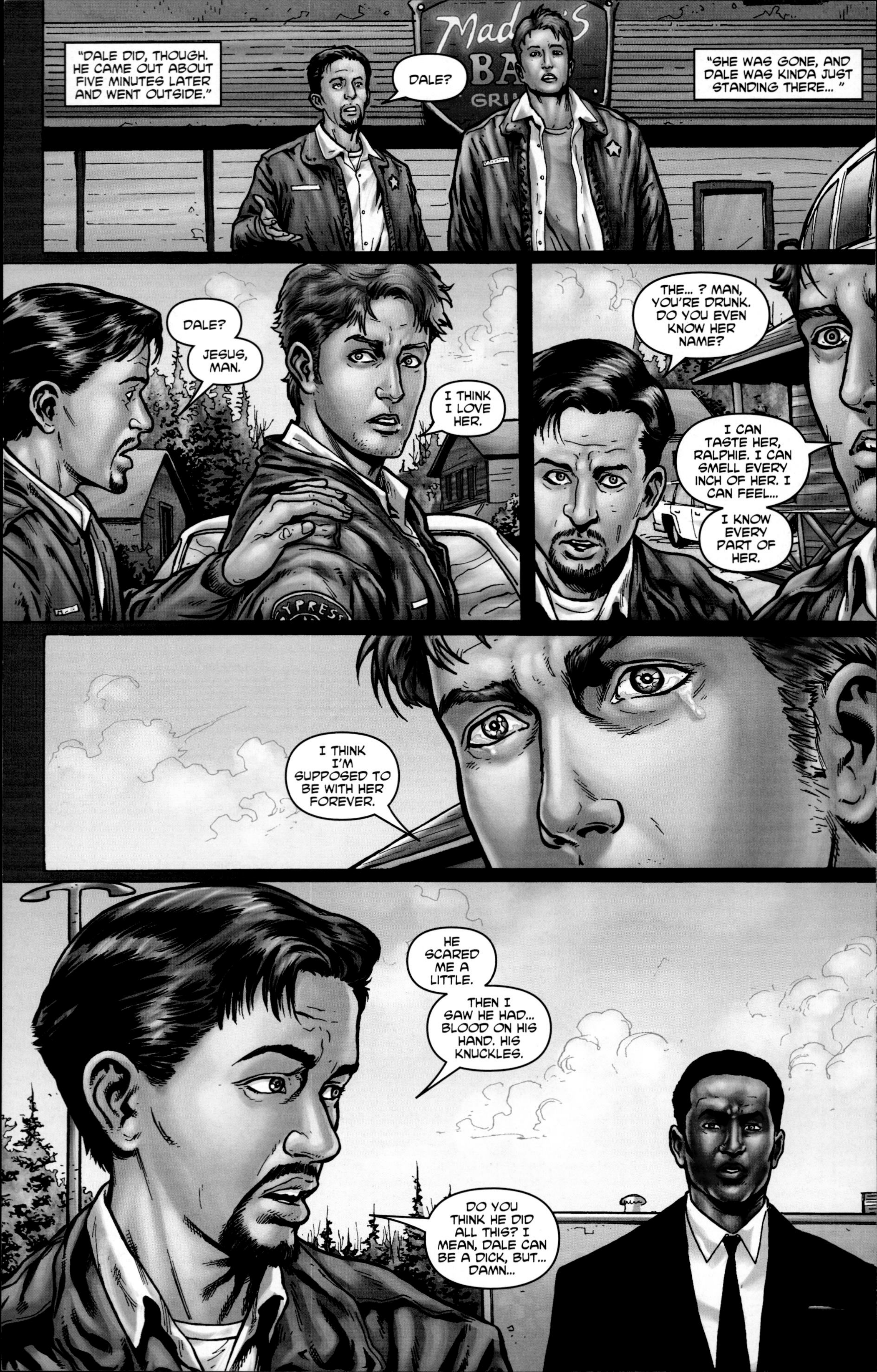
"DALE DID, THOUGH. HE CAME OUT ABOUT FIVE MINUTES LATER AND WENT OUTSIDE."
DALE?
"SHE WAS GONE, AND DALE WAS KINDA JUST STANDING THERE..."
DALE?
JESUS, MAN.
I THINK I LOVE HER.
THE... ? MAN, YOU'RE DRUNK. DO YOU EVEN KNOW HER NAME?
I CAN TASTE HER, RALPHIE. I CAN SMELL EVERY INCH OF HER. I CAN FEEL...
I KNOW EVERY PART OF HER.
I THINK I'M SUPPOSED TO BE WITH HER FOREVER.
HE SCARED ME A LITTLE.
THEN I SAW HE HAD... BLOOD ON HIS HAND. HIS KNUCKLES.
DO YOU THINK HE DID ALL THIS? I MEAN, DALE CAN BE A DICK, BUT... DAMN...

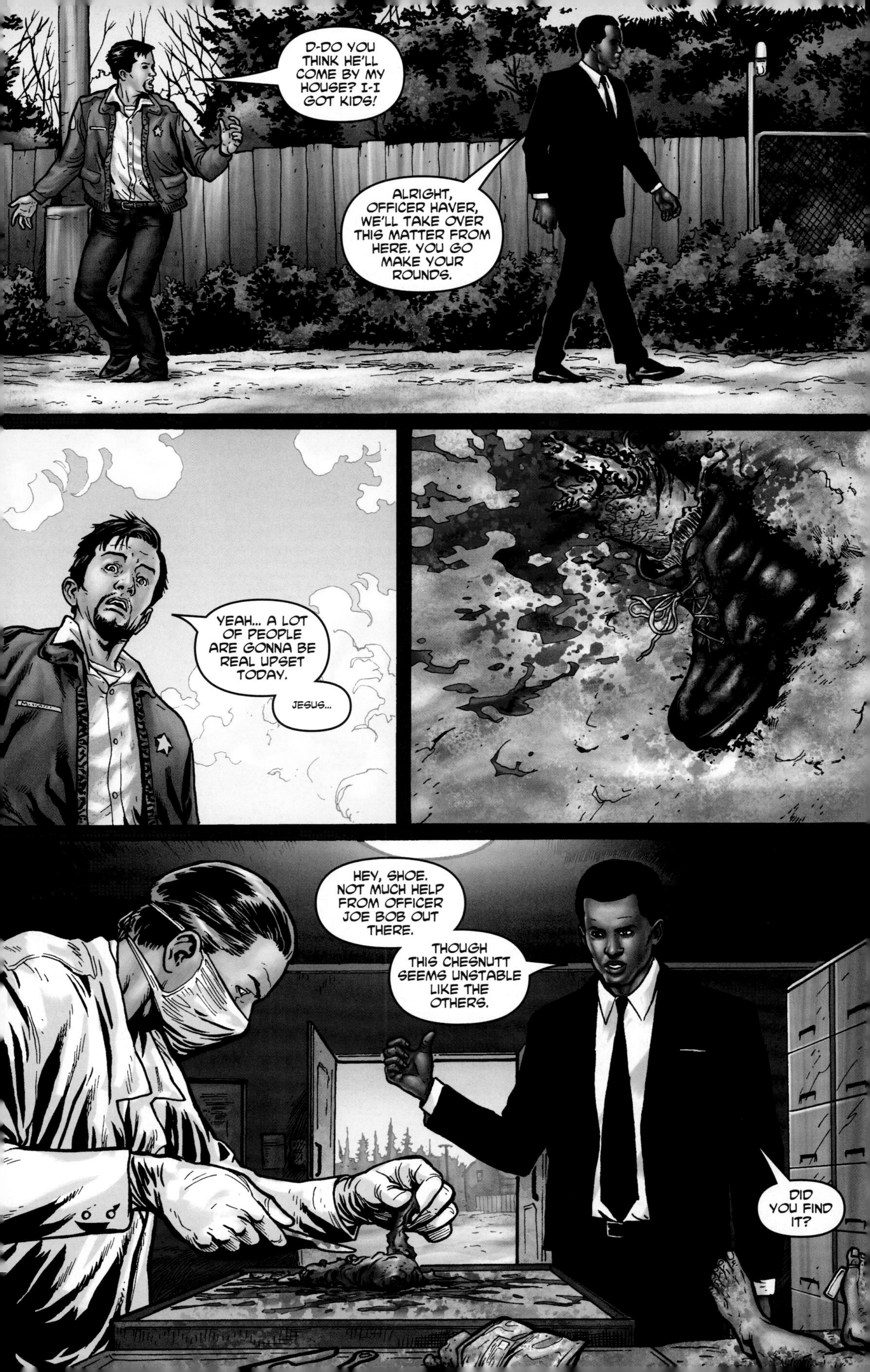
D-DO YOU THINK HE'LL COME BY MY HOUSE? I-I GOT KIDS!
ALRIGHT, OFFICER HAVER, WE'LL TAKE OVER THIS MATTER FROM HERE. YOU GO MAKE YOUR ROUNDS.
YEAH... A LOT OF PEOPLE ARE GONNA BE REAL UPSET TODAY.
JESUS...
HEY, SHOE. NOT MUCH HELP FROM OFFICER JOE BOB OUT THERE.
THOUGH THIS CHESNUTT SEEMS UNSTABLE LIKE THE OTHERS.
DID YOU FIND IT?

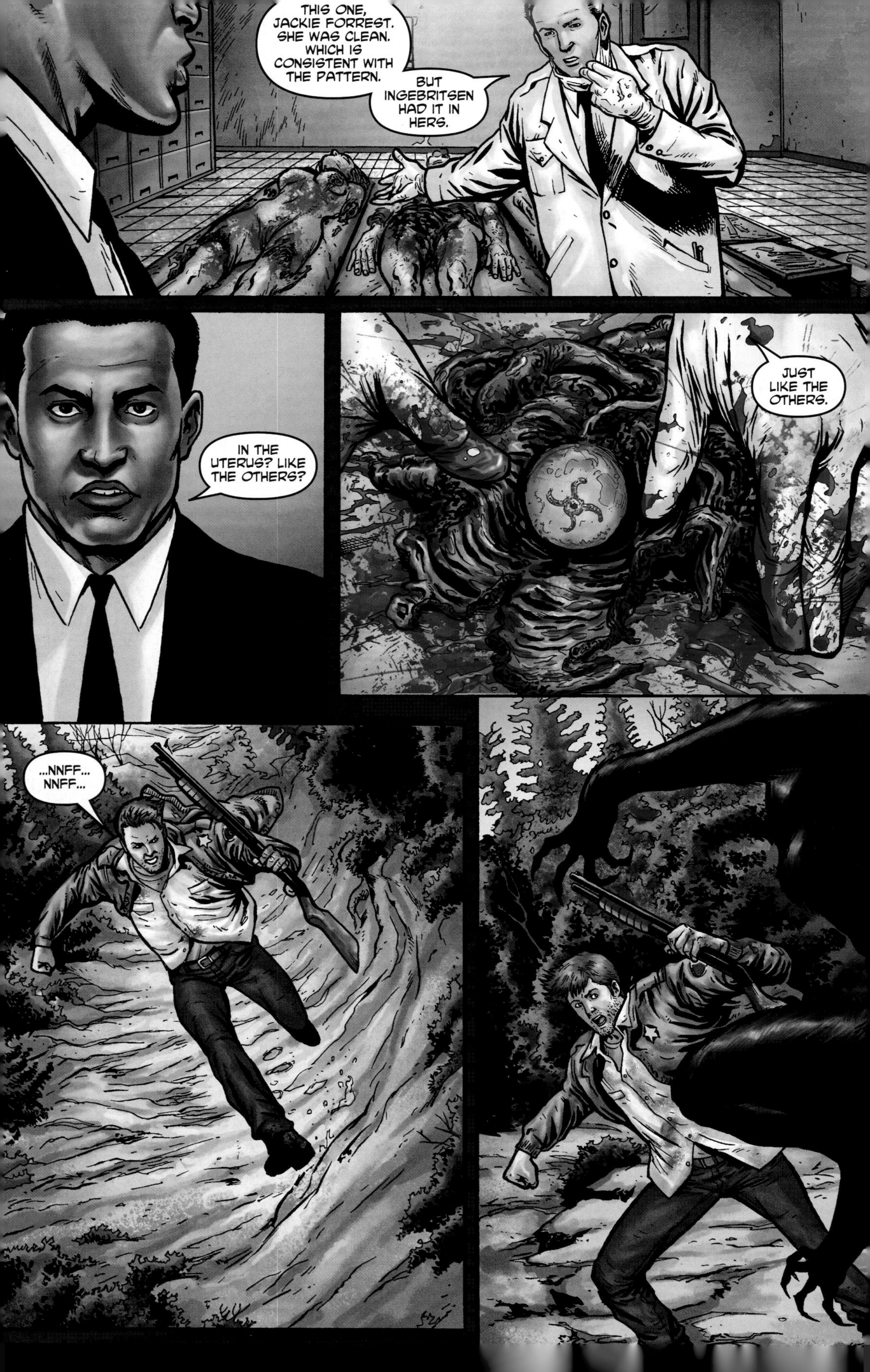
THIS ONE, JACKIE FORREST. SHE WAS CLEAN. WHICH IS CONSISTENT WITH THE PATTERN.
BUT INGEBRITSEN HAD IT IN HERS.
IN THE UTERUS? LIKE THE OTHERS?
JUST LIKE THE OTHERS.
...NNFF... NNFF...

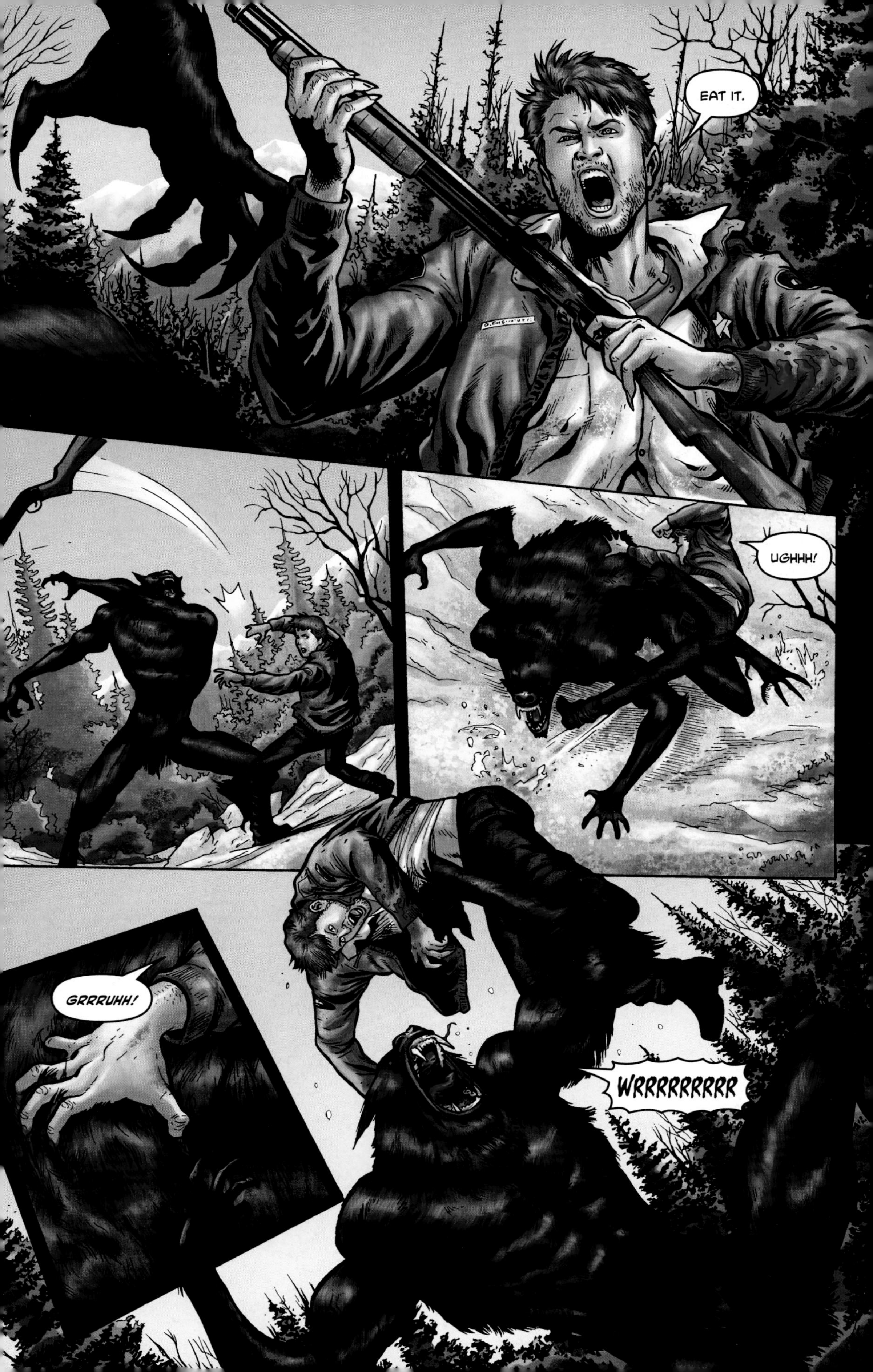
EAT IT.
UGHHH!
GRRRUHH!
WRRRRRRRRR

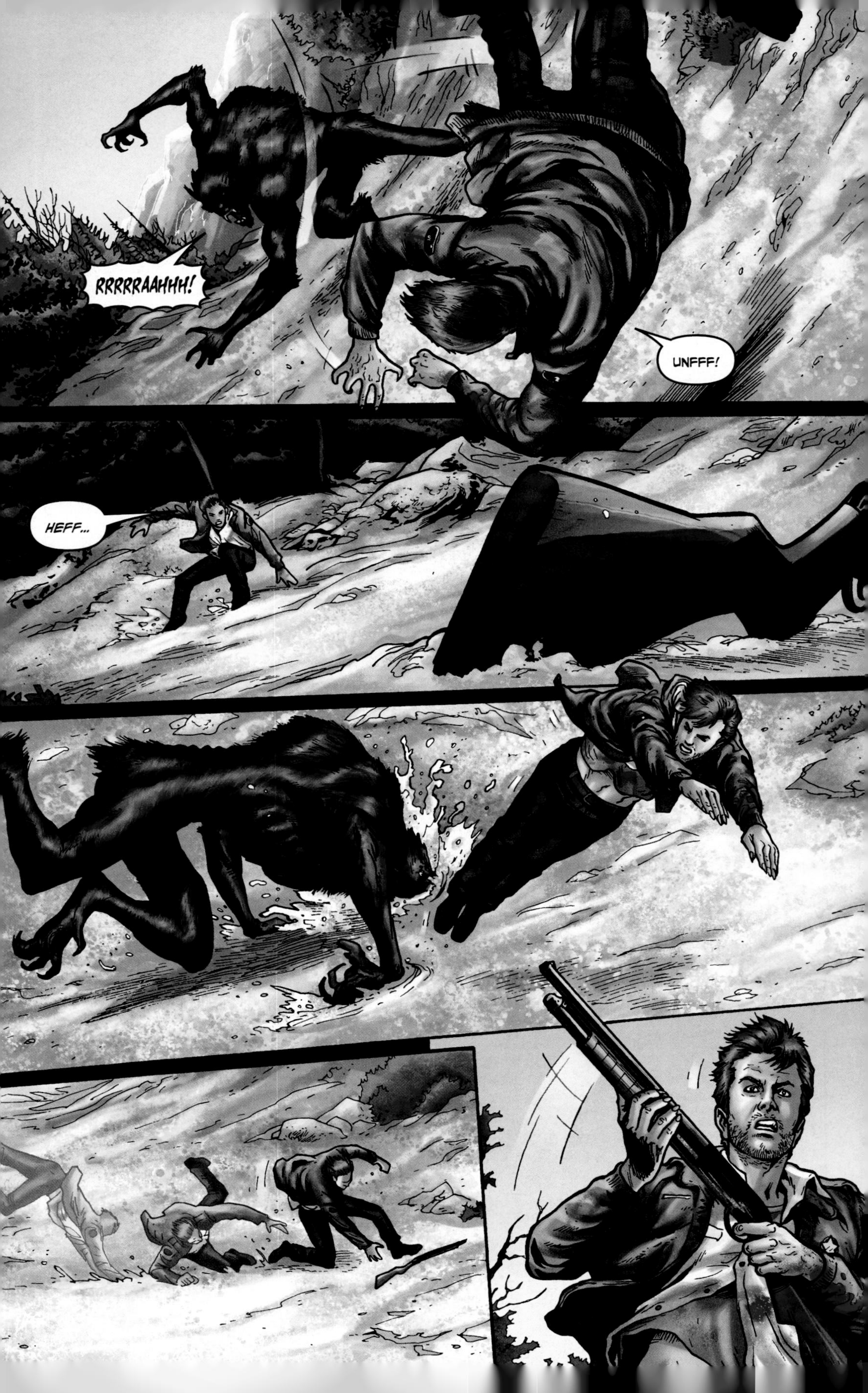
RRRRRAAHHH!
UNFFF!
HEFF...

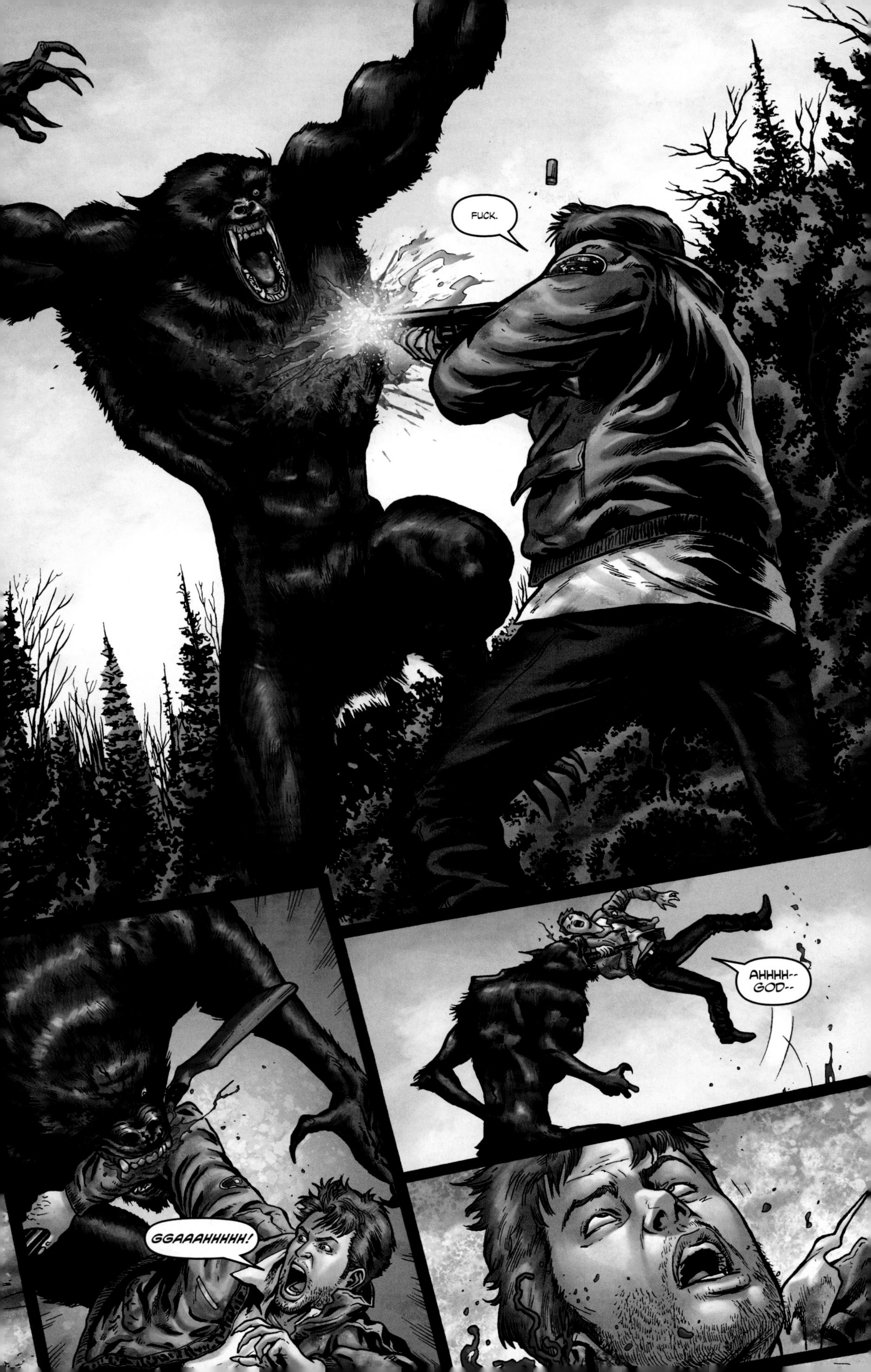
FUCK.
GGAAAHHHHH!
AHHHH--
GOD--

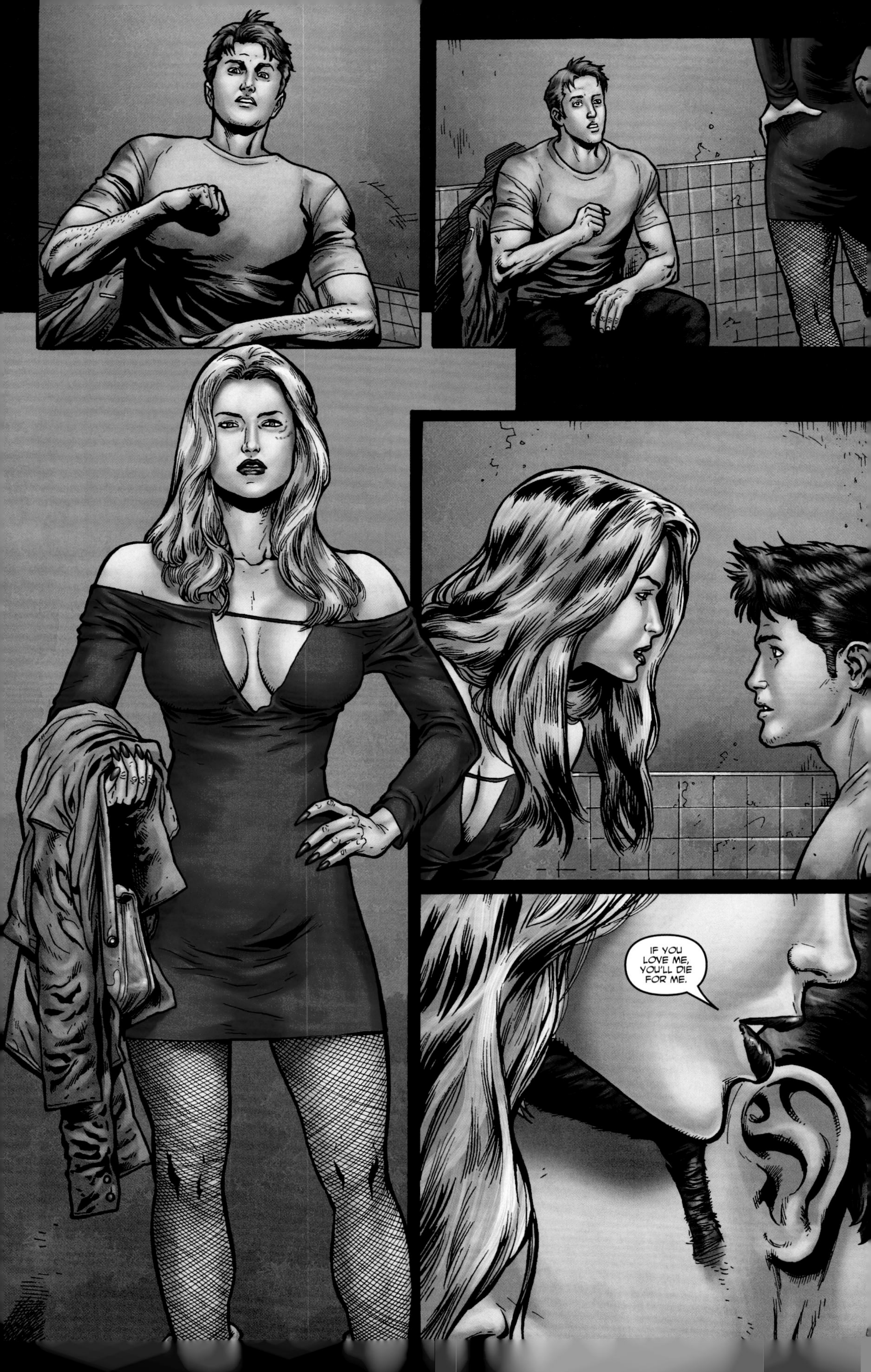
IF YOU LOVE ME, YOU'LL DIE FOR ME.

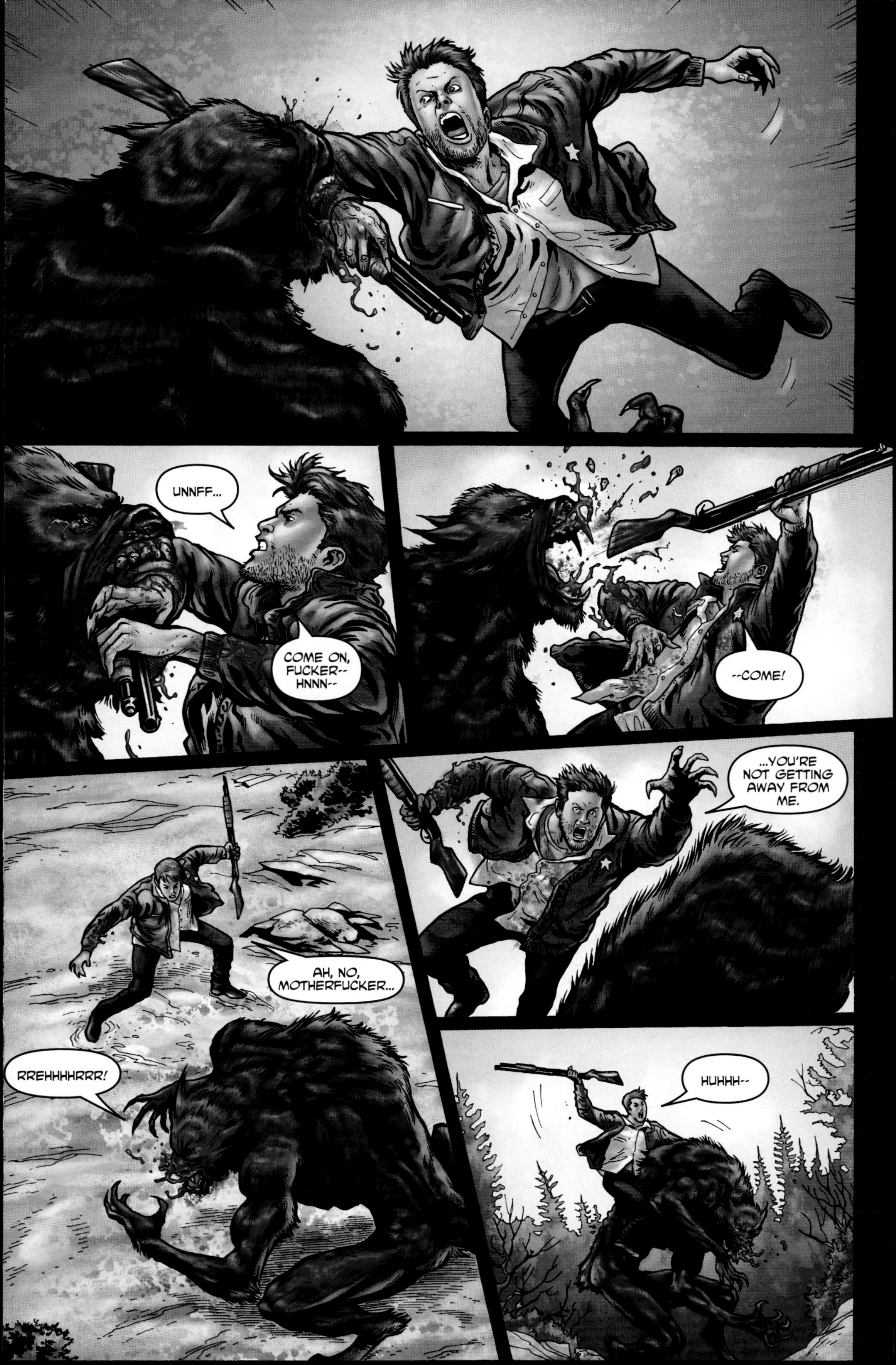
UNNFF...
COME ON, FUCKER-- HNNN--
--COME!
AH, NO, MOTHERFUCKER...
RREHHHHRRR!
...YOU'RE NOT GETTING AWAY FROM ME.
HUHHH--

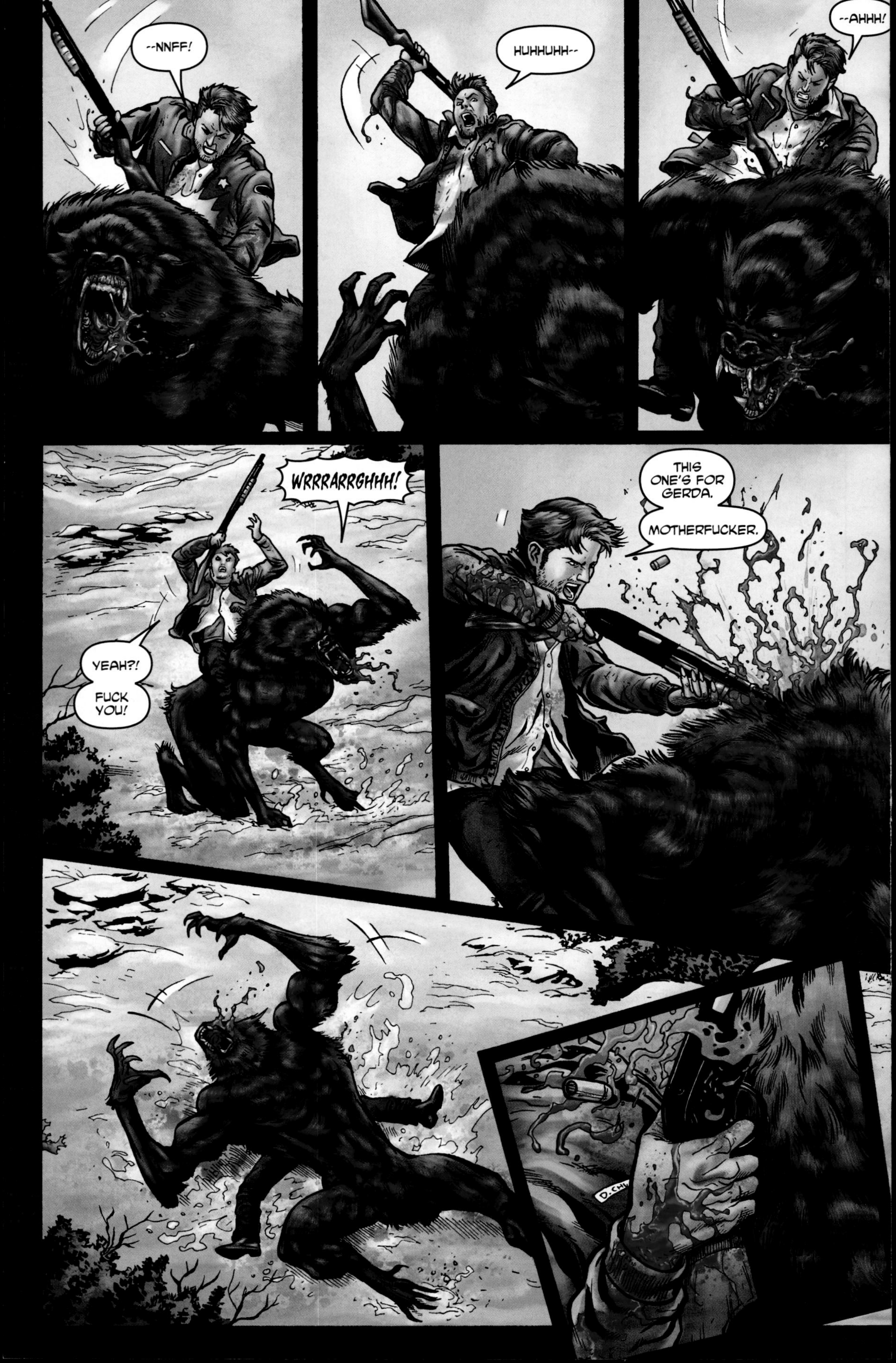
--NNFF!
HUHHUHH--
--AHHH!
WRRRARRGHHH!
YEAH?!
FUCK YOU!
THIS ONE'S FOR GERDA.
MOTHERFUCKER.

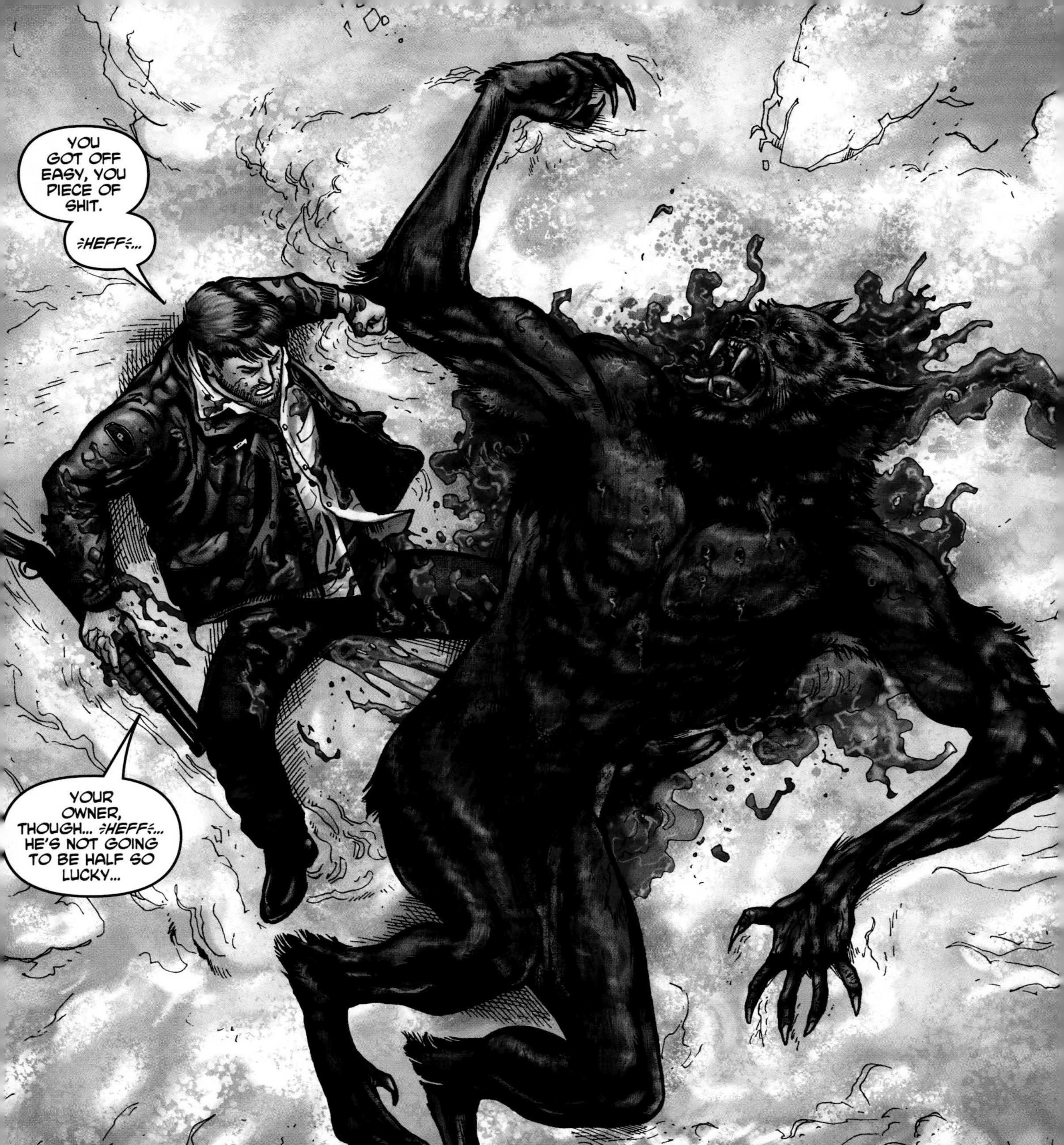
YOU GOT OFF EASY, YOU PIECE OF SHIT.
HEFF...
YOUR OWNER, THOUGH... *HEFF*... HE'S NOT GOING TO BE HALF SO LUCKY...

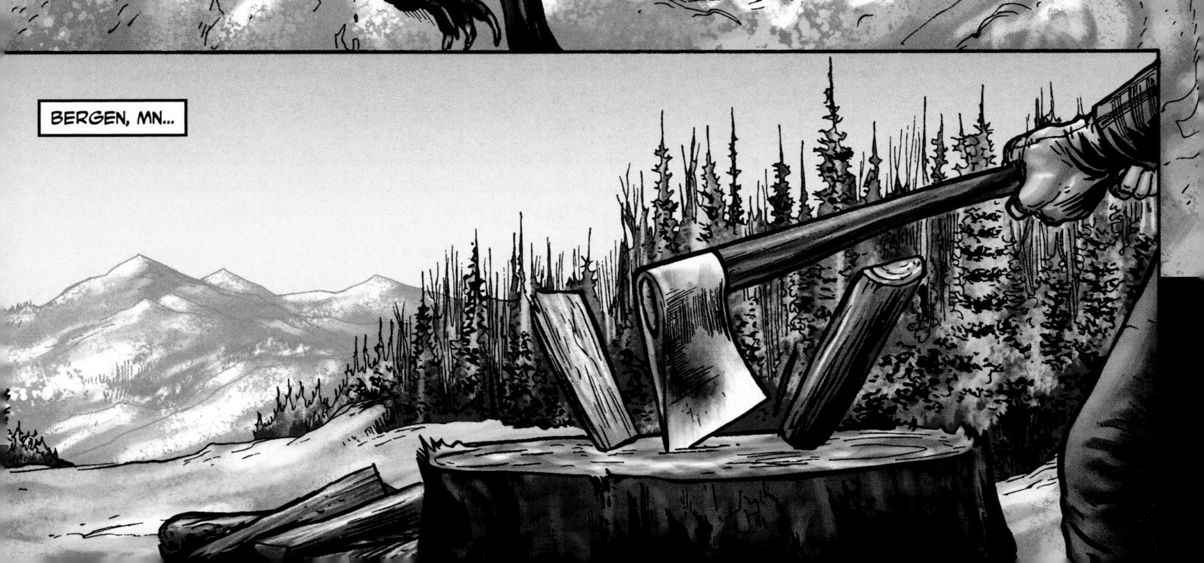
BERGEN, MN...

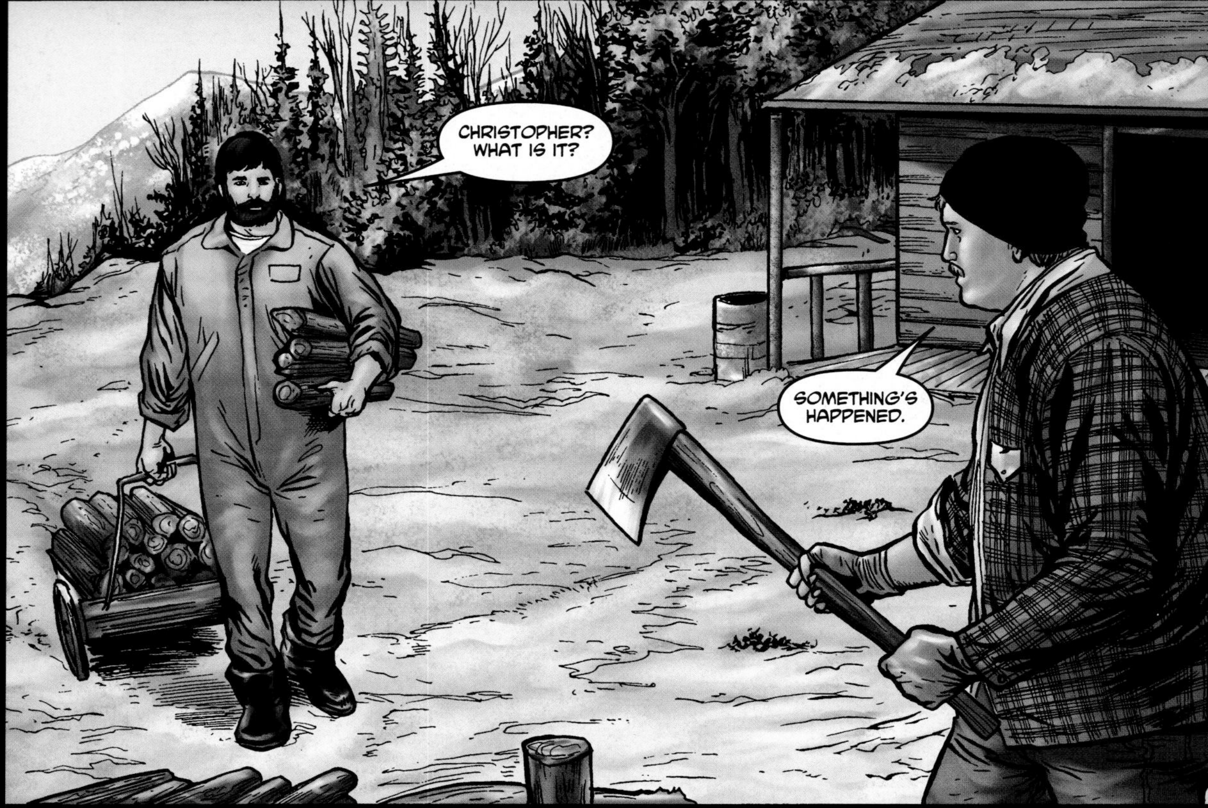
CHRISTOPHER? WHAT IS IT?
SOMETHING'S HAPPENED.

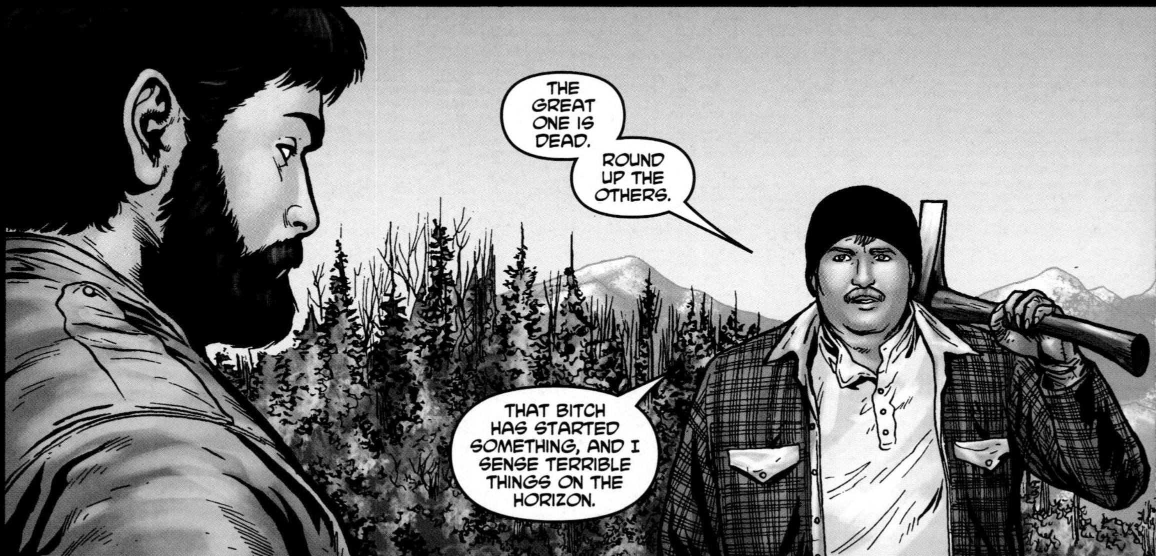
THE GREAT ONE IS DEAD.
ROUND UP THE OTHERS.
THAT BITCH HAS STARTED SOMETHING, AND I SENSE TERRIBLE THINGS ON THE HORIZON.

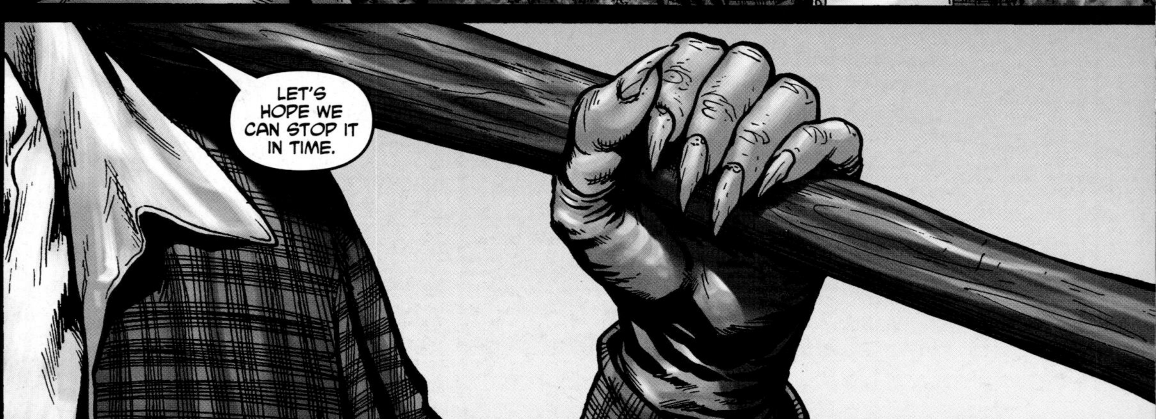
LET'S HOPE WE CAN STOP IT IN TIME.

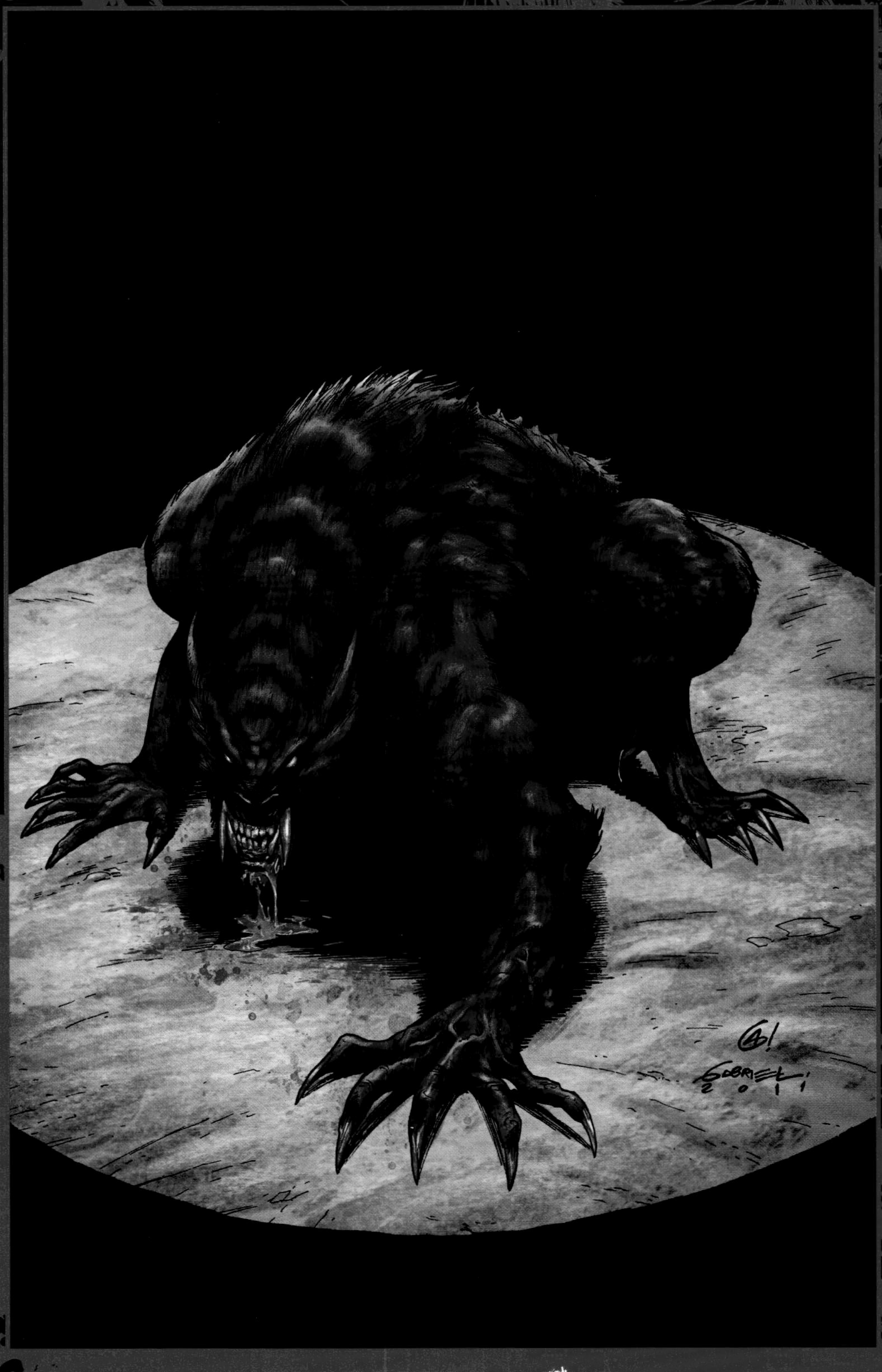

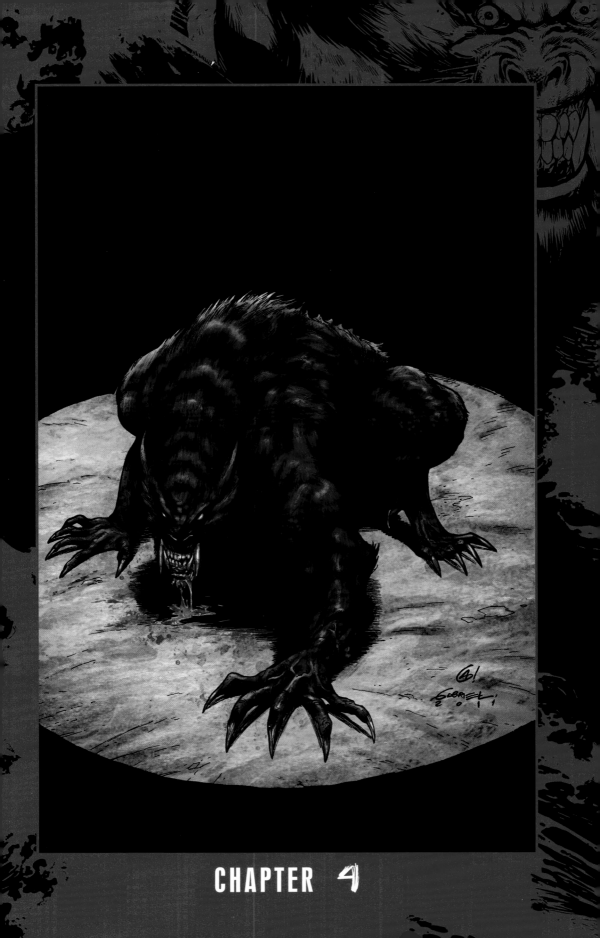

CHAPTER 4

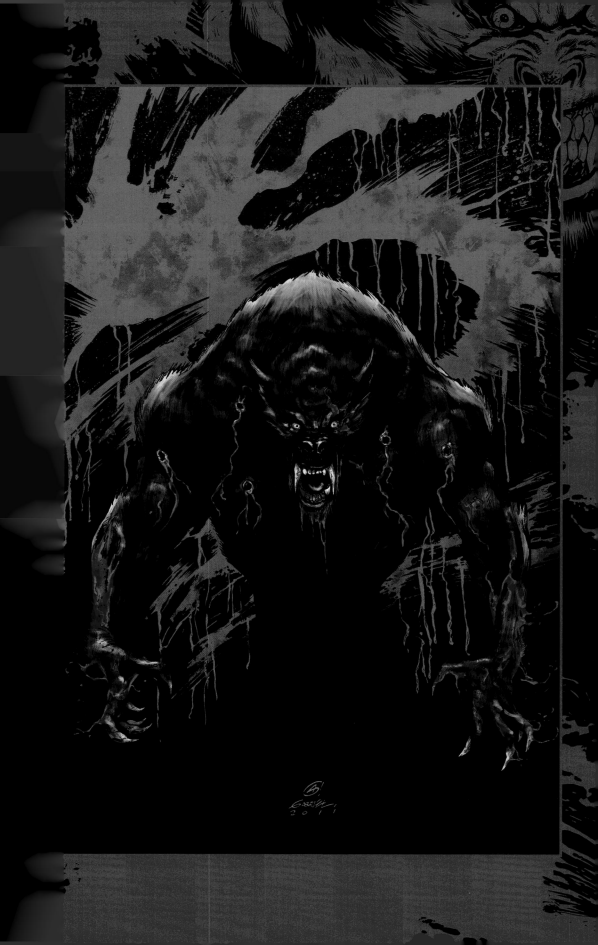

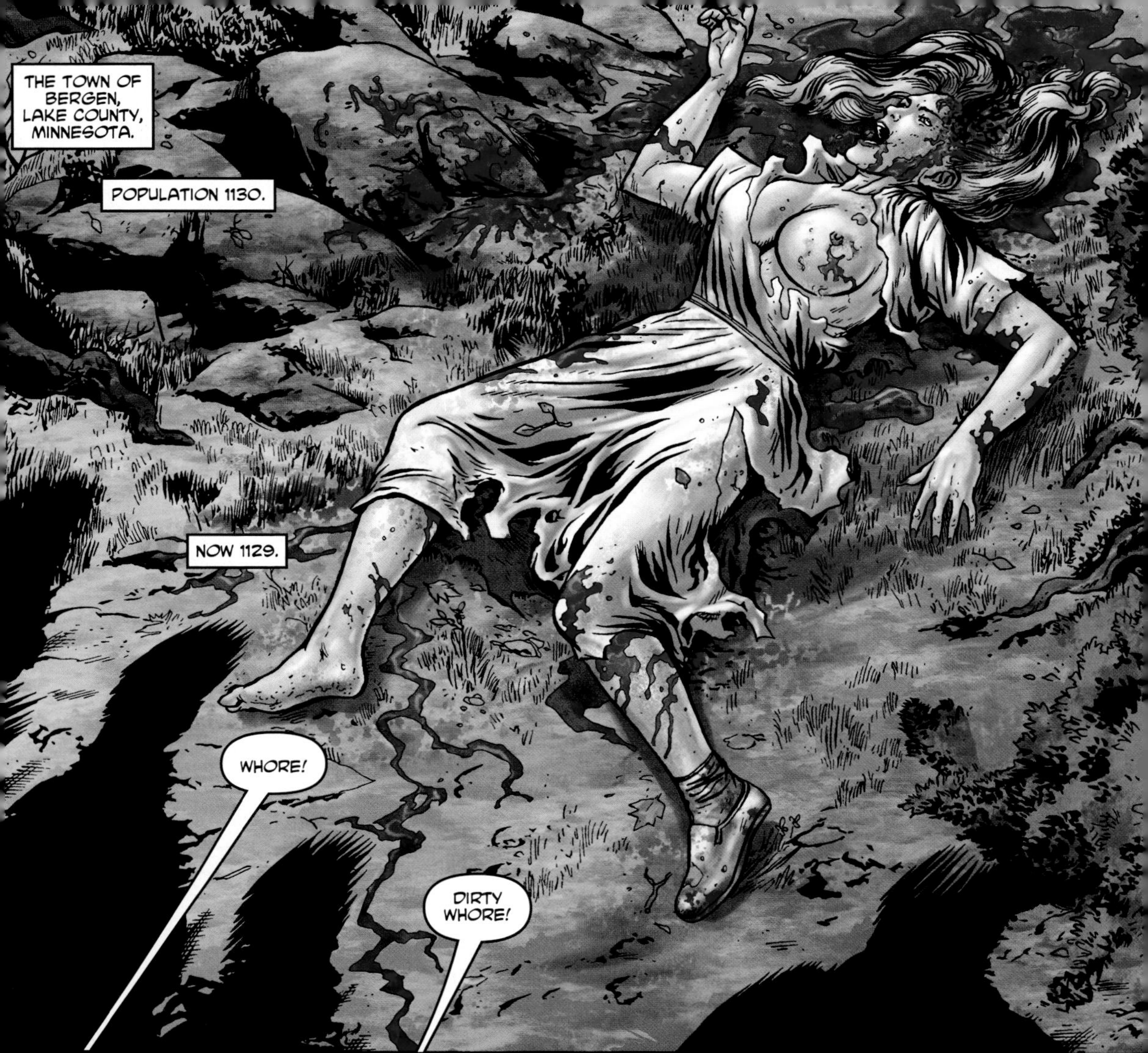
THE TOWN OF BERGEN, LAKE COUNTY, MINNESOTA.
POPULATION 1130.
NOW 1129.
WHORE!
DIRTY WHORE!

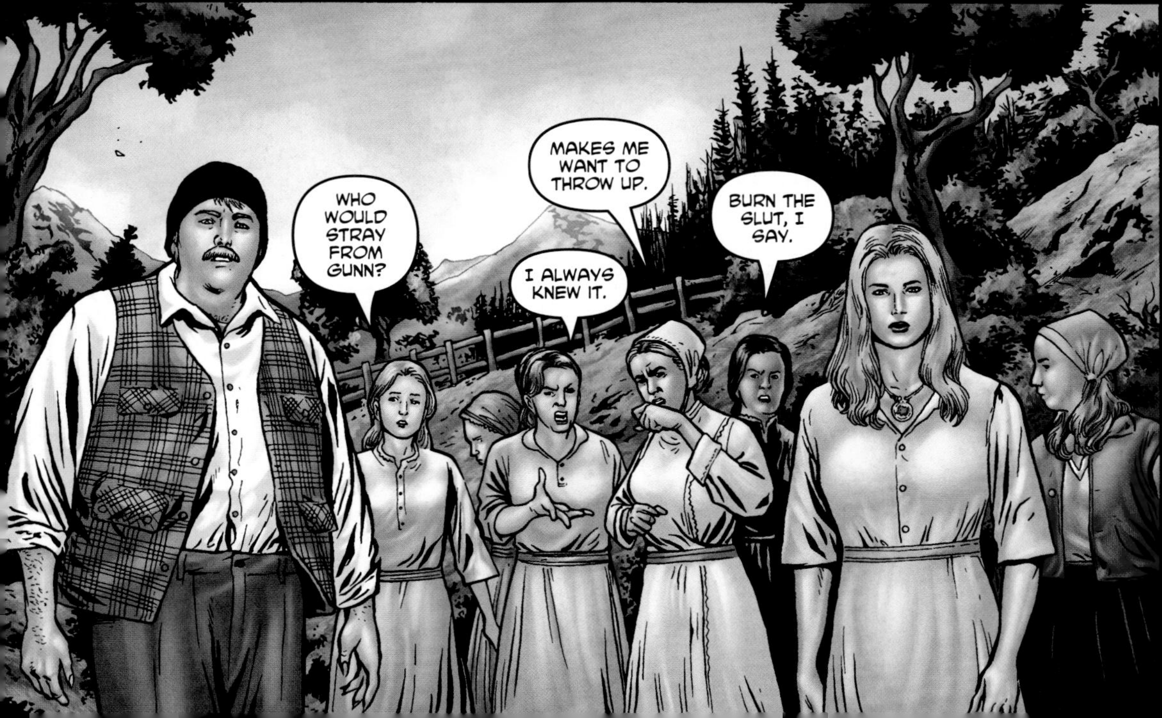
WHO WOULD STRAY FROM GUNN?
I ALWAYS KNEW IT.
MAKES ME WANT TO THROW UP.
BURN THE SLUT, I SAY.

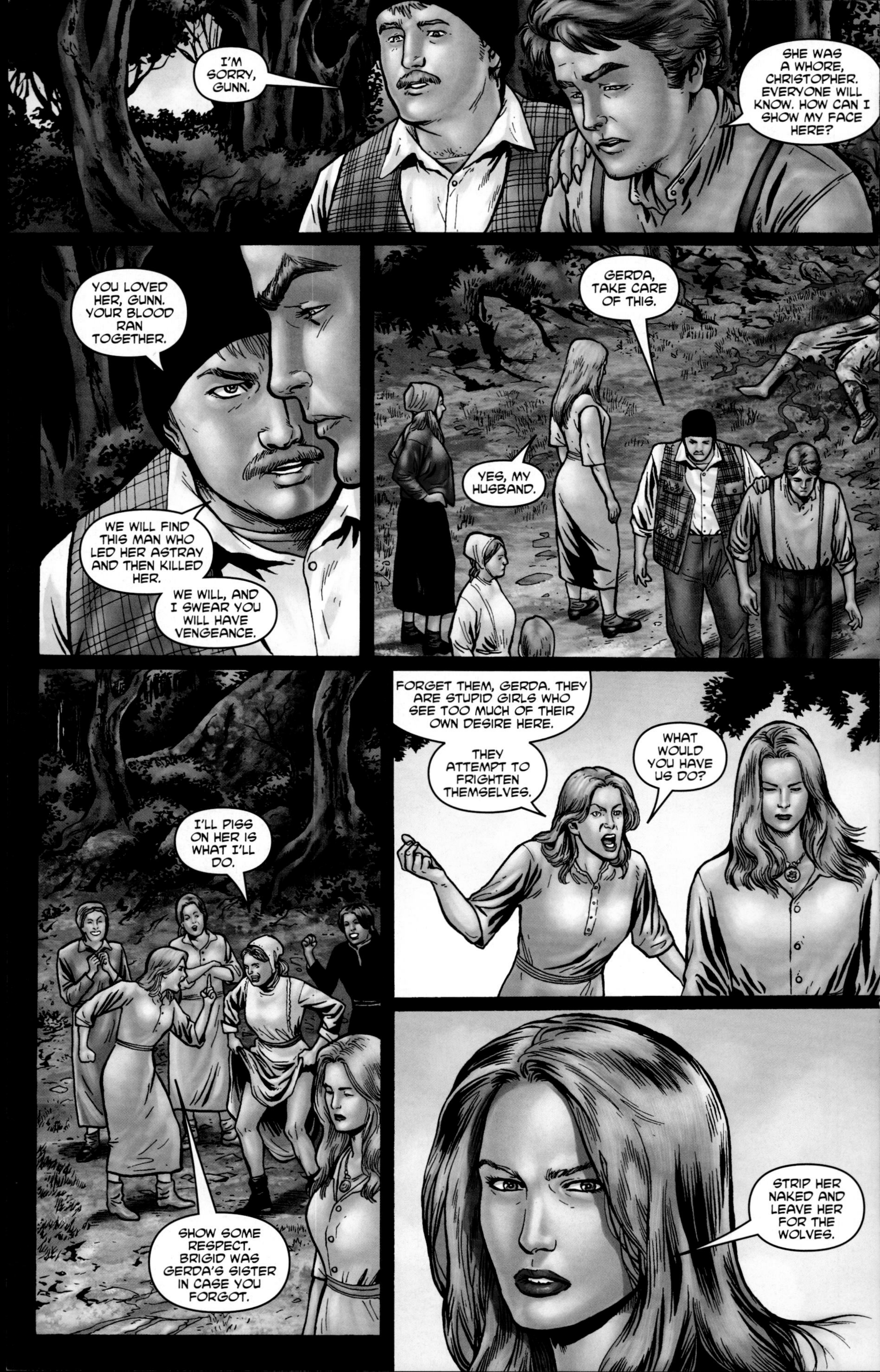
I'M SORRY, GUNN.
SHE WAS A WHORE, CHRISTOPHER. EVERYONE WILL KNOW. HOW CAN I SHOW MY FACE HERE?
YOU LOVED HER, GUNN. YOUR BLOOD RAN TOGETHER.
WE WILL FIND THIS MAN WHO LED HER ASTRAY AND THEN KILLED HER.
WE WILL, AND I SWEAR YOU WILL HAVE VENGEANCE.
GERDA, TAKE CARE OF THIS.
YES, MY HUSBAND.
I'LL PISS ON HER IS WHAT I'LL DO.
SHOW SOME RESPECT. BRIGID WAS GERDA'S SISTER IN CASE YOU FORGOT.
FORGET THEM, GERDA. THEY ARE STUPID GIRLS WHO SEE TOO MUCH OF THEIR OWN DESIRE HERE.
THEY ATTEMPT TO FRIGHTEN THEMSELVES.
WHAT WOULD YOU HAVE US DO?
STRIP HER NAKED AND LEAVE HER FOR THE WOLVES.

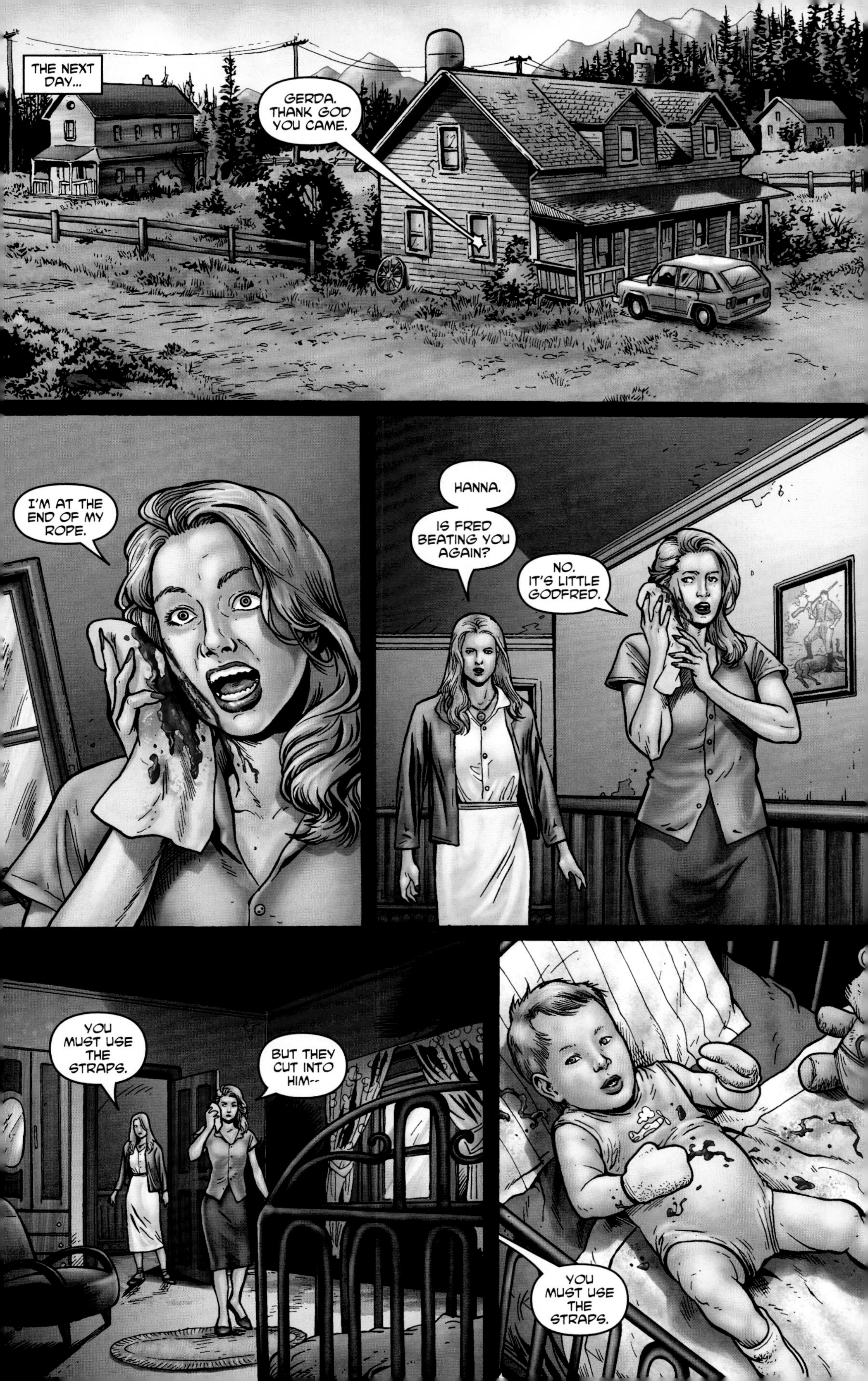
THE NEXT DAY...
GERDA. THANK GOD YOU CAME.
I'M AT THE END OF MY ROPE.
HANNA.
IS FRED BEATING YOU AGAIN?
NO. IT'S LITTLE GODFRED.
YOU MUST USE THE STRAPS.
BUT THEY CUT INTO HIM--
YOU MUST USE THE STRAPS.

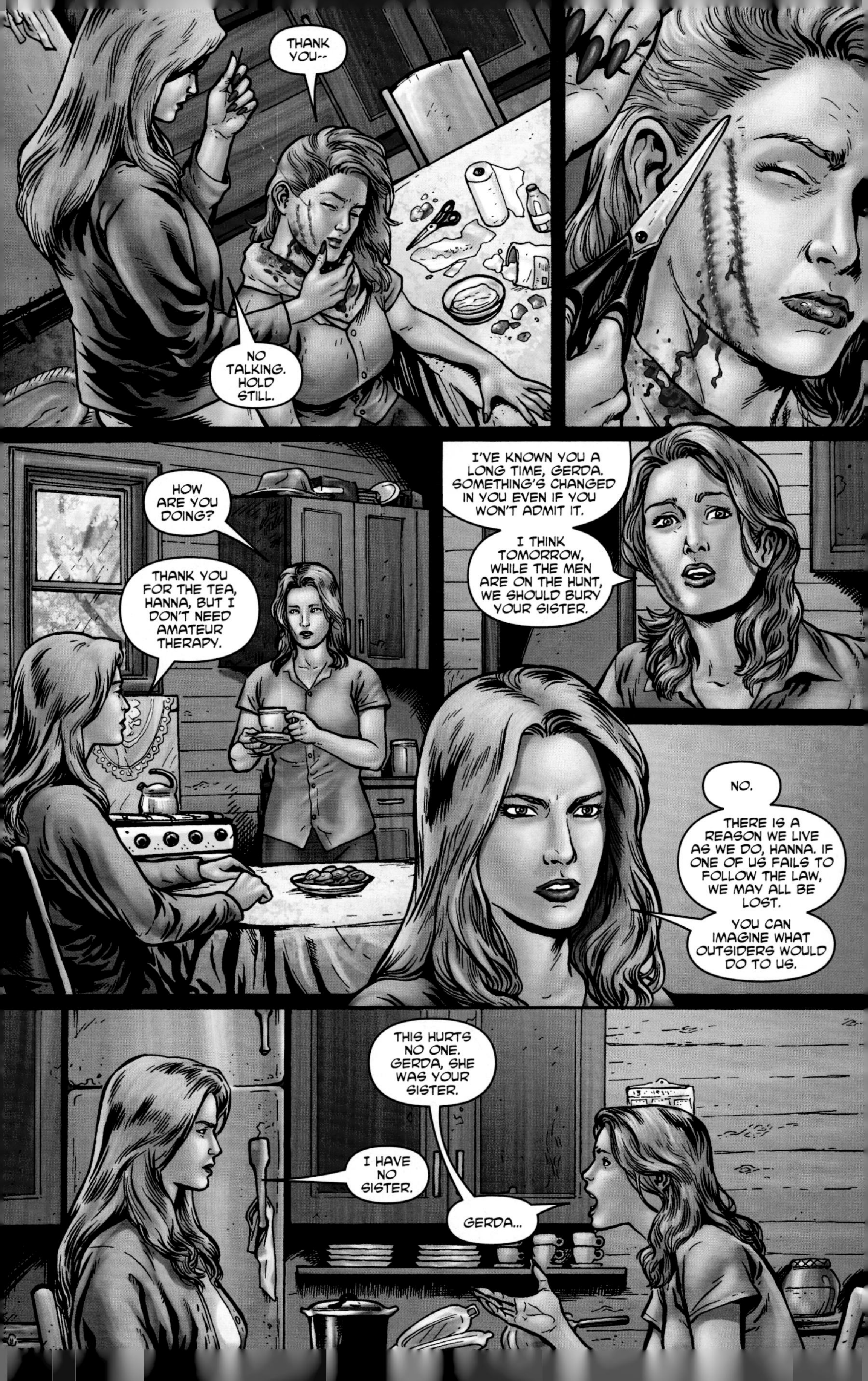
THANK YOU--
NO TALKING. HOLD STILL.
HOW ARE YOU DOING?
THANK YOU FOR THE TEA, HANNA, BUT I DON'T NEED AMATEUR THERAPY.
I'VE KNOWN YOU A LONG TIME, GERDA. SOMETHING'S CHANGED IN YOU EVEN IF YOU WON'T ADMIT IT.
I THINK TOMORROW, WHILE THE MEN ARE ON THE HUNT, WE SHOULD BURY YOUR SISTER.
NO.
THERE IS A REASON WE LIVE AS WE DO, HANNA. IF ONE OF US FAILS TO FOLLOW THE LAW, WE MAY ALL BE LOST.
YOU CAN IMAGINE WHAT OUTSIDERS WOULD DO TO US.
THIS HURTS NO ONE. GERDA, SHE WAS YOUR SISTER.
I HAVE NO SISTER.
GERDA...

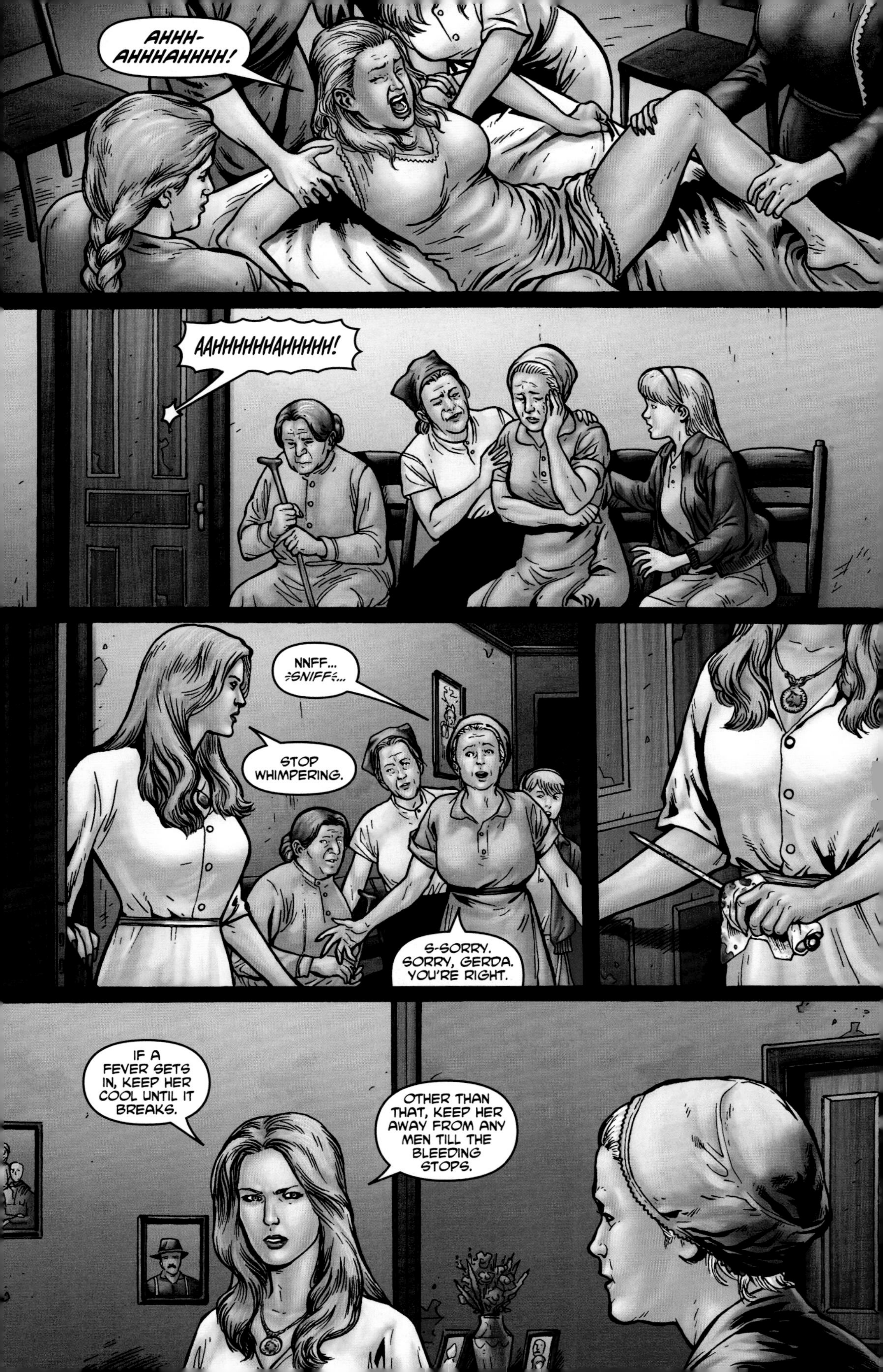
AHHH-
AHHHAHHHH!
AAHHHHHHAHHHHH!
NNFF...
SNIFF...
STOP WHIMPERING.
S-SORRY. SORRY, GERDA. YOU'RE RIGHT.
IF A FEVER SETS IN, KEEP HER COOL UNTIL IT BREAKS.
OTHER THAN THAT, KEEP HER AWAY FROM ANY MEN TILL THE BLEEDING STOPS.

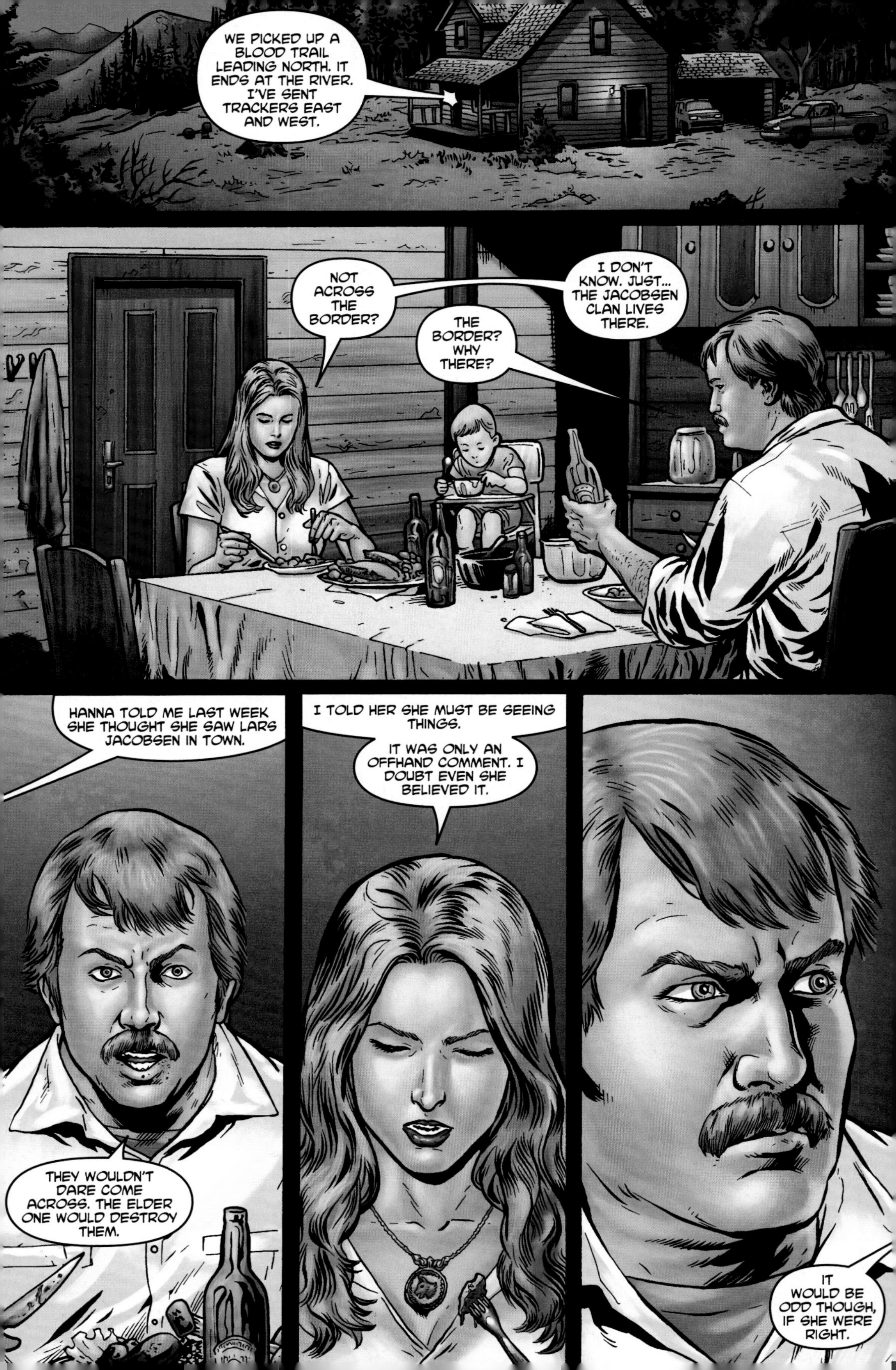
WE PICKED UP A BLOOD TRAIL LEADING NORTH. IT ENDS AT THE RIVER. I'VE SENT TRACKERS EAST AND WEST.
NOT ACROSS THE BORDER?
I DON'T KNOW. JUST... THE JACOBSEN CLAN LIVES THERE.
THE BORDER? WHY THERE?
HANNA TOLD ME LAST WEEK SHE THOUGHT SHE SAW LARS JACOBSEN IN TOWN.
THEY WOULDN'T DARE COME ACROSS. THE ELDER ONE WOULD DESTROY THEM.
I TOLD HER SHE MUST BE SEEING THINGS.
IT WAS ONLY AN OFFHAND COMMENT. I DOUBT EVEN SHE BELIEVED IT.
IT WOULD BE ODD THOUGH, IF SHE WERE RIGHT.

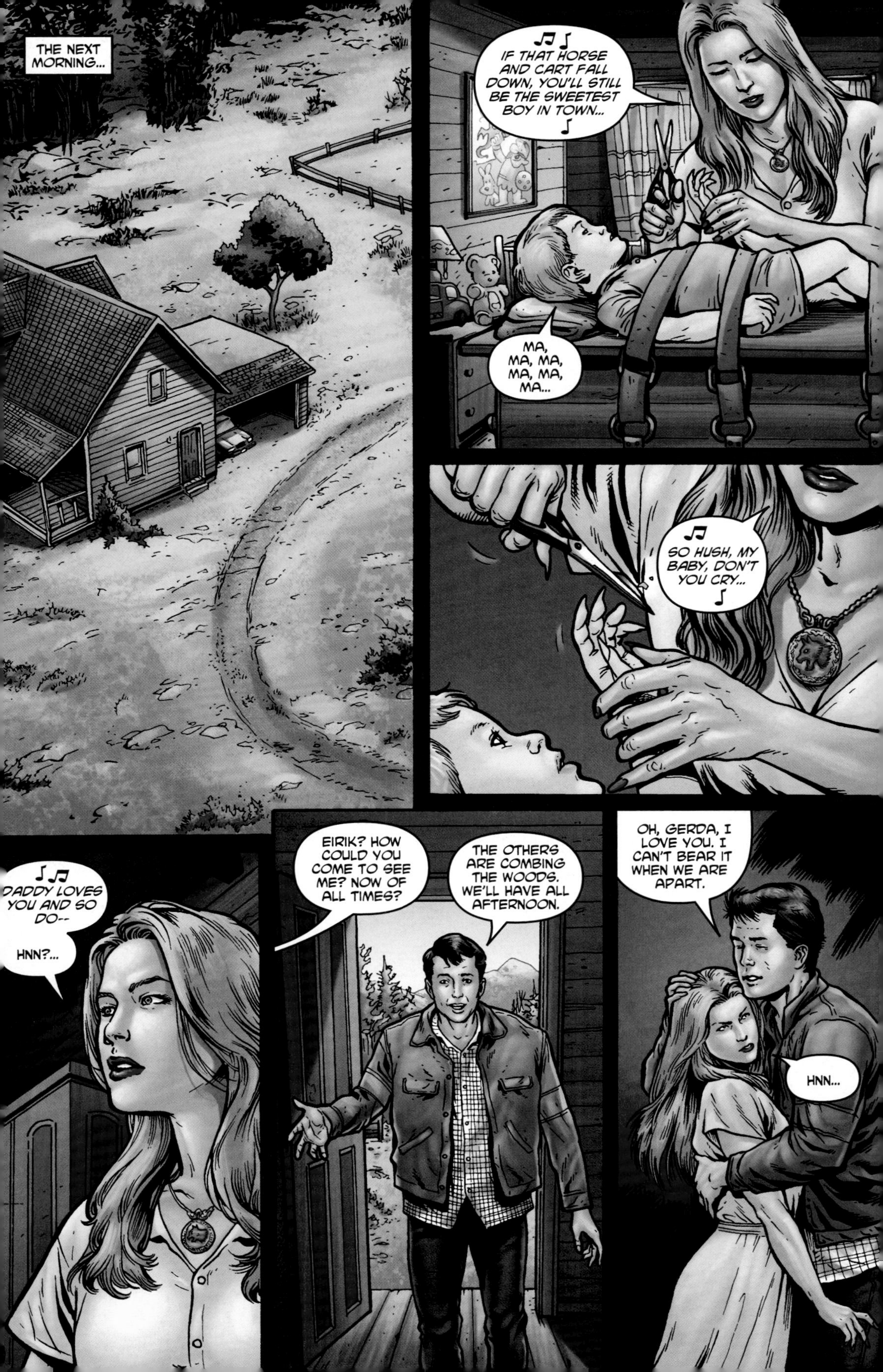
THE NEXT MORNING...
IF THAT HORSE AND CART FALL DOWN, YOU'LL STILL BE THE SWEETEST BOY IN TOWN...
MA, MA, MA, MA, MA, MA...
SO HUSH, MY BABY, DON'T YOU CRY...
DADDY LOVES YOU AND SO DO--
HNN?...
EIRIK? HOW COULD YOU COME TO SEE ME? NOW OF ALL TIMES?
THE OTHERS ARE COMBING THE WOODS. WE'LL HAVE ALL AFTERNOON.
OH, GERDA, I LOVE YOU. I CAN'T BEAR IT WHEN WE ARE APART.
HNN...

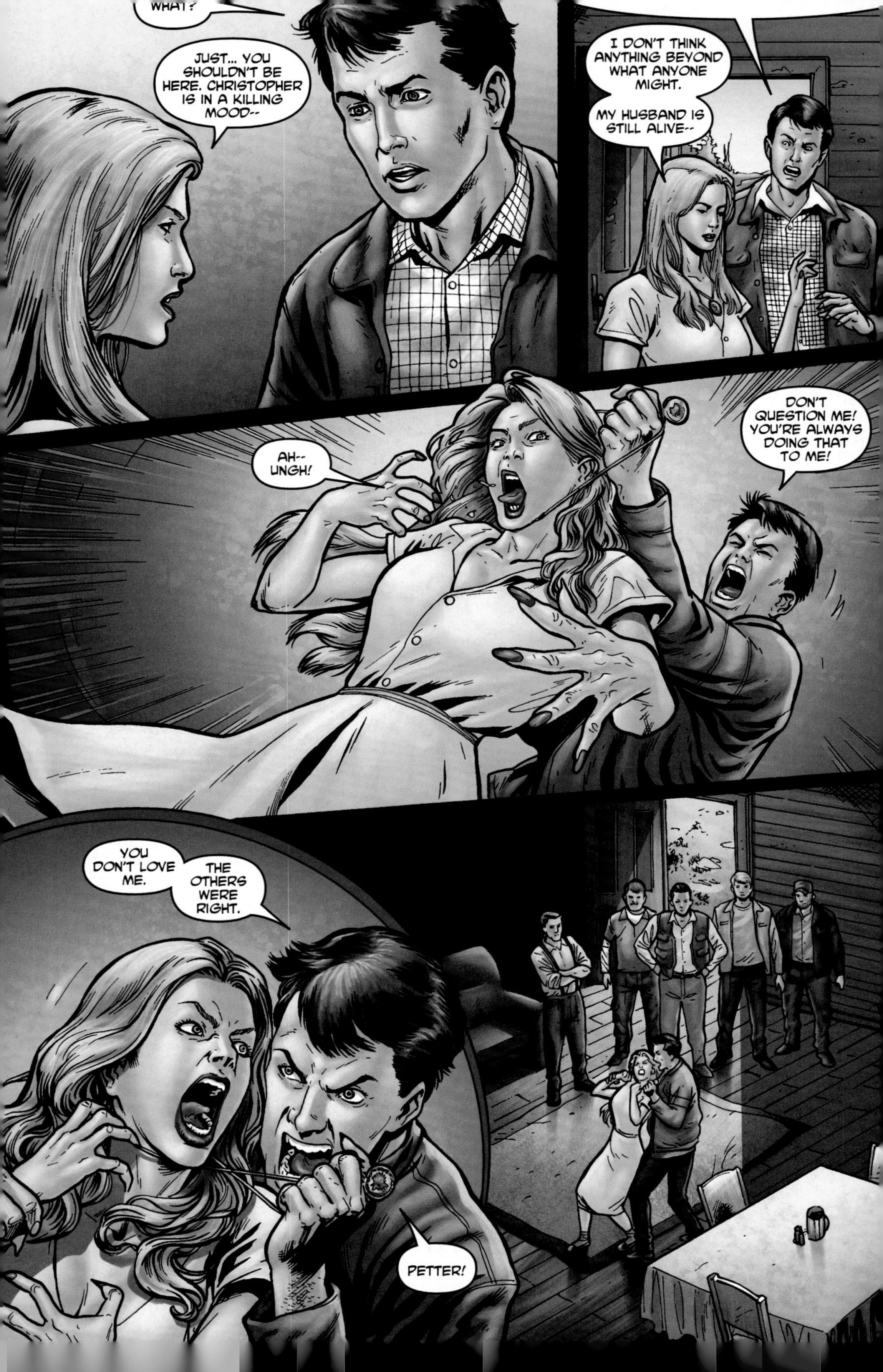
WHAT?
JUST... YOU SHOULDN'T BE HERE. CHRISTOPHER IS IN A KILLING MOOD--
I DON'T THINK ANYTHING BEYOND WHAT ANYONE MIGHT.
MY HUSBAND IS STILL ALIVE--
AH-- UNGH!
DON'T QUESTION ME! YOU'RE ALWAYS DOING THAT TO ME!
YOU DON'T LOVE ME.
THE OTHERS WERE RIGHT.
PETTER!

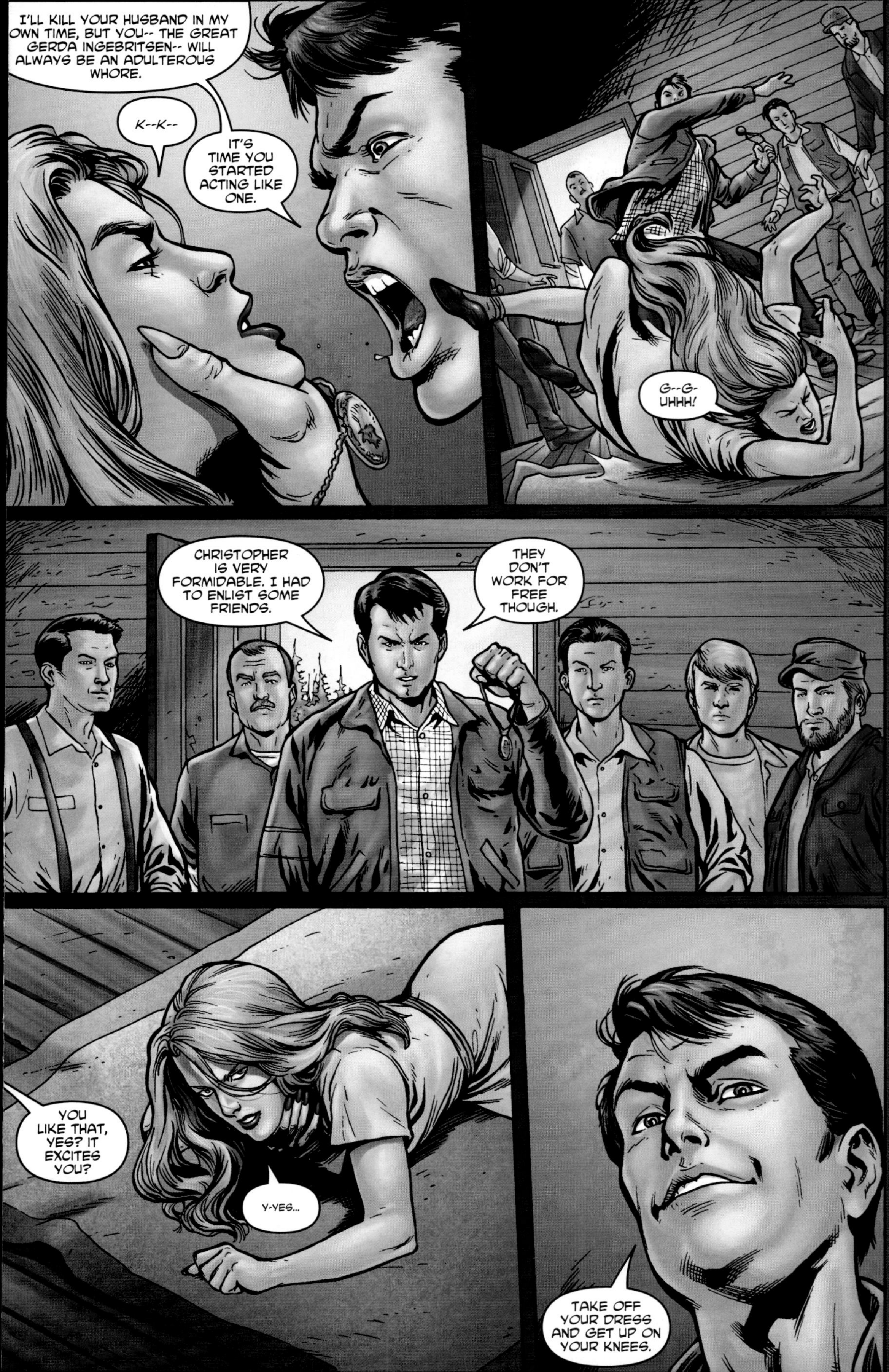
I'LL KILL YOUR HUSBAND IN MY OWN TIME, BUT YOU-- THE GREAT GERDA INGEBRITSEN-- WILL ALWAYS BE AN ADULTEROUS WHORE.
K--K--
IT'S TIME YOU STARTED ACTING LIKE ONE.
G--G-UHHH!
CHRISTOPHER IS VERY FORMIDABLE. I HAD TO ENLIST SOME FRIENDS.
THEY DON'T WORK FOR FREE THOUGH.
YOU LIKE THAT, YES? IT EXCITES YOU?
Y-YES...
TAKE OFF YOUR DRESS AND GET UP ON YOUR KNEES.

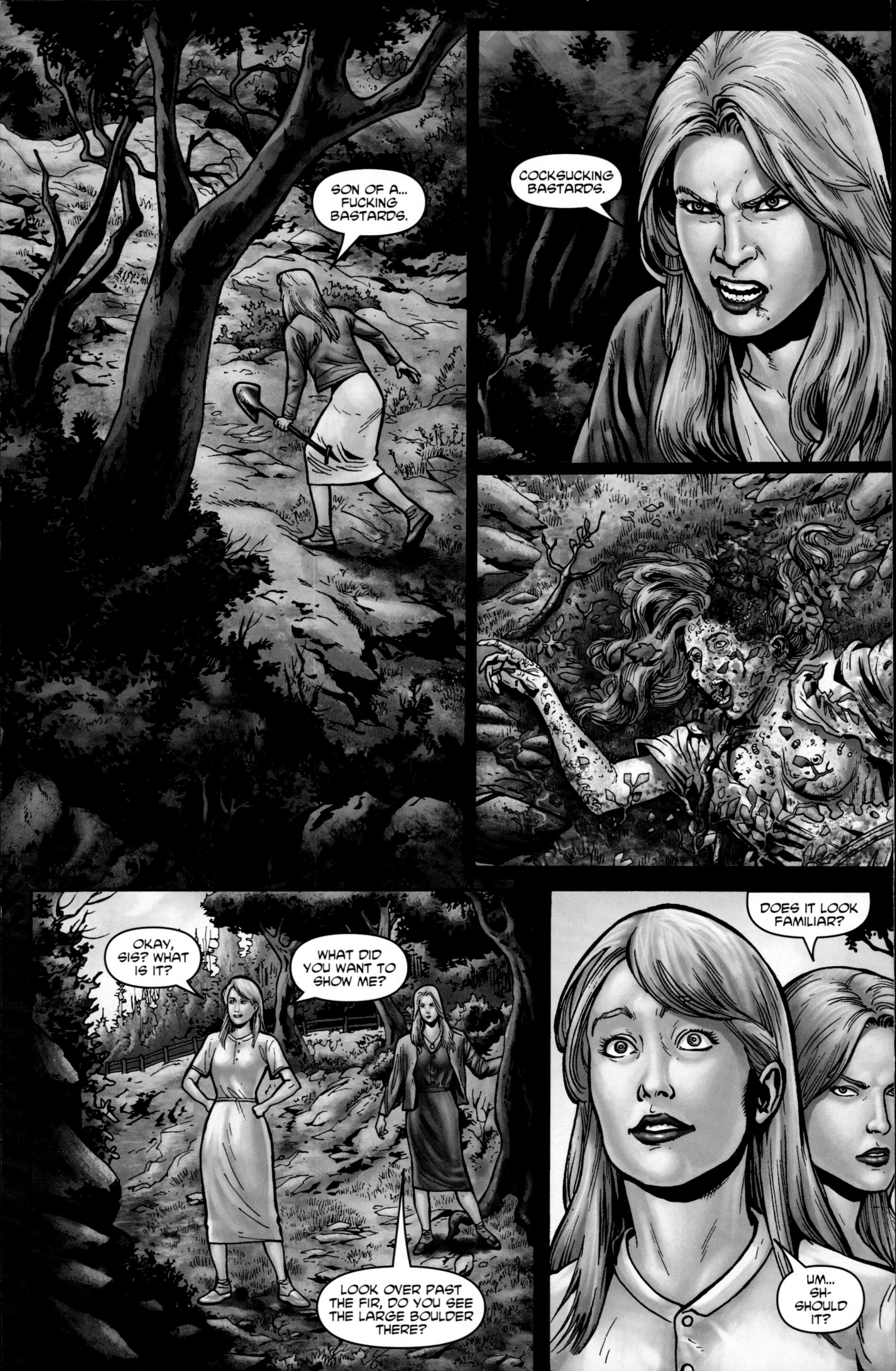
SON OF A... FUCKING BASTARDS.
COCKSUCKING BASTARDS.
OKAY, SIS? WHAT IS IT?
WHAT DID YOU WANT TO SHOW ME?
LOOK OVER PAST THE FIR, DO YOU SEE THE LARGE BOULDER THERE?
DOES IT LOOK FAMILIAR?
UM... SH- SHOULD IT?

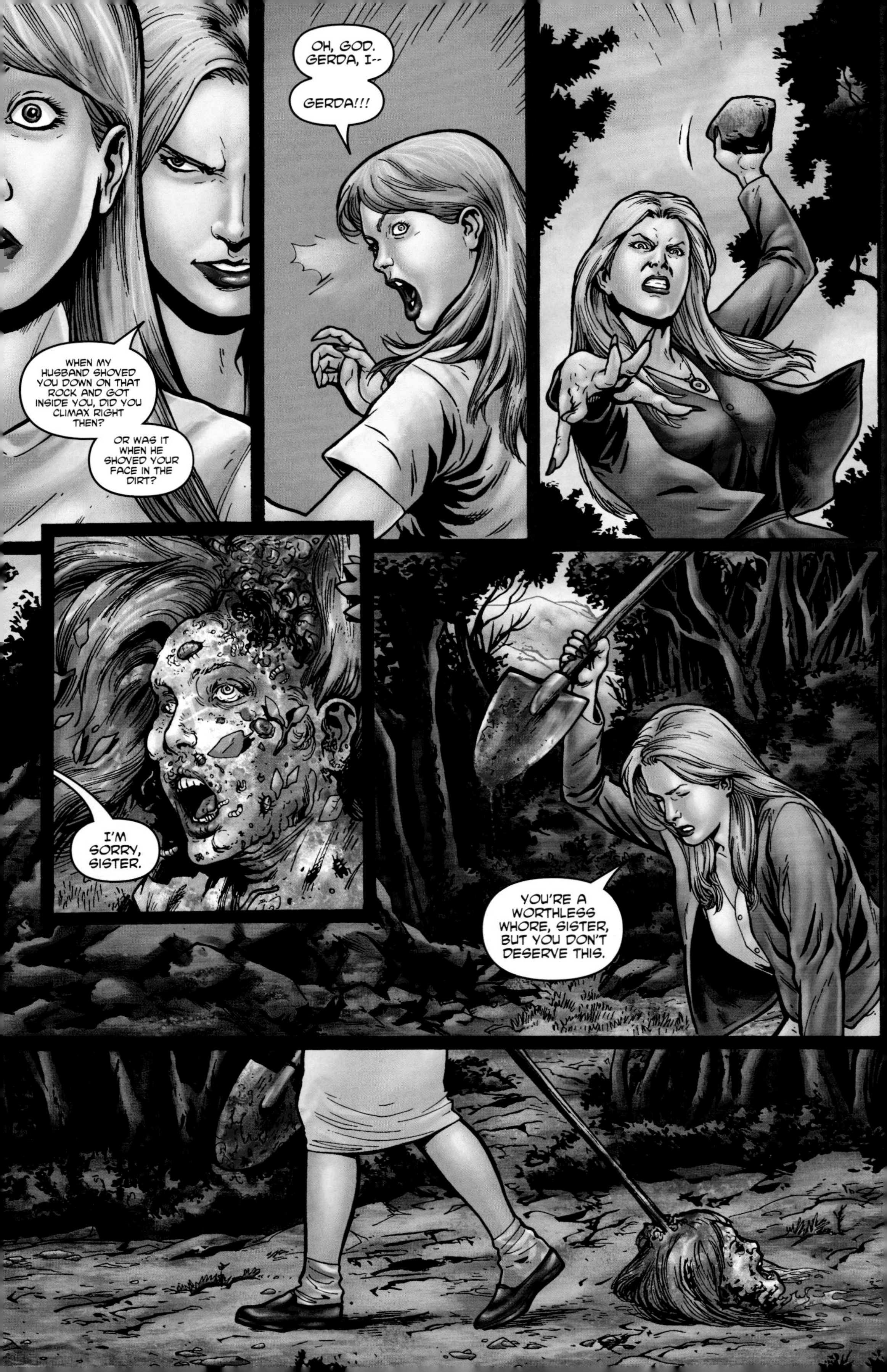
WHEN MY HUSBAND SHOVED YOU DOWN ON THAT ROCK AND GOT INSIDE YOU, DID YOU CLIMAX RIGHT THEN?
OR WAS IT WHEN HE SHOVED YOUR FACE IN THE DIRT?
OH, GOD. GERDA, I--
GERDA!!!
I'M SORRY, SISTER.
YOU'RE A WORTHLESS WHORE, SISTER, BUT YOU DON'T DESERVE THIS.

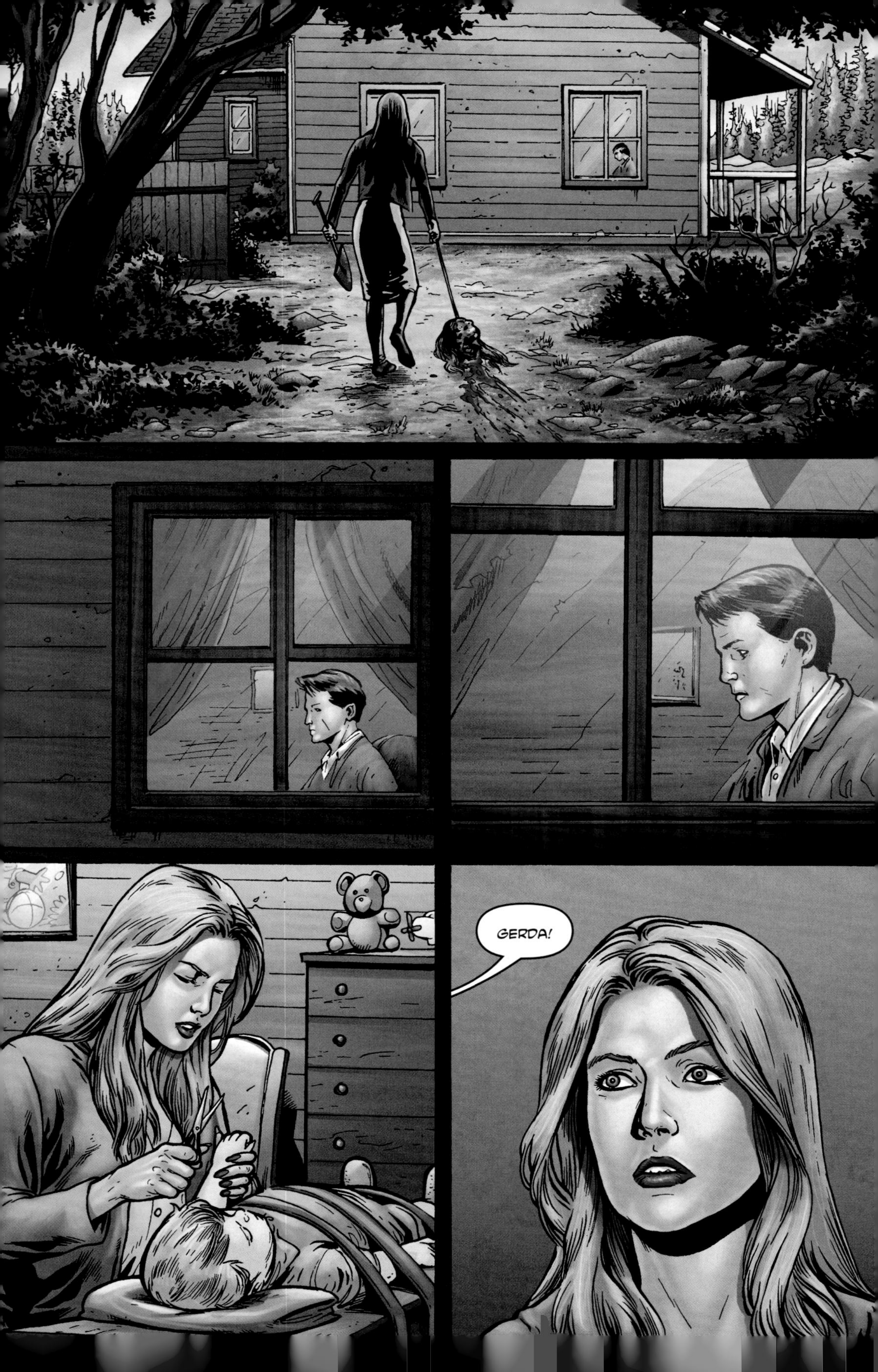
GERDA!

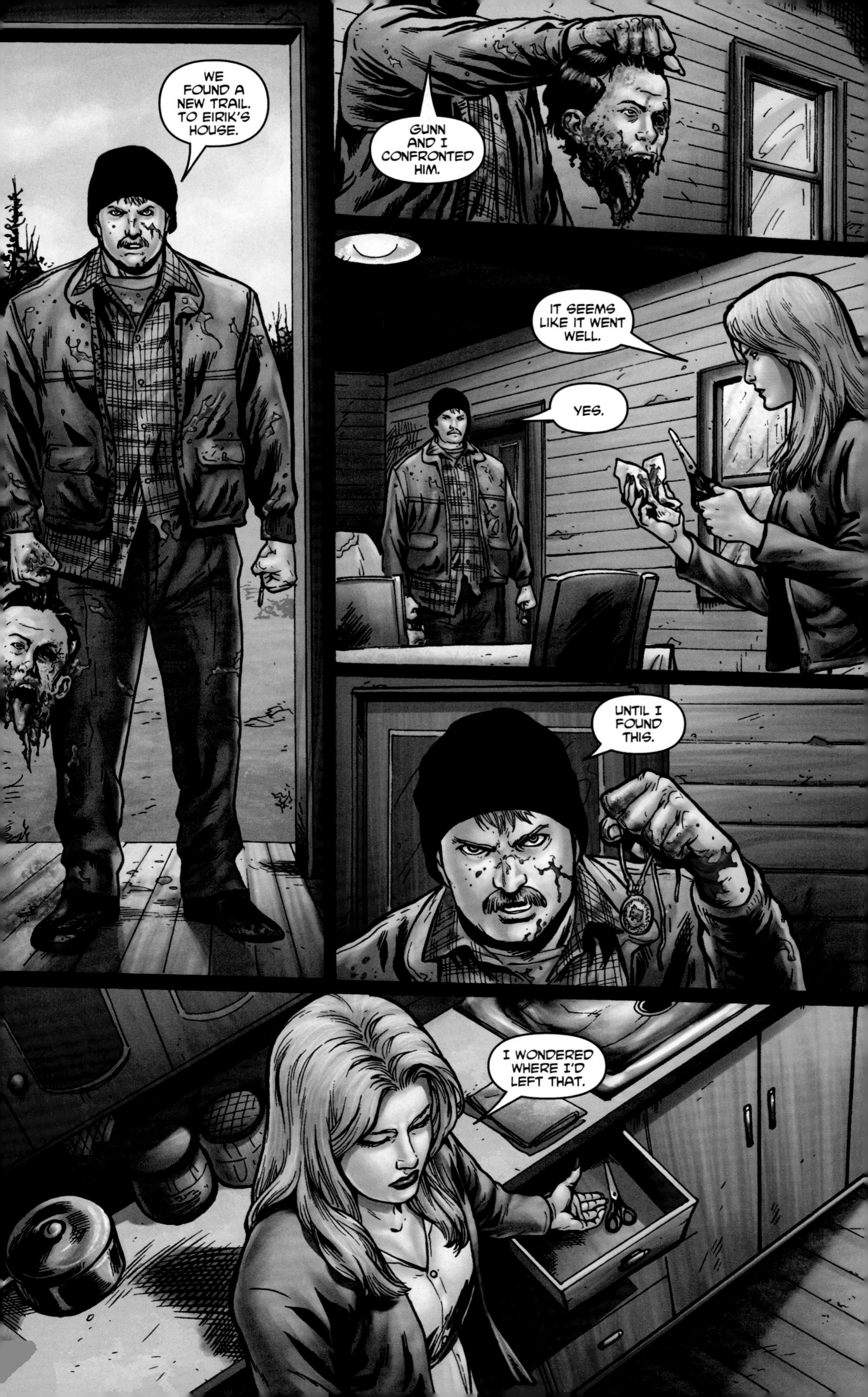
WE FOUND A NEW TRAIL. TO EIRIK'S HOUSE.
GUNN AND I CONFRONTED HIM.
IT SEEMS LIKE IT WENT WELL.
YES.
UNTIL I FOUND THIS.
I WONDERED WHERE I'D LEFT THAT.

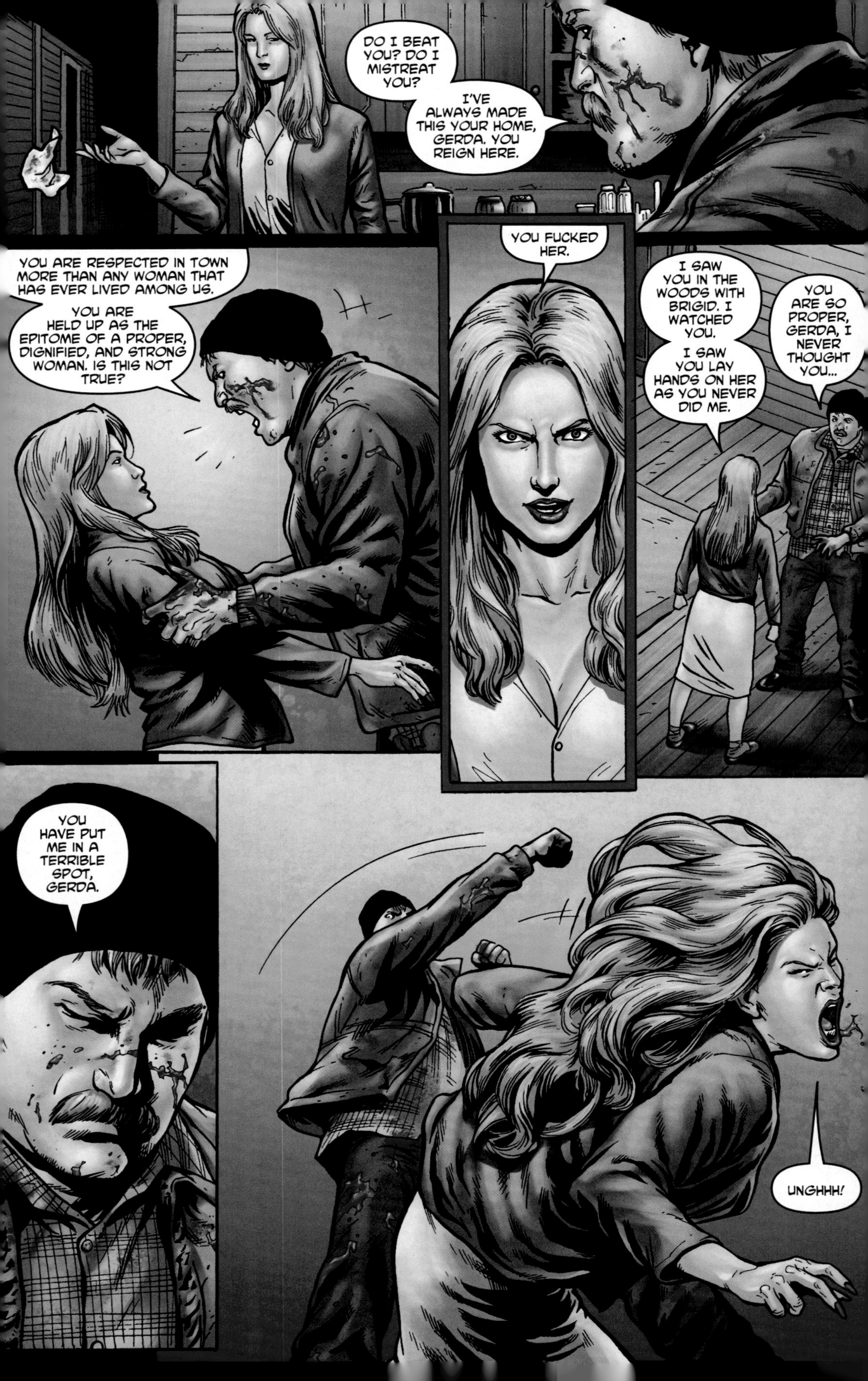
DO I BEAT YOU? DO I MISTREAT YOU?
I'VE ALWAYS MADE THIS YOUR HOME, GERDA. YOU REIGN HERE.
YOU ARE RESPECTED IN TOWN MORE THAN ANY WOMAN THAT HAS EVER LIVED AMONG US.
YOU ARE HELD UP AS THE EPITOME OF A PROPER, DIGNIFIED, AND STRONG WOMAN. IS THIS NOT TRUE?
YOU FUCKED HER.
I SAW YOU IN THE WOODS WITH BRIGID. I WATCHED YOU.
I SAW YOU LAY HANDS ON HER AS YOU NEVER DID ME.
YOU ARE SO PROPER, GERDA, I NEVER THOUGHT YOU...
YOU HAVE PUT ME IN A TERRIBLE SPOT, GERDA.
UNGHHH!

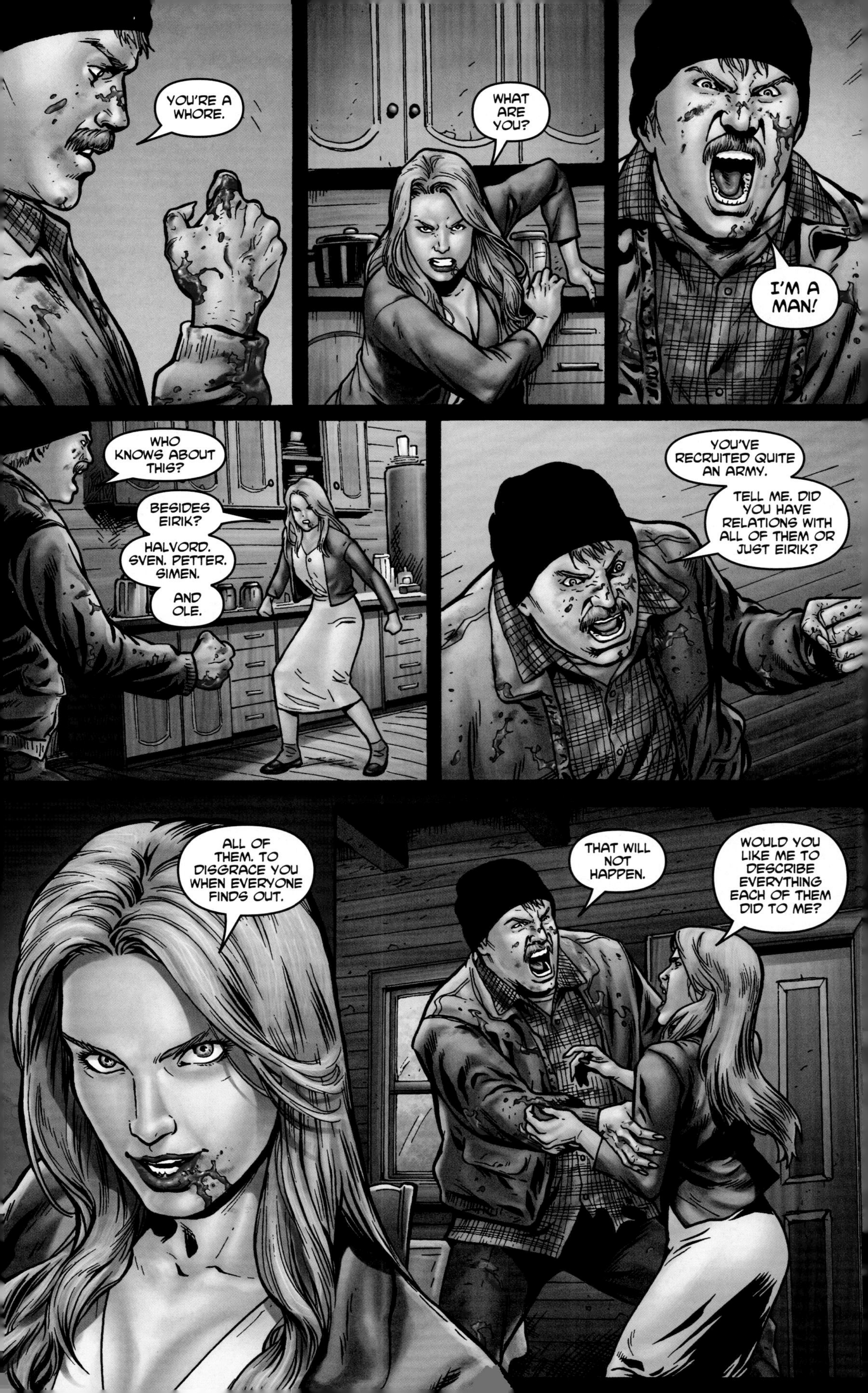
YOU'RE A WHORE.
WHAT ARE YOU?
I'M A MAN!
WHO KNOWS ABOUT THIS?
BESIDES EIRIK?
HALVORD. SVEN. PETTER. SIMEN.
AND OLE.
YOU'VE RECRUITED QUITE AN ARMY.
TELL ME. DID YOU HAVE RELATIONS WITH ALL OF THEM OR JUST EIRIK?
ALL OF THEM. TO DISGRACE YOU WHEN EVERYONE FINDS OUT.
THAT WILL NOT HAPPEN.
WOULD YOU LIKE ME TO DESCRIBE EVERYTHING EACH OF THEM DID TO ME?

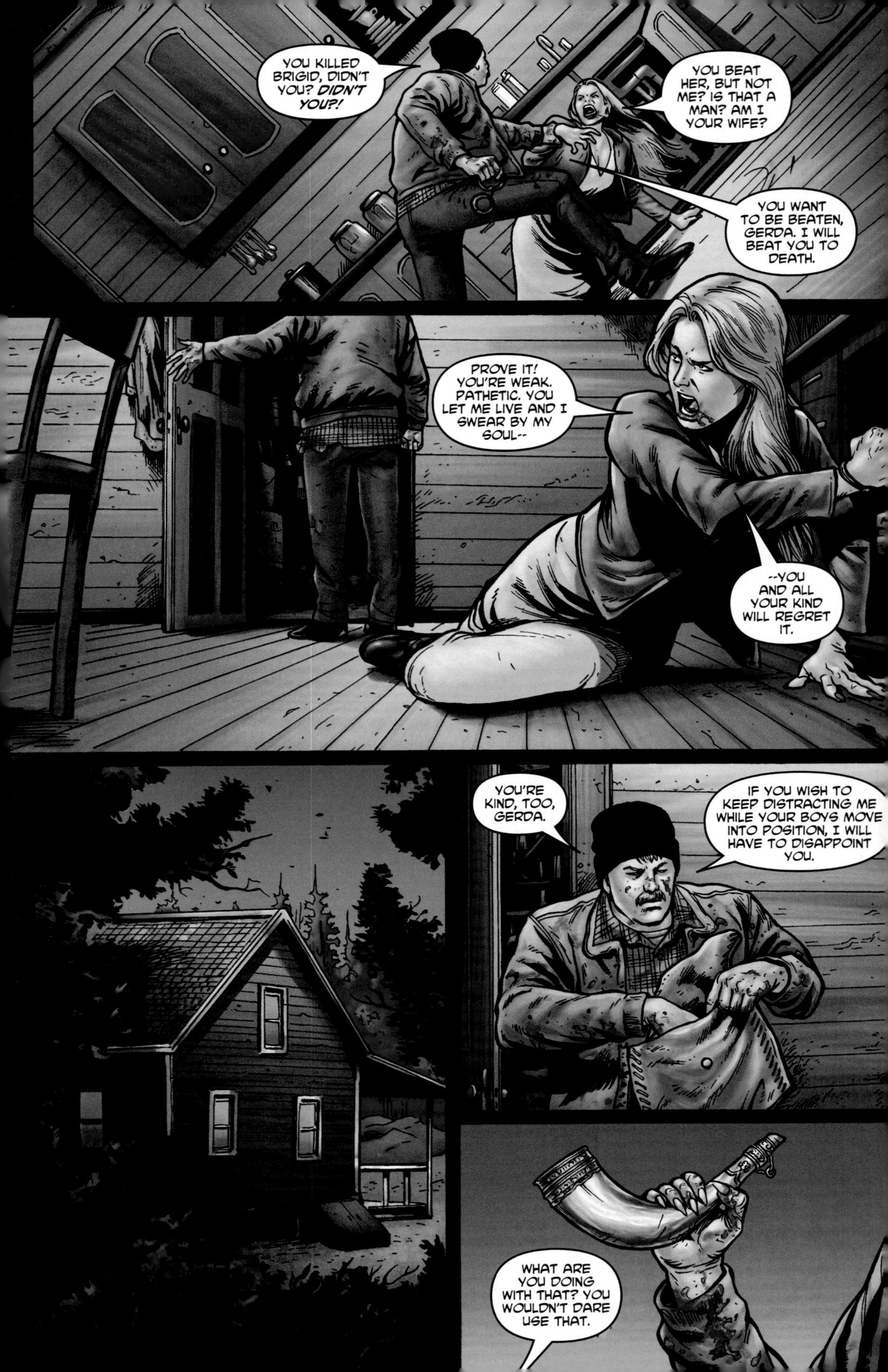
YOU KILLED BRIGID, DIDN'T YOU? *DIDN'T YOU?!*
YOU BEAT HER, BUT NOT ME? IS THAT A MAN? AM I YOUR WIFE?
YOU WANT TO BE BEATEN, GERDA. I WILL BEAT YOU TO DEATH.
PROVE IT! YOU'RE WEAK. PATHETIC. YOU LET ME LIVE AND I SWEAR BY MY SOUL--
--YOU AND ALL YOUR KIND WILL REGRET IT.
YOU'RE KIND, TOO, GERDA.
IF YOU WISH TO KEEP DISTRACTING ME WHILE YOUR BOYS MOVE INTO POSITION, I WILL HAVE TO DISAPPOINT YOU.
WHAT ARE YOU DOING WITH THAT? YOU WOULDN'T DARE USE THAT.

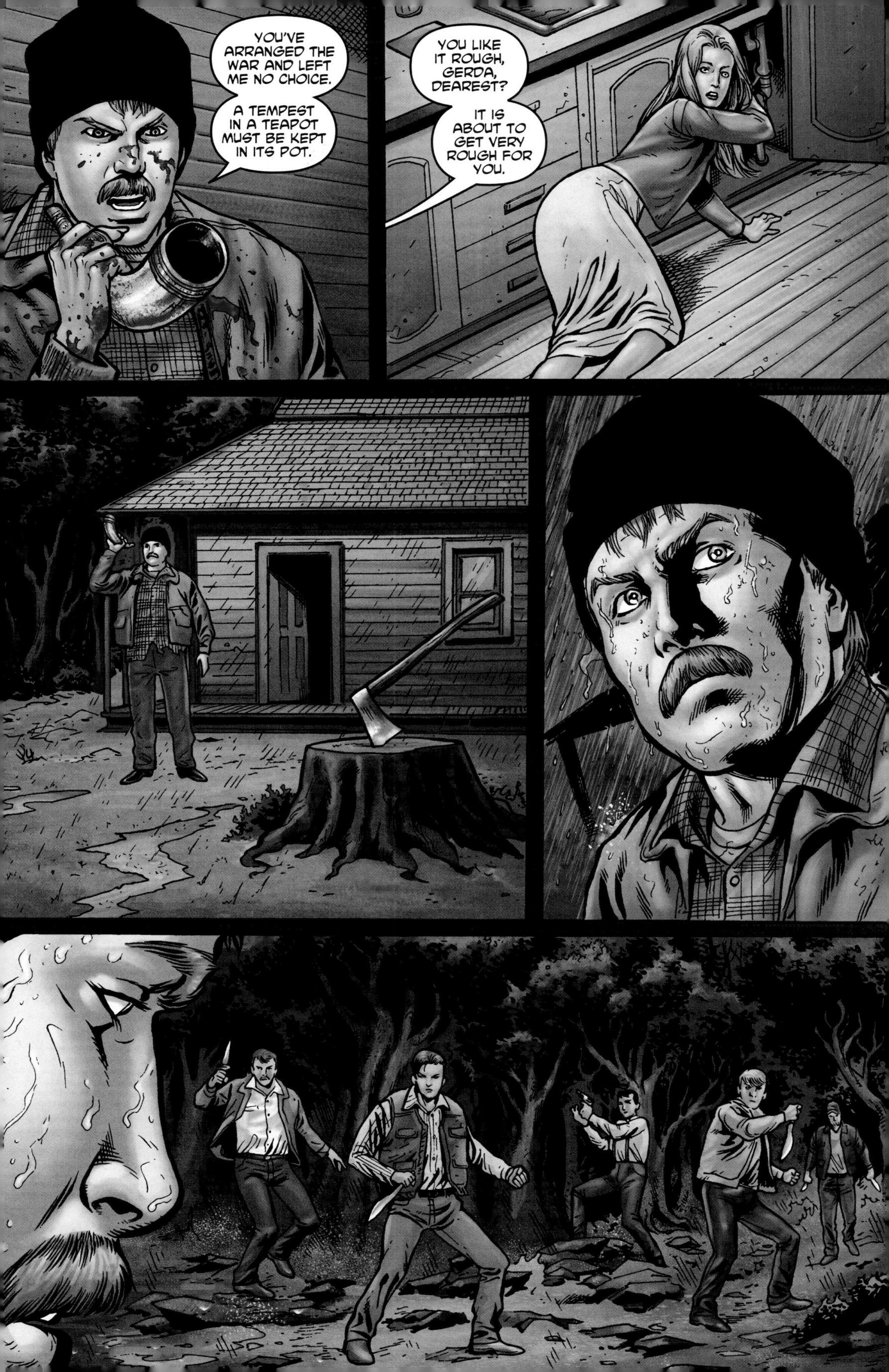
YOU'VE ARRANGED THE WAR AND LEFT ME NO CHOICE.
A TEMPEST IN A TEAPOT MUST BE KEPT IN ITS POT.
YOU LIKE IT ROUGH, GERDA, DEAREST?
IT IS ABOUT TO GET VERY ROUGH FOR YOU.

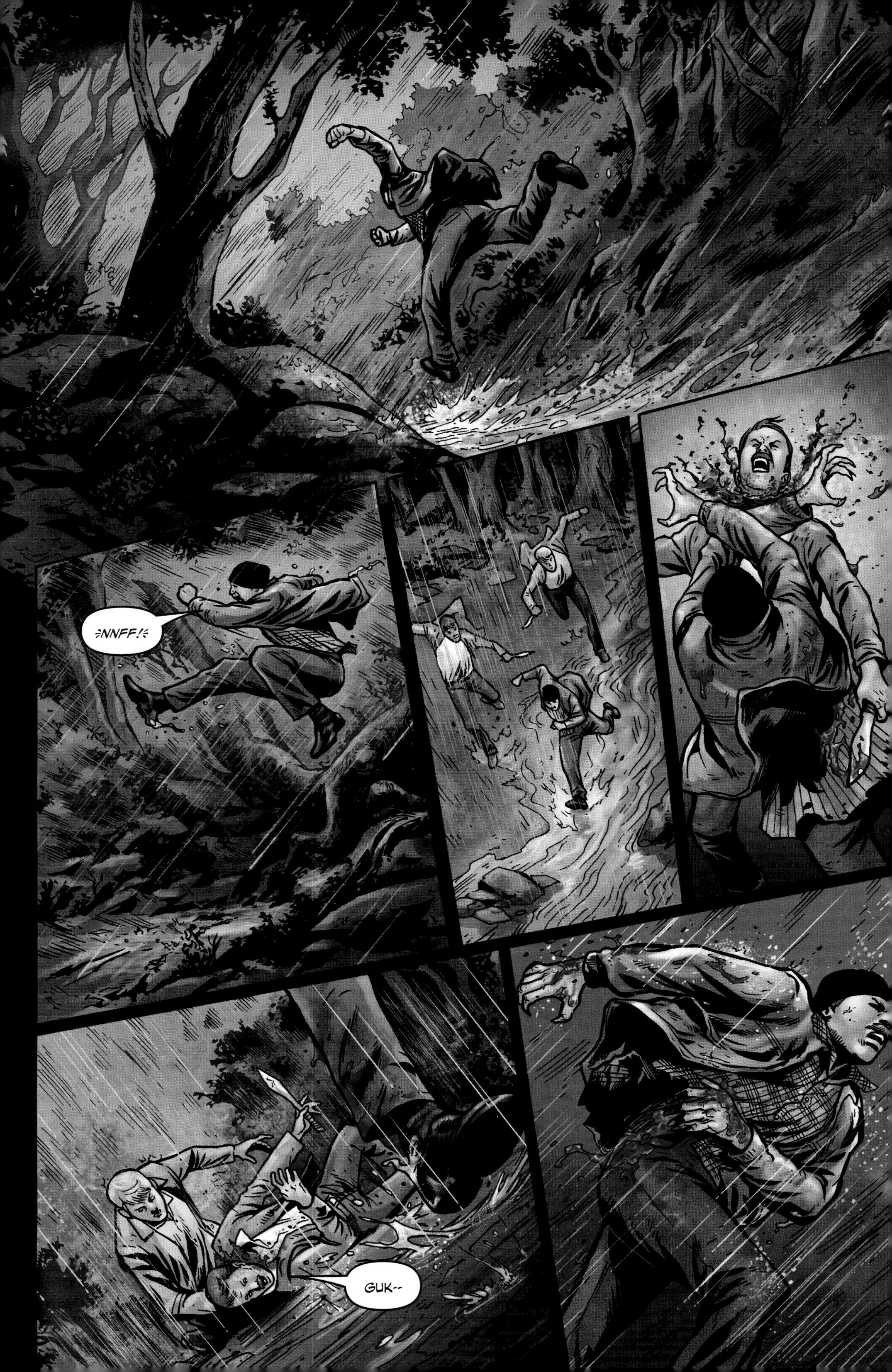
NNFF!
GUK--

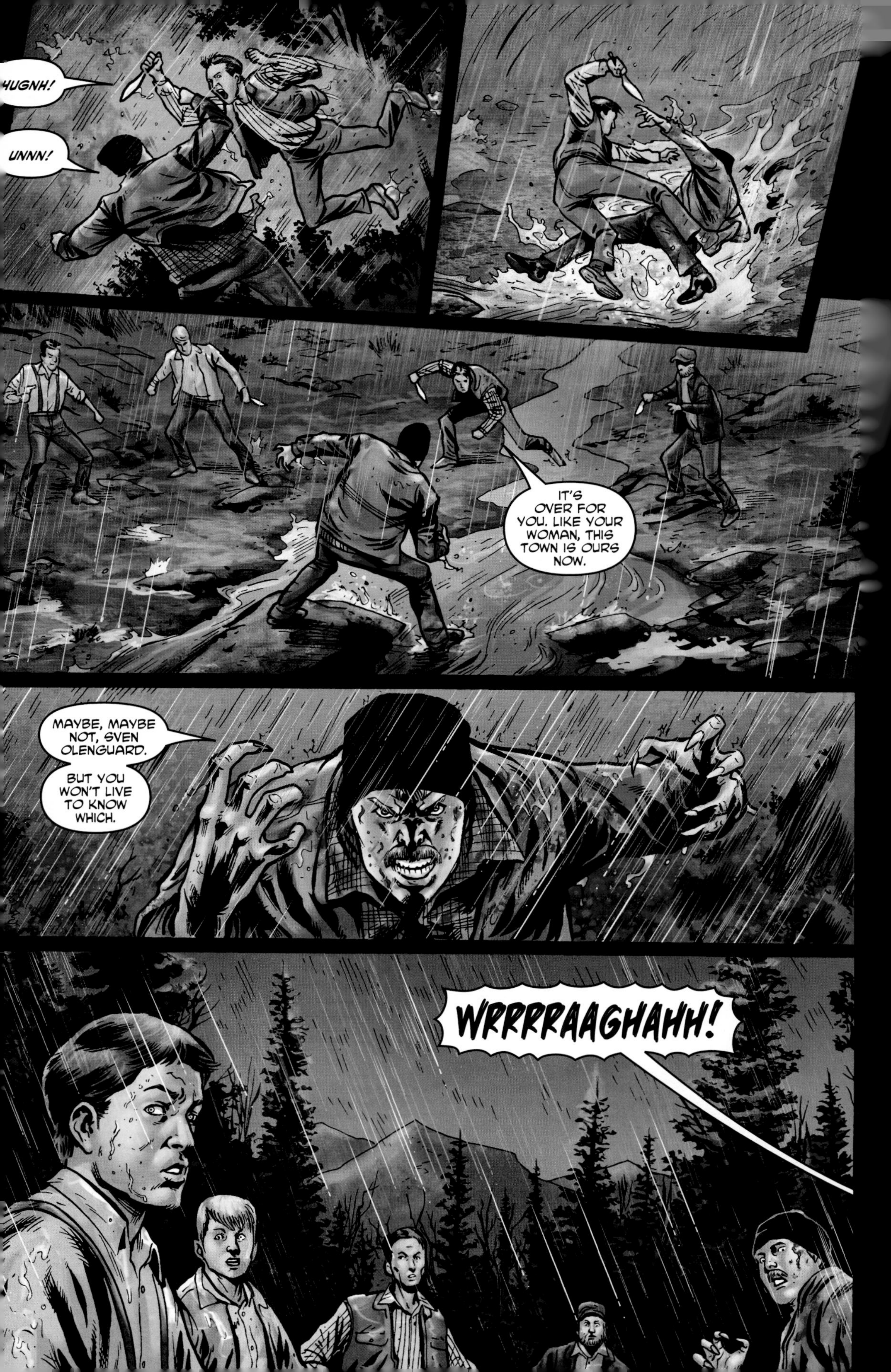
HUGNH!
UNNN!
IT'S OVER FOR YOU. LIKE YOUR WOMAN, THIS TOWN IS OURS NOW.
MAYBE, MAYBE NOT, SVEN OLENGUARD.
BUT YOU WON'T LIVE TO KNOW WHICH.
WRRRRAAGHAHH!

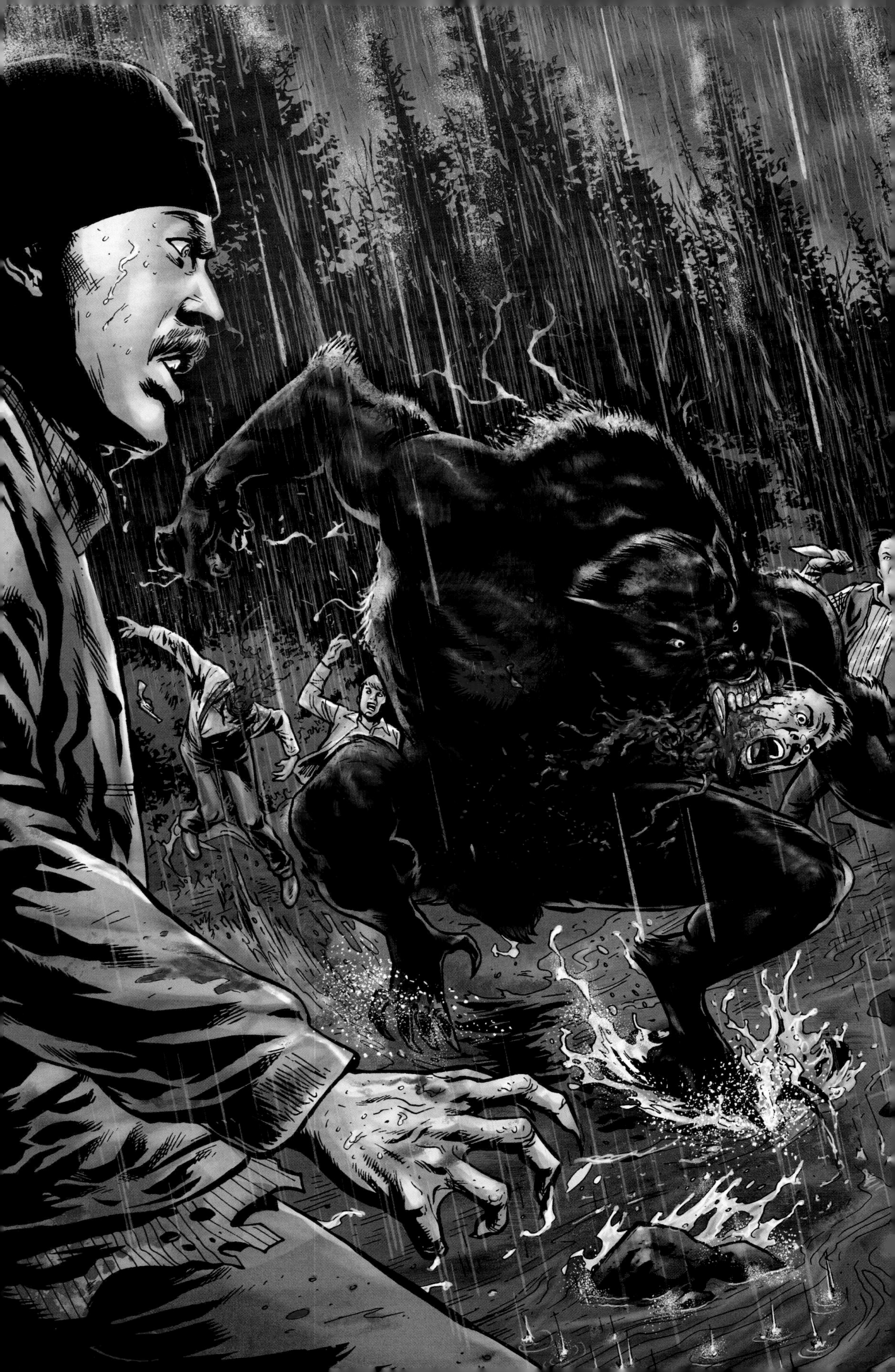

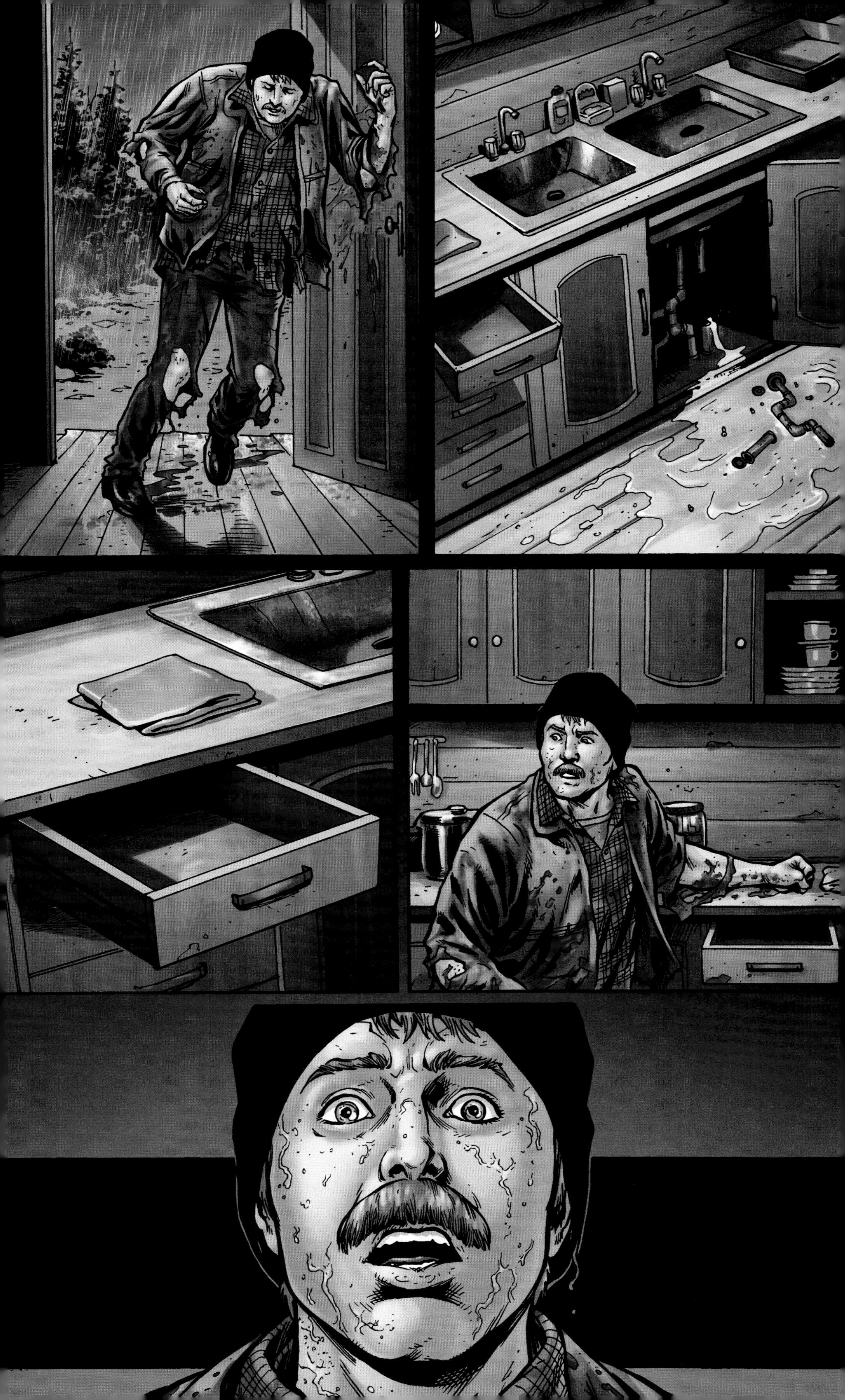

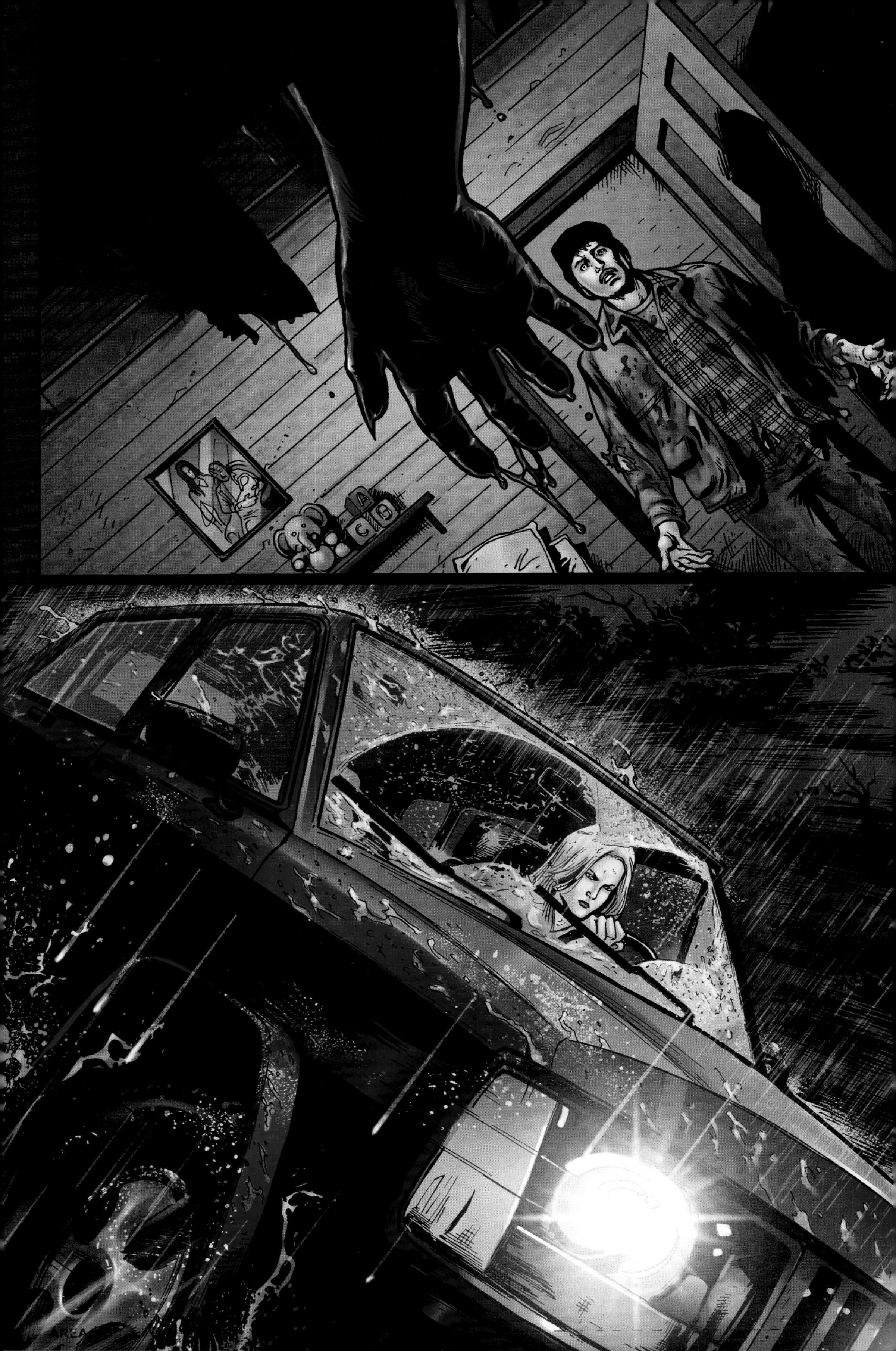

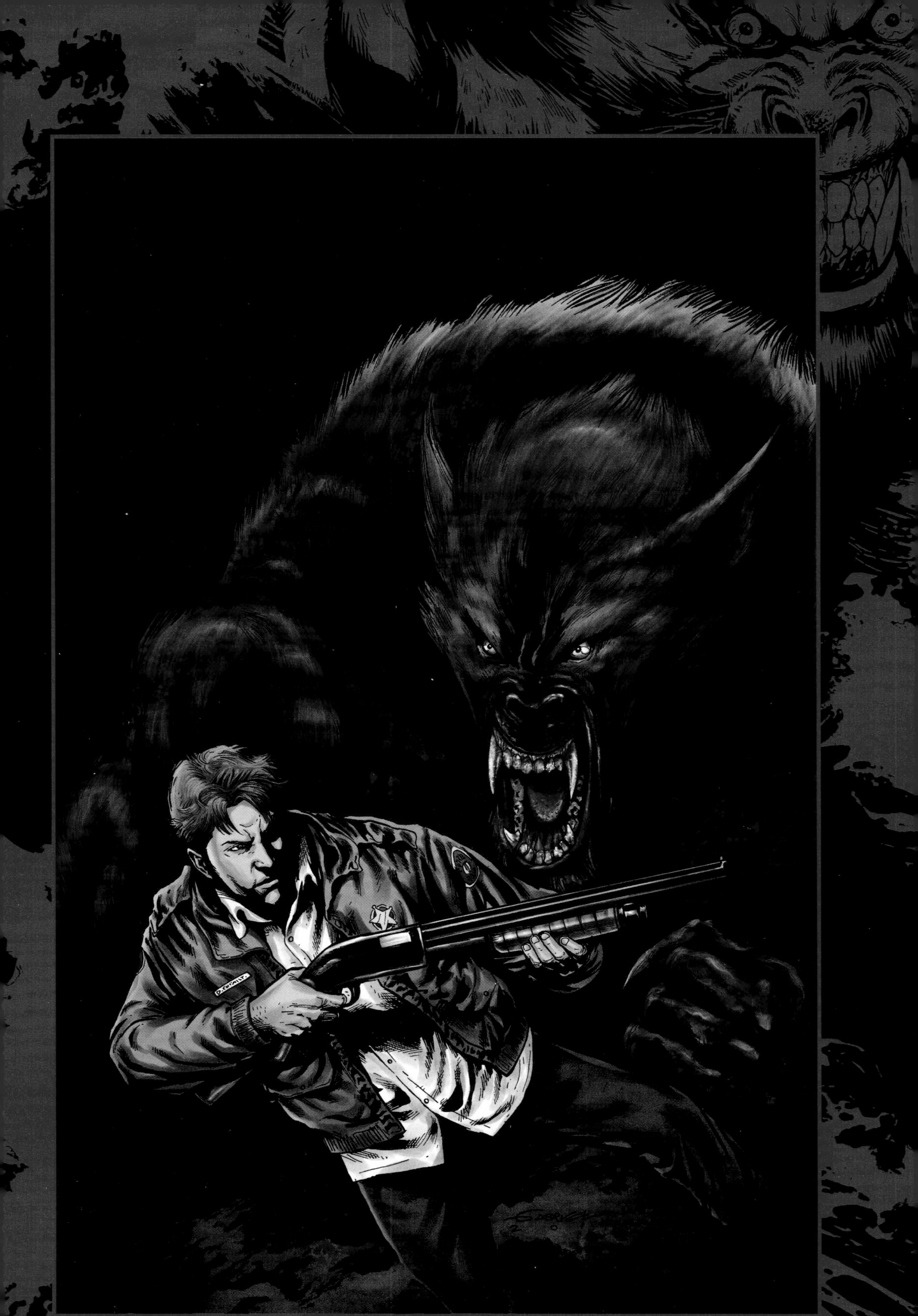

CHAPTER 5

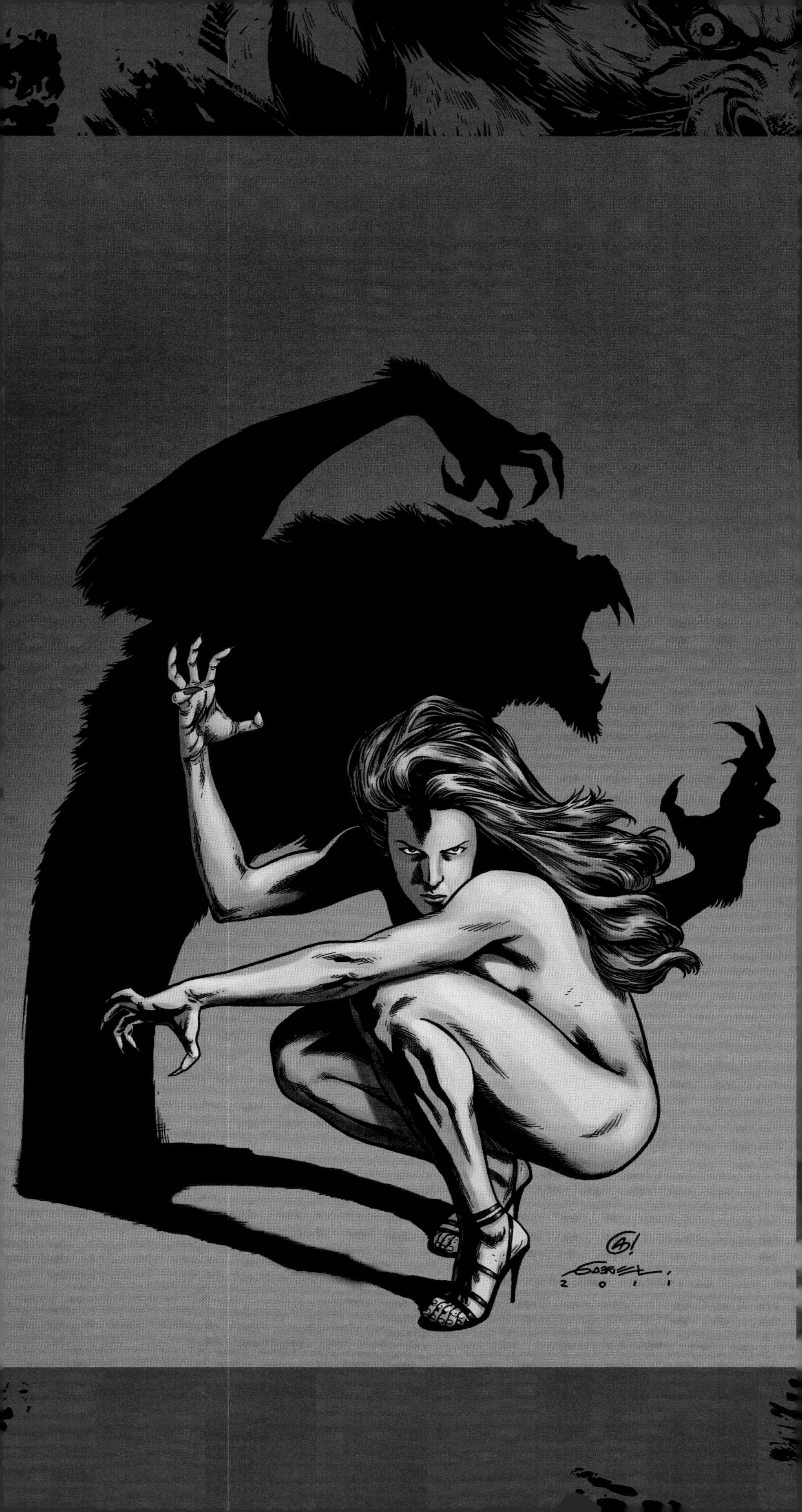
GABRIEL
2011

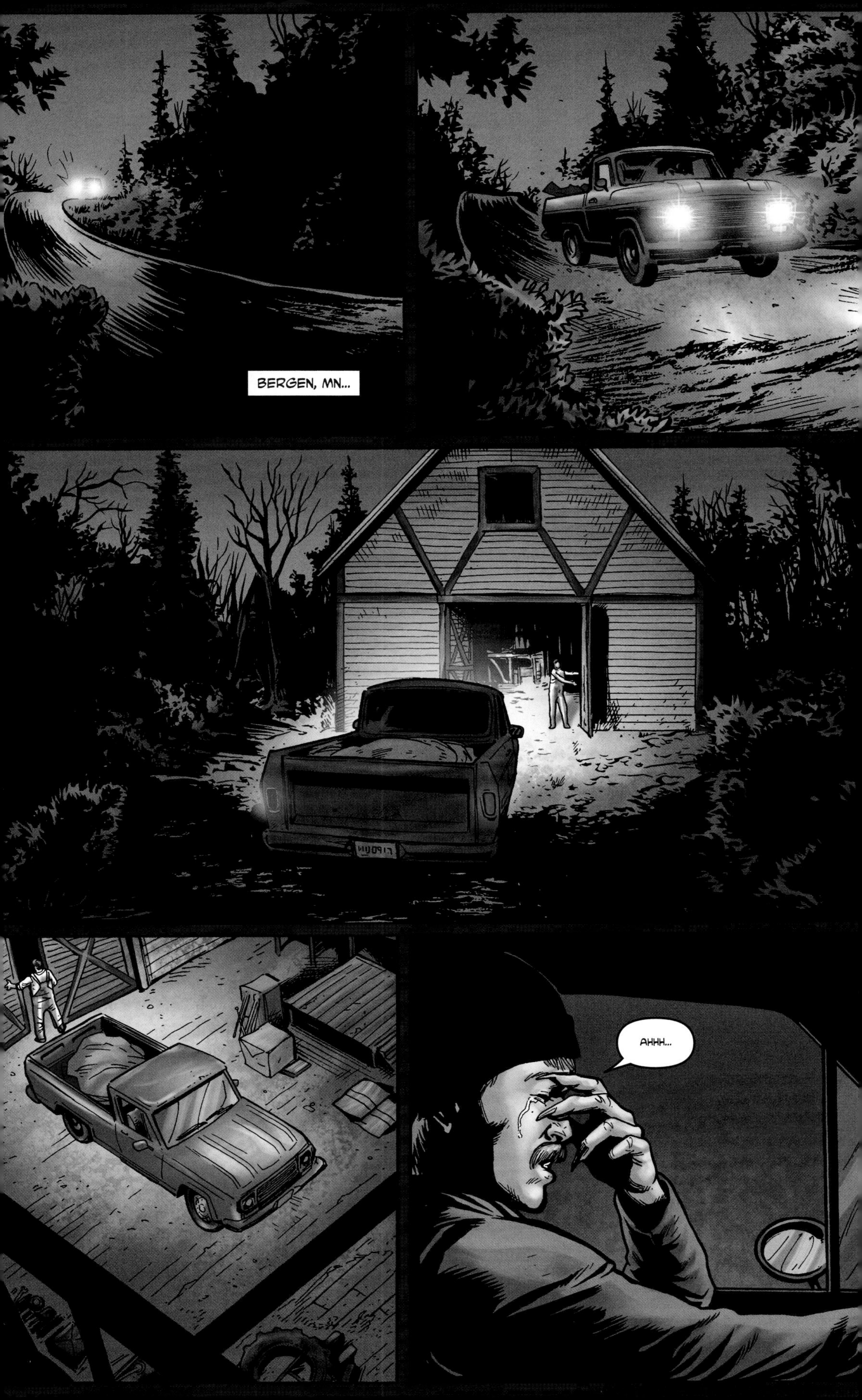
BERGEN, MN...
AHHH...

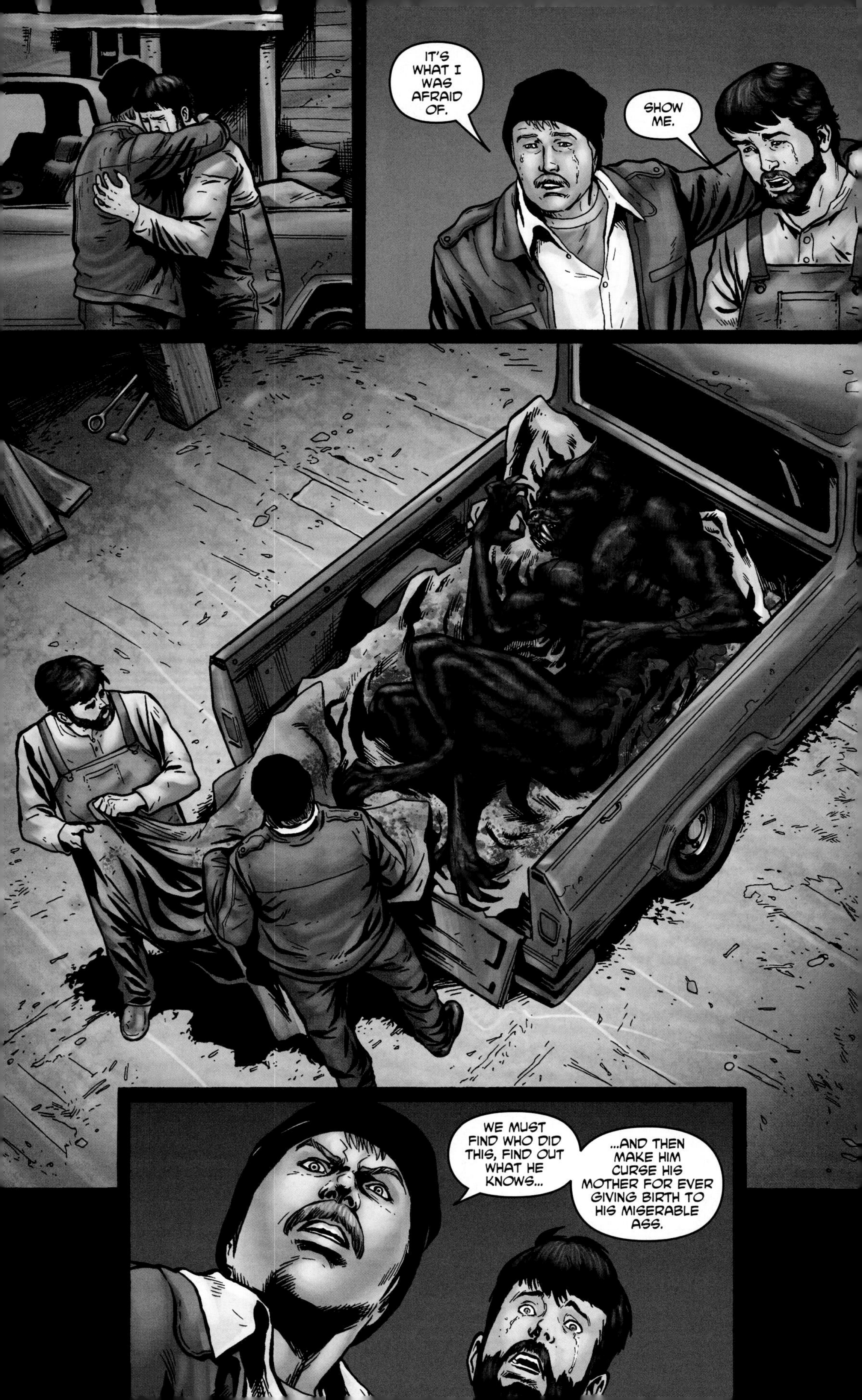
IT'S WHAT I WAS AFRAID OF.
SHOW ME.
WE MUST FIND WHO DID THIS, FIND OUT WHAT HE KNOWS...
...AND THEN MAKE HIM CURSE HIS MOTHER FOR EVER GIVING BIRTH TO HIS MISERABLE ASS.

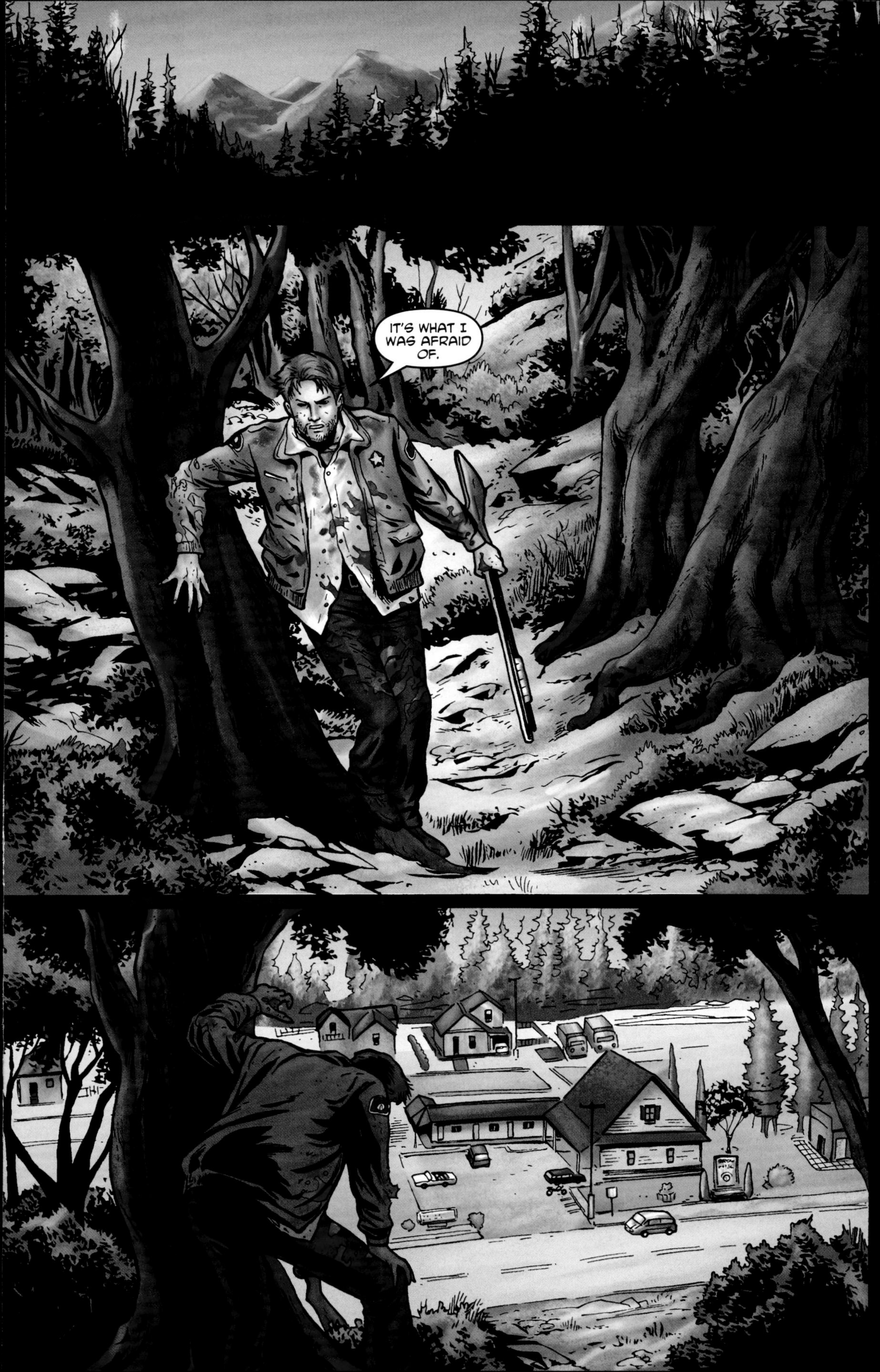
IT'S WHAT I WAS AFRAID OF.

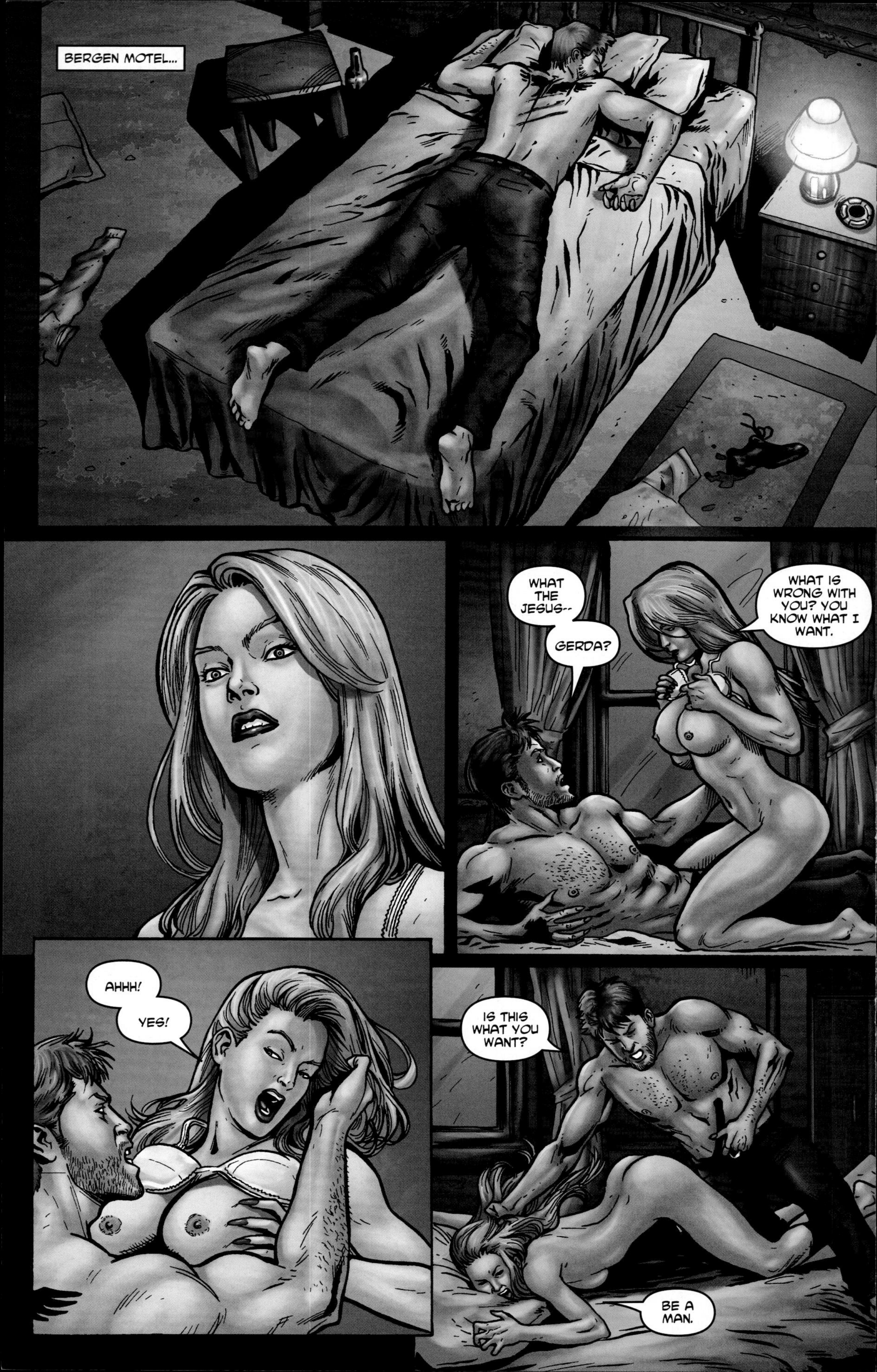
BERGEN MOTEL...
WHAT THE JESUS--
GERDA?
WHAT IS WRONG WITH YOU? YOU KNOW WHAT I WANT.
AHHH!
YES!
IS THIS WHAT YOU WANT?
BE A MAN.

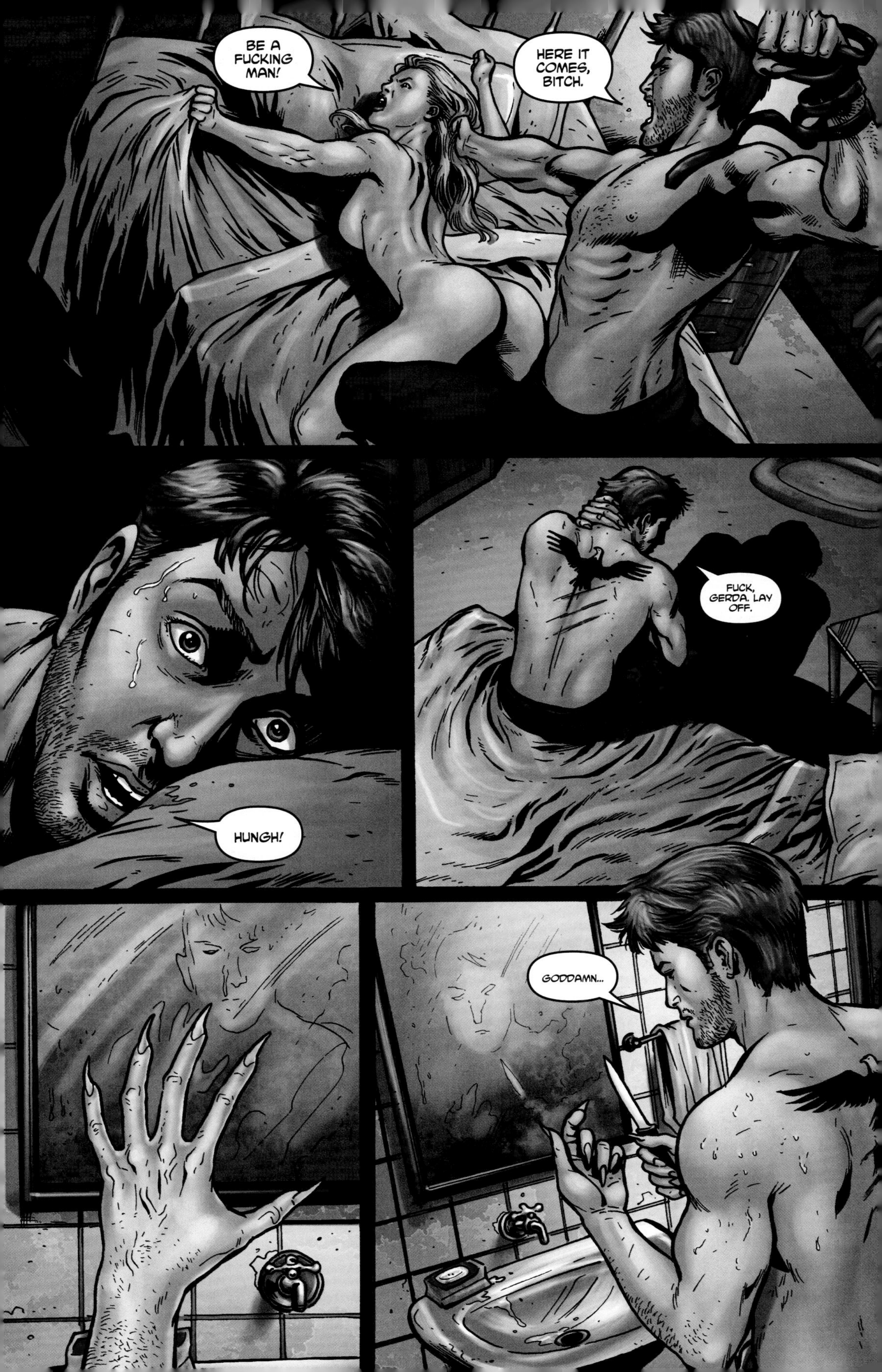
BE A FUCKING MAN!
HERE IT COMES, BITCH.
HUNGH!
FUCK, GERDA. LAY OFF.
GODDAMN...

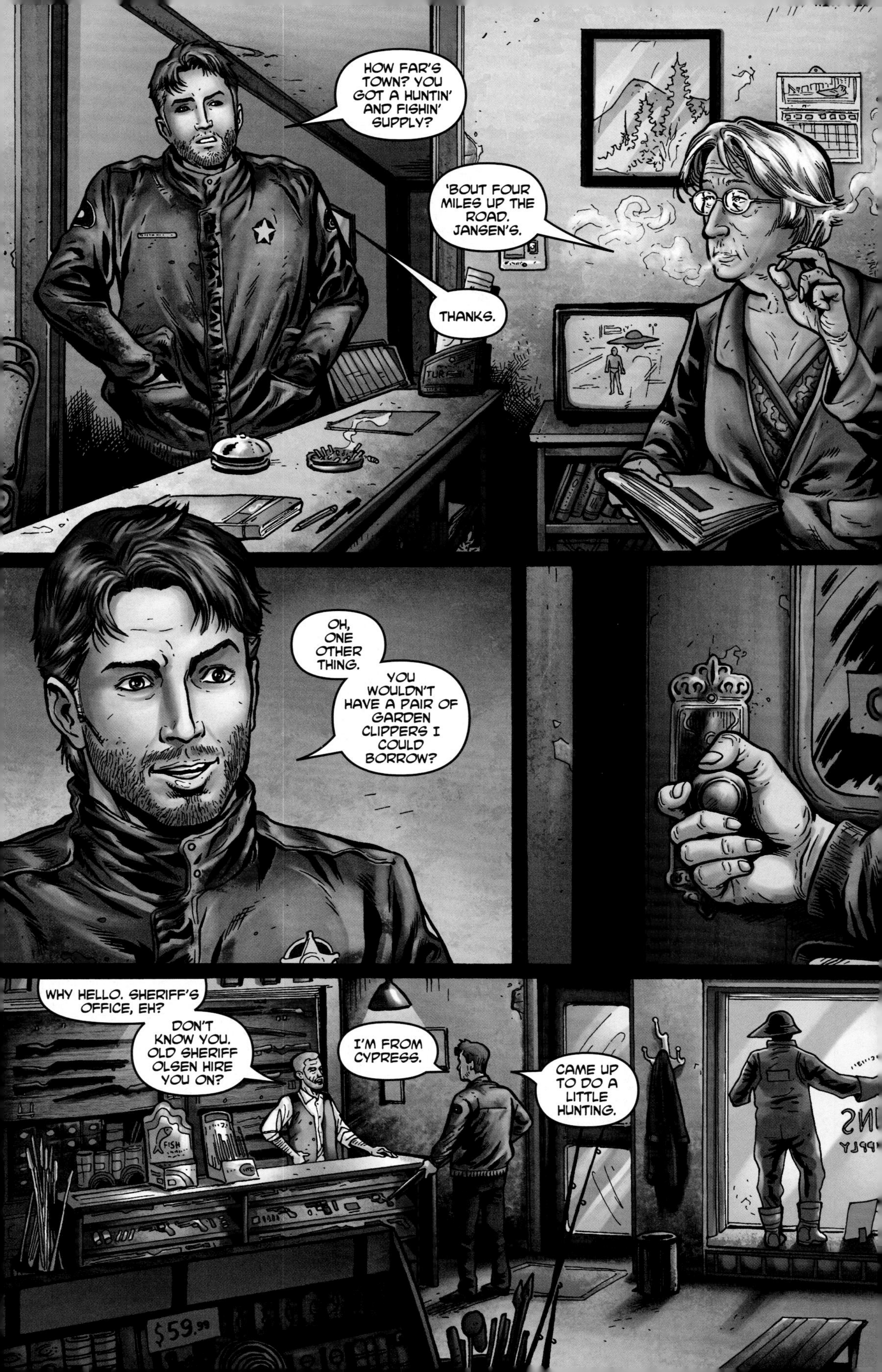

HOW FAR'S TOWN? YOU GOT A HUNTIN' AND FISHIN' SUPPLY?
'BOUT FOUR MILES UP THE ROAD. JANSEN'S.
THANKS.
OH, ONE OTHER THING.
YOU WOULDN'T HAVE A PAIR OF GARDEN CLIPPERS I COULD BORROW?
WHY HELLO. SHERIFF'S OFFICE, EH?
DON'T KNOW YOU. OLD SHERIFF OLSEN HIRE YOU ON?
I'M FROM CYPRESS.
CAME UP TO DO A LITTLE HUNTING.
FISH
$59.99

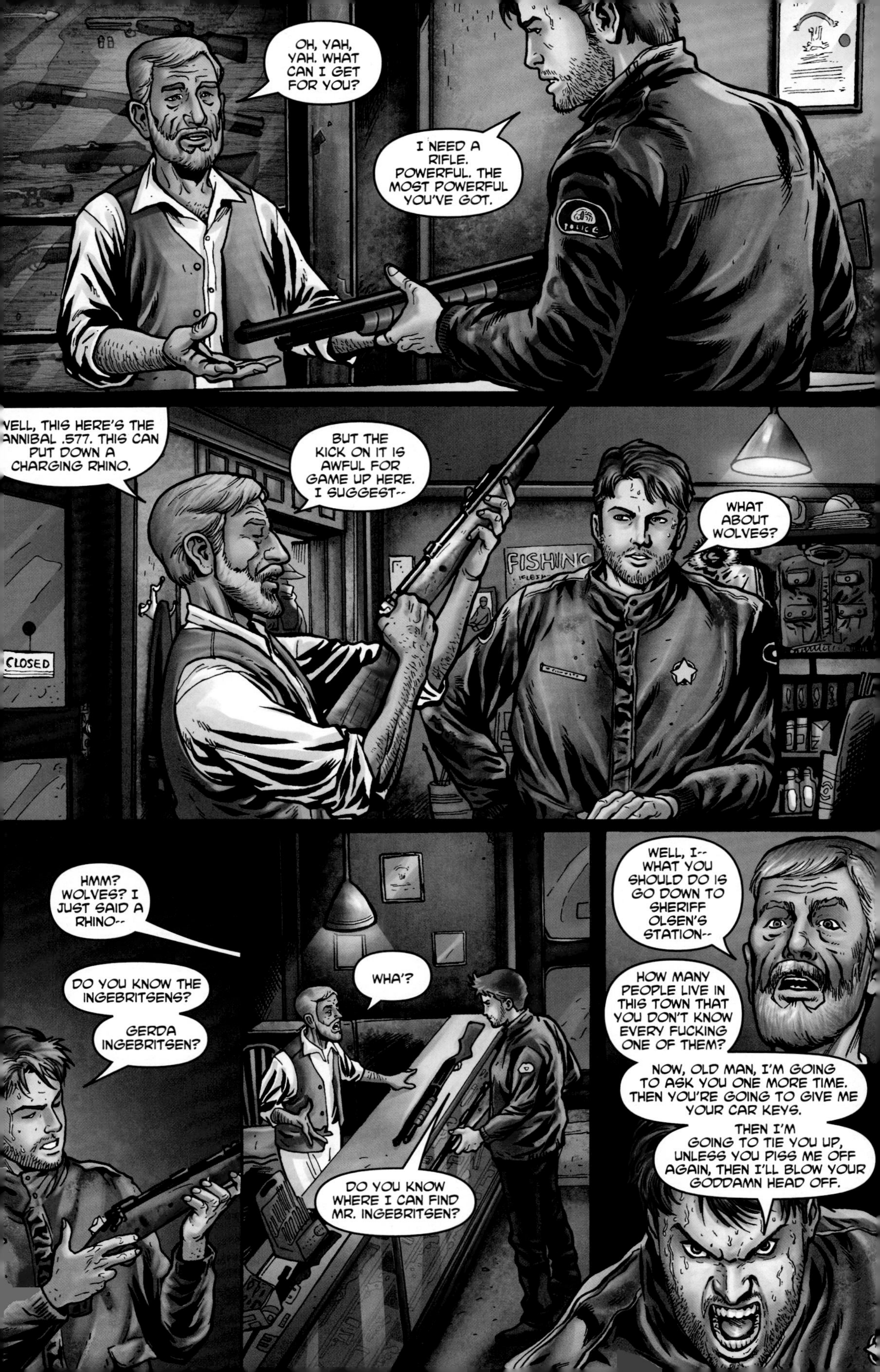
OH, YAH, YAH. WHAT CAN I GET FOR YOU?
I NEED A RIFLE. POWERFUL. THE MOST POWERFUL YOU'VE GOT.
WELL, THIS HERE'S THE ANNIBAL .577. THIS CAN PUT DOWN A CHARGING RHINO.
BUT THE KICK ON IT IS AWFUL FOR GAME UP HERE. I SUGGEST--
WHAT ABOUT WOLVES?
FISHING
CLOSED
HMM? WOLVES? I JUST SAID A RHINO--
DO YOU KNOW THE INGEBRITSENS?
GERDA INGEBRITSEN?
WHA'?
DO YOU KNOW WHERE I CAN FIND MR. INGEBRITSEN?
WELL, I-- WHAT YOU SHOULD DO IS GO DOWN TO SHERIFF OLSEN'S STATION--
HOW MANY PEOPLE LIVE IN THIS TOWN THAT YOU DON'T KNOW EVERY FUCKING ONE OF THEM?
NOW, OLD MAN, I'M GOING TO ASK YOU ONE MORE TIME. THEN YOU'RE GOING TO GIVE ME YOUR CAR KEYS.
THEN I'M GOING TO TIE YOU UP, UNLESS YOU PISS ME OFF AGAIN, THEN I'LL BLOW YOUR GODDAMN HEAD OFF.

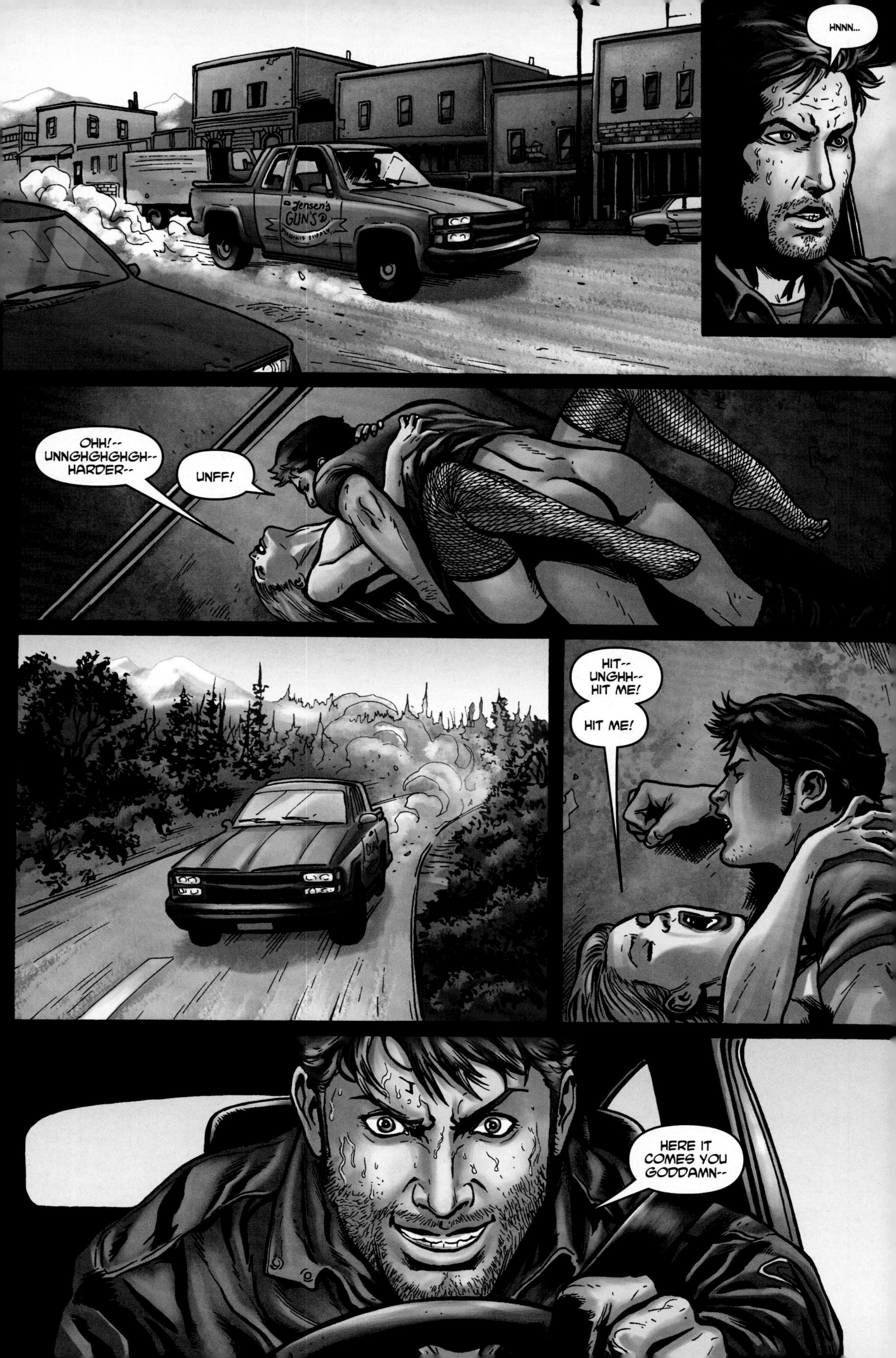

Jensen's GUN'S
HNNN...
OHH!-- UNNGHGHGHGH-- HARDER--
UNFF!
HIT-- UNGHH-- HIT ME!
HIT ME!
HERE IT COMES YOU GODDAMN--

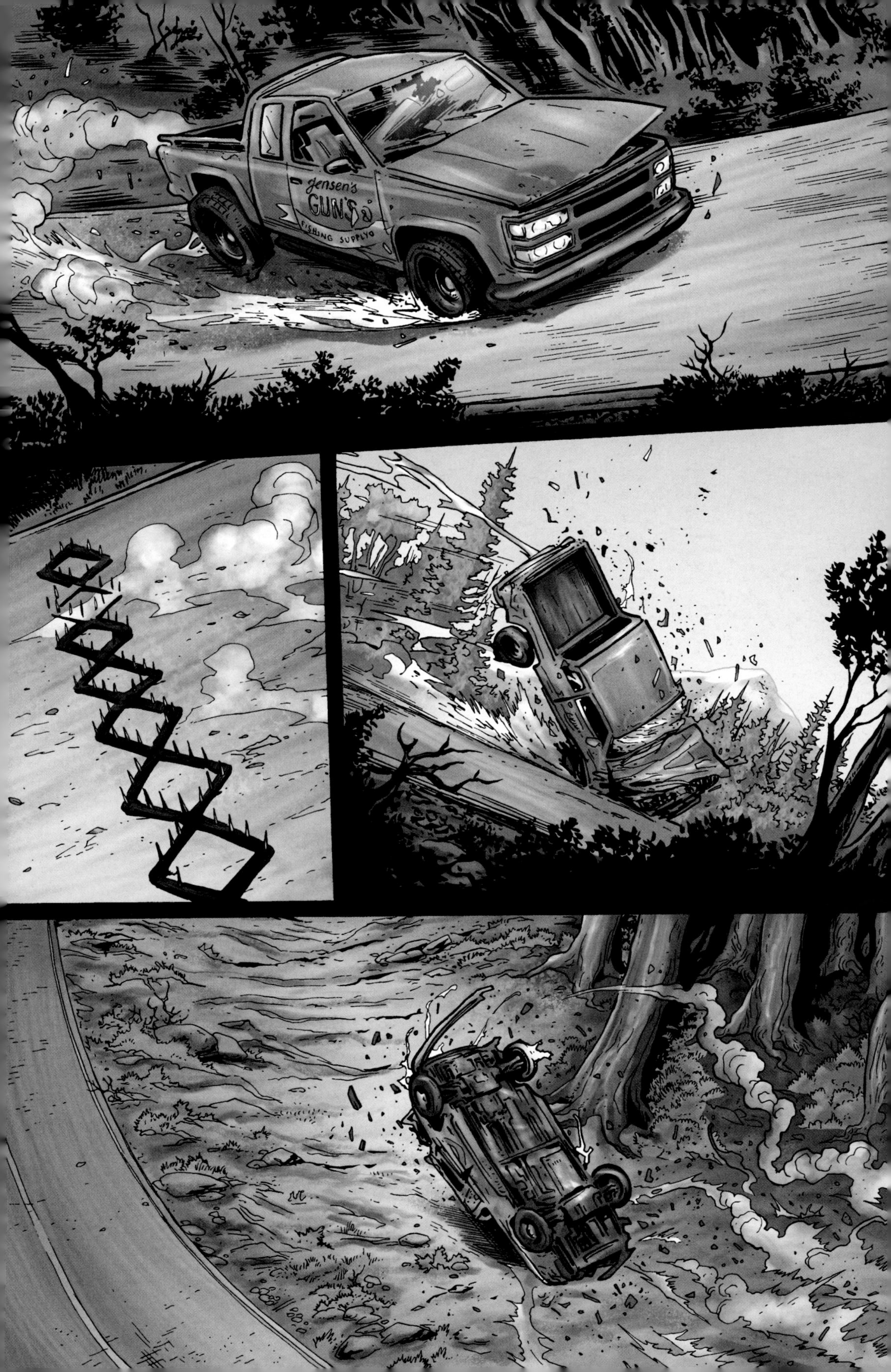
Jensen's
GUNS &
FISHING SUPPLY

MEANWHILE...

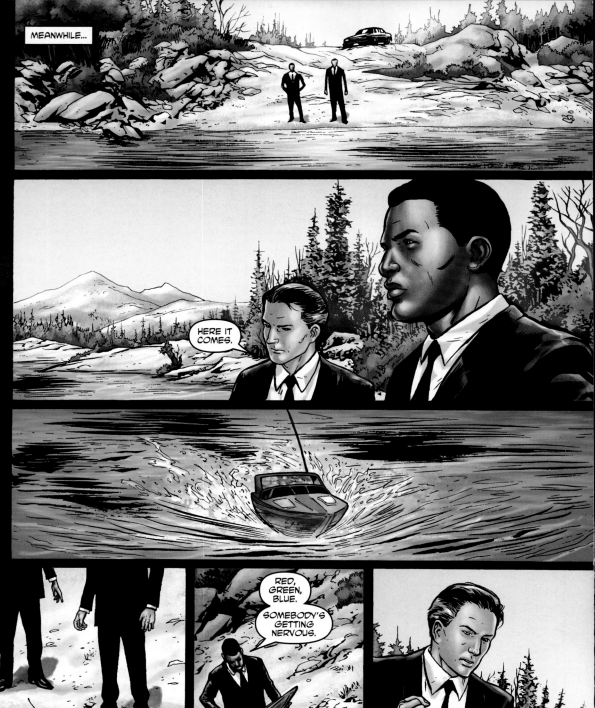

HERE IT COMES.

RED, GREEN, BLUE.

SOMEBODY'S GETTING NERVOUS.

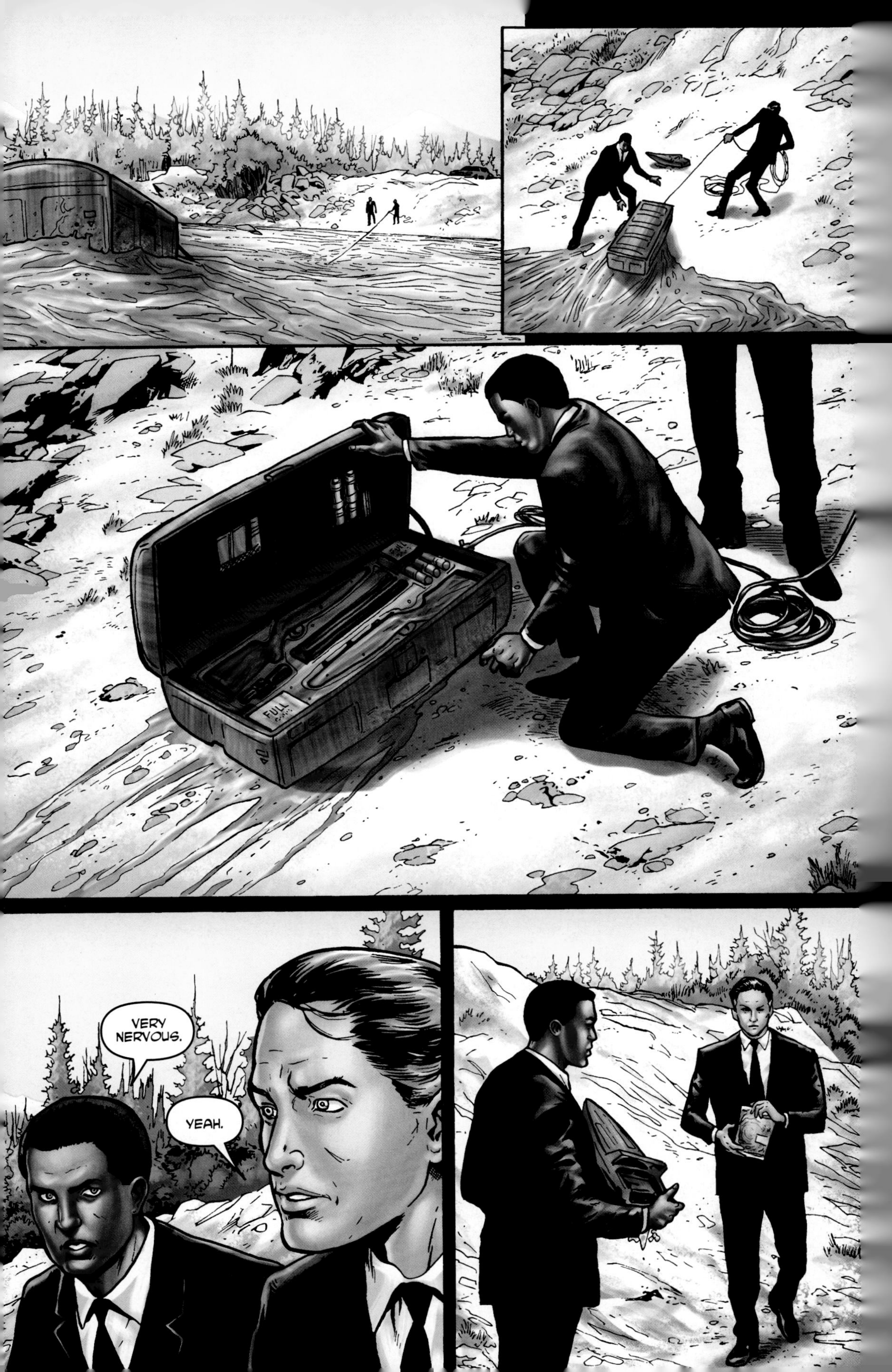
FULL
VERY NERVOUS.
YEAH.

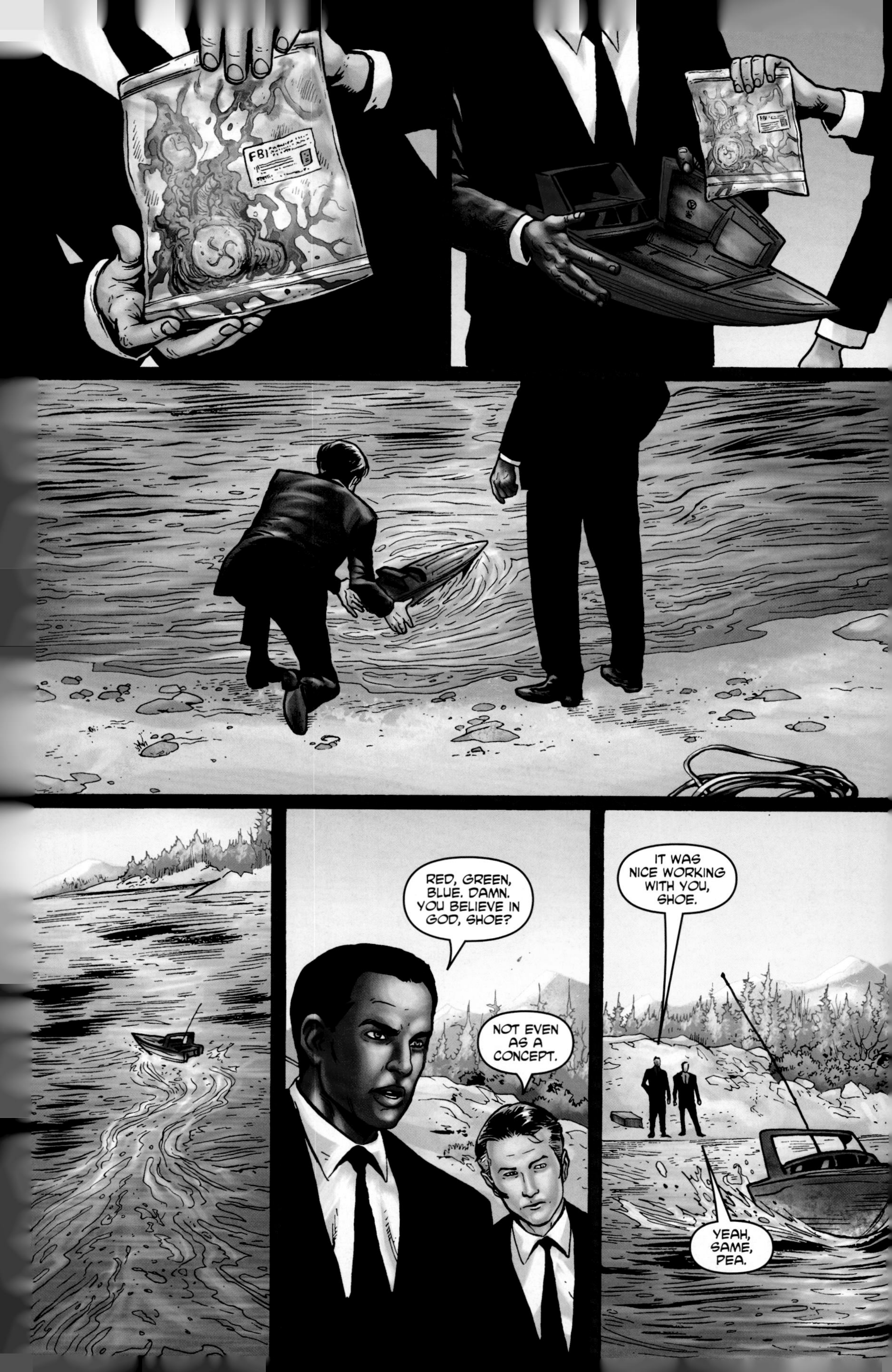
FBI
RED, GREEN, BLUE. DAMN. YOU BELIEVE IN GOD, SHOE?
NOT EVEN AS A CONCEPT.
IT WAS NICE WORKING WITH YOU, SHOE.
YEAH, SAME, PEA.

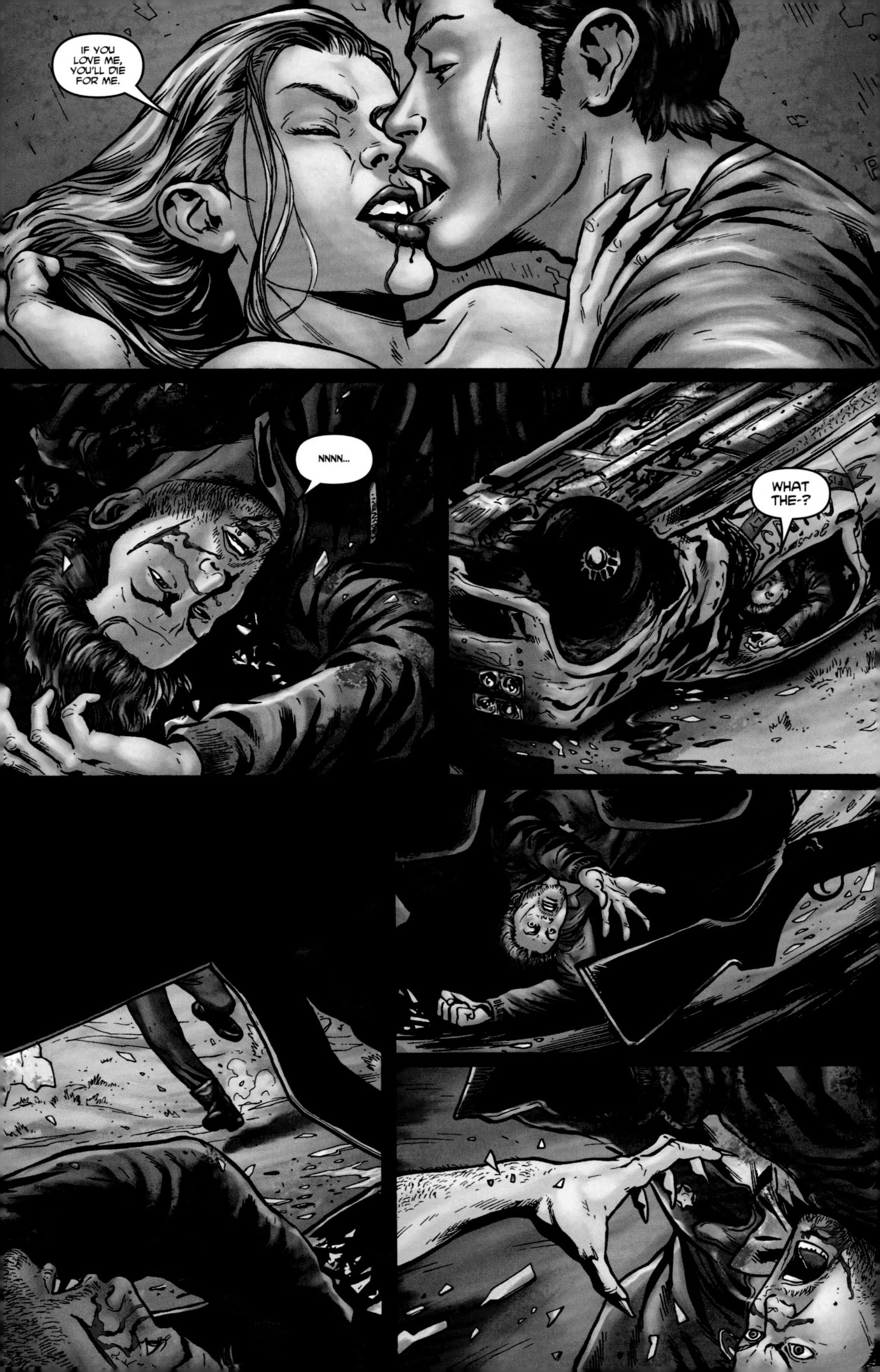
IF YOU LOVE ME, YOU'LL DIE FOR ME.
NNNN...
WHAT THE-?

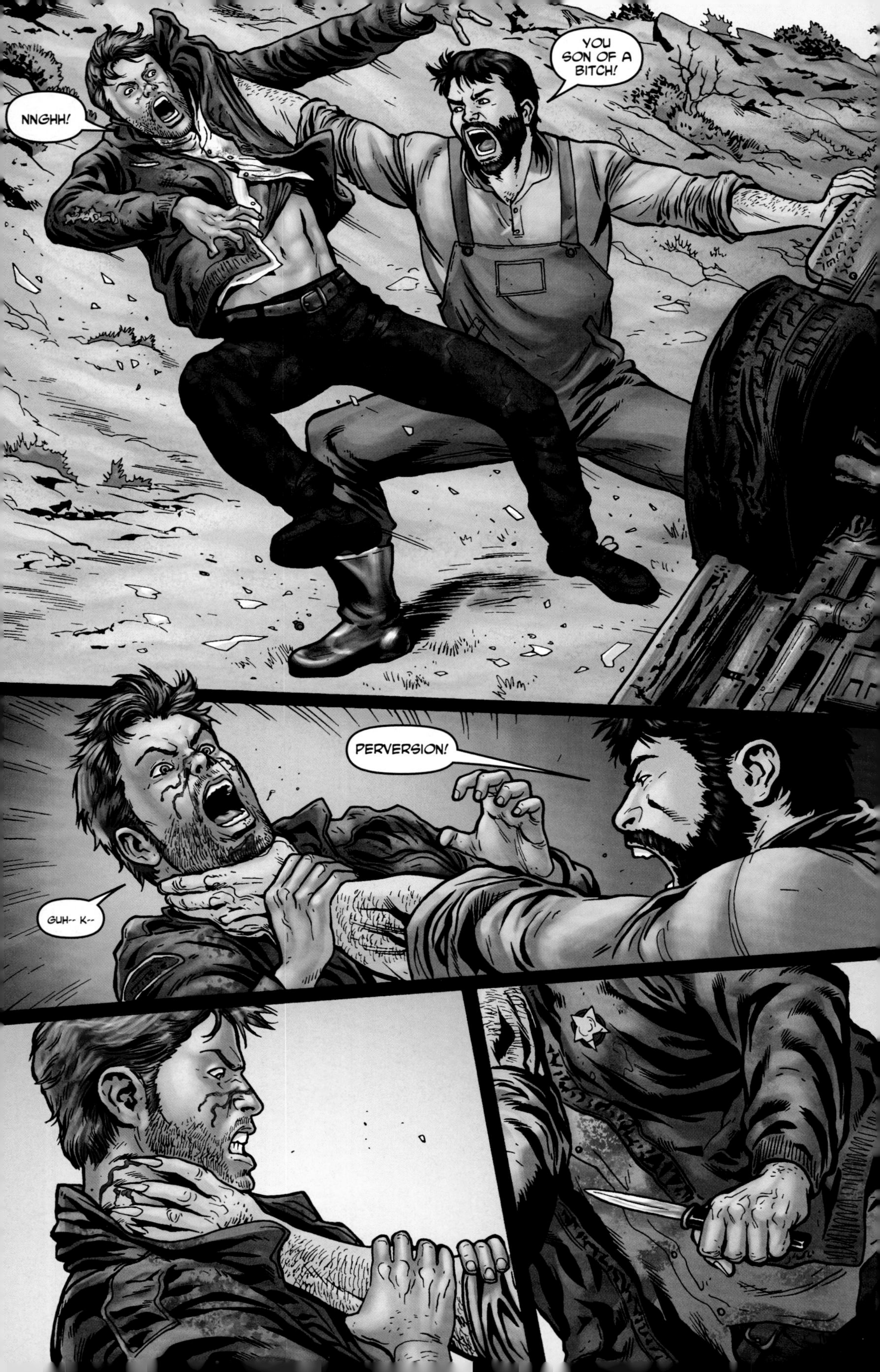
YOU SON OF A BITCH!
NNGHH!
PERVERSION!
GUH-- K--

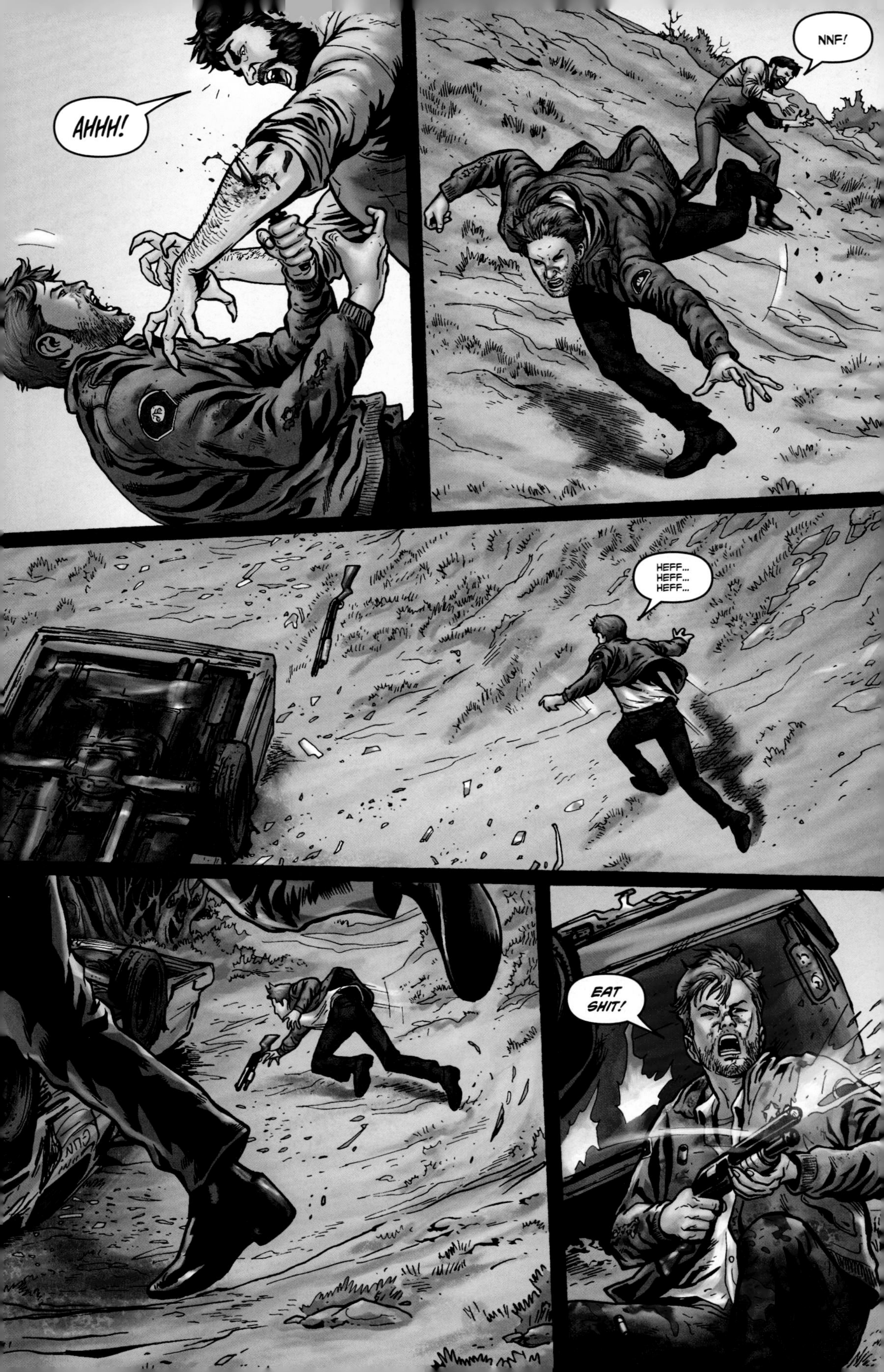
AHHH!
NNF!
HEFF... HEFF... HEFF...
EAT SHIT!

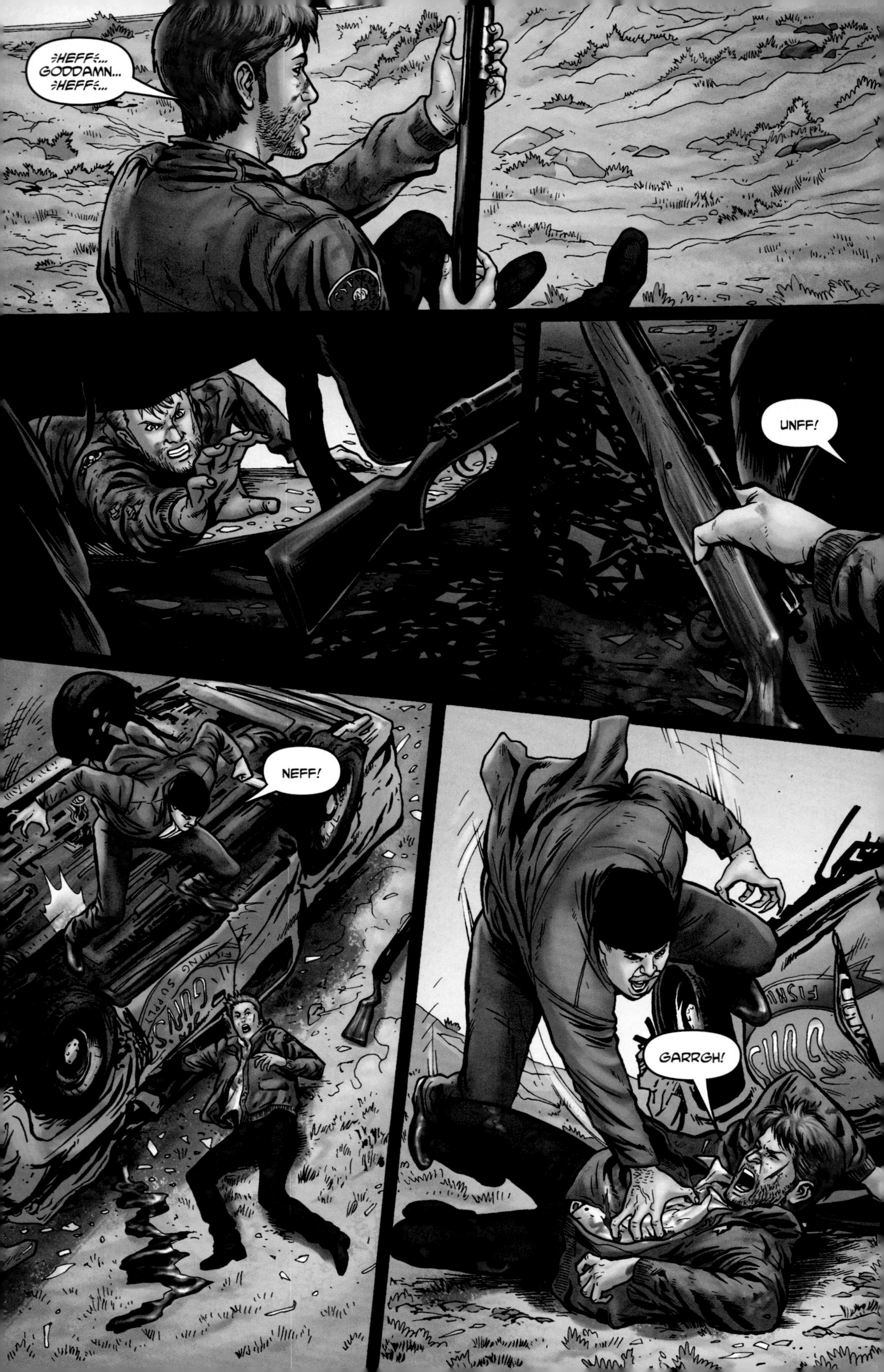

HEFF... GODDAMN... HEFF...
UNFF!
NEFF!
GARRGH!

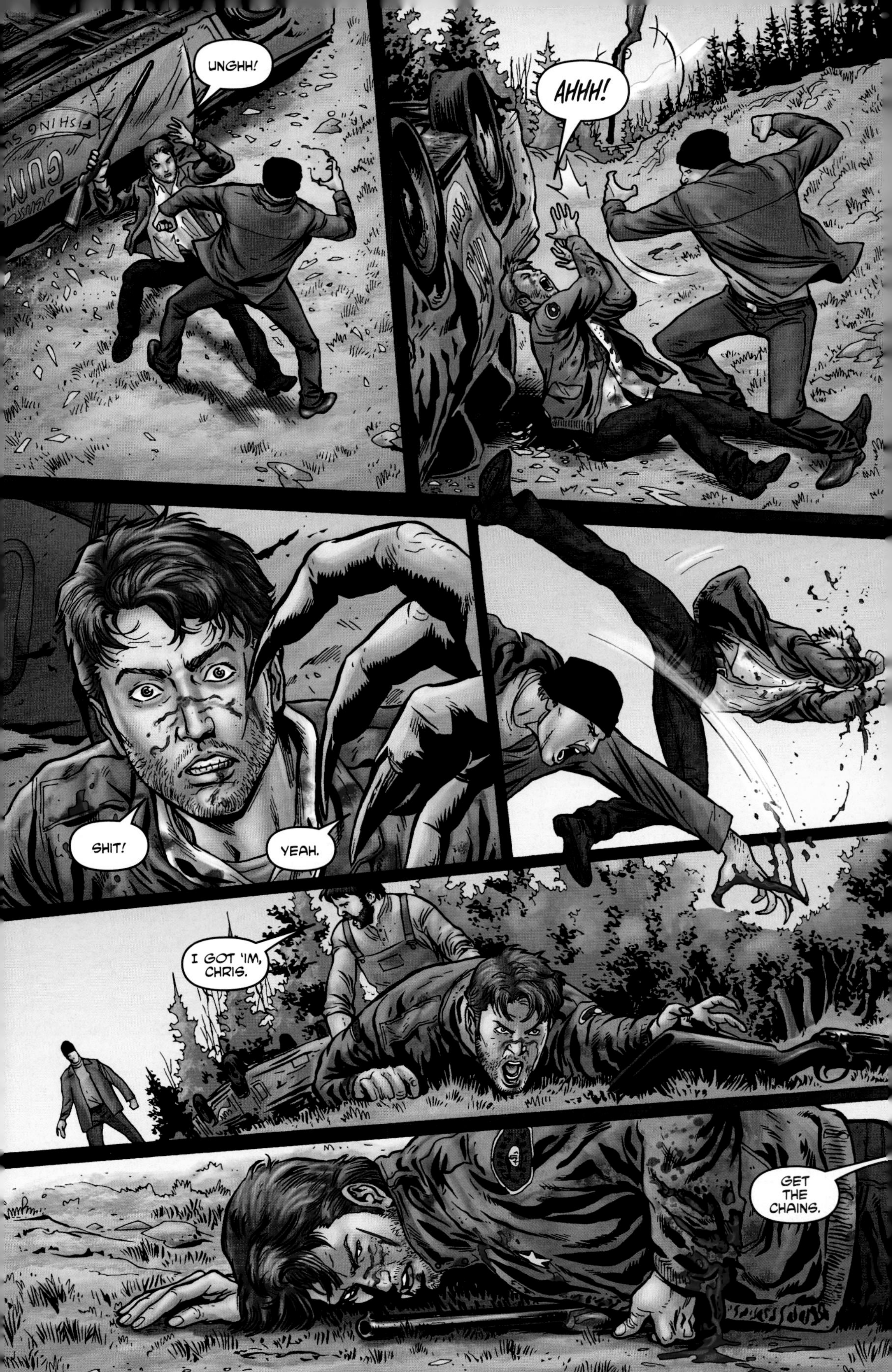
UNGHH!
FISHING SU
GUN
AHHH!
SHIT!
YEAH.
I GOT 'IM, CHRIS.
GET THE CHAINS.

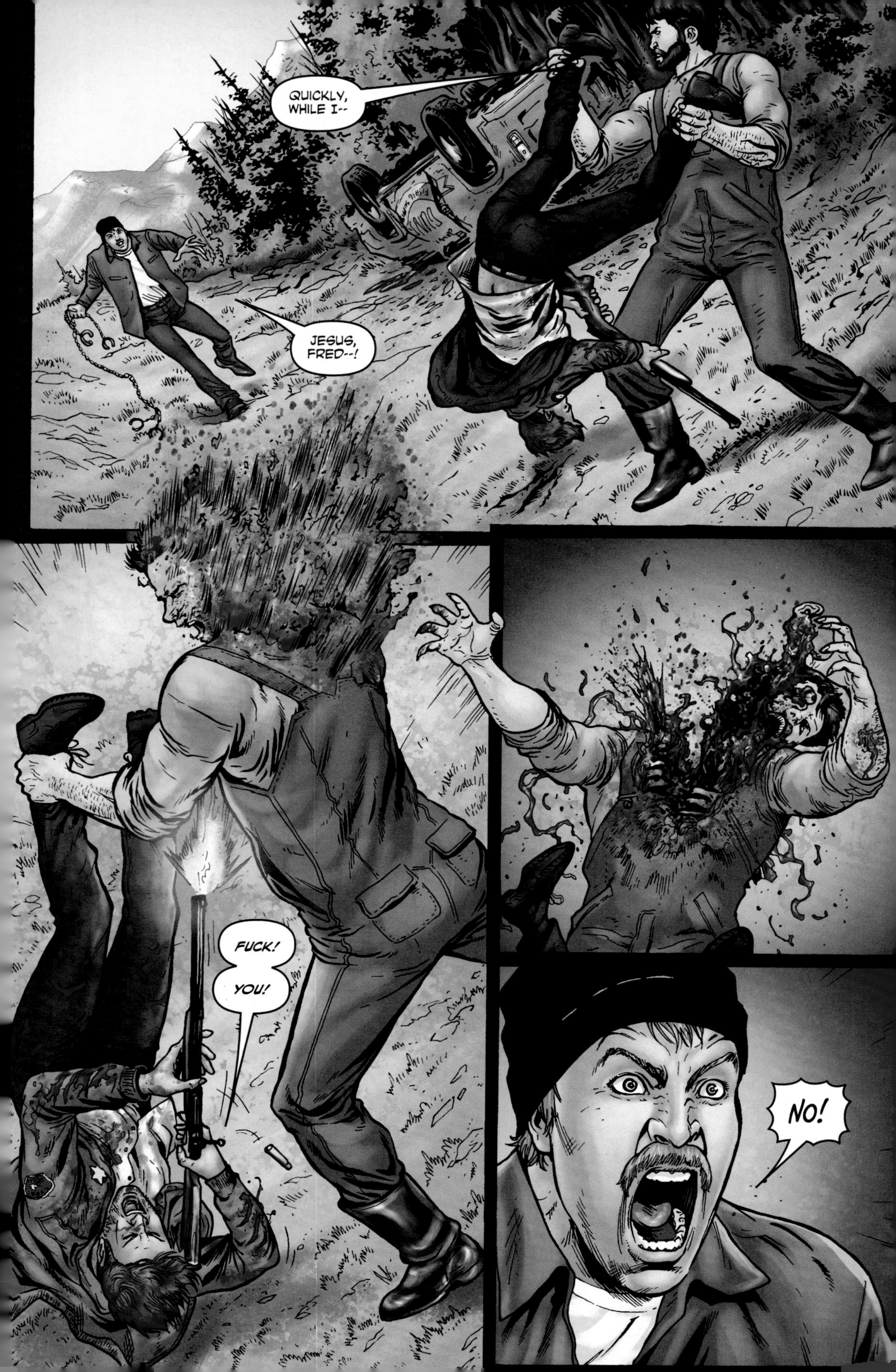
QUICKLY, WHILE I--
JESUS, FRED--!
FUCK!
YOU!
NO!

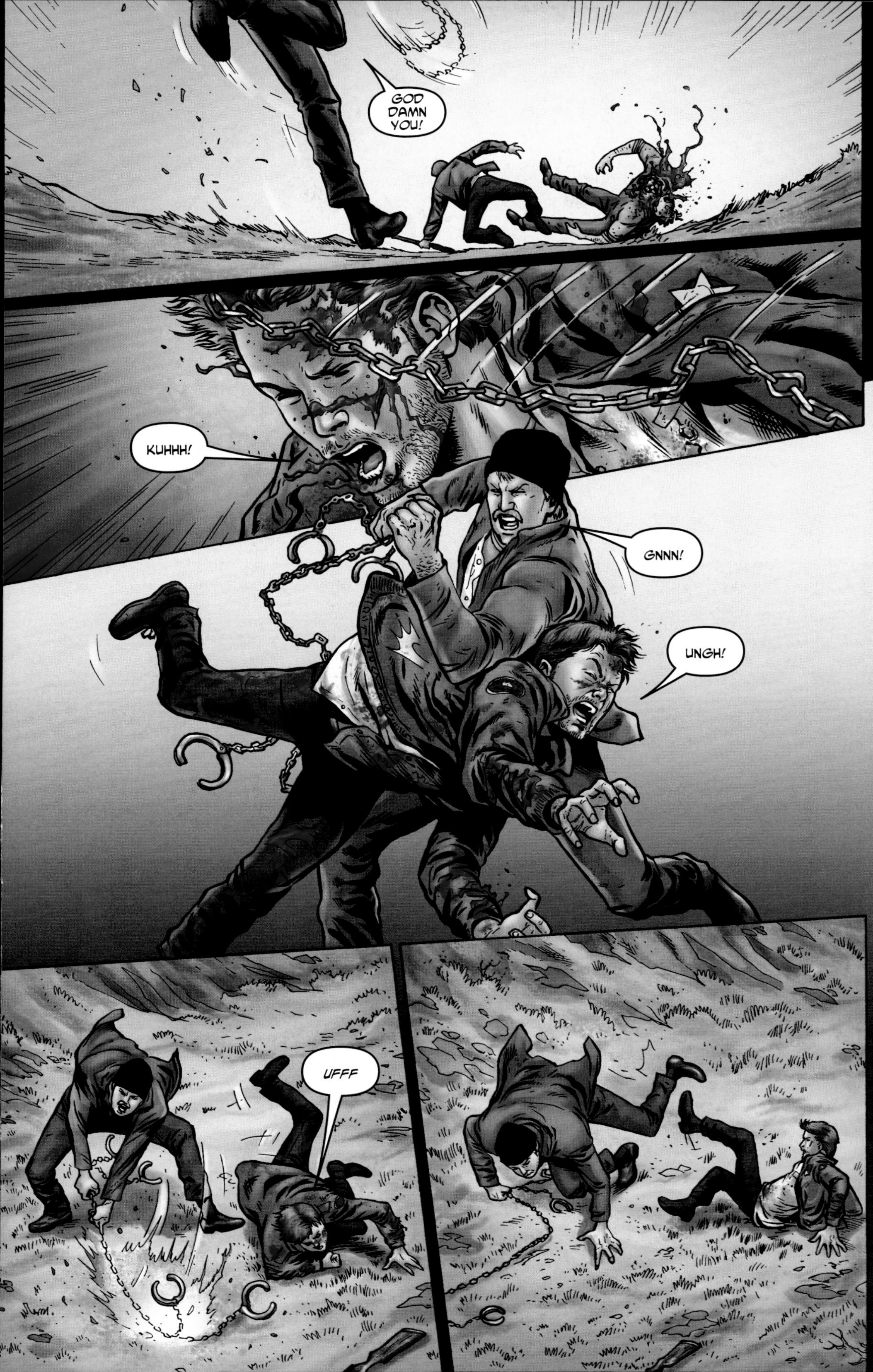
GOD DAMN YOU!
KUHHH!
GNNN!
UNGH!
UFFF

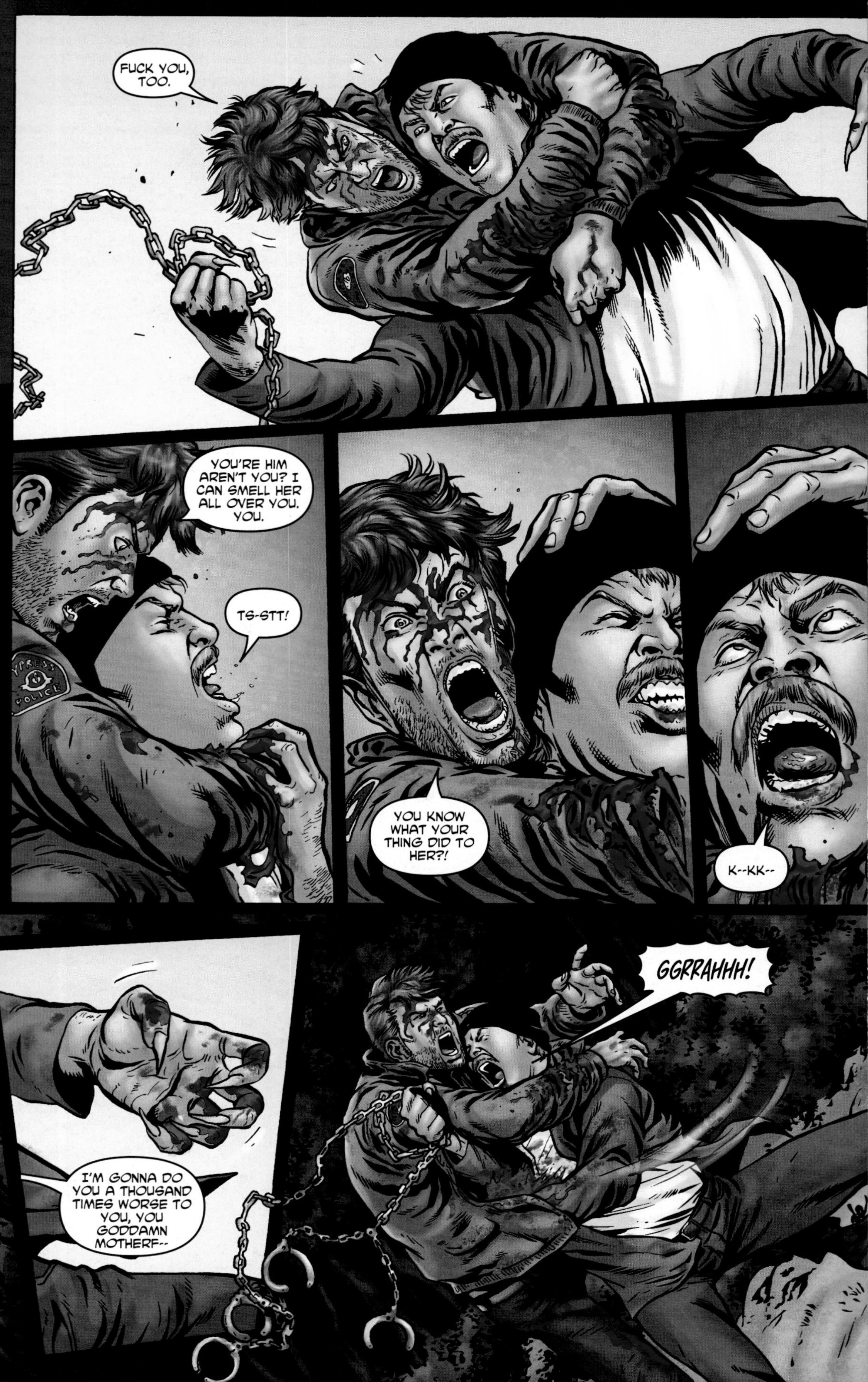
FUCK YOU, TOO.
YOU'RE HIM AREN'T YOU? I CAN SMELL HER ALL OVER YOU. YOU.
TS-STT!
YOU KNOW WHAT YOUR THING DID TO HER?!
K--KK--
I'M GONNA DO YOU A THOUSAND TIMES WORSE TO YOU, YOU GODDAMN MOTHERF--
GGRRAHHH!

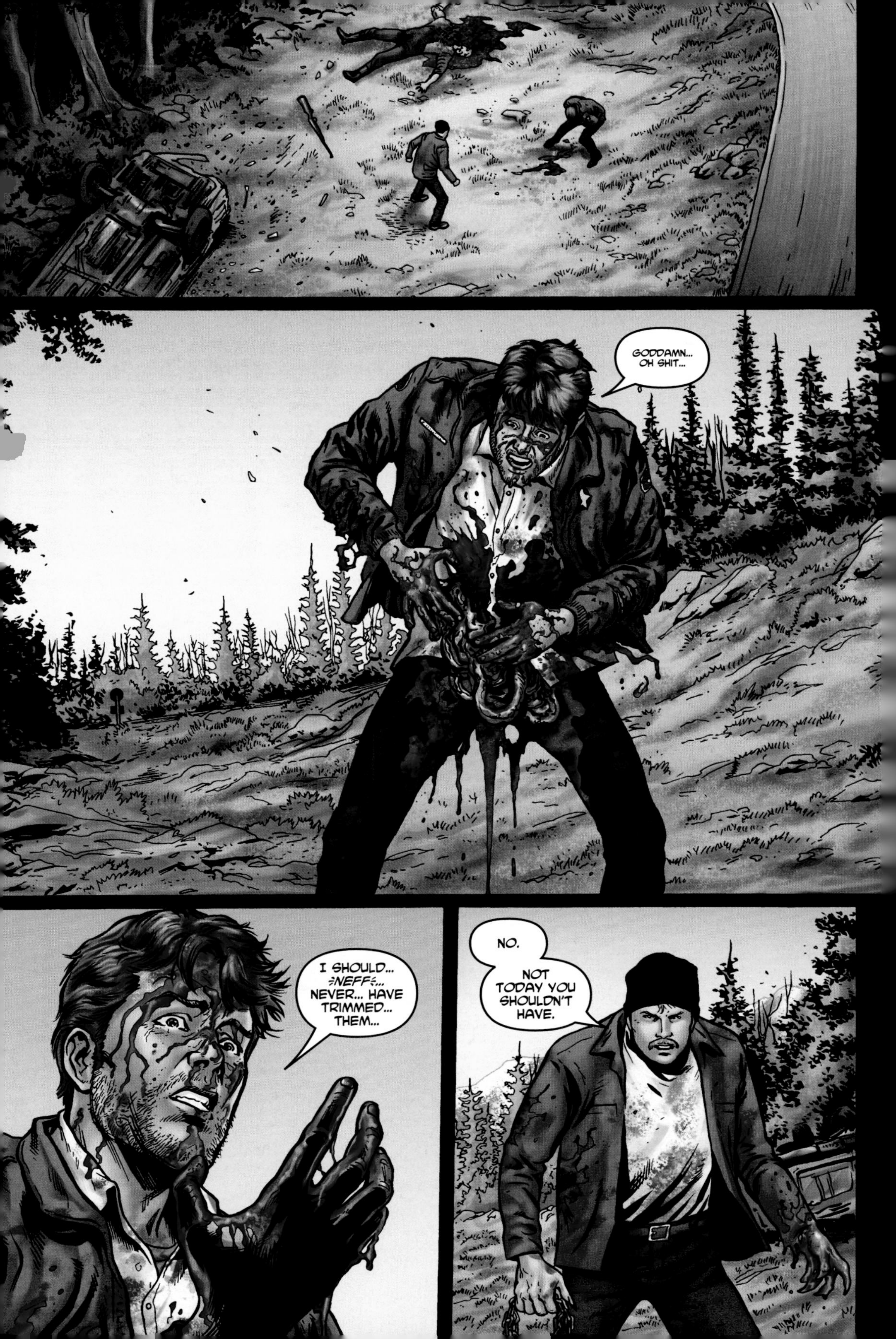
GODDAMN... OH SHIT...
I SHOULD... NEFF... NEVER... HAVE TRIMMED... THEM...
NO.
NOT TODAY YOU SHOULDN'T HAVE.

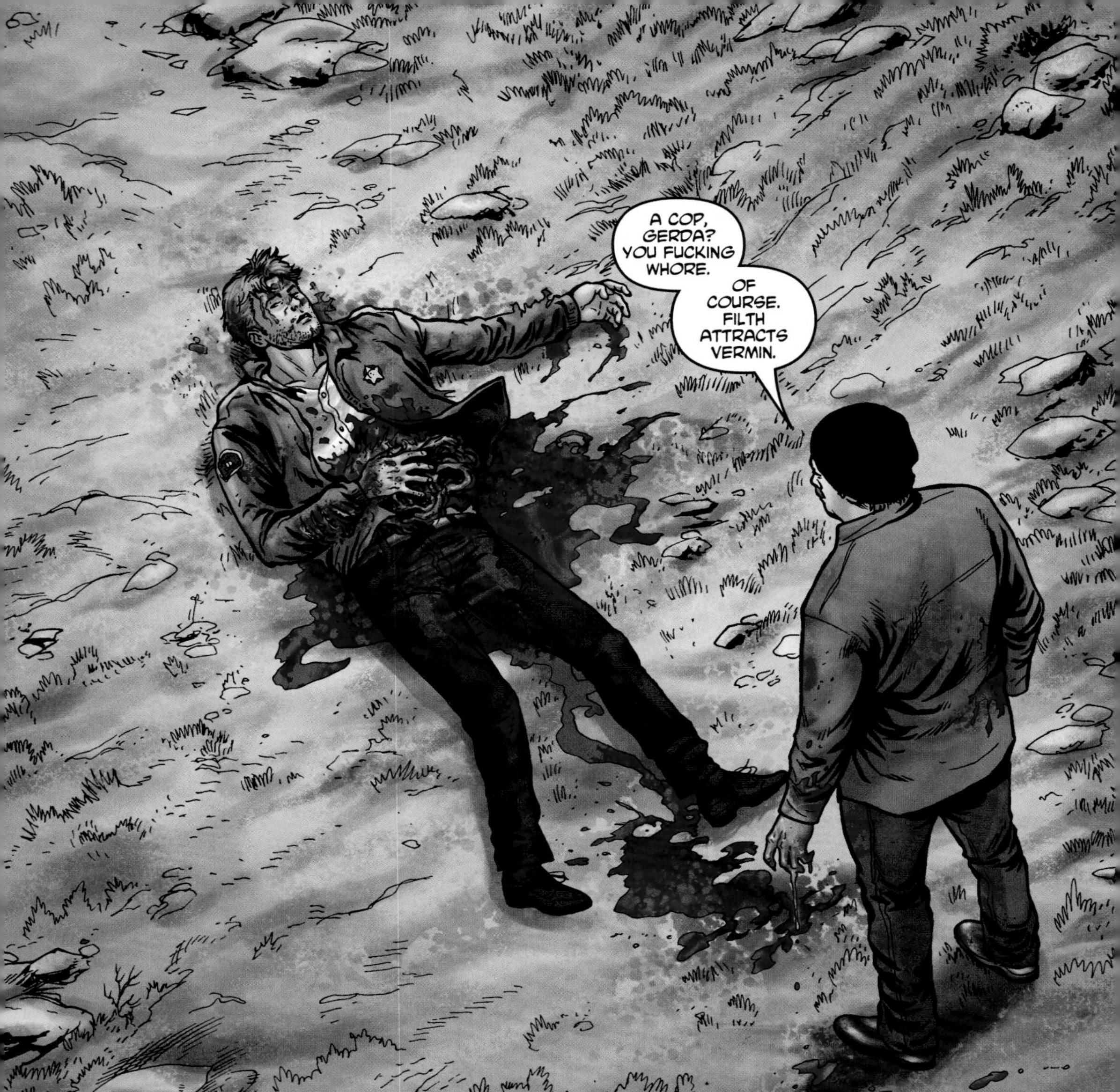
A COP, GERDA? YOU FUCKING WHORE.
OF COURSE. FILTH ATTRACTS VERMIN.

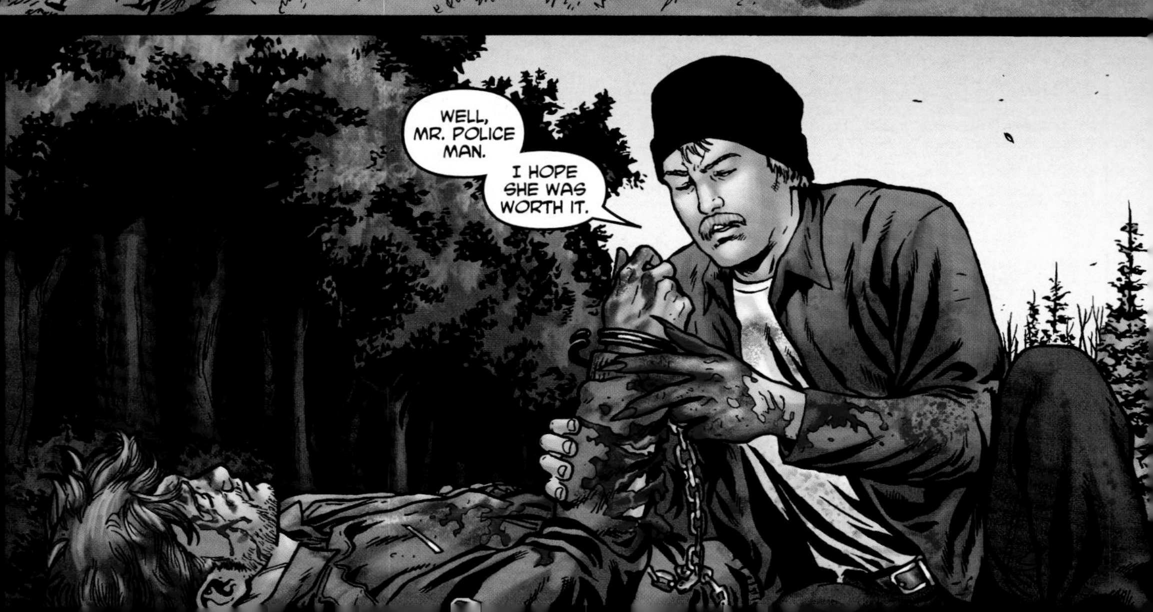
WELL, MR. POLICE MAN.
I HOPE SHE WAS WORTH IT.

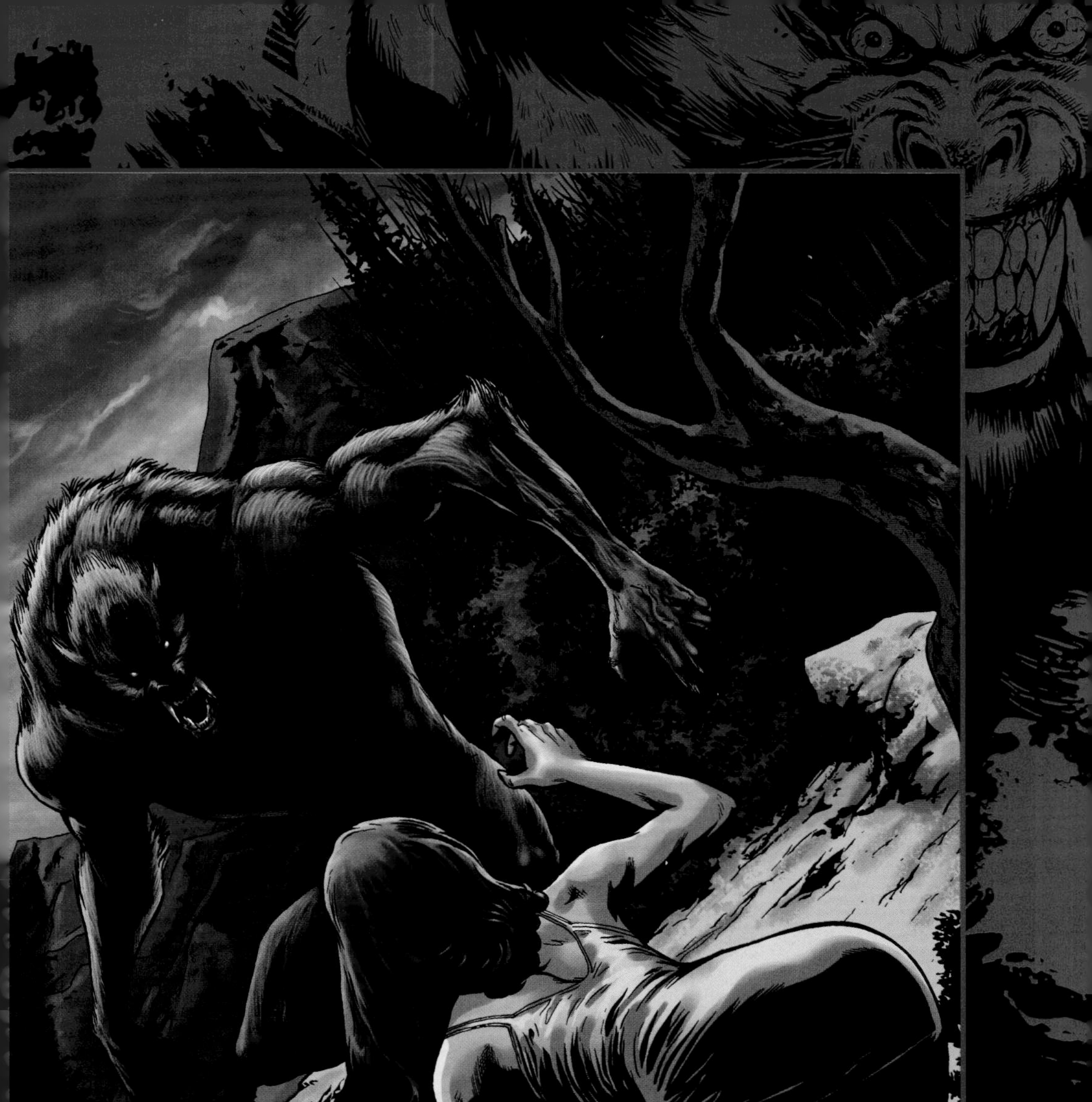
GABRIEL
2012

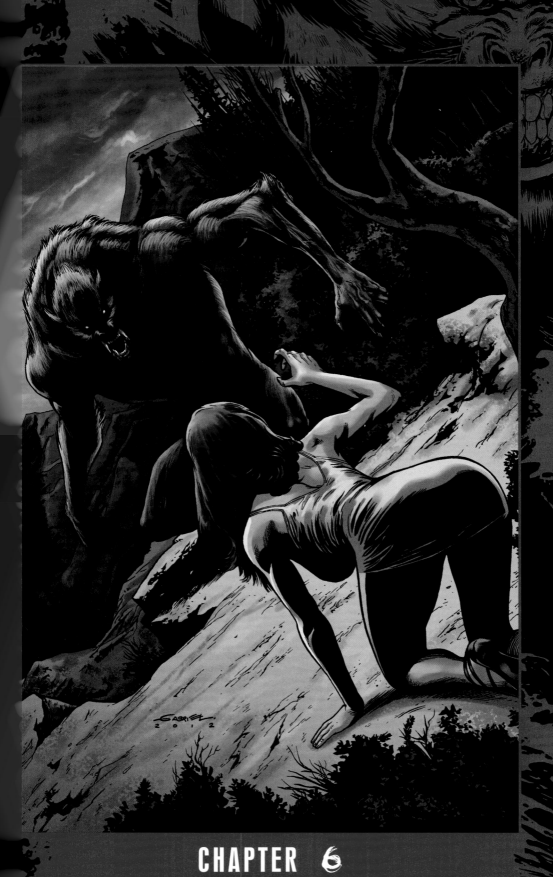

CHAPTER 6

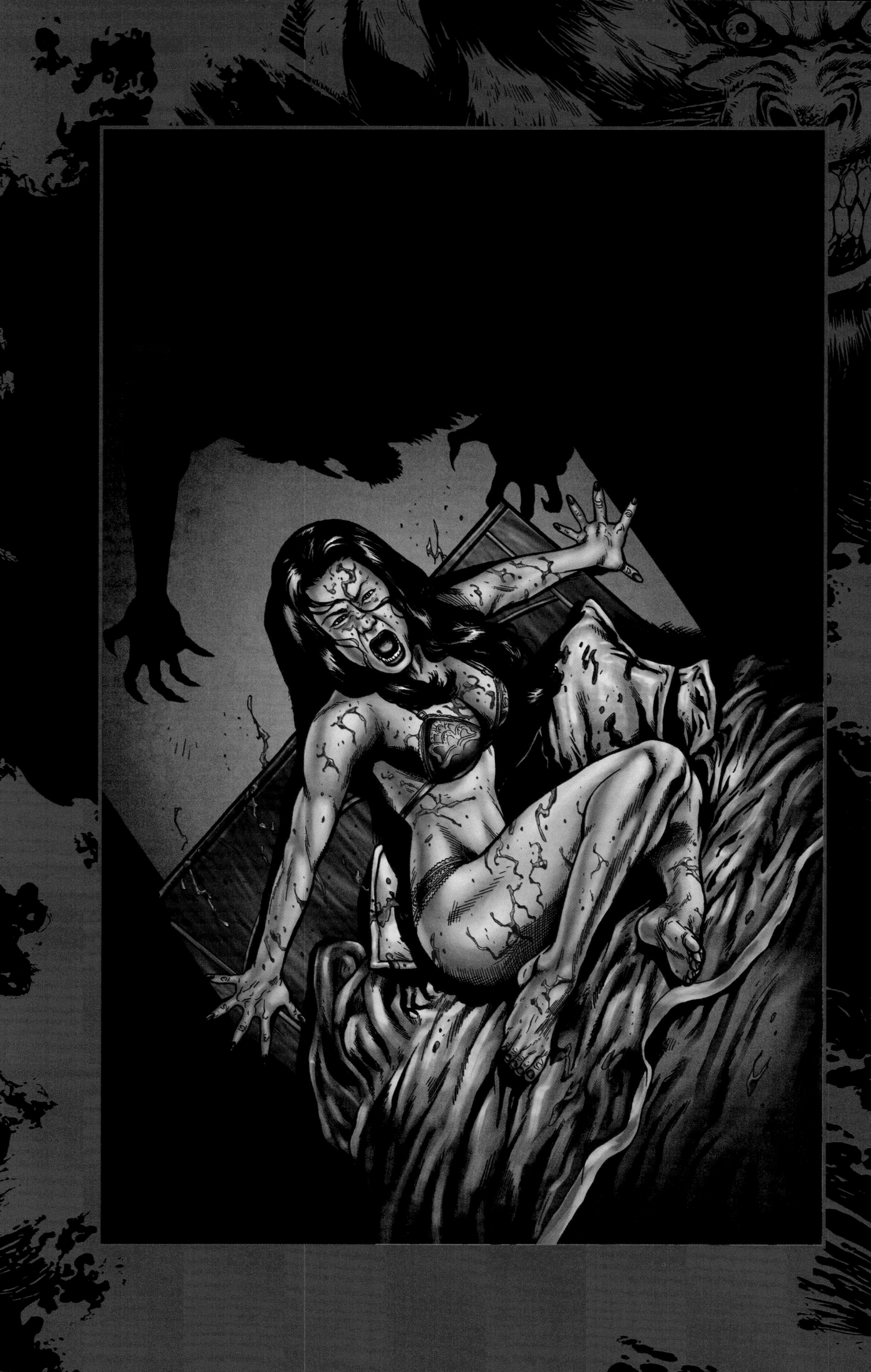

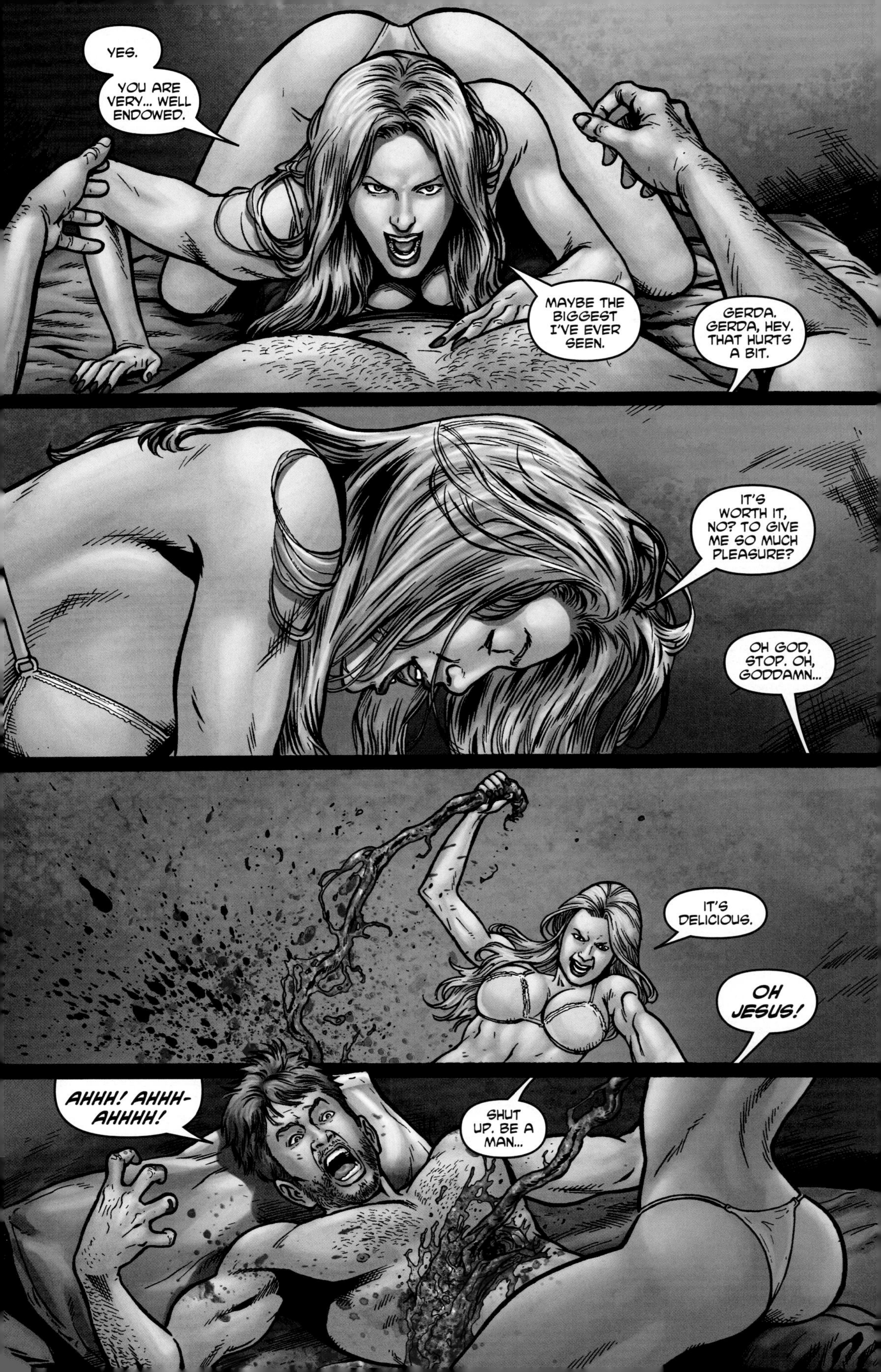
YES.
YOU ARE VERY... WELL ENDOWED.
MAYBE THE BIGGEST I'VE EVER SEEN.
GERDA. GERDA, HEY. THAT HURTS A BIT.
IT'S WORTH IT, NO? TO GIVE ME SO MUCH PLEASURE?
OH GOD, STOP. OH, GODDAMN...
IT'S DELICIOUS.
OH JESUS!
AHHH! AHHH-AHHHH!
SHUT UP. BE A MAN...

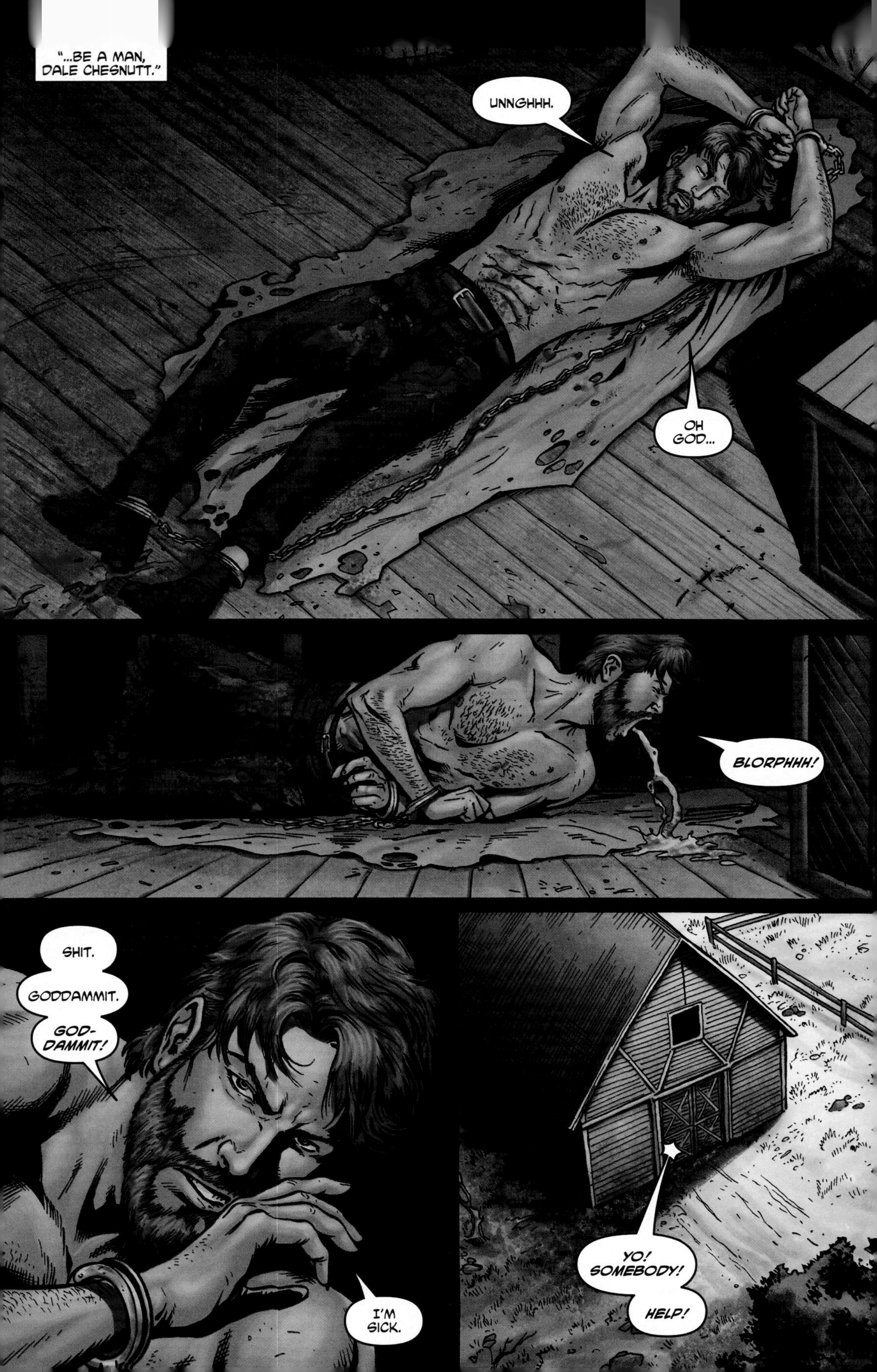
"...BE A MAN, DALE CHESNUTT."
UNNGHHH.
OH GOD...
BLORPHHH!
SHIT.
GODDAMMIT.
GOD-DAMMIT!
I'M SICK.
YO! SOMEBODY!
HELP!

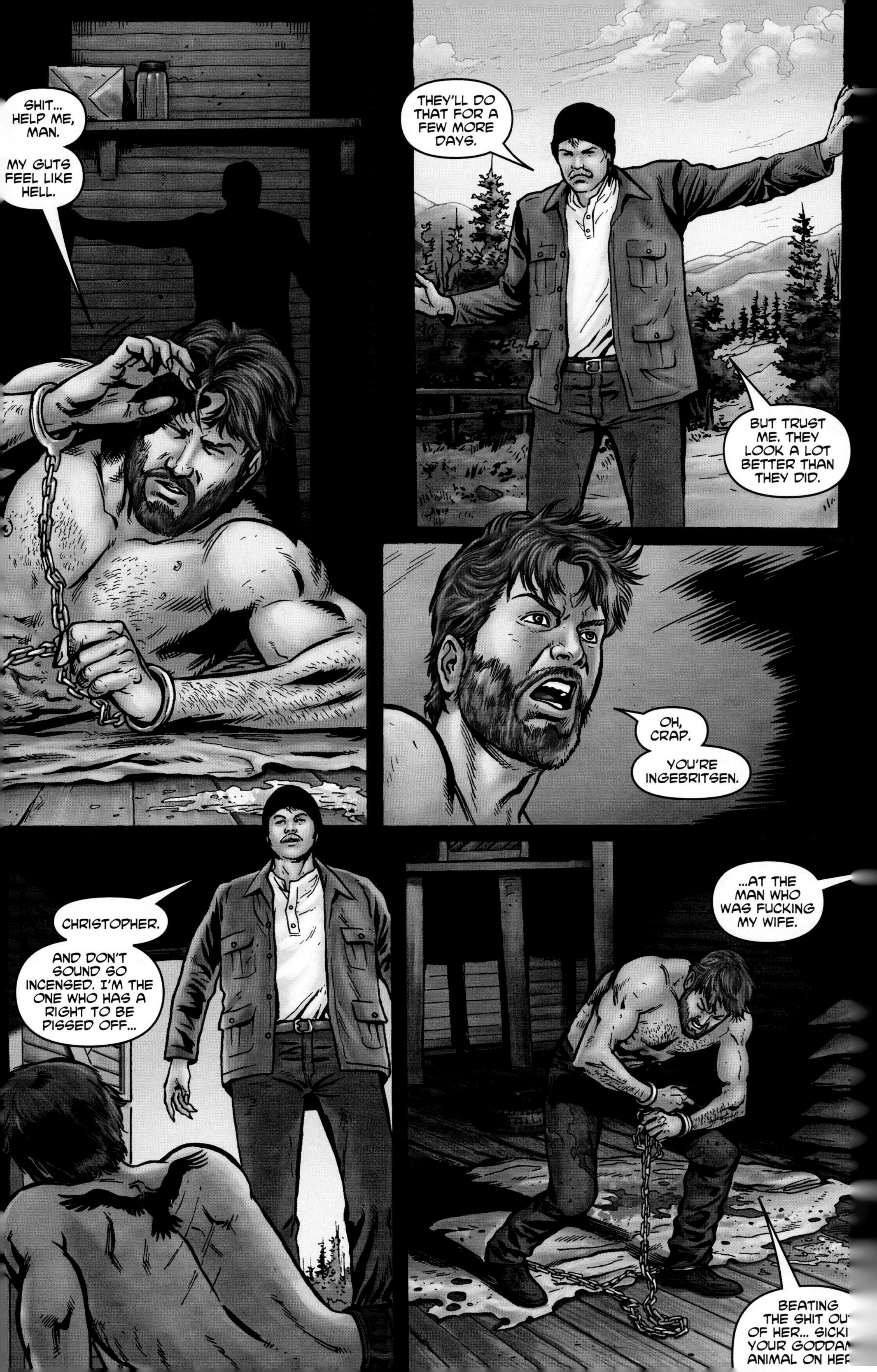
SHIT... HELP ME, MAN.
MY GUTS FEEL LIKE HELL.
THEY'LL DO THAT FOR A FEW MORE DAYS.
BUT TRUST ME. THEY LOOK A LOT BETTER THAN THEY DID.
OH, CRAP.
YOU'RE INGEBRITSEN.
CHRISTOPHER.
AND DON'T SOUND SO INCENSED. I'M THE ONE WHO HAS A RIGHT TO BE PISSED OFF...
...AT THE MAN WHO WAS FUCKING MY WIFE.
BEATING THE SHIT OU OF HER... SICKI YOUR GODDAM ANIMAL ON HEF

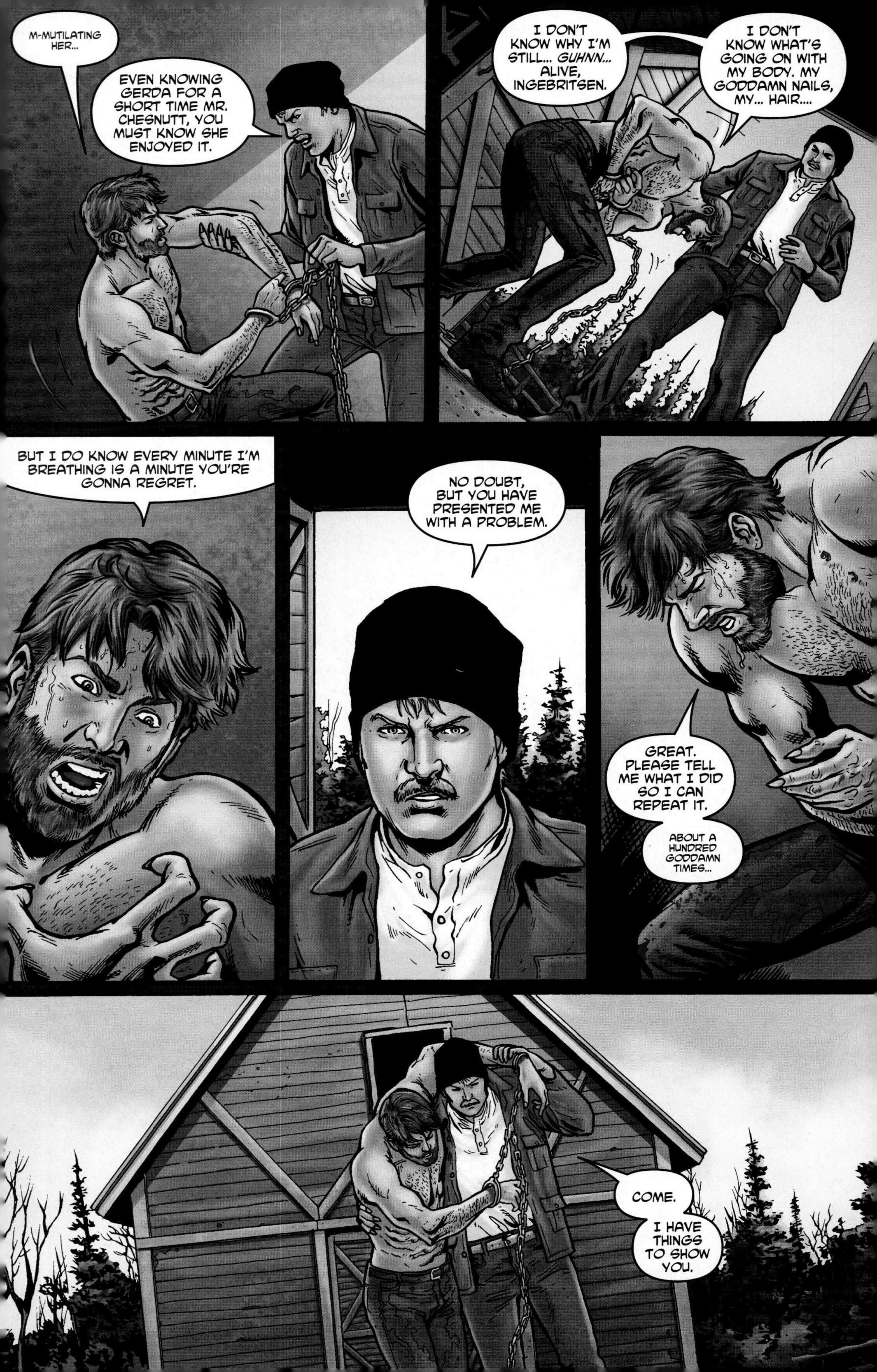
M-MUTILATING HER...
EVEN KNOWING GERDA FOR A SHORT TIME MR. CHESNUTT, YOU MUST KNOW SHE ENJOYED IT.
I DON'T KNOW WHY I'M STILL... *GUHNN...* ALIVE, INGEBRITSEN.
I DON'T KNOW WHAT'S GOING ON WITH MY BODY. MY GODDAMN NAILS, MY... HAIR....
BUT I DO KNOW EVERY MINUTE I'M BREATHING IS A MINUTE YOU'RE GONNA REGRET.
NO DOUBT, BUT YOU HAVE PRESENTED ME WITH A PROBLEM.
GREAT. PLEASE TELL ME WHAT I DID SO I CAN REPEAT IT.
ABOUT A HUNDRED GODDAMN TIMES...
COME.
I HAVE THINGS TO SHOW YOU.

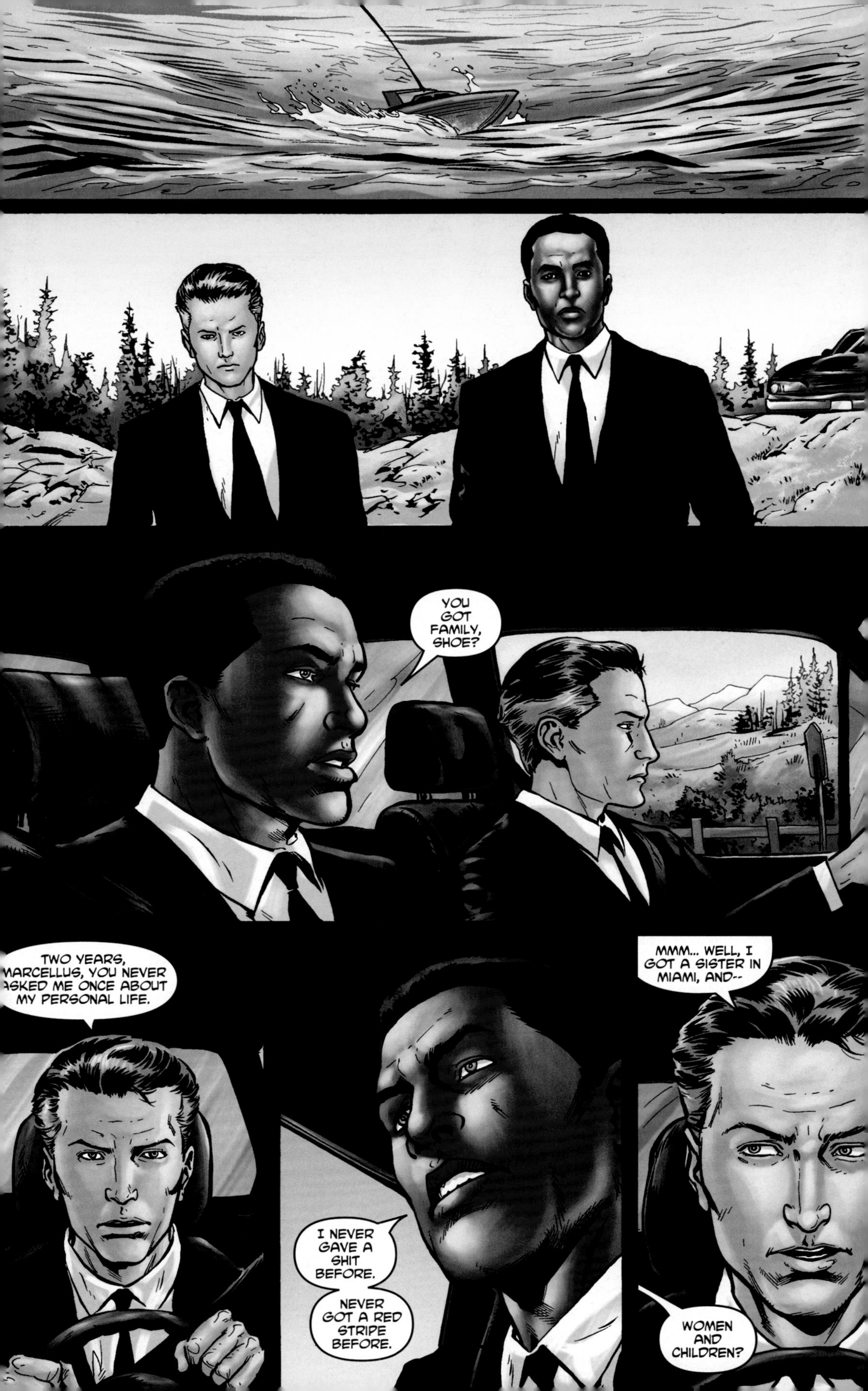
YOU GOT FAMILY, SHOE?
TWO YEARS, MARCELLUS, YOU NEVER ASKED ME ONCE ABOUT MY PERSONAL LIFE.
I NEVER GAVE A SHIT BEFORE.
NEVER GOT A RED STRIPE BEFORE.
MMM... WELL, I GOT A SISTER IN MIAMI, AND--
WOMEN AND CHILDREN?

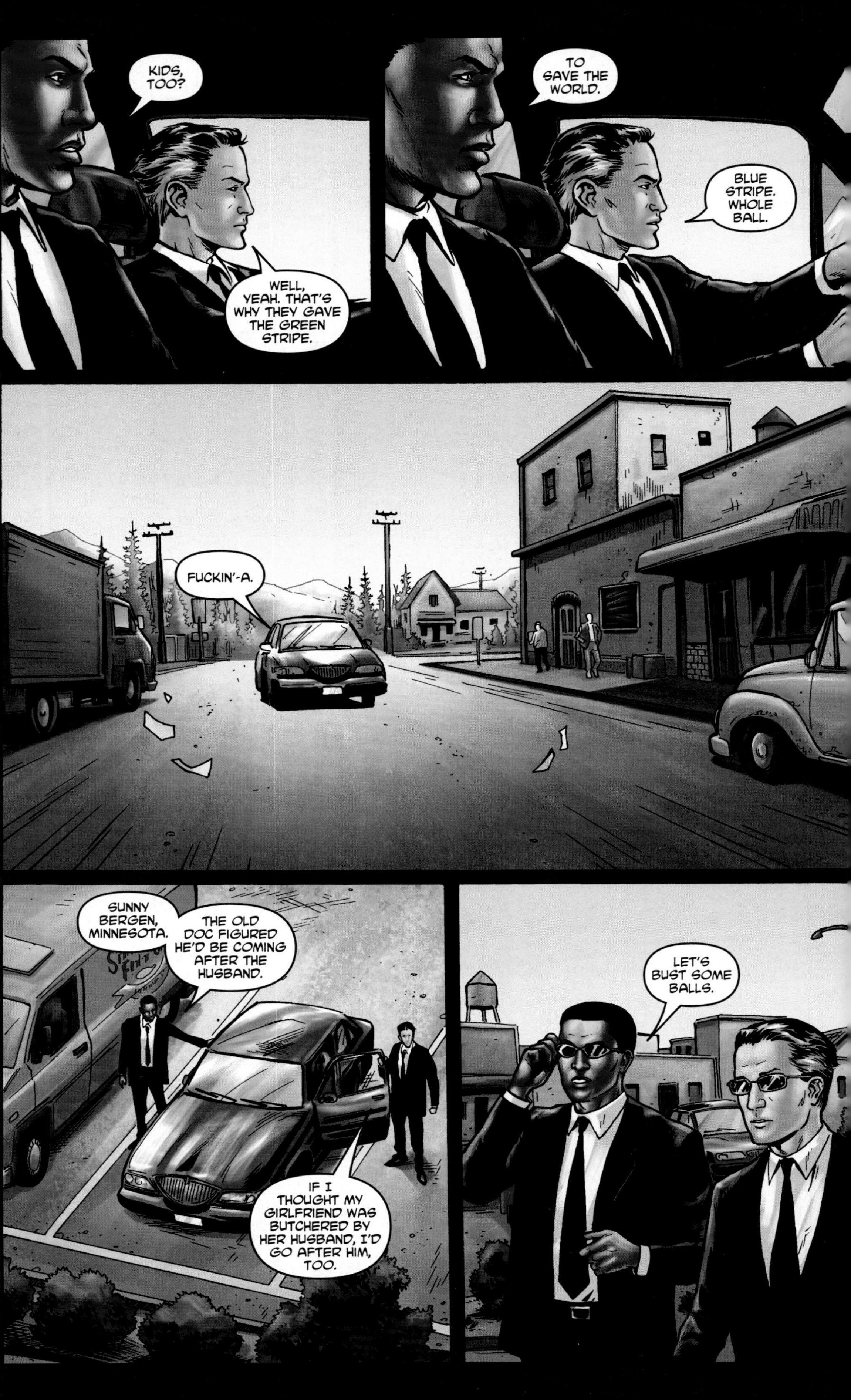
KIDS, TOO?
WELL, YEAH. THAT'S WHY THEY GAVE THE GREEN STRIPE.
TO SAVE THE WORLD.
BLUE STRIPE. WHOLE BALL.
FUCKIN'-A.
SUNNY BERGEN, MINNESOTA.
THE OLD DOC FIGURED HE'D BE COMING AFTER THE HUSBAND.
IF I THOUGHT MY GIRLFRIEND WAS BUTCHERED BY HER HUSBAND, I'D GO AFTER HIM, TOO.
LET'S BUST SOME BALLS.

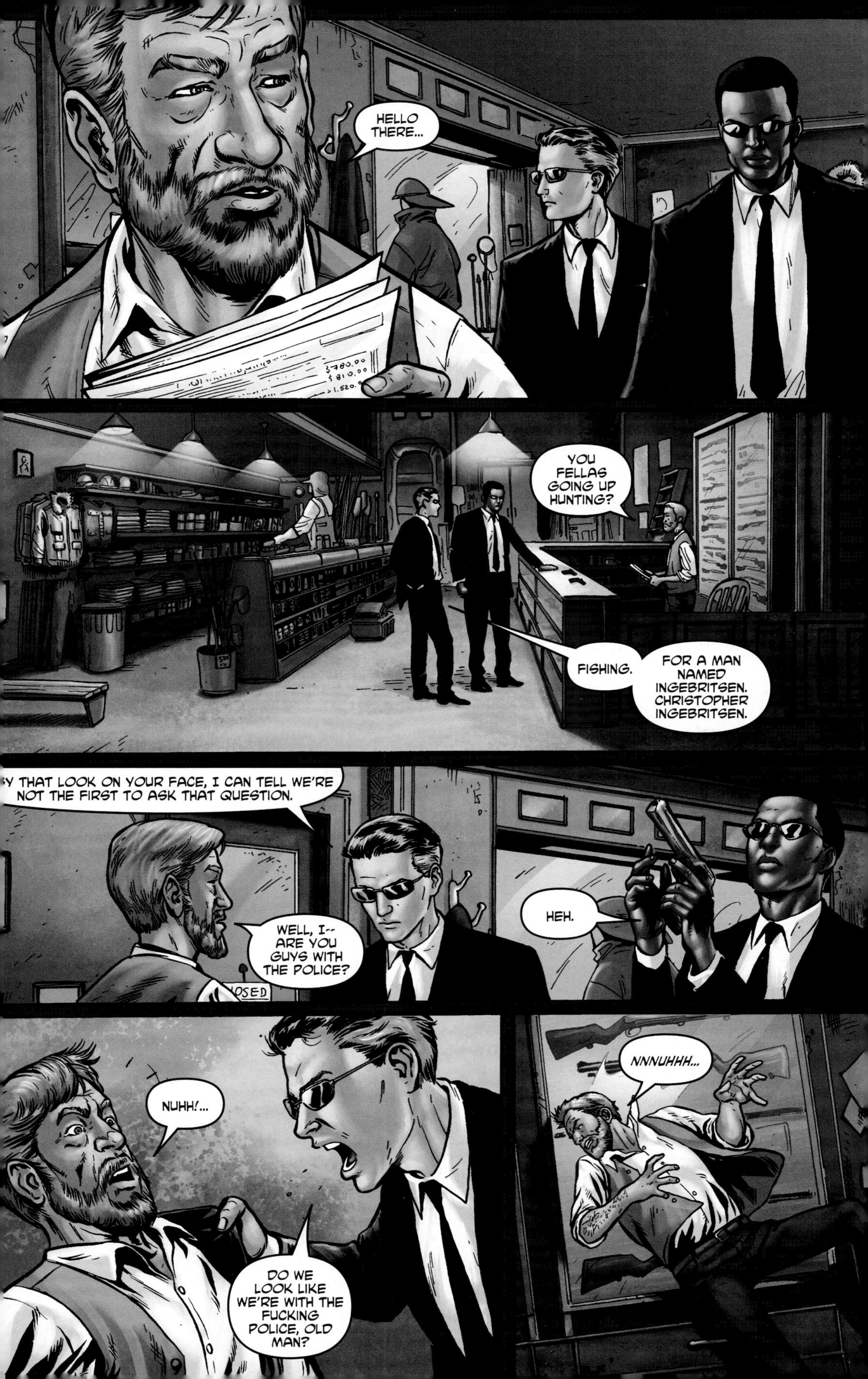
HELLO THERE...
YOU FELLAS GOING UP HUNTING?
FISHING.
FOR A MAN NAMED INGEBRITSEN. CHRISTOPHER INGEBRITSEN.
Y THAT LOOK ON YOUR FACE, I CAN TELL WE'RE NOT THE FIRST TO ASK THAT QUESTION.
WELL, I-- ARE YOU GUYS WITH THE POLICE?
HEH.
OSED
NUHH!...
DO WE LOOK LIKE WE'RE WITH THE FUCKING POLICE, OLD MAN?
NNNUHHH...

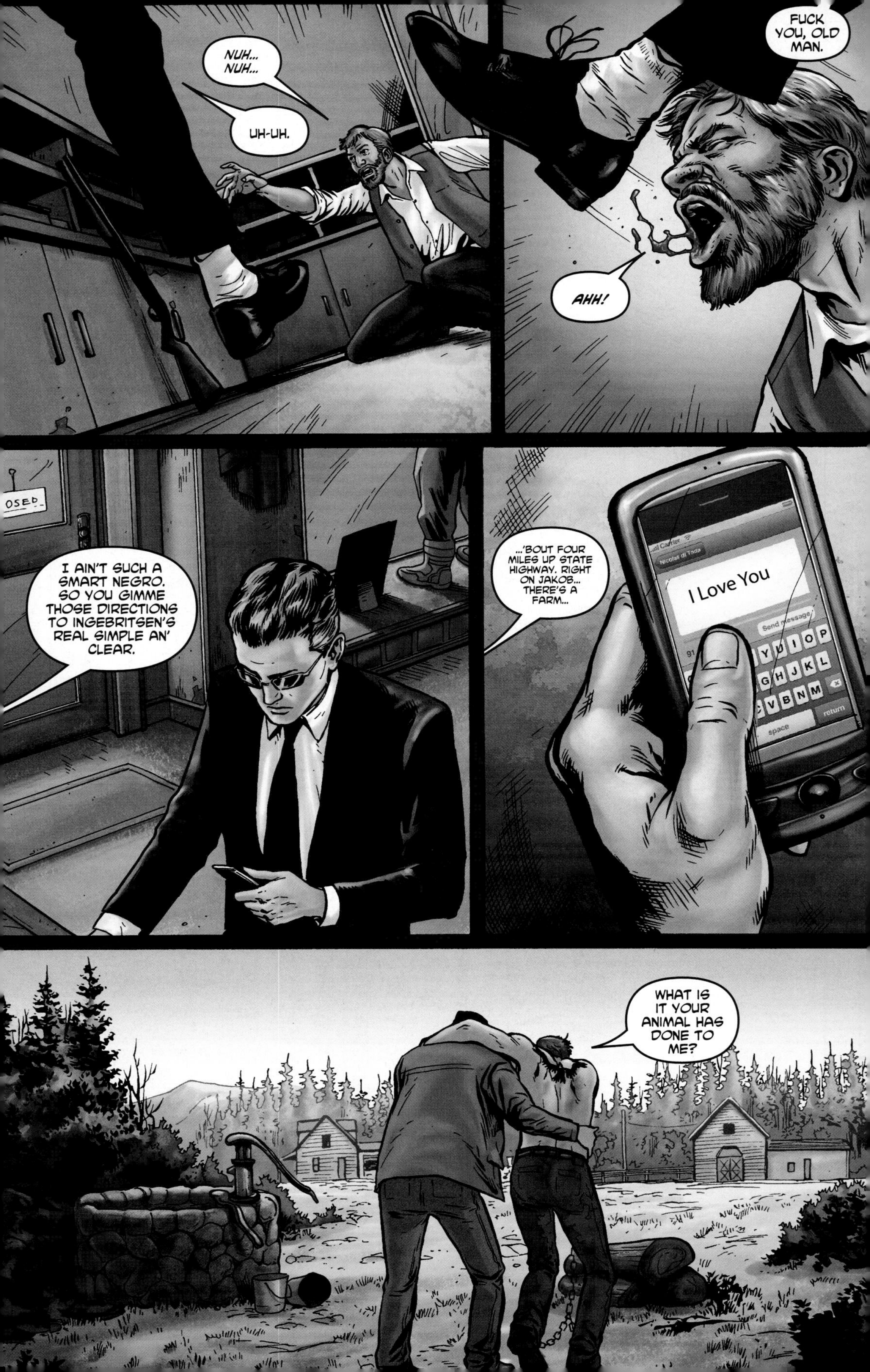
NUH... NUH...
UH-UH.
FUCK YOU, OLD MAN.
AHH!
I AIN'T SUCH A SMART NEGRO. SO YOU GIMME THOSE DIRECTIONS TO INGEBRITSEN'S REAL SIMPLE AN' CLEAR.
...'BOUT FOUR MILES UP STATE HIGHWAY. RIGHT ON JAKOB... THERE'S A FARM...
I Love You
WHAT IS IT YOUR ANIMAL HAS DONE TO ME?

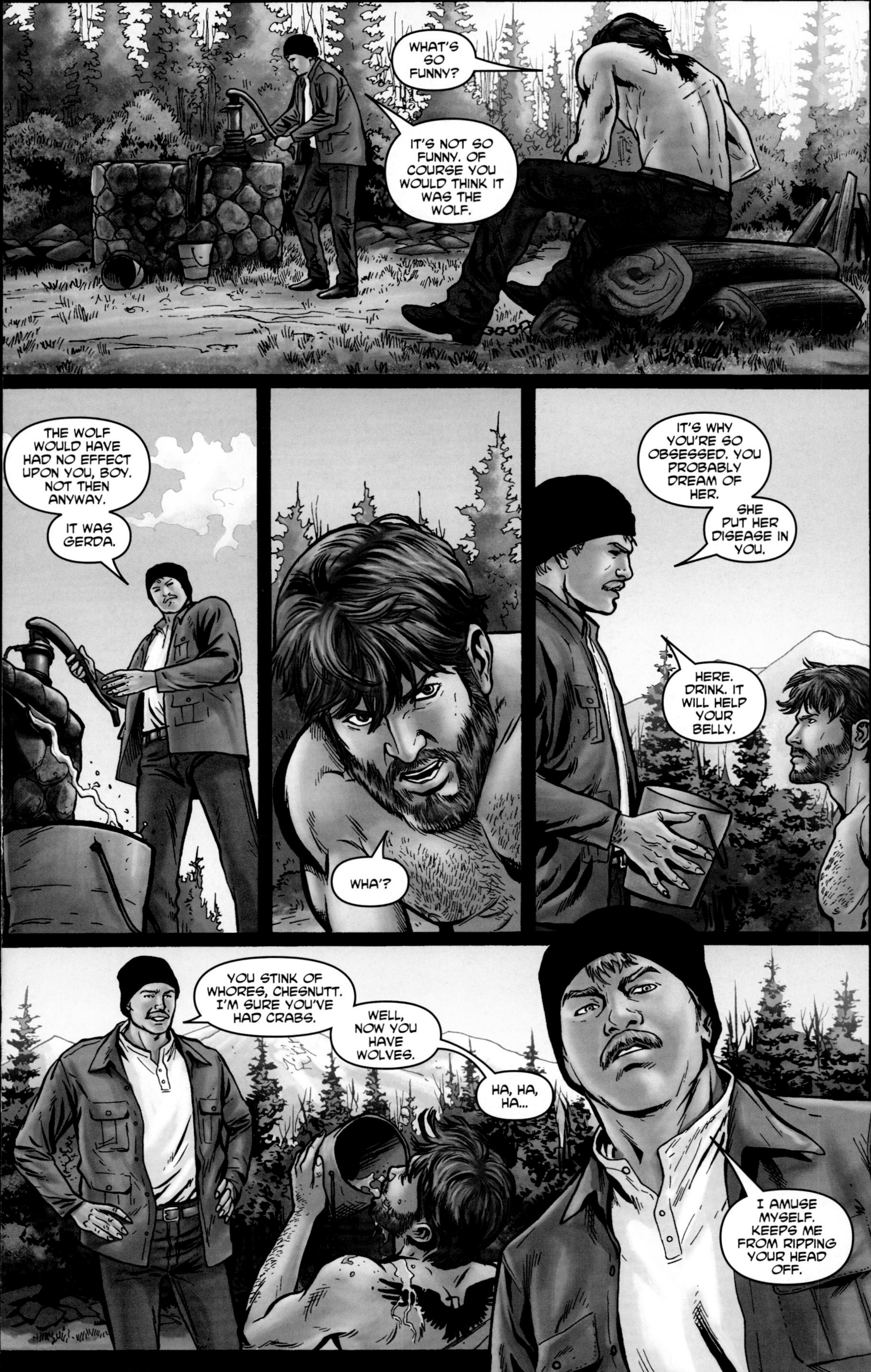
WHAT'S SO FUNNY?
IT'S NOT SO FUNNY. OF COURSE YOU WOULD THINK IT WAS THE WOLF.
THE WOLF WOULD HAVE HAD NO EFFECT UPON YOU, BOY. NOT THEN ANYWAY.
IT WAS GERDA.
WHA'?
IT'S WHY YOU'RE SO OBSESSED. YOU PROBABLY DREAM OF HER.
SHE PUT HER DISEASE IN YOU.
HERE. DRINK. IT WILL HELP YOUR BELLY.
YOU STINK OF WHORES, CHESNUTT. I'M SURE YOU'VE HAD CRABS.
WELL, NOW YOU HAVE WOLVES.
HA, HA, HA...
I AMUSE MYSELF. KEEPS ME FROM RIPPING YOUR HEAD OFF.

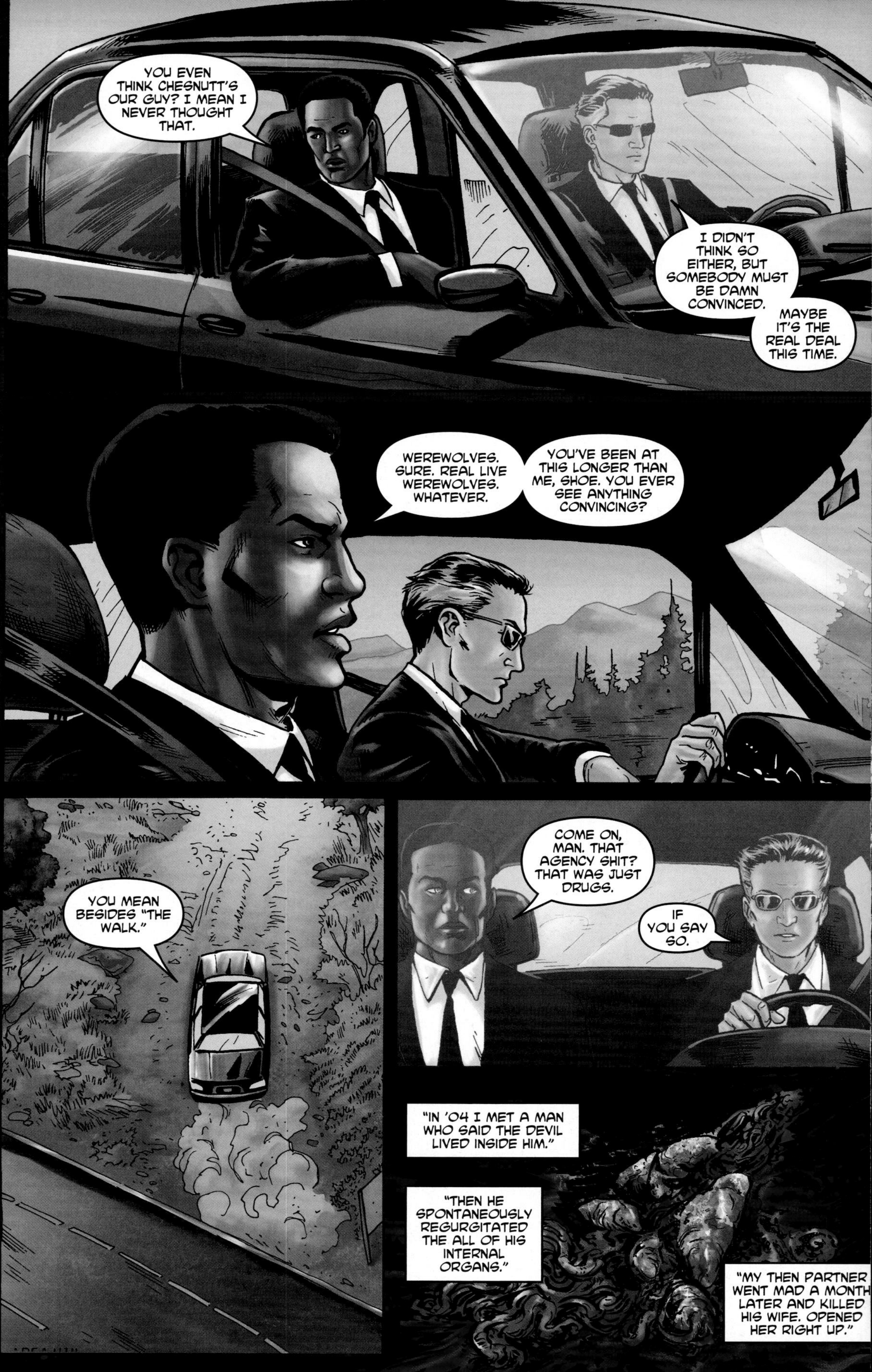
YOU EVEN THINK CHESNUTT'S OUR GUY? I MEAN I NEVER THOUGHT THAT.
I DIDN'T THINK SO EITHER, BUT SOMEBODY MUST BE DAMN CONVINCED.
MAYBE IT'S THE REAL DEAL THIS TIME.
WEREWOLVES. SURE. REAL LIVE WEREWOLVES. WHATEVER.
YOU'VE BEEN AT THIS LONGER THAN ME, SHOE. YOU EVER SEE ANYTHING CONVINCING?
YOU MEAN BESIDES "THE WALK."
COME ON, MAN. THAT AGENCY SHIT? THAT WAS JUST DRUGS.
IF YOU SAY SO.
"IN '04 I MET A MAN WHO SAID THE DEVIL LIVED INSIDE HIM."
"THEN HE SPONTANEOUSLY REGURGITATED THE ALL OF HIS INTERNAL ORGANS."
"MY THEN PARTNER WENT MAD A MONTH LATER AND KILLED HIS WIFE. OPENED HER RIGHT UP."

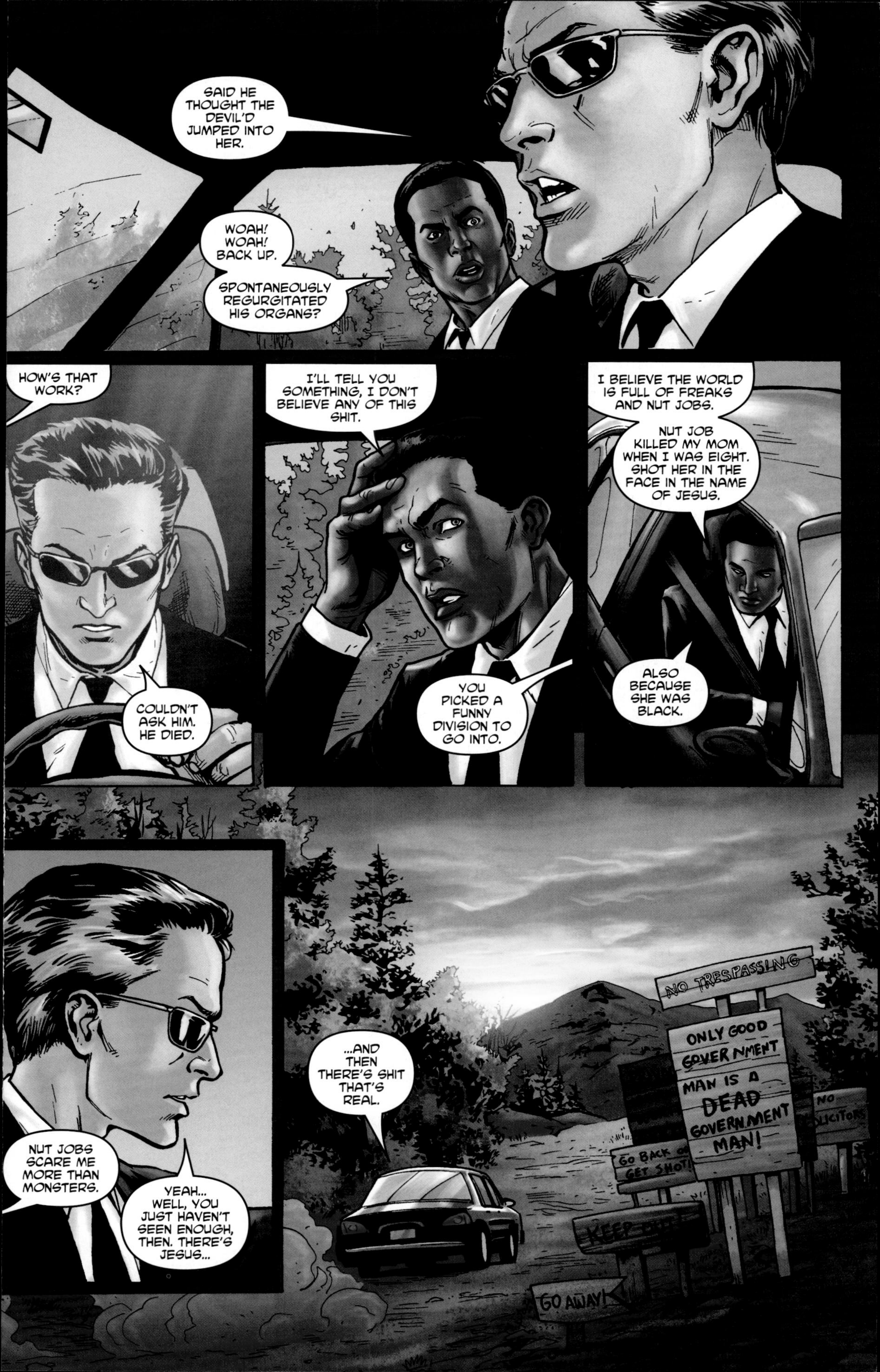
SAID HE THOUGHT THE DEVIL'D JUMPED INTO HER.
WOAH! WOAH! BACK UP.
SPONTANEOUSLY REGURGITATED HIS ORGANS?
HOW'S THAT WORK?
COULDN'T ASK HIM. HE DIED.
I'LL TELL YOU SOMETHING, I DON'T BELIEVE ANY OF THIS SHIT.
YOU PICKED A FUNNY DIVISION TO GO INTO.
I BELIEVE THE WORLD IS FULL OF FREAKS AND NUT JOBS.
NUT JOB KILLED MY MOM WHEN I WAS EIGHT. SHOT HER IN THE FACE IN THE NAME OF JESUS.
ALSO BECAUSE SHE WAS BLACK.
NUT JOBS SCARE ME MORE THAN MONSTERS.
YEAH... WELL, YOU JUST HAVEN'T SEEN ENOUGH, THEN. THERE'S JESUS...
...AND THEN THERE'S SHIT THAT'S REAL.
NO TRESPASSING
ONLY GOOD GOVERNMENT MAN IS A DEAD GOVERNMENT MAN!
GO AWAY!

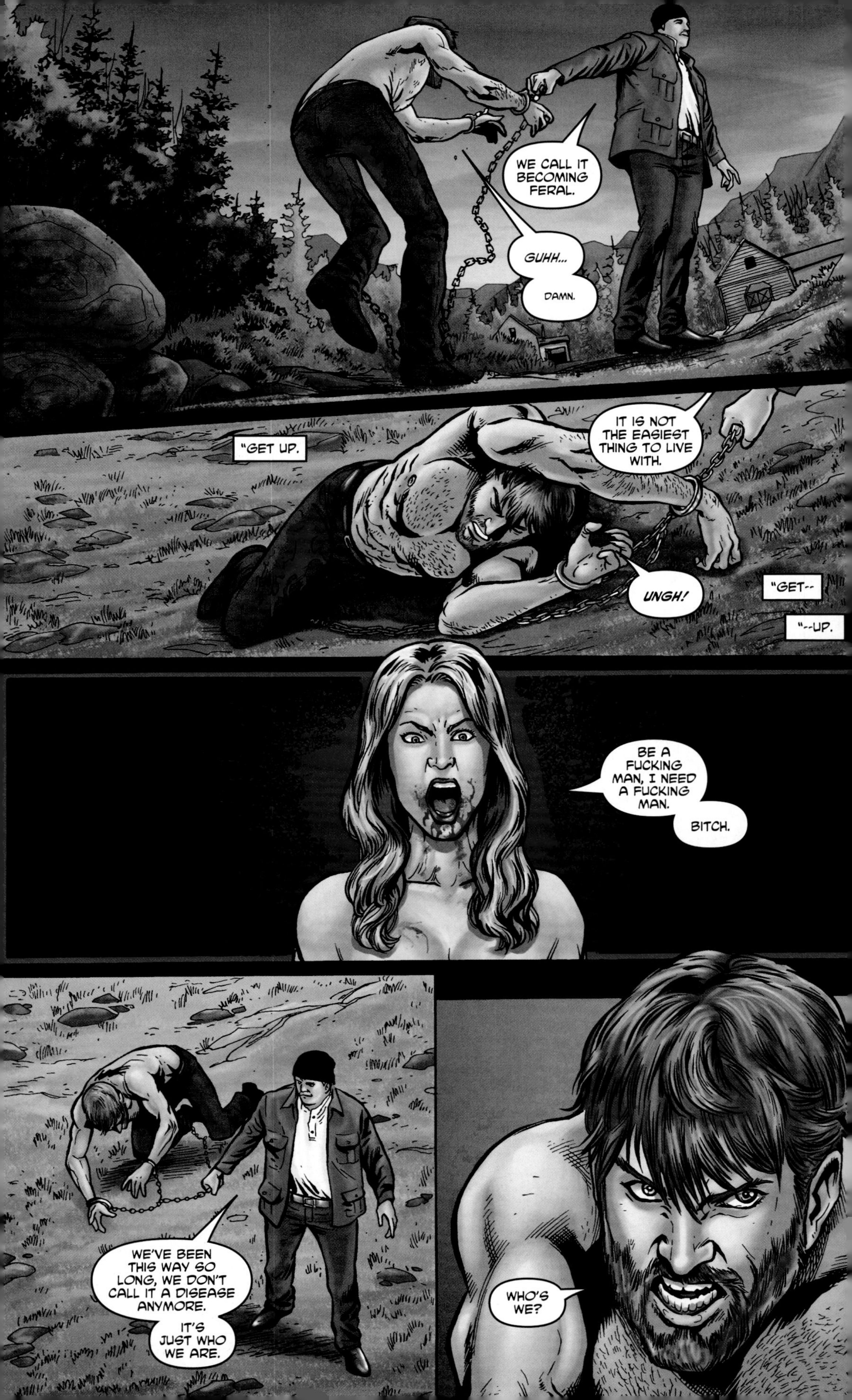
WE CALL IT BECOMING FERAL.
GUHH...
DAMN.
"GET UP.
IT IS NOT THE EASIEST THING TO LIVE WITH.
UNGH!
"GET--
"--UP.
BE A FUCKING MAN, I NEED A FUCKING MAN.
BITCH.
WE'VE BEEN THIS WAY SO LONG, WE DON'T CALL IT A DISEASE ANYMORE.
IT'S JUST WHO WE ARE.
WHO'S WE?

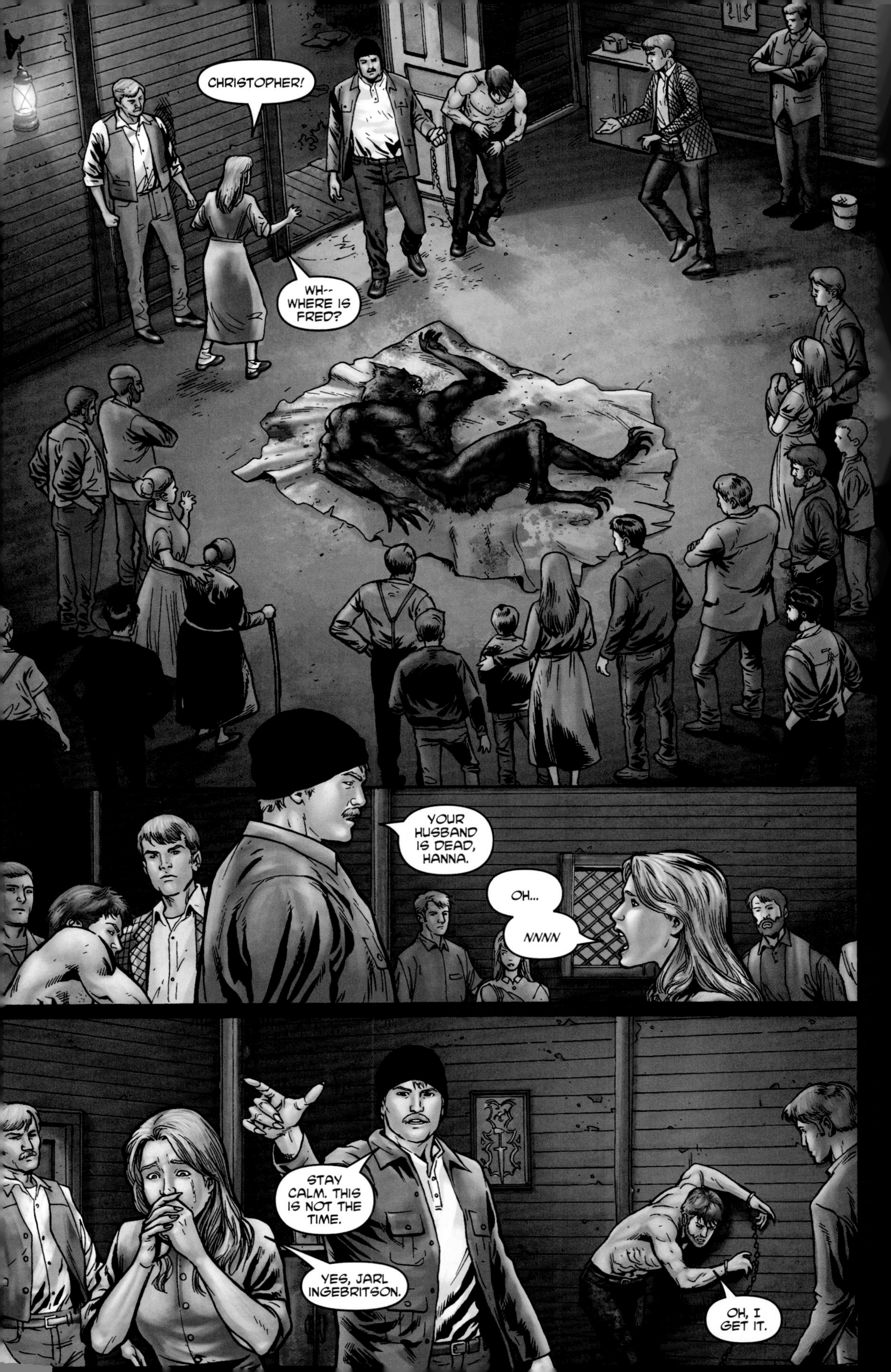
CHRISTOPHER!
WH-- WHERE IS FRED?
YOUR HUSBAND IS DEAD, HANNA.
OH...
NNNN
STAY CALM. THIS IS NOT THE TIME.
YES, JARL INGEBRITSON.
OH, I GET IT.

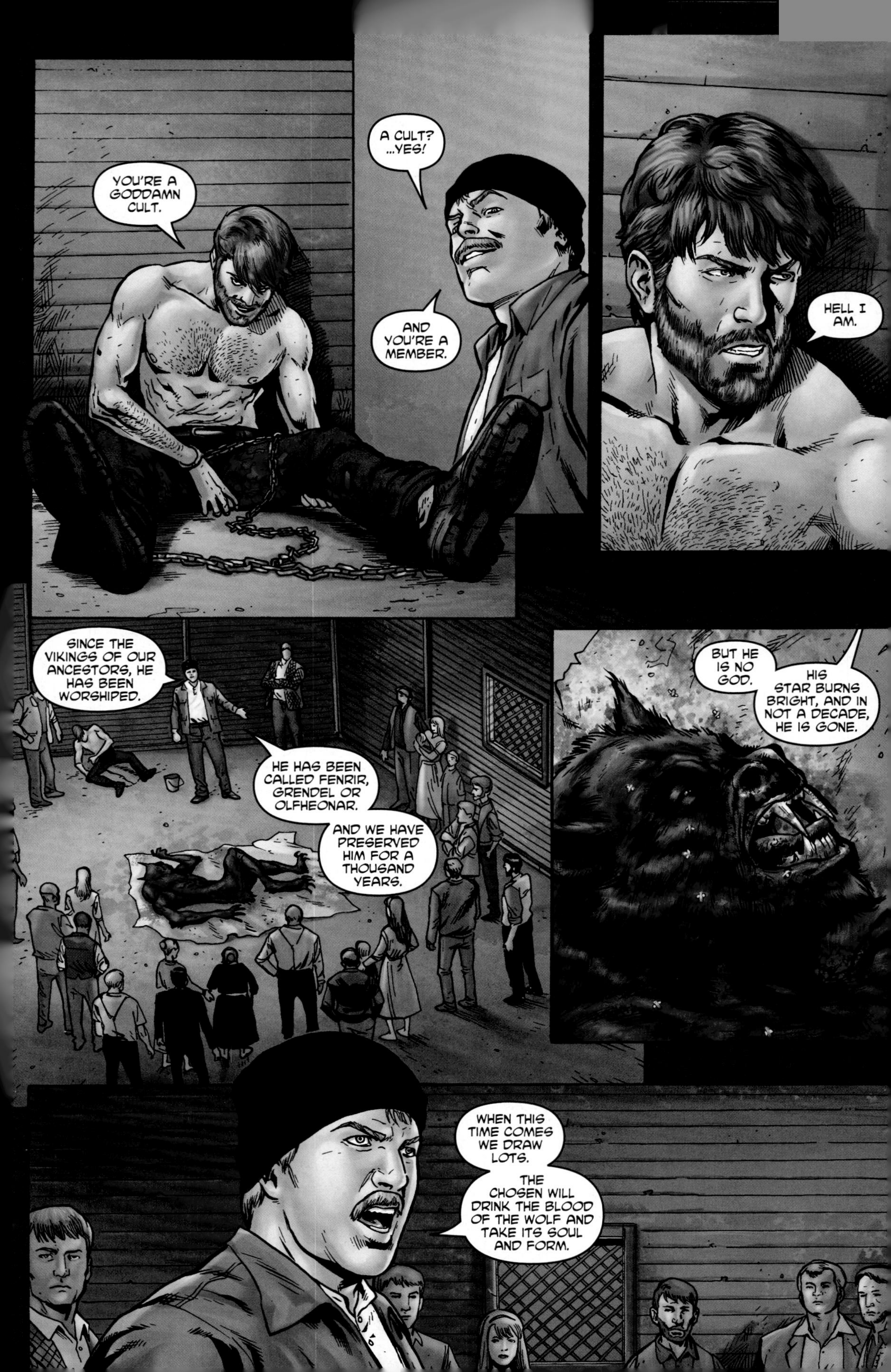
YOU'RE A GODDAMN CULT.
A CULT? ...YES!
AND YOU'RE A MEMBER.
HELL I AM.
SINCE THE VIKINGS OF OUR ANCESTORS, HE HAS BEEN WORSHIPED.
HE HAS BEEN CALLED FENRIR, GRENDEL OR OLFHEONAR.
AND WE HAVE PRESERVED HIM FOR A THOUSAND YEARS.
BUT HE IS NO GOD.
HIS STAR BURNS BRIGHT, AND IN NOT A DECADE, HE IS GONE.
WHEN THIS TIME COMES WE DRAW LOTS.
THE CHOSEN WILL DRINK THE BLOOD OF THE WOLF AND TAKE ITS SOUL AND FORM.

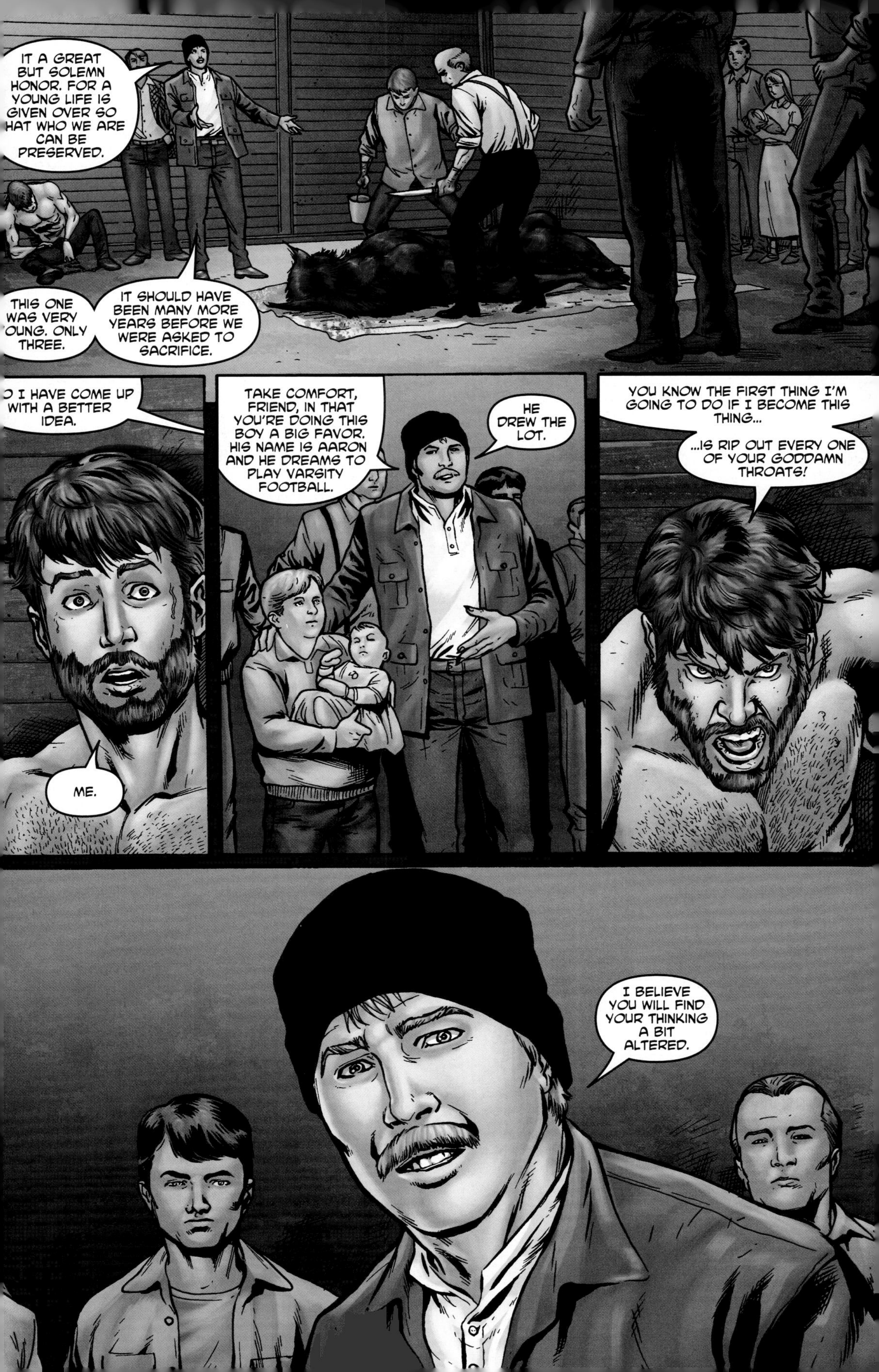
IT A GREAT BUT SOLEMN HONOR. FOR A YOUNG LIFE IS GIVEN OVER SO HAT WHO WE ARE CAN BE PRESERVED.
THIS ONE WAS VERY OUNG. ONLY THREE.
IT SHOULD HAVE BEEN MANY MORE YEARS BEFORE WE WERE ASKED TO SACRIFICE.
O I HAVE COME UP WITH A BETTER IDEA.
ME.
HE DREW THE LOT.
TAKE COMFORT, FRIEND, IN THAT YOU'RE DOING THIS BOY A BIG FAVOR. HIS NAME IS AARON AND HE DREAMS TO PLAY VARSITY FOOTBALL.
YOU KNOW THE FIRST THING I'M GOING TO DO IF I BECOME THIS THING...
...IS RIP OUT EVERY ONE OF YOUR GODDAMN THROATS!
I BELIEVE YOU WILL FIND YOUR THINKING A BIT ALTERED.

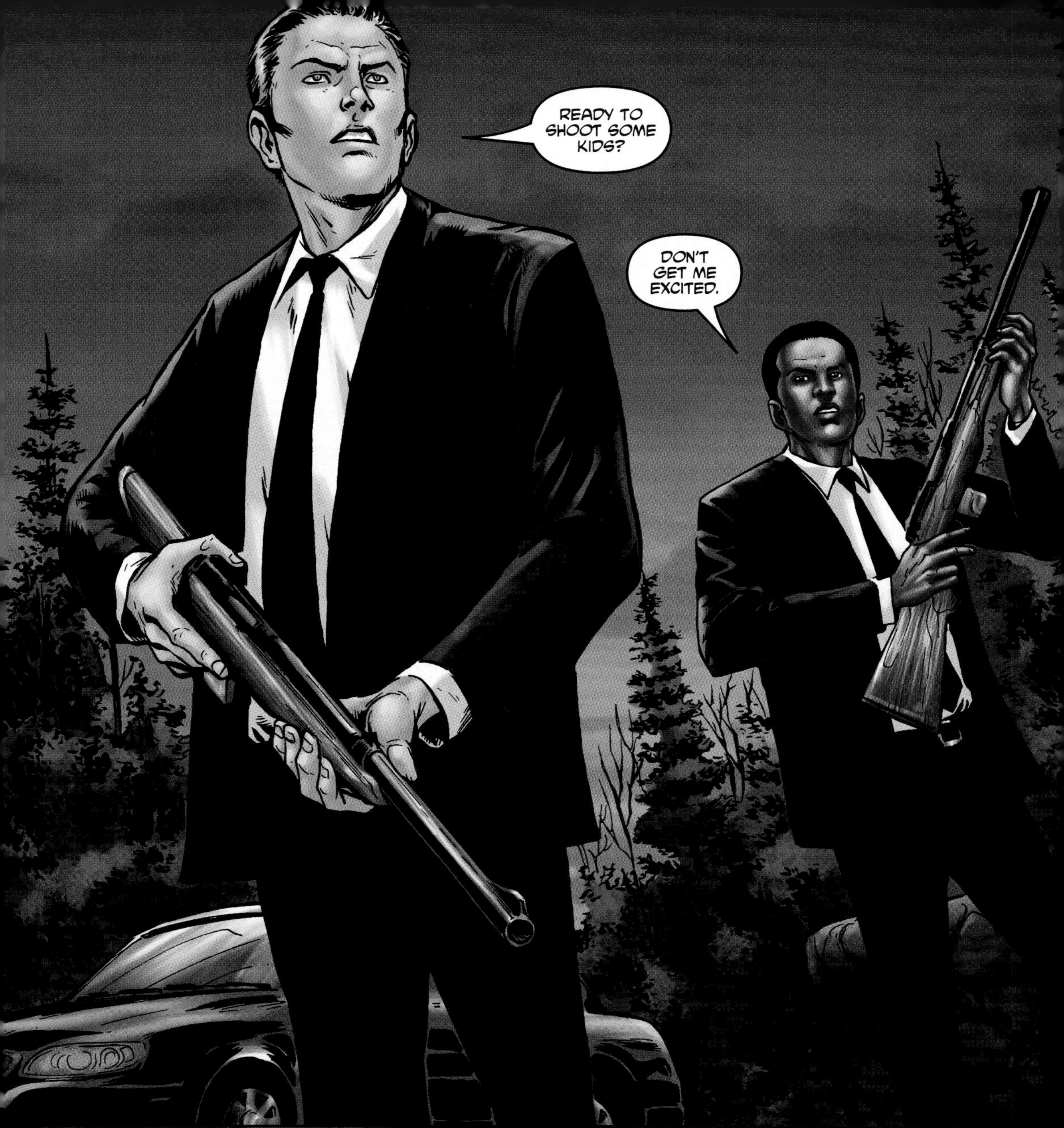
READY TO SHOOT SOME KIDS?
DON'T GET ME EXCITED.

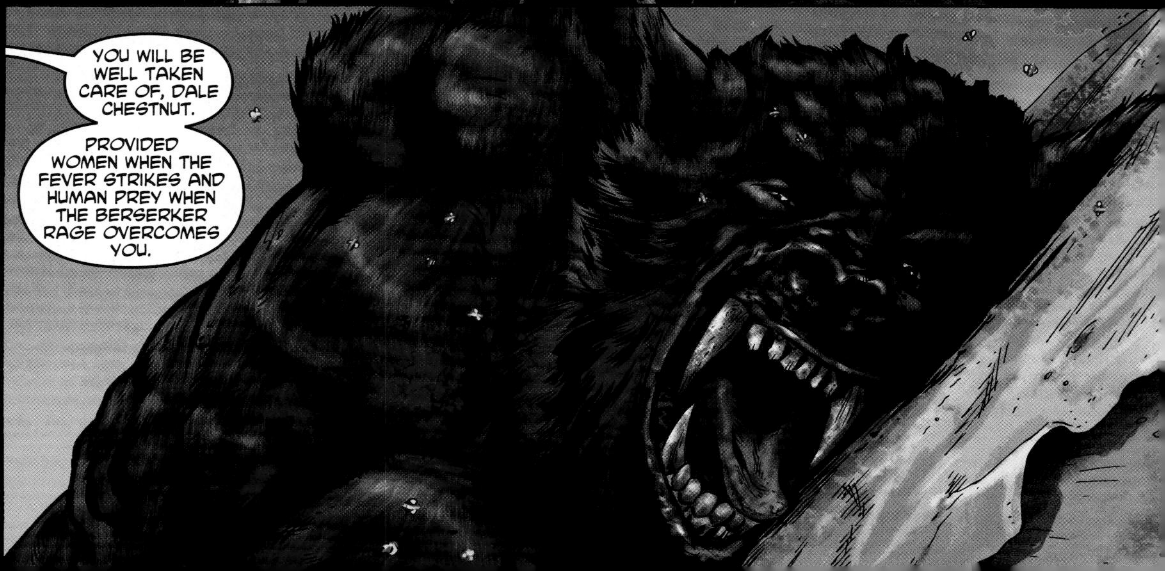
YOU WILL BE WELL TAKEN CARE OF, DALE CHESTNUT.
PROVIDED WOMEN WHEN THE FEVER STRIKES AND HUMAN PREY WHEN THE BERSERKER RAGE OVERCOMES YOU.

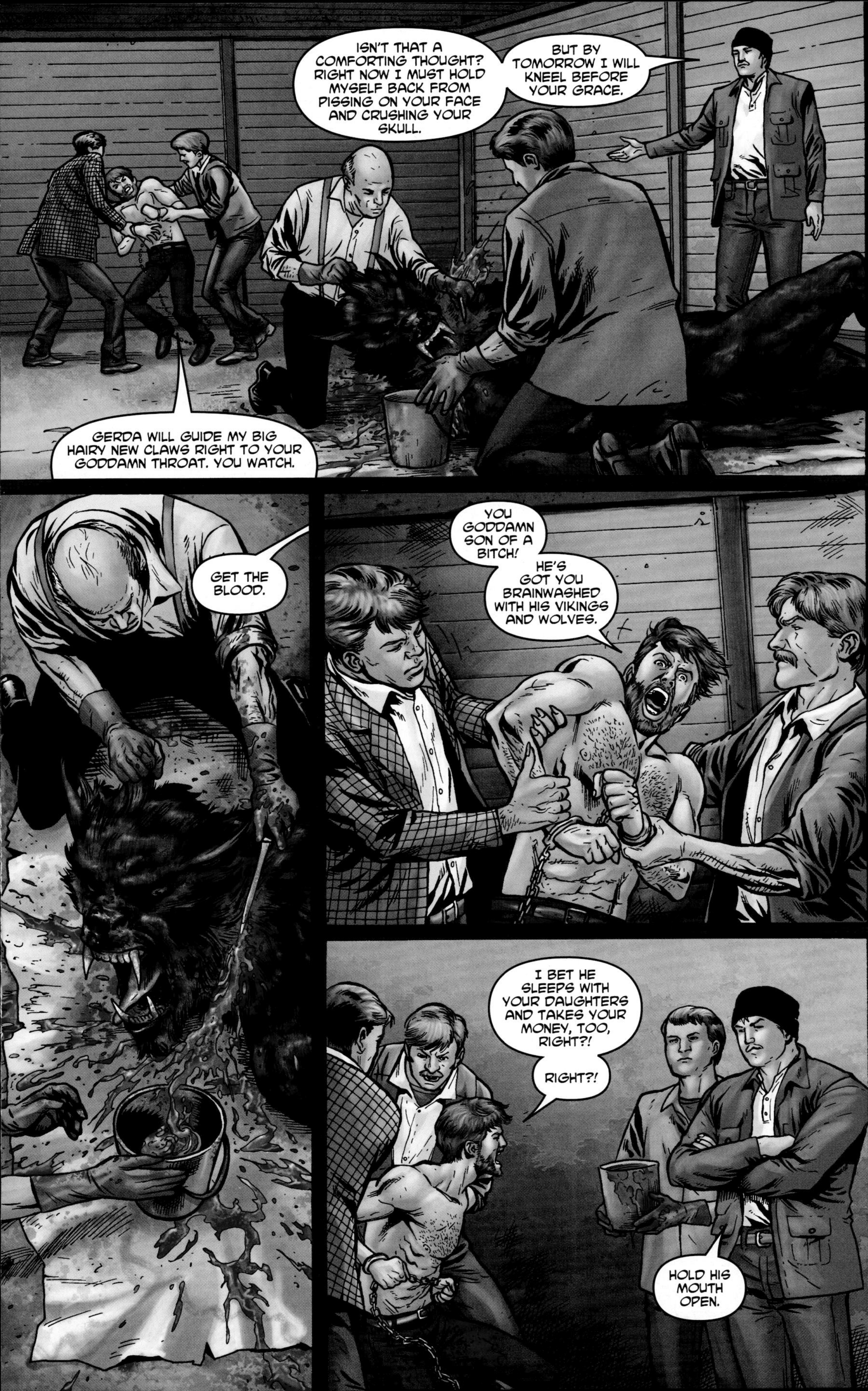
ISN'T THAT A COMFORTING THOUGHT? RIGHT NOW I MUST HOLD MYSELF BACK FROM PISSING ON YOUR FACE AND CRUSHING YOUR SKULL.
BUT BY TOMORROW I WILL KNEEL BEFORE YOUR GRACE.
GERDA WILL GUIDE MY BIG HAIRY NEW CLAWS RIGHT TO YOUR GODDAMN THROAT. YOU WATCH.
GET THE BLOOD.
YOU GODDAMN SON OF A BITCH!
HE'S GOT YOU BRAINWASHED WITH HIS VIKINGS AND WOLVES.
I BET HE SLEEPS WITH YOUR DAUGHTERS AND TAKES YOUR MONEY, TOO, RIGHT?!
RIGHT?!
HOLD HIS MOUTH OPEN.

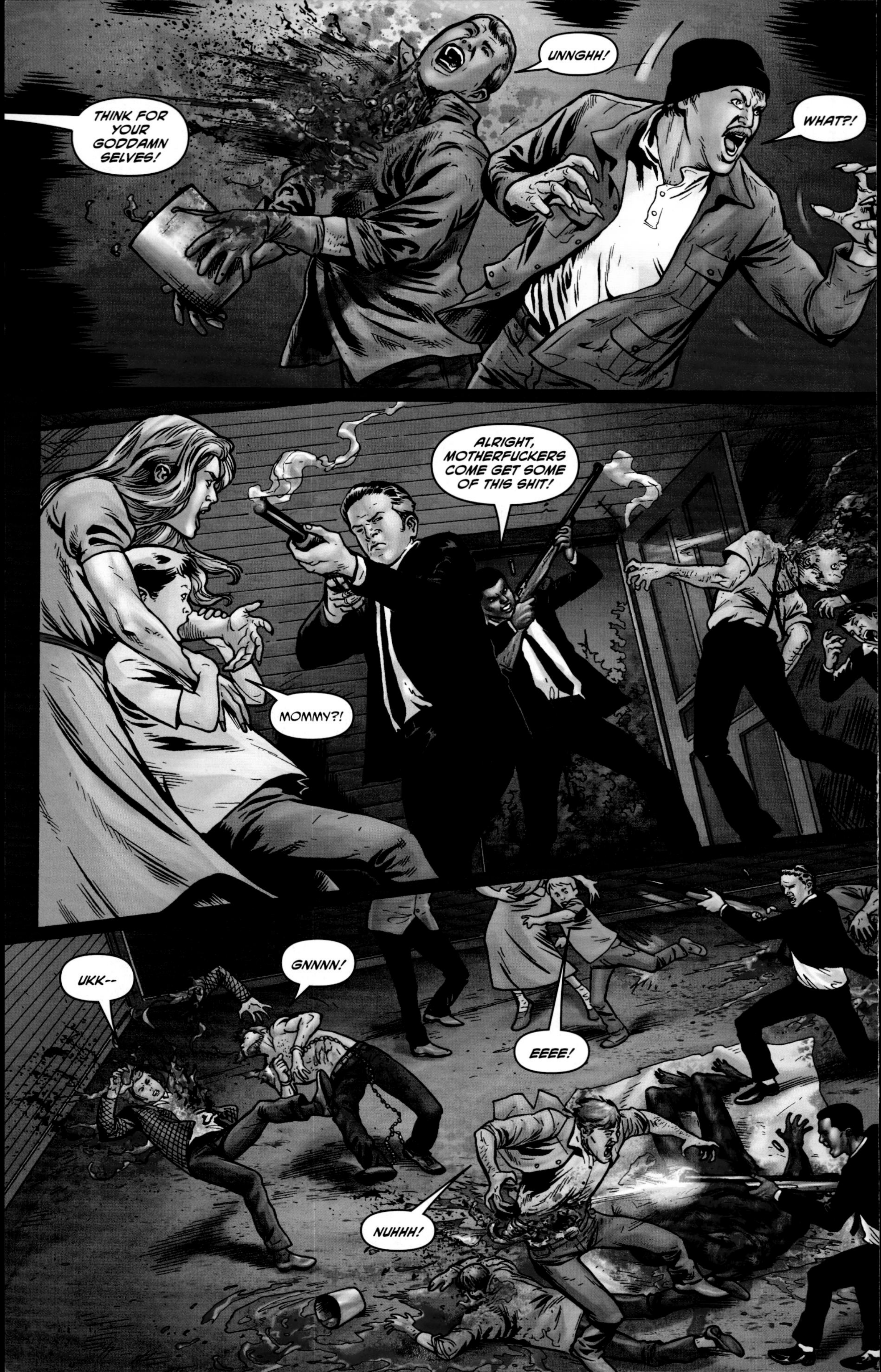
UNNGHH!
THINK FOR YOUR GODDAMN SELVES!
WHAT?!
ALRIGHT, MOTHERFUCKERS COME GET SOME OF THIS SHIT!
MOMMY?!
UKK--
GNNNN!
EEEE!
NUHHH!

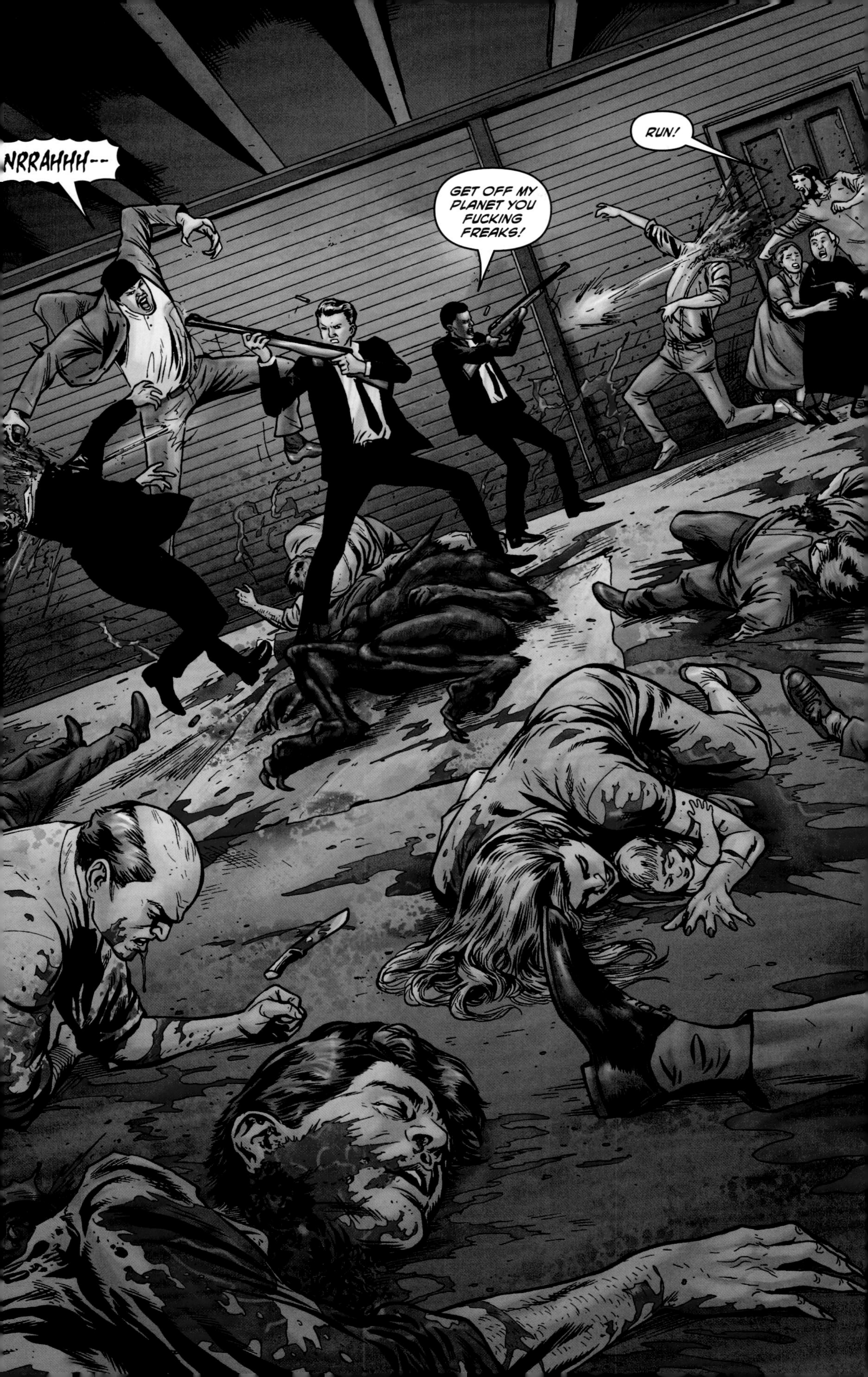
NRRAHHH--
GET OFF MY PLANET YOU FUCKING FREAKS!
RUN!

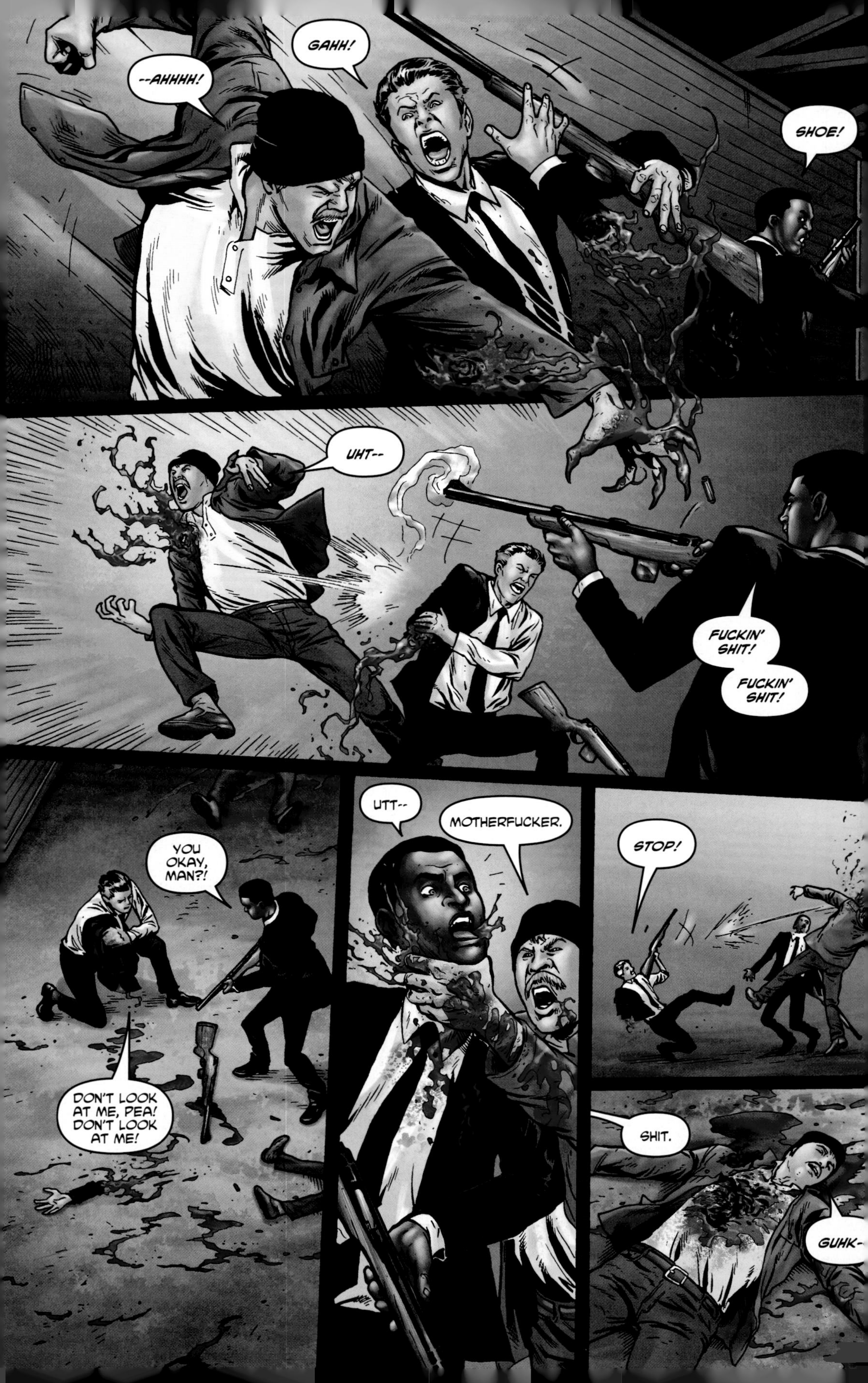
--AHHHH!
GAHH!
SHOE!
UHT--
FUCKIN' SHIT!
FUCKIN' SHIT!
YOU OKAY, MAN?!
DON'T LOOK AT ME, PEA! DON'T LOOK AT ME!
UTT--
MOTHERFUCKER.
STOP!
SHIT.
GUHK-

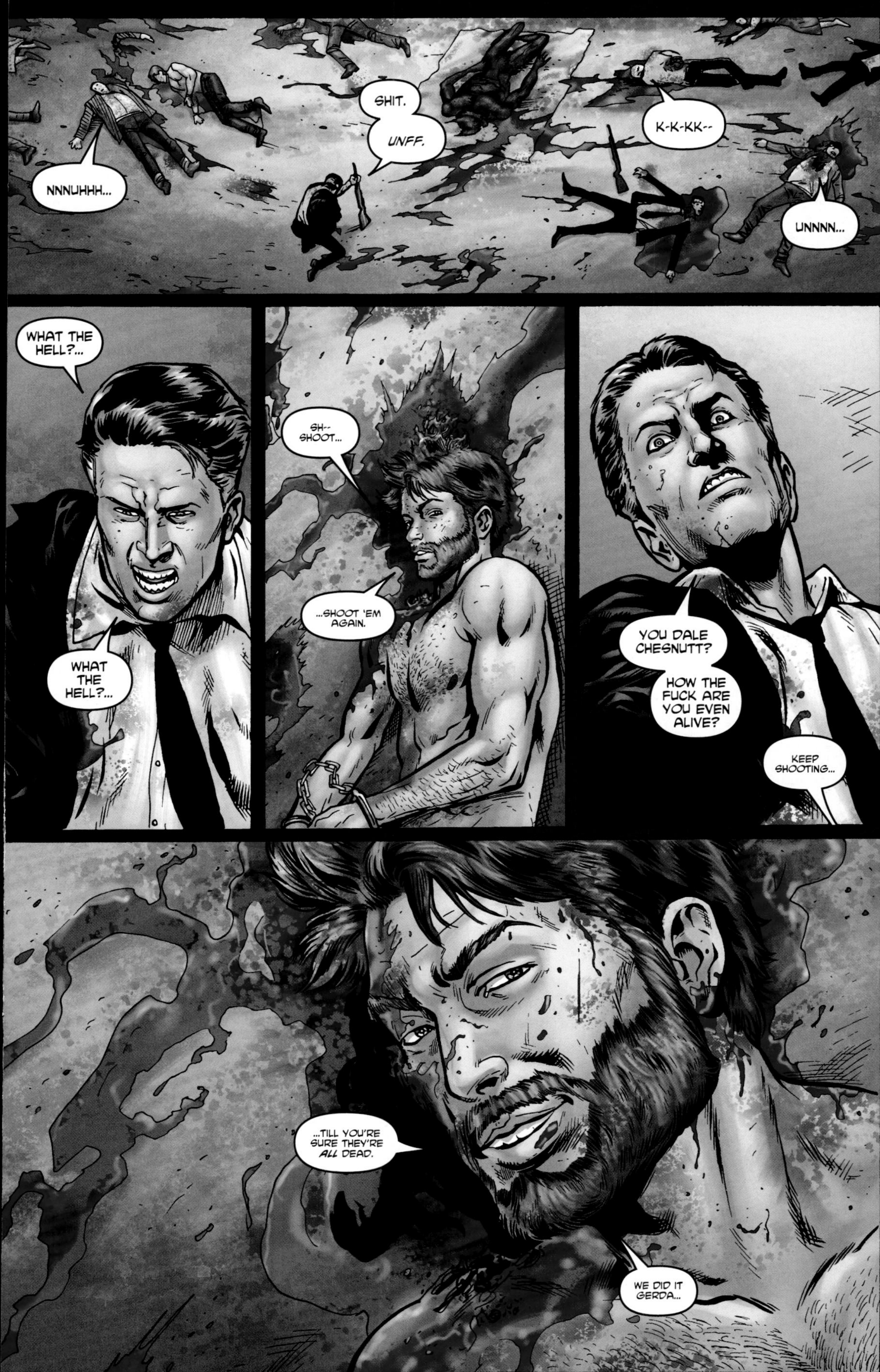
NNNUHHH...
SHIT.
UNFF.
K-K-KK--
UNNNN...
WHAT THE HELL?...
WHAT THE HELL?...
SH-- SHOOT...
...SHOOT 'EM AGAIN.
YOU DALE CHESNUTT?
HOW THE FUCK ARE YOU EVEN ALIVE?
KEEP SHOOTING...
...TILL YOU'RE SURE THEY'RE *ALL* DEAD.
WE DID IT GERDA...

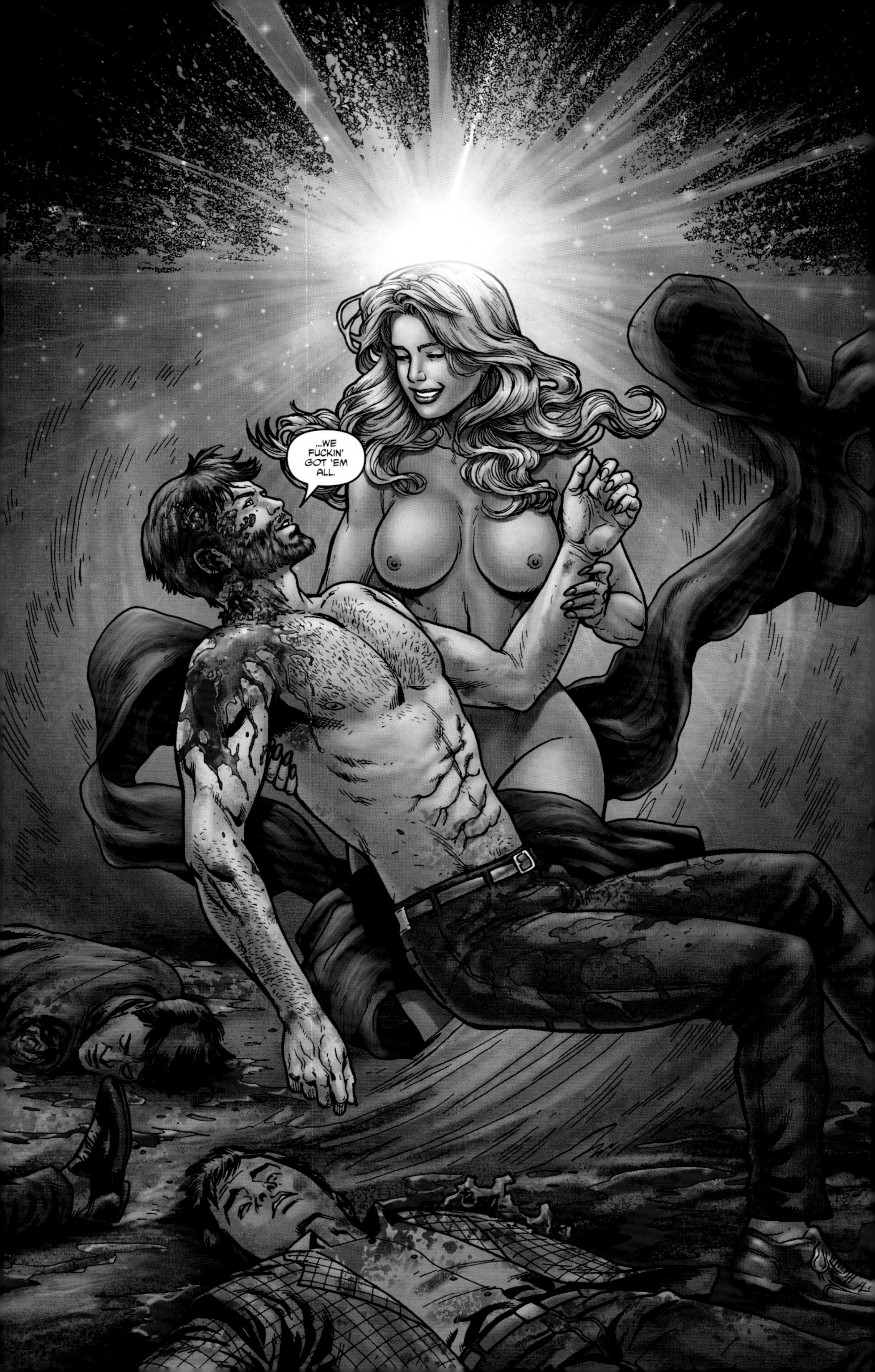
...WE FUCKIN' GOT 'EM ALL.

COVER GALLERY

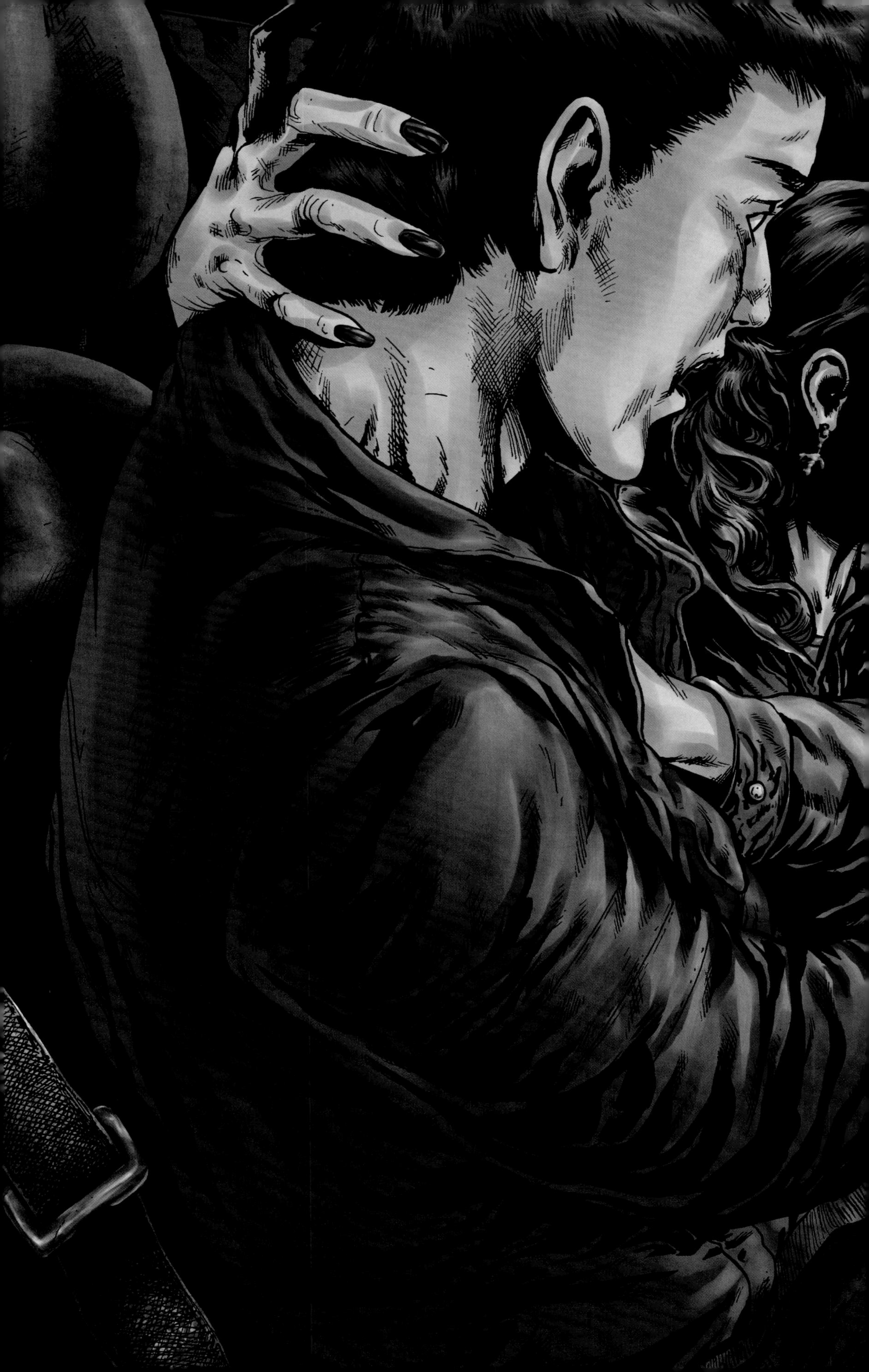

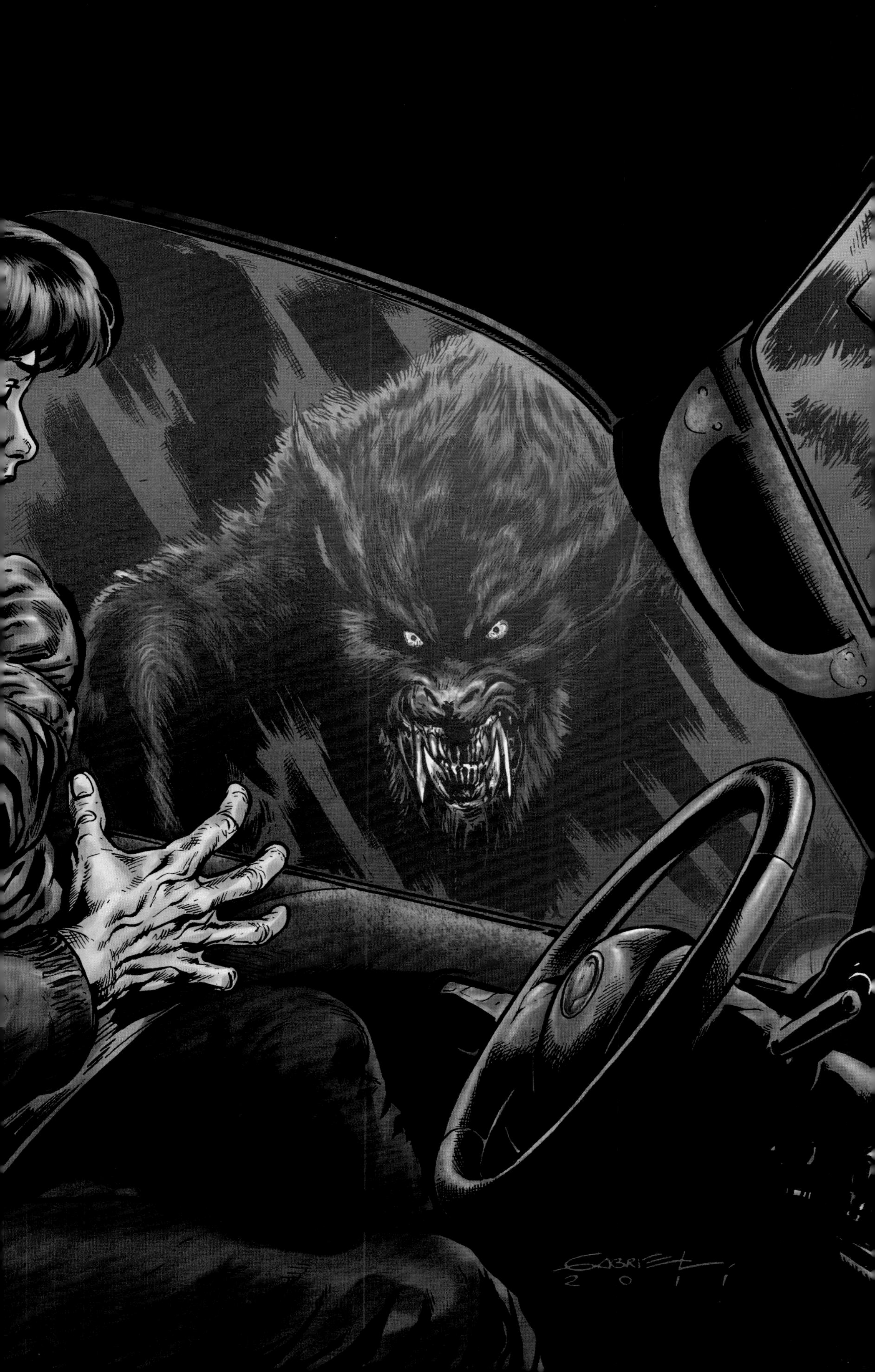
GABRIEL
2011

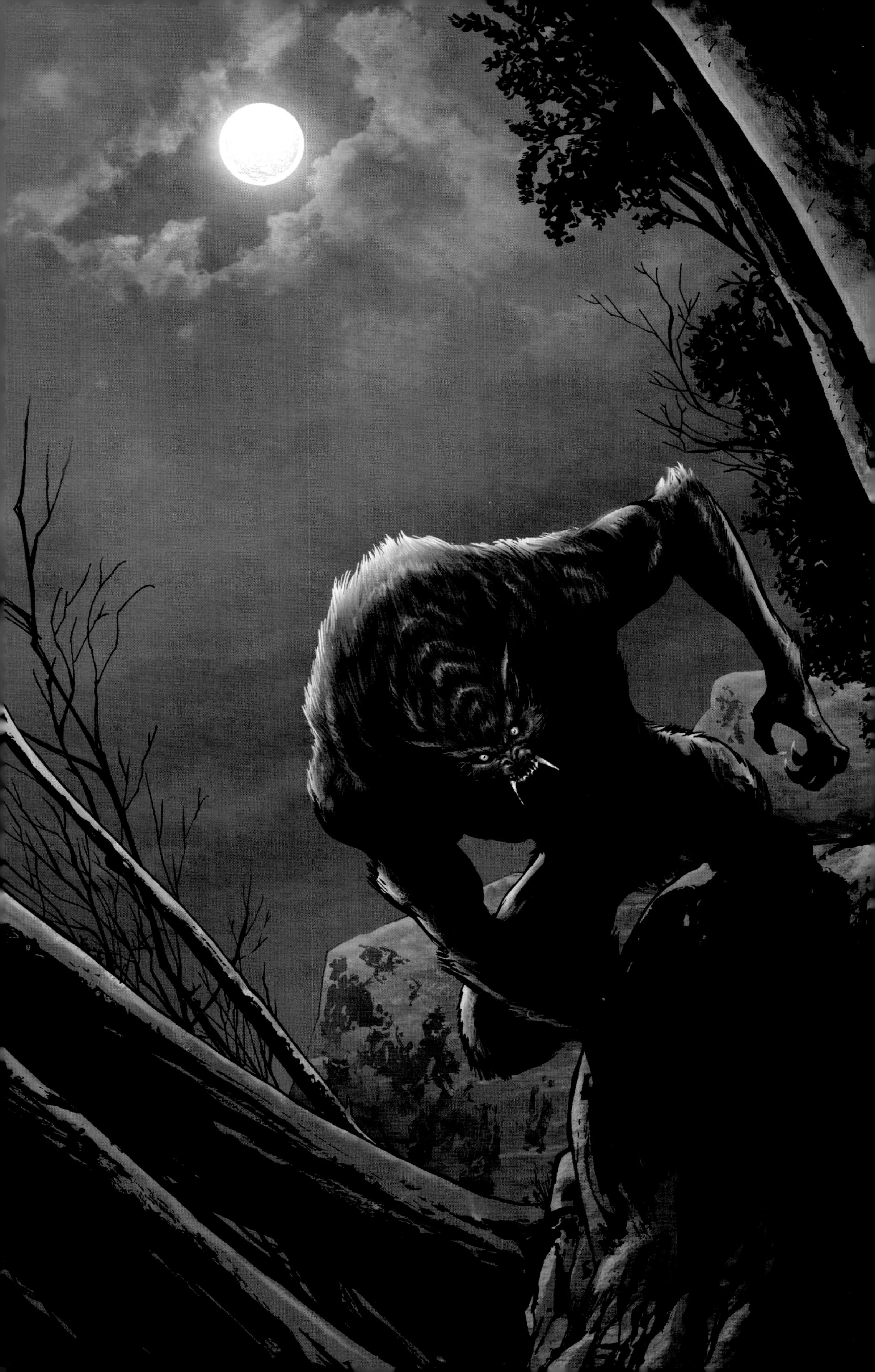

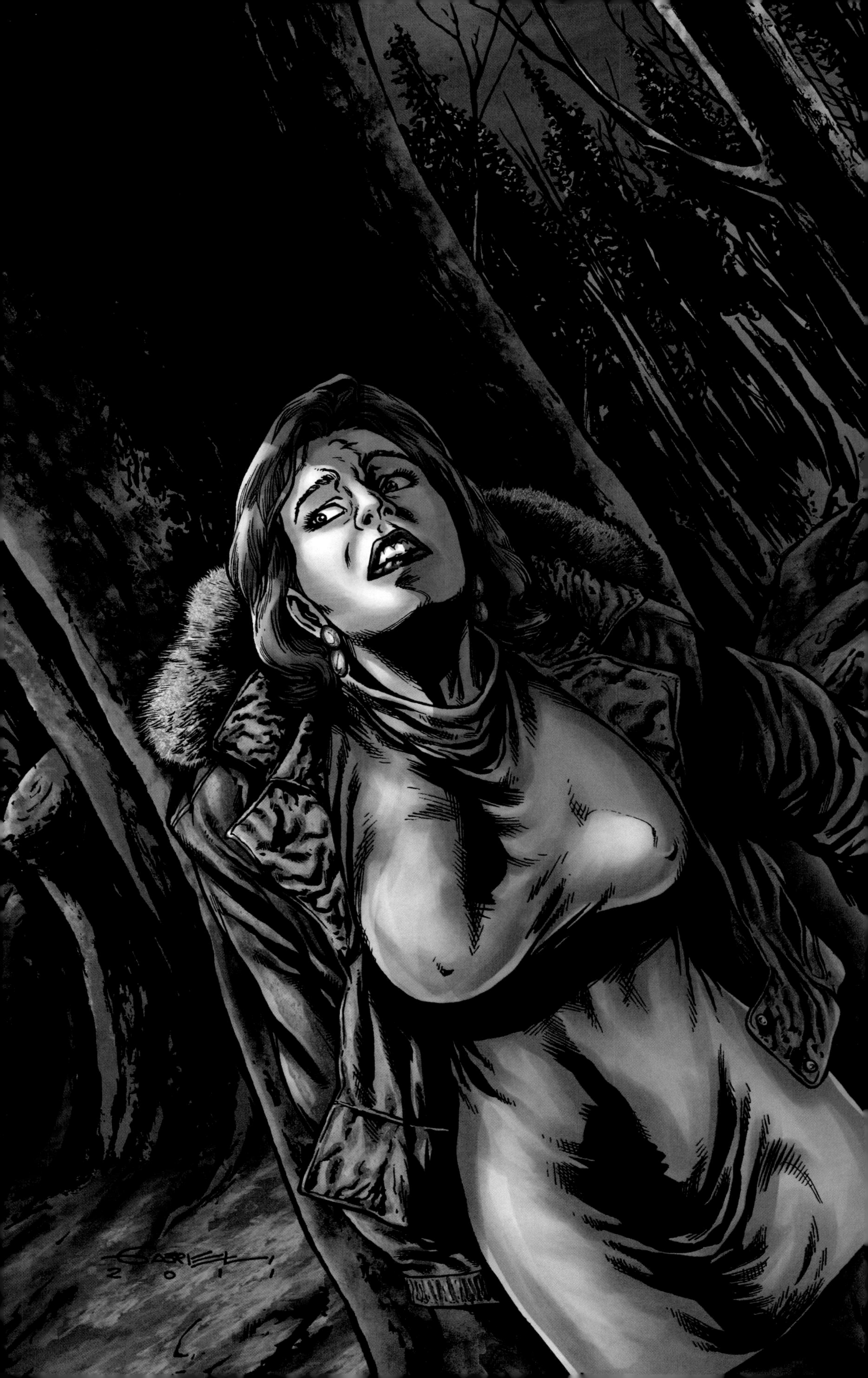
GABRIEL
2011

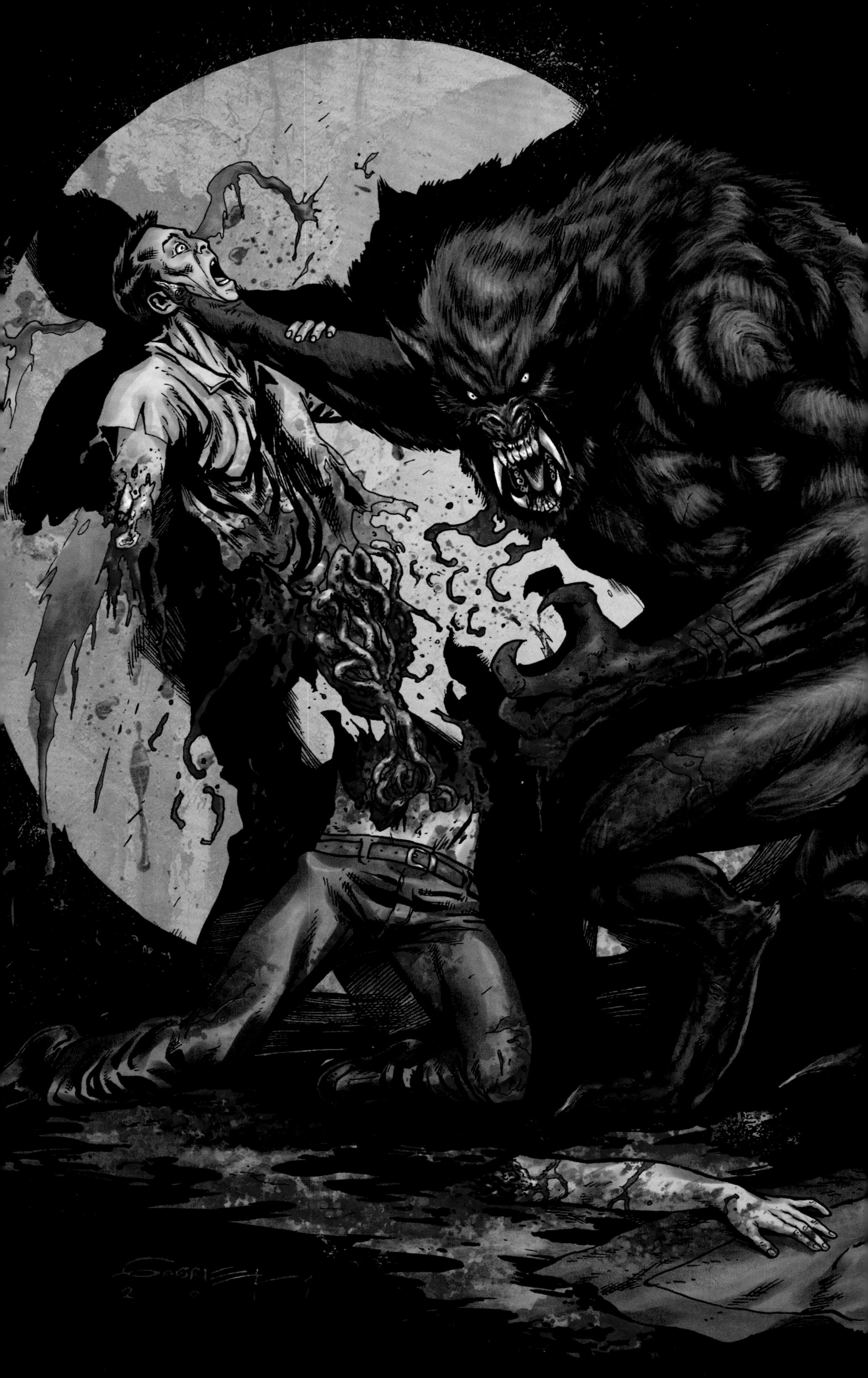

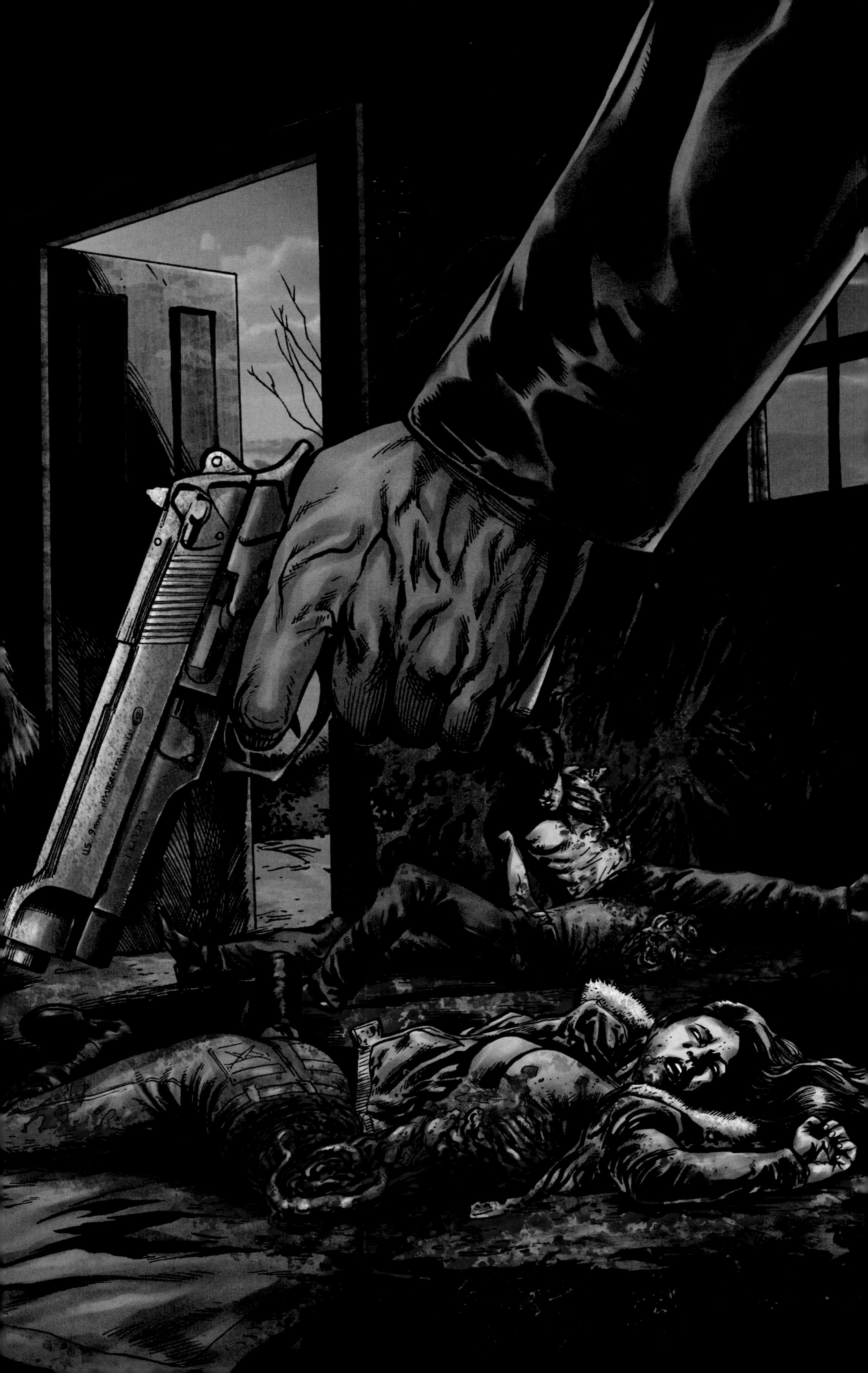

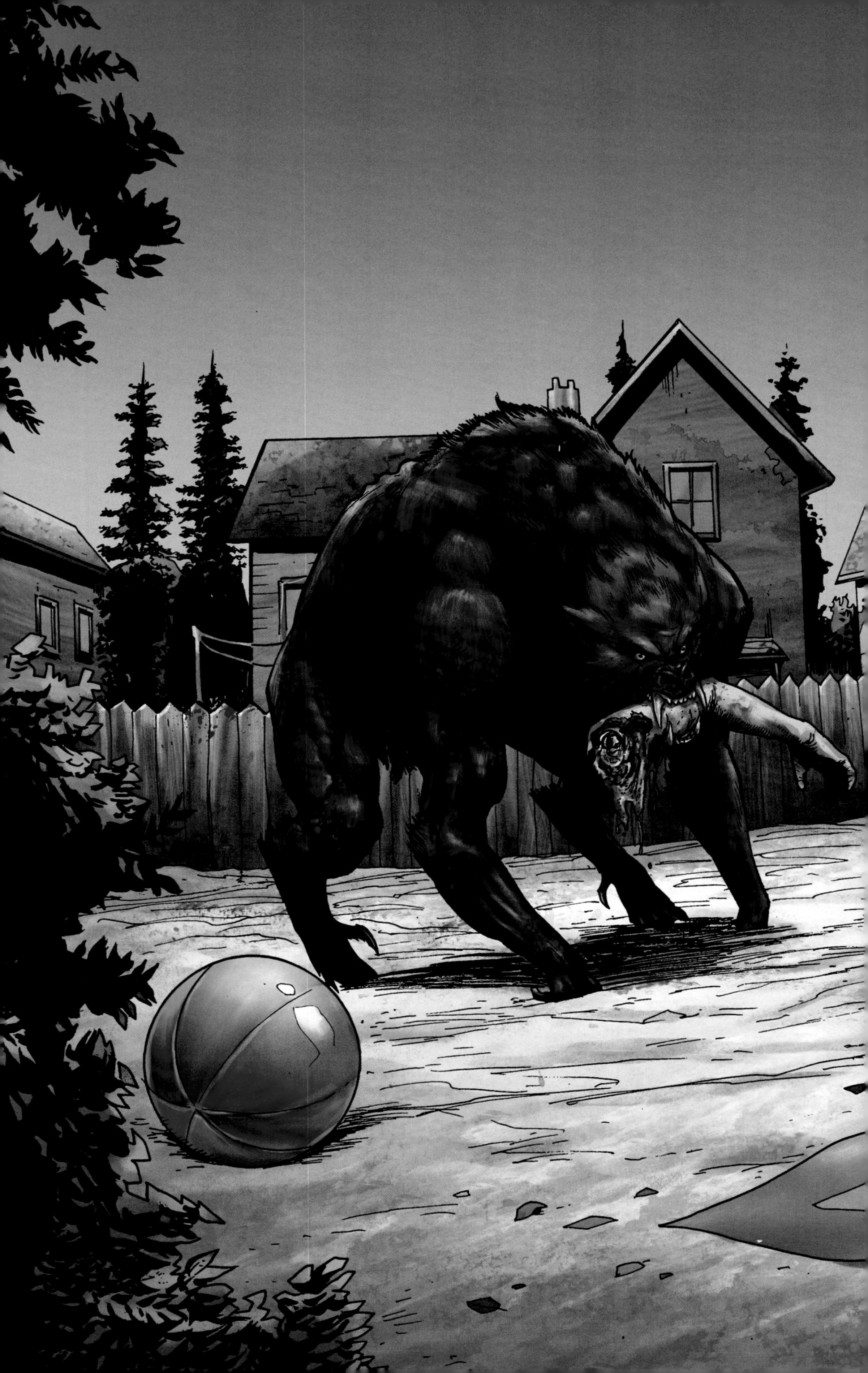

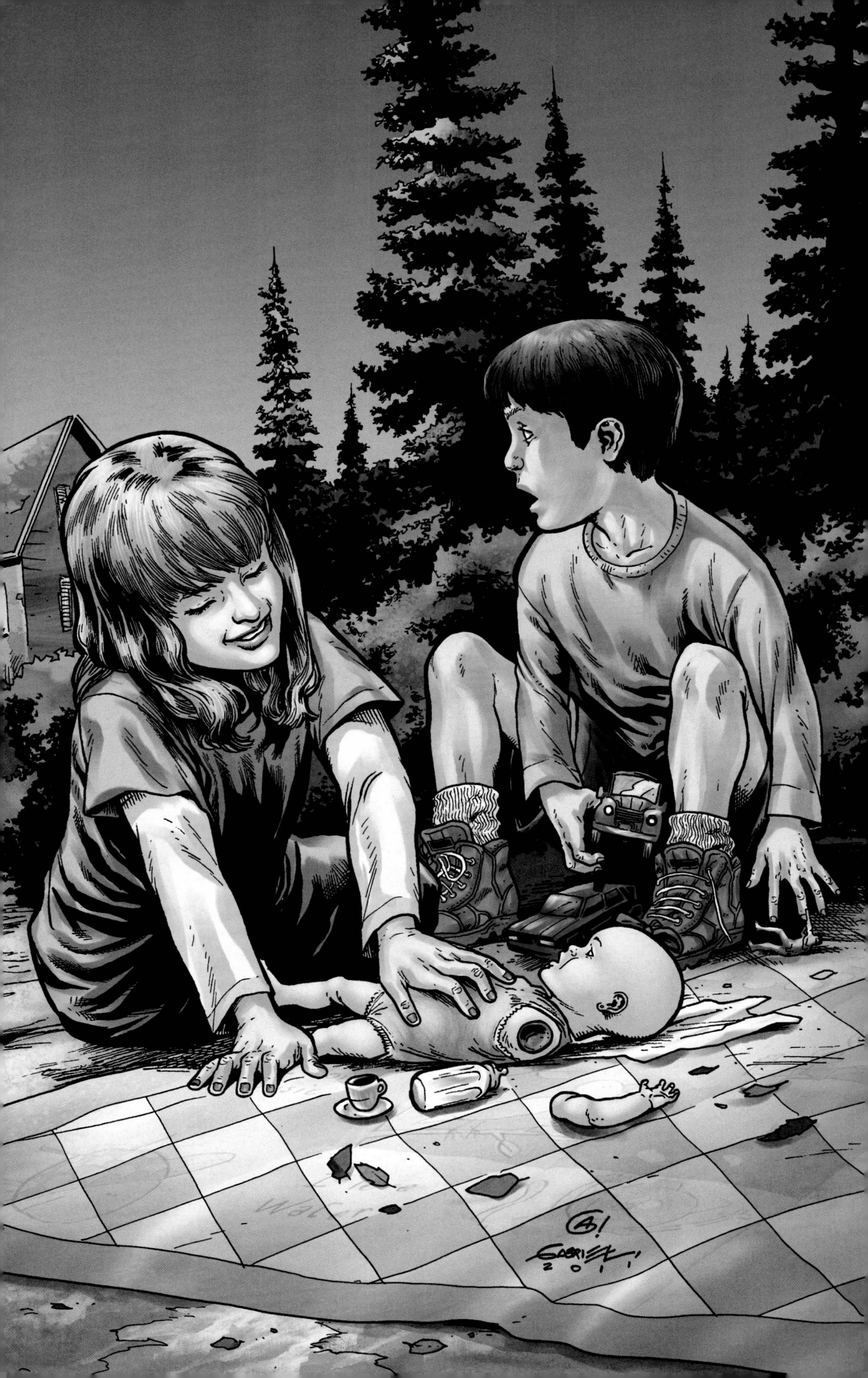
GABRIEL
2011

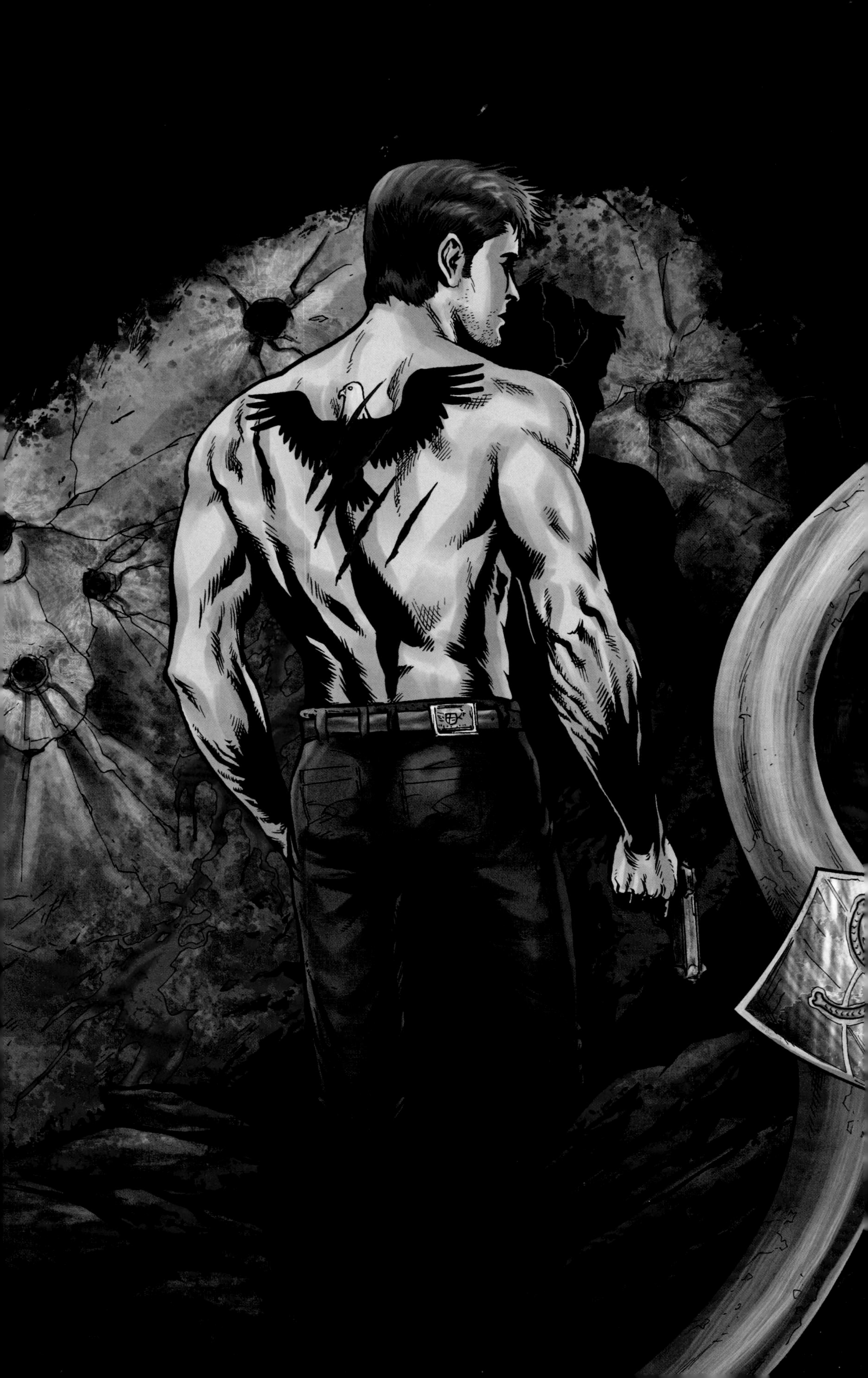

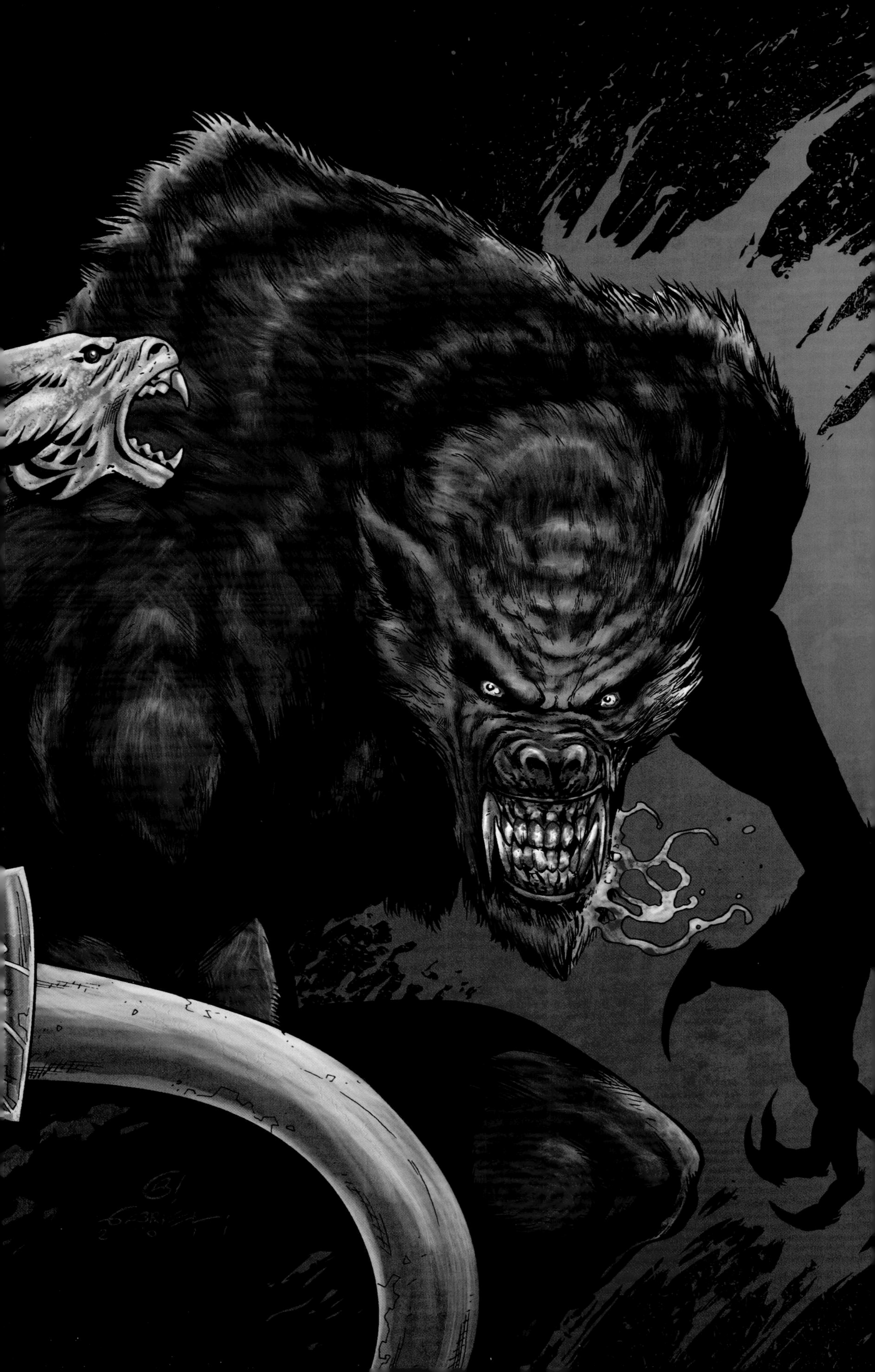

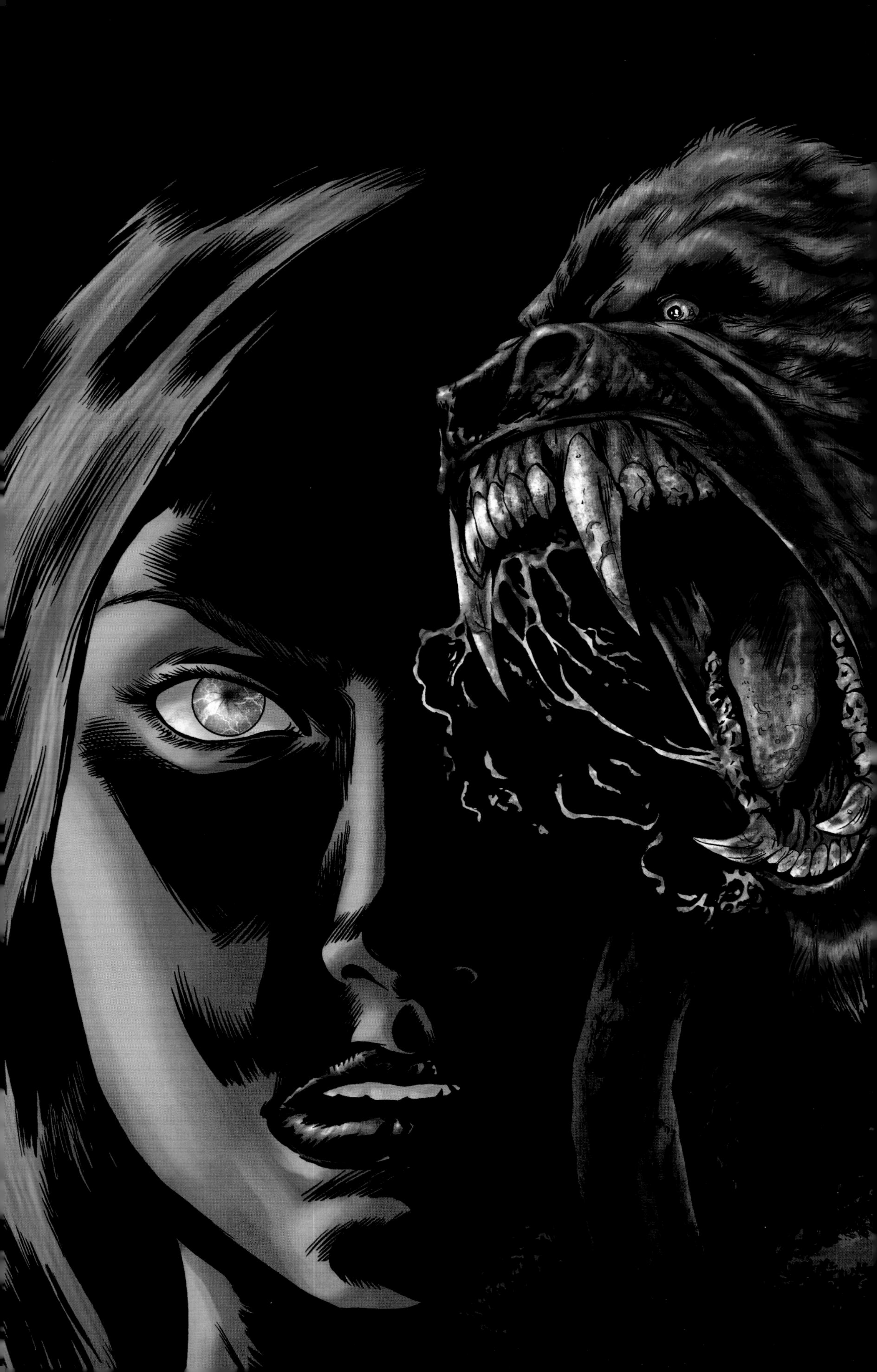

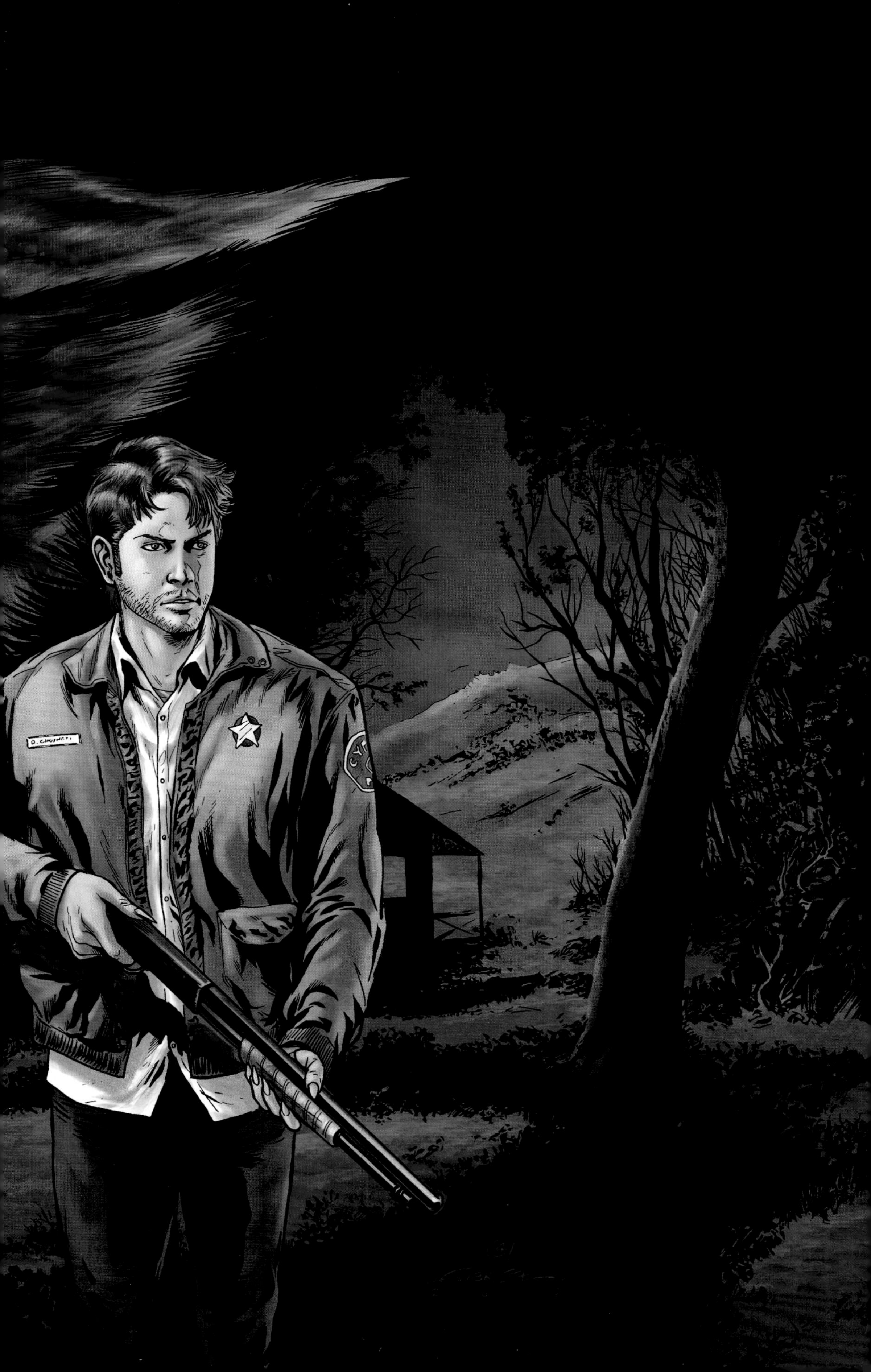

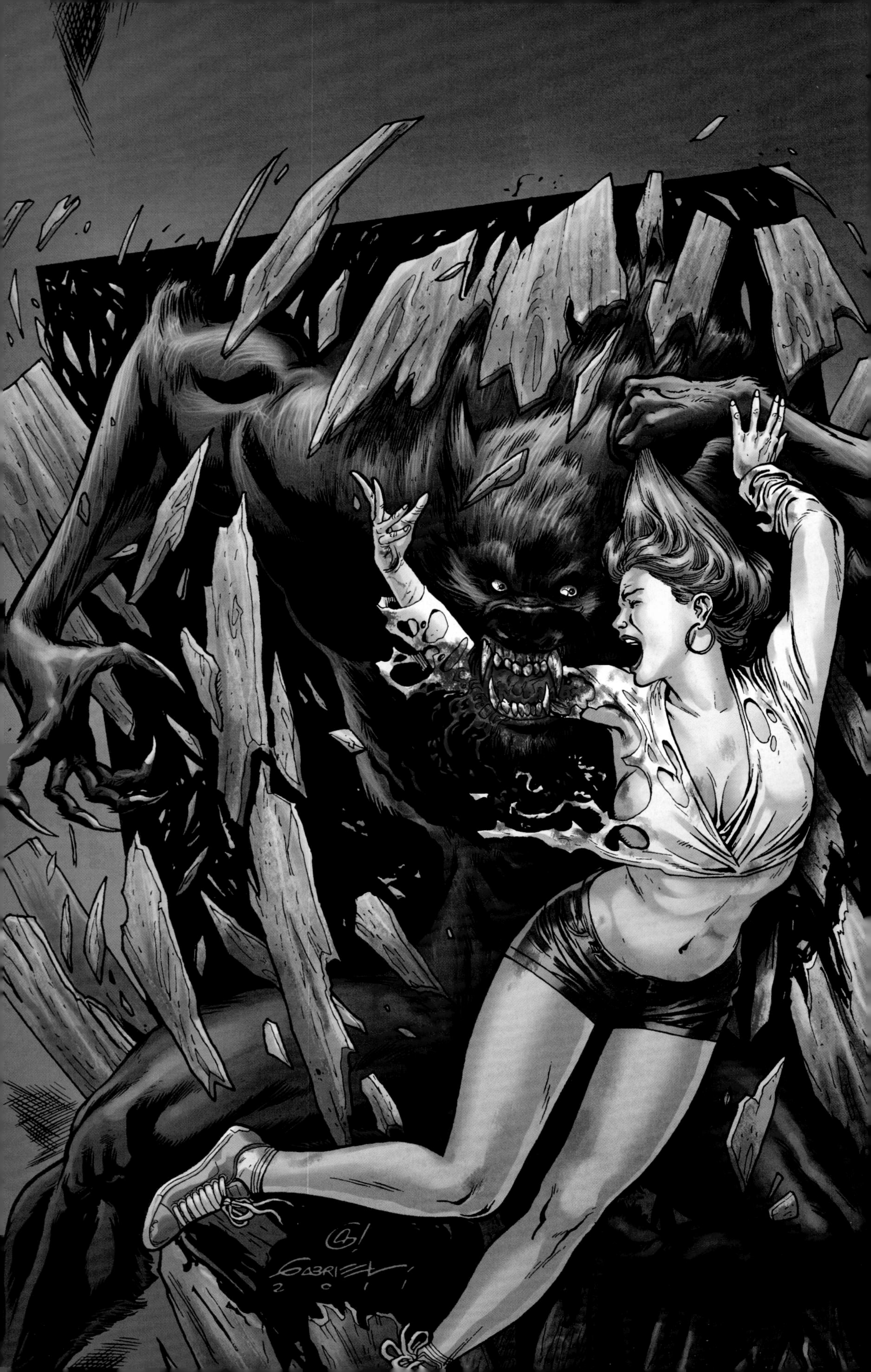

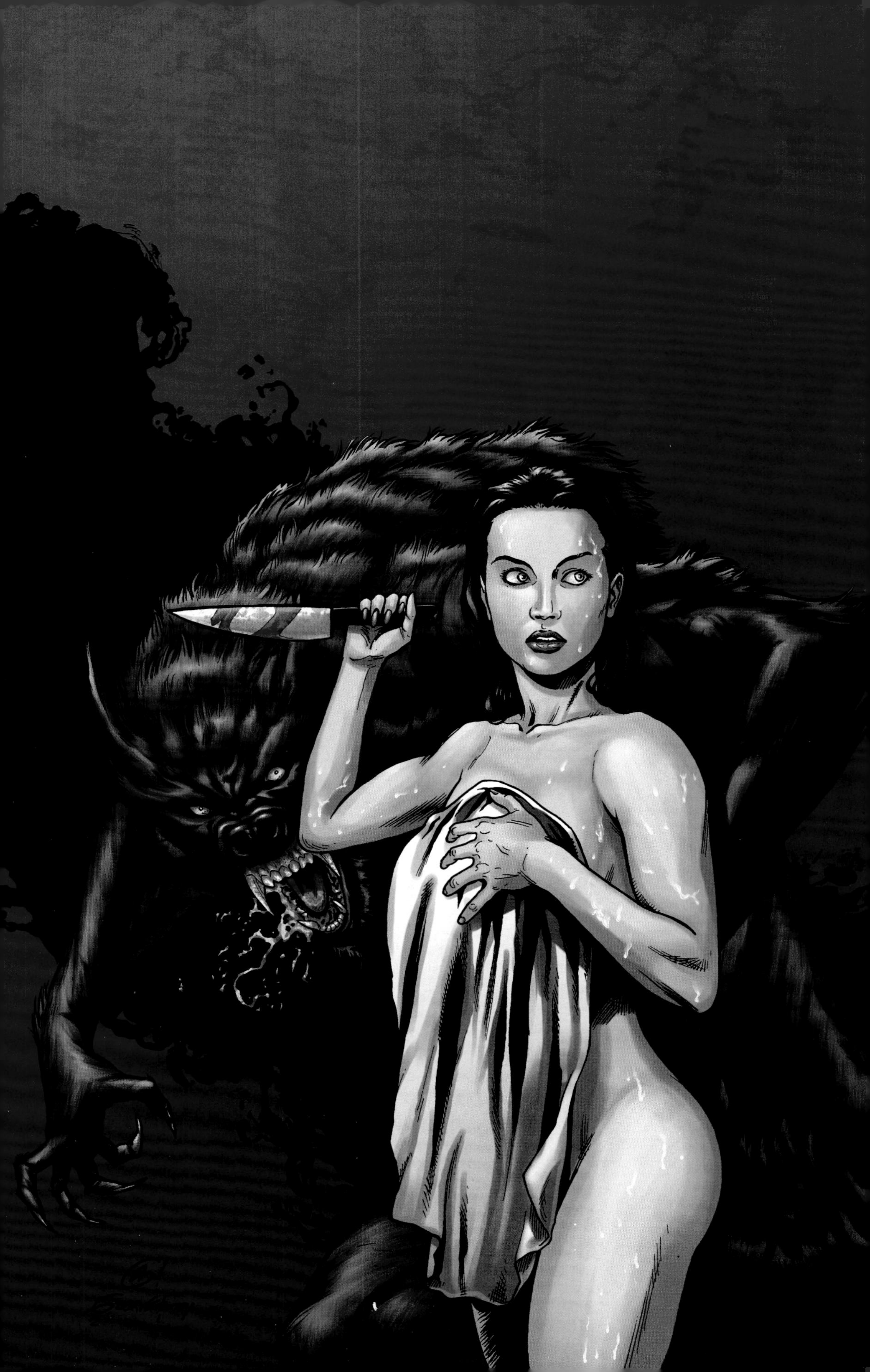

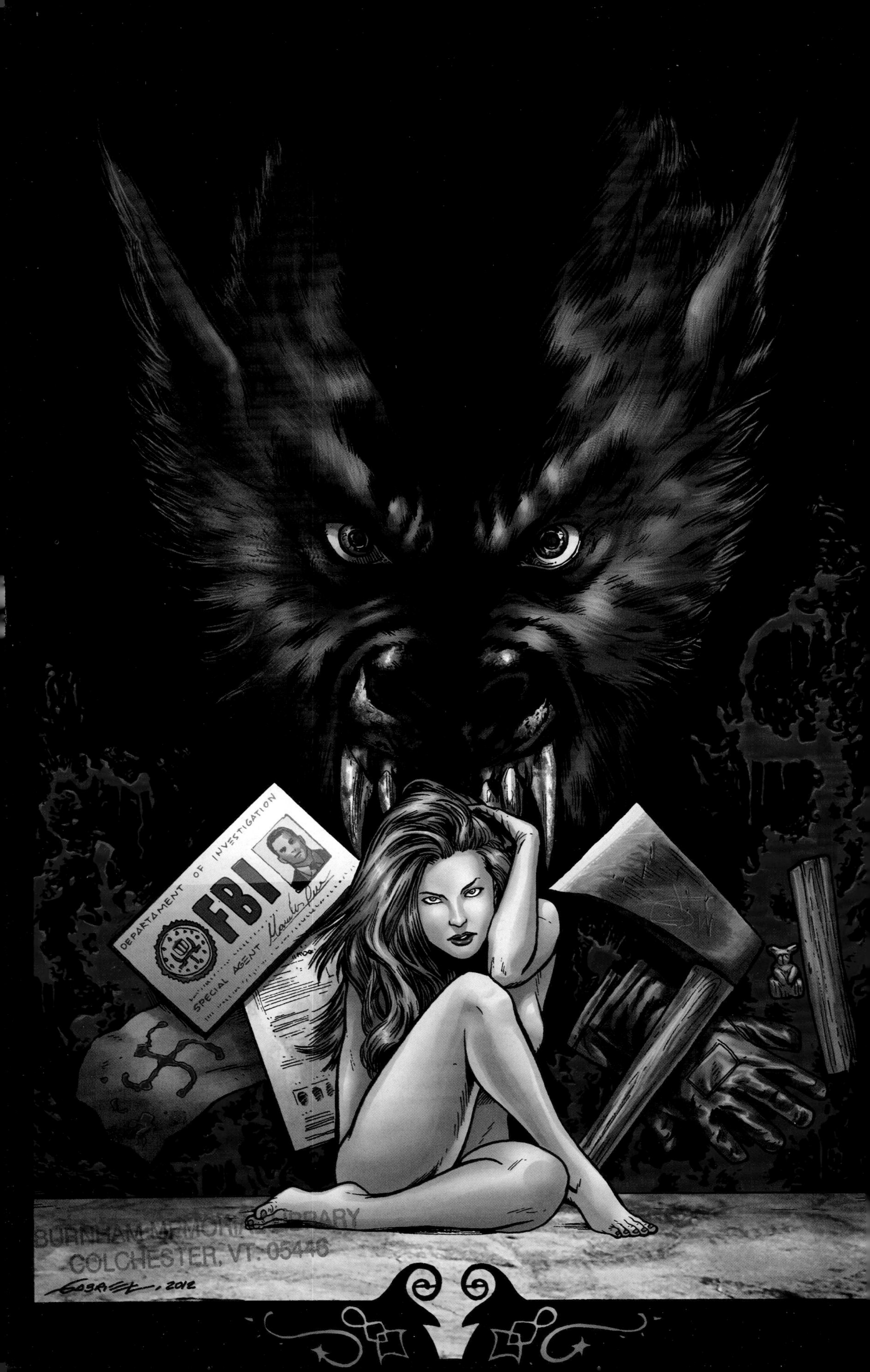
DEPARTMENT OF INVESTIGATION
FBI
SPECIAL AGENT